BASICS

Computer Concepts

Dolores Wells-Pusins

Ann Peele Ambrose

D1468491

**South-Western
Computer Education**
an imprint of Course Technology

Thomson Learning™

Australia • Canada • Mexico • Singapore • Spain • United Kingdom • United States

Publishing Team Leader:	Kristen Duerr
Senior Project Manager:	Dave Lafferty
Production Coordinator:	Jennifer Goguen
Marketing Manager:	Kimberly Woods
Cover Design:	Lou Ann Thesing
Production Services:	Thompson Steele, Inc.

Copyright © 2001
By Thomson Learning/Course Technology
Cambridge, MA

ISBN: 0-538-69501-3
2 3 4 5 6 7 8 9 10 BM 08 07 06 05 04 03 02 01 00
Printed in the United States of America

South-Western is an imprint of Course Technology, a division of Thomson Learning.

For permission to use material from this text or product, contact us by
Web: www.thomsonrights.com
Phone: 1-800-730-2214
Fax: 1-800-730-2215

Cover all the Basics...

With these exciting new products from South-Western!

Our exciting new series of short, application suite books will provide everything needed to learn this software. Other books include:

NEW! Microsoft® Office 2000 BASICS by Morrison
35+ hours of instruction for beginning through intermediate features
0-538-72412-9	Text, Hard Spiral Bound
0-538-72413-7	Text, Perfect Bound, packaged with Data CD-ROM
0-538-72415-3	Activities Workbook
0-538-72414-5	Electronic Instructorís Manual Package (Manual and CD-ROM)
0-538-72516-1	Testing CD Package

NEW! Microsoft® Works 2000 BASICS by Pasewark & Pasewark
35+ hours of instruction for beginning through intermediate features
0-538-72340-8	Text, Hard Spiral Bound
0-538-72411-0	Text, Perfect Bound, packaged with Data CD-ROM
0-538-72342-4	Activities Workbook
0-538-72341-6	Electronic Instructorís Manual Package (Manual and CD-ROM)
0-538-72343-2	Testing CD Package

NEW! Microsoft® Office 98 Macintosh BASICS by Murphy
35+ hours of instruction for beginning through intermediate features
0-538-72431-5	Text, Hard Spiral Bound
0-538-72432-3	Text, Perfect Bound, packaged with Data CD-ROM
0-538-72434-X	Activities Workbook
0-538-72433-1	Electronic Instructorís Manual Package (Manual and CD-ROM)
0-538-72435-8	Testing CD Package

NEW! Microsoft® Visual Basic BASICS by Knowlton and Collings
35+ hours of instruction for beginning through intermediate features
0-538-69083-6	Text, Hard Spiral Bound
0-538-69086-0	Text, Perfect Bound, packaged with Data Disk
0-538-69084-4	Activities Workbook
0-538-69085-2	Electronic Instructorís Manual Package (Manual and CD-ROM)
0-538-69243-X	Testing CD Package

NEW! Computer Concepts BASICS by Pusins and Ambrose
35+ hours of instruction for beginning through intermediate features
0-538-69501-3	Text, Hard Spiral Bound
0-538-69502-1	Activities Workbook
0-538-69503-X	Electronic Instructorís Manual Package (Manual and CD-ROM)
0-538-69504-8	Testing CD Package

NEW! C++ BASICS by Knowlton
35+ hours of instruction for beginning through intermediate features
0-538-69493-9	Text, Hard Spiral Bound
0-538-69494-7	Text, Perfect Bound, packaged with Data CD-ROM
0-538-69496-3	Activities Workbook
0-538-69495-5	Electronic Instructorís Manual Package (Manual and CD-ROM)
0-538-69497-1	Testing CD Package

Call 800-824-5179 for more information!

South-Western
EDUCATIONAL PUBLISHING
Thomson Learning™

Join Us On the Internet www.course.com/swep

How to Use this Book

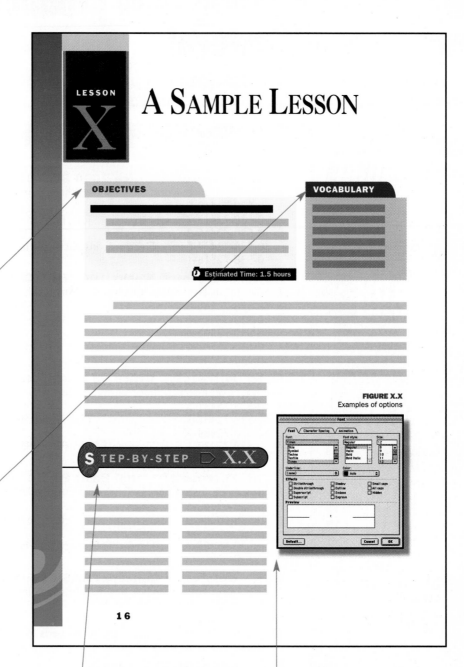

LESSON X

A SAMPLE LESSON

OBJECTIVES

VOCABULARY

Estimated Time: 1.5 hours

FIGURE X.X
Examples of options

S TEP-BY-STEP ▷ **X.X**

16

Objectives–
Objectives are listed at the beginning of each lesson, along with a suggested time for completion of the lesson. This allows you to look ahead to what you will be learning and to pace your work.

Vocabulary–
Vocabulary is listed at the beginning of each lesson.

Step-by-Step Exercises–These exercises that appear throughout the lesson lead learners step-by-step through the procedures introduced.

Enhanced Screen Shots–
Screen shots now come to life on each page with color and depth.

How to Use this Book

Marginal boxes–
These boxes provide additional information. Hot Tips show advanced or alternative ways to perform a task. Did You Know gives extra information about content discussed in the text. Internet tips provide Internet technology and useful Internet information.

Technology Careers–
This Special Feature describes various careers in technology.

Ethics in Technology–
This Special Feature explores ethical questions that have arisen from the use of technology and the Internet.

Summary–At the end of each lesson you will find a summary to prepare you to complete the end-of-lesson activities.

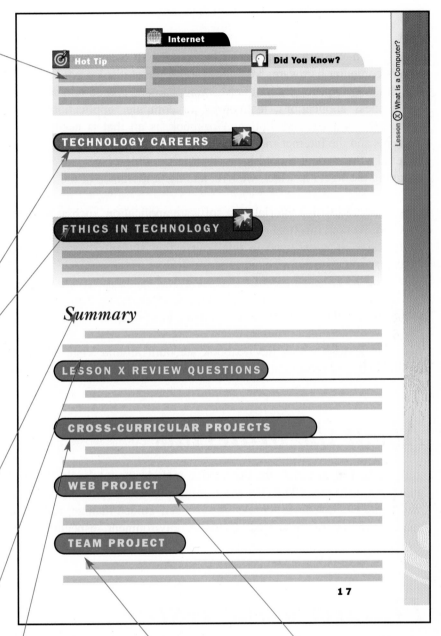

Internet

Hot Tip

Did You Know?

TECHNOLOGY CAREERS

ETHICS IN TECHNOLOGY

Summary

LESSON X REVIEW QUESTIONS

CROSS-CURRICULAR PROJECTS

WEB PROJECT

TEAM PROJECT

Lesson ⊗ What is a Computer?

1 7

Review Questions–
Review material at the end of each lesson enables you to prepare for assessment of the content presented.

Cross-Cirricular Projects–
End-of-lesson applications of lesson material is applied to various subjects for real-world experience of the subject matter.

Team Project–
Each lesson gives you an opportunity to share what has been learned in the lesson by working cooperatively on a project with other class members.

Web Project–
Hands-on application of what has been learned in the lesson that helps your understanding and use of the Internet.

PREFACE

South-Western's Computer Concepts BASICS is a brief introduction to computers. This text covers computer hardware, software, application skills, keyboarding skills, the Internet and Internet searching, Web page creation, networking, careers, and computer ethics. It can be used in any class on business applications, technology, or computer applications. This textbook, along with the Instructor's Manual and Student Workbook, is all that is needed for a brief course on computer concepts and the Internet and can be used for 35 or more hours of instruction. After completing these materials, the student should have an understanding of the basics of computers, how technology is changing the world in which we live, and the importance of the Internet.

Partnered with a tutorial on a software application, such as Microsoft Office, MicrosoftWorks, or ClarisWorks, this text provides a complete course on computer concepts—with hands-on applications. It is assumed in this course that students have no prior experience with computer concepts.

Other possible applications include supplementing a mathematics, science, language arts, or social studies class through the integrated end-of-chapter and workbook activities and exercises.

The lessons within the textbook are built around Vista Multimedia, a video/CD Company. Relating chapter information to this company provides the student a link to the real world.

About the Materials

The full materials for this course include the textbook, the workbook, and the instructor's guide. An instructor CD-ROM and testing software are also available. Although advanced students may complete the course successfully in a self-guided manner, it is recommended that the course be taken in an instructor-guided, hands-on environment, especially for beginning or intermediate students.

Features of the Text

Twenty lessons gradually introduce the skills necessary to learn the fundamentals of what computers are and how they can be used, including how to access and use the Internet and World Wide Web. Step-by-step exercises divide each lesson into conceptual blocks and are accompanied by integrated hands-on exercises that reinforce the presented information. Because the student provides the data used for the exercises, the text can serve as a roadmap for learning the different applications. At the end of each lesson is a summary; review questions, including multiple- choice, true-false, and short answer; Web projects, team projects, and cross-curricular projects. Other features include margins notes on topics such as Did You Know?, Internet tips, and Hot Tips.

Included within each lesson are objectives, vocabulary lists, estimated completion times, screen illustrations for visual reinforcement, and photos and illustrations to provide interest and clarity. Special sections on ethics and careers are included in each lesson.

SCANS

In 1992, the U.S. Department of Labor and Education formed the Secretary's Commission on Achieving Necessary Skills, or SCANS, to study the kinds of competencies and skills that workers must have to success in today's marketplace. The results of the study were published in a document entitled What Work Requires of Schools: A SCANS Report for America 2000. The in-chapter and end-of-chapter exercises in this book are designed to meet the criteria outlined in the SCANS report and thus help prepare students to be successful in today's workplace.

Activities Workbook

The student workbook contains additional exercises and additional review questions. Definitions, short-answer, fill in the blank, and true/false questions are provided in the student workbook as a basis for study, chapter review, or test preparation.

Electronic Instructor

The Electronic Instructor CD-ROM includes solutions to end of lesson exercises and projects, test questions and solutions, and solutions to the workbook exercises.

Acknowledgements

No book is the work of just the authors, but rather an entire team is responsible for bringing it about. Thanks to Cheryl Beck and Dave Lafferty at South-Western for overseeing the project. Special thanks to Cathy Duce at Intel for her lesson review and Elinor Stapleton at Thompson Steele, Inc. for her assistance in developing and producing these materials.

PHOTO CREDITS

Lesson 1
1.1   © PhotoDisc
1.3   Courtesy of International Business Machines Corporation. Unauthorized use not permitted.
1.4   © PhotoDisc
1.5   Rapid Rental Software (1.800.263.0000)
1.6   Compaq Computer Corporation
1.7   Courtesy of International Business Machines Corporation. Unauthorized use not permitted.
1.9   Courtesy of International Business Machines Corporation. Unauthorized use not permitted.
1.10   Courtesy of Cray Research, a Silicon Graphics Company
1.11   © PhotoDisc

Lesson 2
2.3   © PhotoDisc
2.4   © PhotoDisc
2.7   © PhotoDisc

Lesson 3
3.2   © PhotoDisc
3.3   © PhotoDisc
3.4   © PhotoDisc
3.5   © PhotoDisc
3.6   © PhotoDisc
3.7   Lernout & Hauspie Speech Technology Products & Services
3.8   © PhotoDisc
3.9   © PhotoDisc
3.10   © PhotoDisc
3.16   © PhotoDisc

Lesson 5
5.2   © Photonics Kinesis Corporation
5.4   © PhotoDisc

Lesson 10
10.1   © PhotoDisc

Lesson 12
12.4   © PhotoDisc

Lesson 13
13.2   © PhotoDisc

Lesson 15
15.1   © PhotoDisc

Lesson 18
18.1   © PhotoDisc
18.6   © PhotoDisc
18.7   © PhotoDisc

Lesson 19
19.3   Courtesy of IriScan; IriScan's iris recognition technology identifies people by the patterns in the iris of the eye

Lesson 20
20.6   © PhotoDisc
20.10   © PhotoDisc

TABLE OF CONTENTS

iv   How to Use this Book
vi   Preface
viii Photo Credits

LESSON 1 WHAT IS A COMPUTER?

2   What Is a Computer?
3   Why Are Computers So Popular?
3   The History of the Computer
4   How Computers Are Used
6   Types of Computers
8   What Is a Computer System?
9   Data Communications

13   Computers in Our Future
13   Summary
14   Lesson 1 Review Questions
15   Cross-Curricular Projects
16   Web Project
16   Team Project

LESSON 2 HOW DOES A COMPUTER PROCESS DATA?

17   Computer System Components
19   System Components
25   Data Representation
26   Summary

26   Lesson 2 Review Questions
28   Cross-Curricular Projects
28   Web Project
29   Team Project

LESSON 3 HOW DO I INPUT DATA AND OUTPUT AND STORE INFORMATION?

31   Input Devices
37   Output Devices
41   Connecting Input/Output Devices to the Computer
41   Storage Devices
44   Caring for Removable Storage Media

44   Summary
45   Lesson 3 Review Questions
46   Cross-Curricular Projects
47   Web Project
47   Team Project

LESSON 4 WHAT IS SOFTWARE?

48   Hardware vs. Software
49   Types of Software
52   Microcomputer Operating Systems Interfaces
53   Microcomputer Operating Systems

59   Summary
60   Lesson 4 Review Questions
61   Cross-Curricular Projects
62   Web Project
62   Team Project

LESSON 5 HOW DO I KEYBOARD?

64   First Thigs First
67   Developing Beginning Keyboard Skills
69   Additional Concepts
72   Using Your New Keyboarding Skill
74   Summary

75   Lesson 5 Review Questions
76   Cross-Curricular Projects
77   Web Project
77   Team Project

LESSON 6 WHAT BASIC SKILLS DO I NEED TO USE THE COMPUTER?

78 Overview of Graphical User Interface
79 Starting and Shutting Down the GUI
80 Opening a Window
81 Closing a Window
82 Formatting a Disk
85 Files and Folders
86 Starting a Program
91 Managing Files
97 Getting Help
97 Summary
98 Lesson 6 Review Questions
100 Cross-Curricular Projects
100 Web Project
100 Team Project100

LESSON 7 HOW DO I USE WORD PROCESSING SOFTWARE?

101 What Is Word Processing Software?
103 The Word Processing Screen
113 Other Features of Word Processing Software
114 Preparing a Letter
115 Summary
116 Lesson 7 Review Questions
117 Cross-Curricular Projects
118 Web Project
118 Team Project

LESSON 8 HOW DO I USE SPREADSHEET SOFTWARE?

119 What Is the Purpose of Spreadsheets?
120 The Anatomy of a Spreadsheet
122 Moving Around in a Spreadsheet
123 Entering Data into a Spreadsheet
127 Additional Features
129 Using a Spreadsheet
130 Summary
131 Lesson 8 Review Questions
133 Cross-Curricular Projects
134 Web Project
134 Team Project

LESSON 9 HOW DO I USE DATABASE SOFTWARE?

135 What Is Database Software?
136 Creating a Database
138 Entering Data into a Table
140 Querying a Database
140 Modifying the Table Structure
142 Updating a Database
142 Printing a Database
142 Creating and Using Forms
142 Creating and Using a Report
144 Summary
144 Lesson 9 Review Questions
146 Cross-Curricular Projects
147 Web Project
147 Team Project

LESSON 10 HOW DO I USE PRESENTATION GRAPHICS SOFTWARE?

148 Using Visuals in a Presentation
150 Creating a Presentation
153 Working in Different Views
154 Adding a Chart to your Presentation
156 Adding WordArt to a Presentation
158 Adding Design to a Presentation
160 Printing Your Presentation
161 Preparing an Effective Presentation
162 Delivering a Presentation
163 Summary
164 Lesson 10 Review Questions
165 Cross-Curricular Projects
166 Web Project
166 Team Project

LESSON 11 — HOW DO I USE DESKTOP PUBLISHING SOFTWARE?

167 What Is Desktop Publishing?
168 Stages in the Desktop Publishing Process
170 Layout and Design
172 Using Graphics
174 Using Color
174 Using Lines
174 Using Other Elements

176 Desktop Publishing Tips
176 Summary
177 Lesson 11 Review Questions
178 Cross-Curricular Projects
179 Web Project
179 Team Project

LESSON 12 — WHAT IS A NETWORK?

180 Introducing Networks
182 Communications Media
185 Network Hardware
187 Types of Networks
189 Network Topologies
190 Communications Protocols

191 Network Operating Systems Software
191 Summary
192 Lesson 12 Review Questions
194 Cross-Curricular Projects
194 Web Project
194 Team Project

LESSON 13 — WHAT IS THE INTERNET?

195 Evolution of the Internet
196 Accessing the INTERNET—Dial in or Direct Connection
198 How does the Internet Work?
200 Major Features of the Internet

210 Summary
212 Lesson 13 Review Questions
213 Cross-Curricular Projects
214 Web Project
214 Team Project

LESSON 14 — WHAT BASIC SKILLS DO I NEED TO USE THE INTERNET?

215 What Is a Browser?
217 Browser Terminology
218 Browser Basics
229 Copy and Save Text, Web Pages, and Images
234 E-Mail

238 Summary
239 Lesson 14 Review Questions
240 Cross-Curricular Projects
241 Web Project
241 Team Project

LESSON 15 — HOW DO I DO RESEARCH ON THE INTERNET?

242 The Key to a Successful Search
243 Why Search the Internet?
244 Introducing Search Engines
250 Specialty Search Engines
253 Subject Directory Searching
257 Tools and Techniques for Searching the Web

261 Summary
262 Lesson 15 Review Questions
263 Cross-Curricular Projects
264 Web Project
264 Team Project

LESSON 16 — HOW DO I EVALUATE ELECTRONIC INFORMATION?

266 Evaluating Information Found on the Internet
266 Viewing a Page
269 Criteria for Evaluating Electronic Information
270 Types of Internet Resources
271 Citing Internet Resources
273 Internet Detective
273 Evaluation Survey
274 Summary
274 Lesson 16 Review Questions
275 Cross-Curricular Projects
276 Web Project
276 Team Project

LESSON 17 — HOW DO I CREATE A WEB PAGE?

277 How a Web Page Works
279 Plan a Document
279 A Basic Page
282 Page Formatting
286 Text Formatting
291 Hyperlinks
293 Images
299 Backgrounds
299 Publishing Your Web page
300 Summary
301 Lesson 17 Review Questions
302 Cross-Curricular Projects
303 Web Project
303 Team Project

LESSON 18 — HOW CAN I USE TECHNOLOGY TO SOLVE A PROBLEM?

304 How Does Technology Solve Problems for You?
306 What Is Problem Solving?
306 Problem-Solving Steps
307 Problem Solving with Computers in Action
308 Using Technology Tools to Solve Problems
314 Other Technologies
315 Summary
315 Lesson 18 Review Questions
317 Cross-Curricular Projects
317 Web Project
318 Team Project

LESSON 19 — WHAT ARE SOME TECHNOLOGICAL ISSUES?

319 Types of Computer Crimes
322 Privacy
323 Security
324 Software Piracy
325 Protection for Technology Injuries
326 Summary
327 Lesson 19 Review Questions
328 Cross-Curricular Projects
329 Web Project
329 Team Project

LESSON 20 — HOW IS TECHNOLOGY CHANGING THE WORKPLACE AND SOCIETY?

330 Education
337 Scientific Discovery and Technological Innovations
340 Work and Play
344 Summary
345 Lesson 20 Review Questions
346 Cross-Curricular Projects
347 Web Project
347 Team Project

348 Glossary
357 Index

WHAT IS A COMPUTER?

OBJECTIVES

When you have completed this module, you will be able to:

- Define a computer.
- Identify how computers are used in our daily lives.
- Compare the types of computers.
- List the parts of a computer system.
- Explain how the Internet, the World Wide Web, e-mail, and networks affect the use of computers.

🕐 **Estimated Time: 1.5 hours**

VOCABULARY

Computer
Computer system
Data
Data communications
E-mail
Hardware
Internet
Microcomputer
Networks
Software

You have recently been hired to work at Vista Multimedia as a part-time sales assistant. Vista Multimedia rents videos and CDs and provides a service for customers to use computers in the store and to create their own CDs. You will use the computer to perform many of your duties. It appears to be the most important piece of equipment in the store. It is used for recording sales, for maintaining employee records, and to communicate with suppliers; just to name a few applications.

That really should not be a surprise. The computer is probably the single most important invention of the twentieth century! It affects us not only individually but also as a society as a whole. You can see computers almost everywhere!

- In schools they are used to enhance instruction.
- At arcades they can transport you to an imaginary world.
- At banks computers allow you to withdraw cash from your account without having to talk with a teller.
- While watching a football game on television, you can even see an instant replay of a tackle. The list could go on and on.

As technology produces more powerful computers, we will find more ways to use them to enhance our lives. See Figure 1.1.

FIGURE 1.1
One example of the wide variety of ways people use computer systems.

What Is a Computer?

Just what is a *computer?* What does it really do? It is an electronic device that receives data, processes data, stores data, and produces a result (output).

Let's see how this definition fits with the way the computer in the video store is used.

■ *Receives data:* Customers' names and the name of the video rented are entered into the computer.

■ *Processes data:* The computer will change the data from what we entered into what we want the result to be.

■ *Stores data:* The information is stored in the computer's memory or on disk.

■ *Produces a result:* We will see a final display of the information we enter. See Figure 1.2.

FIGURE 1.2
The processing cycle of the computer

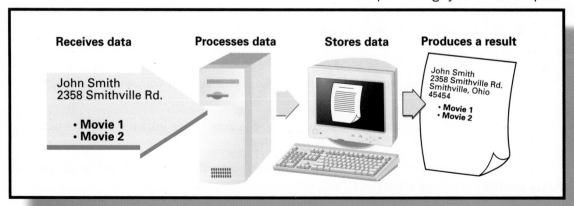

Why Are Computers So Popular?

OK, now you know what a computer is and what it does. But why has it become so popular? Basically, it performs only three operations:

- Arithmetic operations (adding, subtracting, multiplying, and dividing)
- Logical comparison of values (examples: equal to, greater than)
- Storage and retrieval operations

However, what really makes the computer as widely used as it is? Is that it:

- performs these functions very quickly?
- produces accurate and reliable results?
- stores large amounts of data?
- provides versatility in its various applications?
- provides cost-effective applications?
- is becoming more and more powerful and more useful?

 Did You Know?

Charles Babbage is the father of computers.

The History of the Computer

Can you remember a time when computers did not exist? You probably cannot. Computers in the 1950s, 1960s, and 1970s were larger and limited in what they could do. They were temperature sensitive and difficult to repair. Only large companies could afford them and only a few visionary people like Steve Jobs or Bill Gates saw a future for small home computers. See Figure 1.3.

FIGURE 1.3
Early generation computers

Small desktop computers are now the most popular type of computer today. They are much more powerful and less expensive. These home computers are called personal computers because they were designed to be used by one person at a time. The first personal computer was sold in 1977. Now they are in millions of homes and offices.

Internet

Visit the Computer Museum Network's site, www.tcm.org, to locate information about computer history.

How Computers Are Used

Computers have vastly impacted our lives. They have changed the way:

- we bank.
- we buy groceries.
- we shop for toys.
- we do homework.

They are so important in our lives today that without them, our world as we know it would come to a sudden halt. Computers have become necessary tools in almost every type of activity and in almost every type of business. They are capable of performing many different tasks. Think of the many ways computers affect *you* every day. Any time you go to the movies, shop in a grocery store, watch the instant replay of a tackle in a football game, or take a trip on an airplane, you are benefiting from the capabilities of computers. See Figure 1.4.

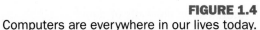
FIGURE 1.4
Computers are everywhere in our lives today.

Hot Tip

Original music can be created using computers. People do not need a lot of musical talent or even specific instruments to make music. They just need to press a button or key on a MIDI keyboard.

4

How Does the Video Store Use Computers?

Since you have been employed at Vista Multimedia as a sales clerk, you have seen the computer used a lot. You thought it was just being used as a cash register and to enter customers' information when they rented a video. If you were to ask your supervisor how the computer is used in the operation of the store, you would probably be surprised at the answer. You would learn that the computer is used to:

- maintain inventory of all the videos.

- maintain records of all the members.

- maintain personnel records.

- maintain the store's budget.

- record sales figures.

- interact with the computers at headquarters.

- order inventory and other items.

- advertise on the Internet.

- communicate with other stores, suppliers, customers, and so on.

See Figure 1.5.

FIGURE 1.5
An employee at Vista Video uses the computer.

Types of Computers

The personal computer is only one type of computer. There are other types more suited for various tasks and organizations. Computers are classified by their size, speed, and application.

The *microcomputer,* also called a personal computer or desktop computer, is the type of computer used at home or at the office by one person. Its size and shape allow it to fit on top or under a desk. The PC is typically used for writing papers or letters, tracking personal finances, playing games, and surfing the Internet. See Figure 1.6.

FIGURE 1.6
Microcomputer

The *notebook computer* has the same capabilities as the desktop computer. However, it is much smaller and more expensive. Because of its small size, it is portable and can run on power from an electrical outlet or batteries. Businesspeople find the notebook computer very convenient to use when they are away from the office. See Figure 1.7.

FIGURE 1.7
Notebook computer

FIGURE 1.8
A personal digital assistant, or palm-top computer

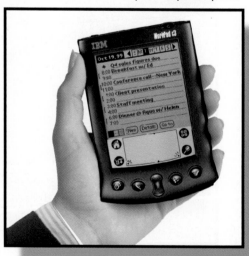

The *personal digital assistant (PDA),* also known as a palm-top computer, is even smaller than the notebook computer. It has limited capabilities and may lack traditional components such as the keyboard. On such a PDA, a touch-sensitive screen accepts characters drawn with your finger. PDAs can connect to desktop computers to exchange and update information. The cost of a PDA is not necessarily lower than a microcomputer. See Figure 1.8.

Minicomputers are larger than microcomputers and basically have the same capabilities. The cost, however, is much higher. A company would choose to use minicomputers rather than microcomputers if there are many users and large amounts of data.

Mainframe computers are much larger and more powerful than minicomputers. They also perform processing tasks for many users. They are used for centralized storage, processing, and management of very large amounts of data. Mainframe computers cost hundreds of thousands of dollars and are used by large institutions and government installations. See Figure 1.9.

Hot Tip

Supercomputers are often used as testers for medical experiments.

Supercomputers are the largest and fastest computers. These computers are used by large corporations with tremendous volumes of data to be processed. The processing speed is much faster than any other type of computer. A supercomputer can cost several million dollars! See Figure 1.10.

FIGURE 1.9
Mainframe computers are capable of performing several billion operations per second.

FIGURE 1.10
The supercomputer was first developed for high-volume computing tasks such as predicting the weather.

What Is a Computer System?

What makes it possible for the computer to perform the work it does? It uses a combination of several parts working together called a ***computer system.*** It consists of four parts:

- ***Hardware*** is the tangible, physical equipment that can be seen and touched. Examples include the keyboard, processor, monitor, and printer.

- ***Software*** is the intangible set of instructions that tells the computer what to do. These sets of instructions are called programs or software programs. There are two types of software programs: system software programs and application software programs.

- ***Data*** is the new facts entered into the computer to be processed. Data consists of the following:

  - text
  - numbers
  - sounds and images

Did You Know?

A computer won a World Chess Championship game against a human.

It is entered into the computer as raw data and the computer manipulates (processes) it into the final form that the user needs. This data can be entered into the computer in several ways including:

- the keyboard
- voice activation
- diskettes
- scanning

Likewise there are various sources from which data can come including:

- handwritten notes
- diskettes
- voice input
- typed reports
- bar codes

- ***People*** are the users of the computers who enter the data and use the output. See Figure 1.11.

FIGURE 1.11
The components of a microcomputer system

Data Communications

In the early years (1950s) of computers, they did not "talk" to each other. There were many reasons for this. One was that they didn't talk the same language. It was as if Computer "A" spoke French and Computer "B" spoke Swedish. As technology expanded, standards were developed that enabled computer to communicate.

Data communications, the technology that enables computers to communicate, is defined as the transmission of text, numeric, voice or video data from one machine to another. Popular examples are the Internet, electronic messages (e-mail), faxes, and electronic or online banking. Data communications has changed the way the world does business and the way we live our lives. This technology has made it possible to communicate around the globe!

These are the four components of data communications:

- *Sender:* the computer that is sending the message.

- *Receiver:* the computer receiving the message.

- *Channel:* the media that carries or transports the message. This could be telephone wire, coaxial cable, microwave signal, or fiber optic.

- *Protocol:* the rules that govern the orderly transfer of the data sent. See Figure 1.12.

FIGURE 1.12
Data communications use modems to send and receive messages.

Networks

One of the most utilized types of data communications in the business world is a ***network*** connection. A network connects one computer to other computers and peripheral devices. This connection enables the computers to share data and resources. If the computers are located in a relatively close location such as in the same building or department, they are part of a local area network. The data and software for these computers are stored on a central computer called the file server. See Figure 1.13.

These local area networks can be expanded to include several local area networks within a city, state, region, territory, country, continent, or the world. These are called ***wide-area networks***.

FIGURE 1.13
A network system consists of workstations, servers, and printers.

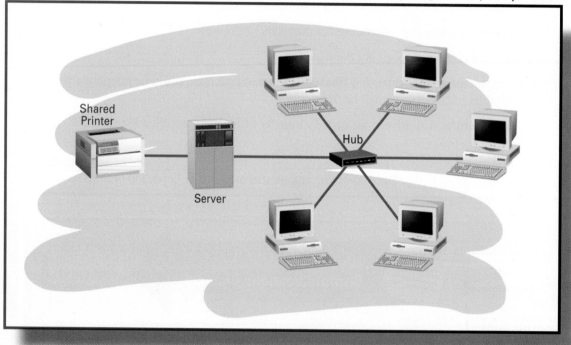

The Internet

The *Internet* was originally developed for the government to enable researchers around the world to be able to share information. Today, it is the largest network (computers connected together) in the world. It is used every day by millions of users. It has become an invaluable communication tool for businesses, individuals, and governments. See Figure 1.14.

 Internet

Visit NASA's site, www.nasa.gov, to learn how computers and computer-related technologies are used in space exploration.

FIGURE 1.14
A graphical representation of the Internet in the United States

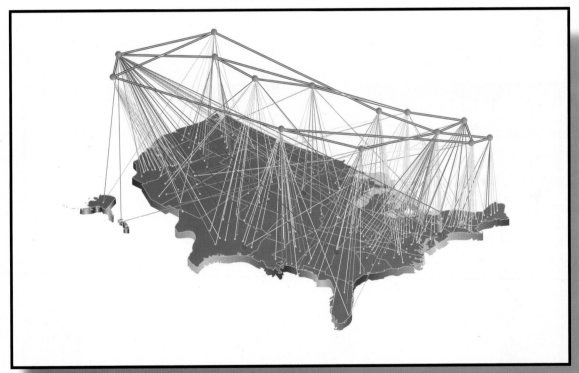

E-MAIL

The most commonly used feature on the Interne is electronic mail, better known as *e-mail*. This is the capability to send a message from one person's computer to another person's computer. E-mail is stored on someone's server and then downloaded to an individual's computer. E-mail messages can be sent to friends, family members, and businesses locally or across the world. E-mail has reduced the number of letters mailed each day and has increased productivity in the workplace. Just about everyone has an e-mail address! See Figure 1.15.

INTRANETS

Many companies have implemented intranets within their own organizations. An intranet is for the exclusive use of users within the organization and contains only company information. Company manuals, handbooks, and newsletters are just a few of the types of documents distributed via an intranet. Online forms are also made available on an intranet. The major advantage of using an intranet is reliability and security—possible because the organization can control access.

EXTRANETS

Extranets are applications that allow outside organizations to access internal information systems. Access is controlled very tightly. These are usually reserved for suppliers or customers.

FIGURE 1.15
E-mail is the most used application of the Internet

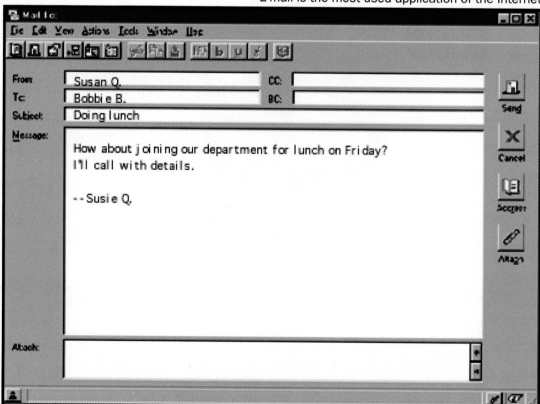

Computers in Our Future

It is a fair assumption that computers of the future will be much more powerful and less expensive. It is also a fair assumption that almost every job will somehow involve a computer.

One of the major areas of change in the computer evolution will be connectivity, the ability to connect with other computers. We will be able to do the things we are now doing with computers but on an even bigger scale. This bigger and better computer age will affect how and where we work, how we communicate with other people, how we shop, as well as how we communicate and share information.

Summary

- A computer is an electronic device that receives data, processes data, and stores data to produce a result.

- The first computers were used by the military and government installations.

- The first personal computer was sold in 1977.

- Computers can be found in almost every aspect of our lives.

- There are different types of computers including microcomputers, notebook computers, personal digital assistants, minicomputers, mainframe computers, and supercomputers.

- Computers are classified by size, speed, and application.

- A computer system consists of the following components:

  - Hardware: tangible, physical equipment that can be seen and touched.

  - Software: the intangible set of instructions that tell the computer what to do. This set of instructions is called a software program.

  - Data: the information entered into a computer to be processed.

  - People: the users who enter the data and use the output.

- Data communication is the transmission of text, numeric, voice, or video data from one machine to another. The four components of data communication are as follows:

  - Sender: the computer that is sending the message

  - Receiver: the computer receiving the message

  - Channel: the media that carries or transports the message. This could be telephone wire, coaxial cable, microwave signal, or fiber optic

  - Protocol: the rules that govern the orderly transfer of the data sent

- A local area network connects multiple computers within a building. It allows the sharing of data and resources.

- The Internet was originally developed so information could be shared by government researchers around the world.

- E-mail is the most common experience most people have with the Internet. It lets us send messages from one computer to another locally and around the world.

- The World Wide Web is a huge database of information that allows public access.

MULTIPLE CHOICE

1. The first personal computer was sold in _____.
   A. 1967
   B. 1977
   C. 1987
   D. 1999

2. The Internet's most popular feature is _____.
   A. e-mail
   B. buying on the Web
   C. viewing videos
   D. creating Web pages

3. A _____ consists of hardware, software, data, and users.
   A. computer
   B. computer system
   C. telecommunications
   D. Web pages

4. The _____ was developed for government researchers.
   A. Internet
   B. mainframe computer
   C. electronic mail
   D. World Wide Web

5. _____ computers share files, data, and software.
   A. Apple
   B. IBM
   C. Networked
   D. Protocol

TRUE/FALSE

Circle the T if the statement is true. Circle F if it is false.

T F 1. Computers have been a part of society for over 100 years.

T F 2. The Internet was first developed for government use.

T F 3. Computers are classified by size, cost, and Internet abilities.

T F 4. Because notebook computers are much smaller than microcomputers, they are less expensive than microcomputers.

T F 5. Software is a set of instructions that tells the computer how to perform certain tasks.

SHORT ANSWER

1. The basic functions of a computer are _____

    _____

2. List four types of computers. _____

    _____

3. List the components of a computer system. _____

    _____

4. What is e-mail? _____

    _____

5. What is a network? _____

    _____

LESSON 1 PROJECTS

Cross-Curricular

MATH

Select a career in the field of mathematics such as teachers or statisticians. Use the Internet or other resources to research information explaining how computers are being used in a specific mathematics career. Write a two-page report. Use the keyword *mathematics careers* with one or two search engines (Excite, Mamma, askjeeves, etc.).

SCIENCE

Use the Internet and other resources to locate information regarding computers in our future. We know that computers are getting more and more powerful every day and are making our lives easier. One example is robotics. These computerized helpers perform many activities that may be dangerous or unpleasant for humans to perform. What are some other capabilities we can anticipate? Write a one- to two-page report describing these capabilities. Use www.AskJeeves.com to ask for information for this report.

SOCIAL STUDIES

Using the Internet or other resources, see what information you can find on computers that were developed in the early 1950s and 1960s. Write a one- to two-page report on the capabilities of these computers. Also include specific uses of these early computers. Visit www.looksmart.com to locate information regarding earlier computers. The Obsolete Computer Museum will also be helpful.

LANGUAGE ARTS

The computer has greatly influenced the way we communicate. Use the Internet and other resources to locate information on some of these ways. Write a two-page report on your findings.

WEB PROJECT

E-mail is a tool that allows you to communicate with friends and family members using the Internet. E-mail has other capabilities such as replying to messages. If you have access to e-mail, study the e-mail screen and identify and describe the various options available. Also use the Internet to find the names of at least three providers of e-mail services, such as America On-Line. Prepare a two-page report on your findings.

TEAM PROJECT

Your supervisor is considering putting a computer in her office as well as one in the office used by the part-time supervisor and other employees. She wants to look into the possibilities of having these two computers networked with the main computer in the store. She knows this is possible, but she is not really sure about what is involved.

She needs to know if there is a minimum number of computers needed to be networked. What kind of information and resources can be shared? What special hardware is required? Working with the other part-time sales clerk, research information on local area networks and find answers to your supervisor's questions. You may also include any other information about networks you think will be beneficial. Prepare a written report of your findings. You may find useful information at www.office-lans.com/Office_lan.htm and at www.AskJeeves.com.

HOW DOES A COMPUTER PROCESS DATA?

LESSON 2

A topic often discussed by employees at Vista Multimedia relates to how a computer processes data. They wonder if it's really important for them to know what happens inside the computer. Someday we won't need to worry about what's inside the system. With today's technology, however, a little knowledge about what's inside can make you a more effective user and help you select the right computer for the job you need it to do. In this module you will learn how the CPU processes data and turns it into information. And you will learn about some of the basic components contained on the computer's motherboard.

Computer System Components

We use computers for all kinds of tasks—to predict weather, to fly airplanes, to control traffic lights, to play games, to access the Internet, to send e-mail, and so on. You might wonder how a machine can do so many things.

To understand what a computer really does takes a degree in computer engineering. But most of us don't need that level of understanding. Instead, we need an overview for a basic understanding.

Just how does the computer work and how can the computer help you? Let's look at just one example. In your job at Vista Multimedia Company, you work with new customers who are continually coming into the store. The manager wants to track the names of the customers and keep a record of the products they purchase.

- The customers fill out a form with their name, address, and telephone number.

- You use your computer to input this data.

- Once the data is stored in the computer, you can ask the computer to provide you with a list of all of the customers.

- The computer processes the data and turns it into information.

- The computer outputs the information and sends it to the printer or monitor.

- You then ask the computer to store the information so you can use it again.

So, what happened here? You just experienced how a computer works. It took raw data and changed it into information that could be used by Vista Multimedia.

Just about all computers, regardless of size, perform these same general operations: input, process, output, and storage (IPOS). For example,

- You input data with some type of input device.

- The computer processes it to turn it into information.

- You output the information to some type of output device.

- You store it for later retrieval.

Hot Tip

Research companies and universities are designing wearable computer systems.

Input, output, and processing devices grouped together represent a computer system. In this module, we look at the components that the computer uses to process data. These components are contained within the system case. See Figure 2.1.

FIGURE 2.1
Computer system components

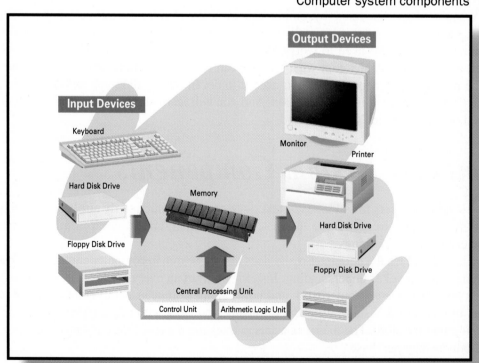

System Components

The PC system case is the metal and plastic case that houses the main system components of the computer. Central to all of this is the **motherboard** or system board that mounts into the case. The motherboard is a circuit board that contains many integral components. A circuit board is simply a thin plate or board that contains electronic components. See Figure 2.2. Some of the most important of these components are as follows:

- The central processing unit
- Memory
- Basic controllers
- Expansion ports and expansion slots

FIGURE 2.2
Simplified motherboard

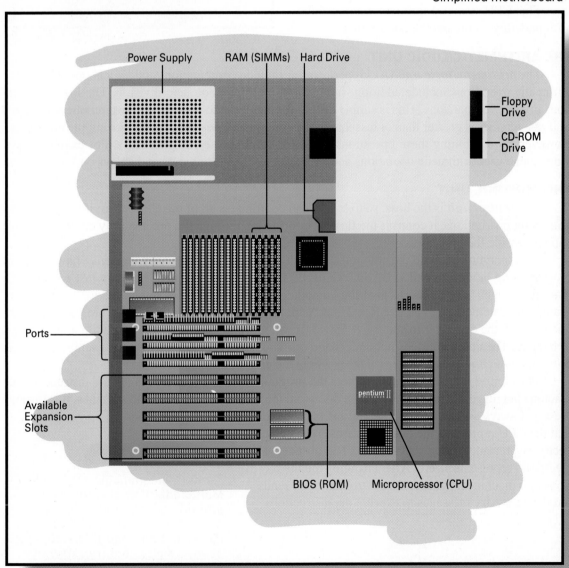

The Central Processing Unit

The *central processing unit*, also called the microprocessor, the processor, or central processor, is the brains of the computer. The CPU is housed on a tiny silicon chip. See Figure 2.3. This chip contains millions of switches and pathways that help your computer make important decisions. The switches control the flow of the electricity as it travels across the miles of pathways. The CPU knows which switches to turn on and which to turn off because it receives its instructions from computer programs. Programs are a set of special instructions written by programmers that control the activities of the computer. Programs are also known as software.

The CPU has two primary sections: the arithmetic/logic unit and the control unit.

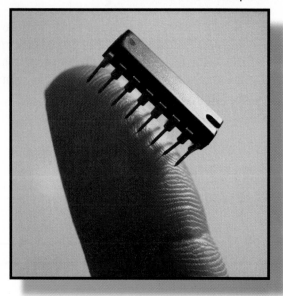

FIGURE 2.3
The brains of the computer

THE ARITHMETIC/LOGIC UNIT

The *arithmetic/logic unit* (ALU) performs arithmetic computations and logical operations. The arithmetic operations include addition, subtraction, multiplication, and division. The logical operations involve comparisons. This is simply asking the computer to determine if two numbers are equal or if one number is greater than or less than another number. These may seem like simple operations. However, by combining these operations, the ALU can execute complex tasks. For example, your video game uses arithmetic operations and comparisons to determine what displays on your screen.

THE CONTROL UNIT

The *control unit* is the boss, so to speak, and coordinates all of the CPU's activities. Using programming instructions, it controls the flow of information through the processor by controlling what happens inside the processor.

We communicate with the computer through programming languages. You may have heard of programming languages called BASIC, COBOL, C++, or Visual Basic. These are just a few of the many languages we can use to give the computer instructions. For example, we may have a programming statement such as Let X = 2 + 8. With this statement, we are using a programming language to ask the computer to add 2 + 8. However, when we input this instruction, something else has to happen. The computer does not understand our language. It only understands machine language, or binary, which is ones and zeros. This is where the control unit takes over.

The control unit reads and interprets the program instruction and changes the instruction into machine language. Recall that earlier we discussed the CPU and pathways and switches. It is through these pathways and the turning on and off of switches that the CPU represents the ones and zeros. When electricity is present, it represents a one. The absence of electricity represents a zero. After changing the instructions into machine language, the control unit then sends out the necessary messages to execute the instructions.

 Internet

Jones Telecommunications and Multimedia Encyclopedia Web site has a wealth of information on computer history and development. You can find this Web site at www.digitalcentury.com/ency-clo/update/comp_hd.html.

Memory

Memory is also found on the motherboard. Sometimes understanding memory can be confusing because it can mean different things to different people. The easiest way to understand memory is to think of it as "short term" or "long term." When you want to store a file or information permanently, you use secondary storage devices such as the computer's hard disk drive or a floppy disk. You might think of this as long term.

RANDOM ACCESS MEMORY

You can think about the memory on the motherboard as short term. This type of memory is called *random access memory,* or *RAM*. You may have heard someone ask, "How much memory is in your computer?" Most likely they are asking how much RAM is in your computer. Data, information, and program instructions are stored temporarily on a RAM chip or a set of RAM chips. See Figure 2.4.

When the computer is turned off or if there is a loss of power, whatever is stored in the RAM memory chips disappears. Therefore, it is considered volatile. The computer can read from and write to this type of memory. RAM is also referred to as *main memory* and primary memory.

FIGURE 2.4
RAM Chip: memory

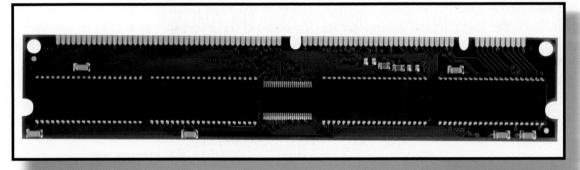

STEP-BY-STEP ▷ 2.1

To better understand how RAM works and how the computer processes data, think about our earlier example when you created the list of names and addresses for Vista Multimedia. Let's assume you use a word processing program to create your list.

1. You start your word processing program.

2. The computer loads your word processing program instructions into RAM.

3. You input the names, addresses, and telephone numbers (your data). Your data is also stored in RAM.

4. You give your word processing program a command to process your data by arranging it in a special format. This command and your processed data, or information, is also now stored in RAM.

5. You click the Print button. Instructions to print are transmitted to RAM and your document is sent to your printer.

(continued on next page)

6. You click the Save button. Instructions to provide you with an opportunity to name and save your file are loaded into RAM.

7. You save your file, exit your word processing program, and turn off the computer.

This step-by-step process is known as the Instruction cycle or I-cycle and the Execution cycle or E-cycle. When the CPU receives an instruction to perform a specified task, such as in step 4, the instruction cycle is the amount of time it takes to retrieve the instruction and complete the command. The execution cycle refers to the amount of time it takes the CPU to execute the instruction and store the results in RAM. See Figure 2.5.

Together, the instruction cycle and one or more execution cycles create a machine cycle. Machine cycles are measured in microseconds (millionths of a second), nanoseconds (billionths of a second), and even pico seconds (trillionths of a second) in some of the larger computers. The faster the machine cycle, the faster your computer processes data. The speed of the processor has a lot to do with the speed of the machine cycle. However, the amount of RAM in your computer can also help increase how fast the computer processes data. The more RAM you have, the faster the computer processes data. See Figure 2.6.

8. All instructions, data, and information are erased from RAM.

Hot Tip

Can't afford that new computer, but need more speed? Try adding more RAM. Or purchase one of the optimizer software programs.

FIGURE 2.5
Processing Cycle

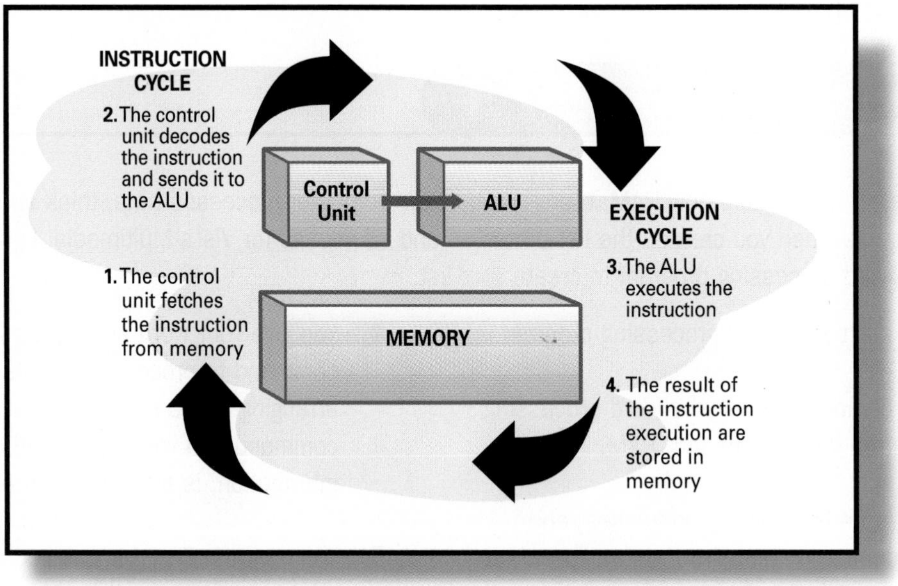

INSTRUCTION CYCLE

2. The control unit decodes the instruction and sends it to the ALU

Control Unit → ALU

1. The control unit fetches the instruction from memory

MEMORY

EXECUTION CYCLE

3. The ALU executes the instruction

4. The result of the instruction execution are stored in memory

FIGURE 2.6
Machine Cycle

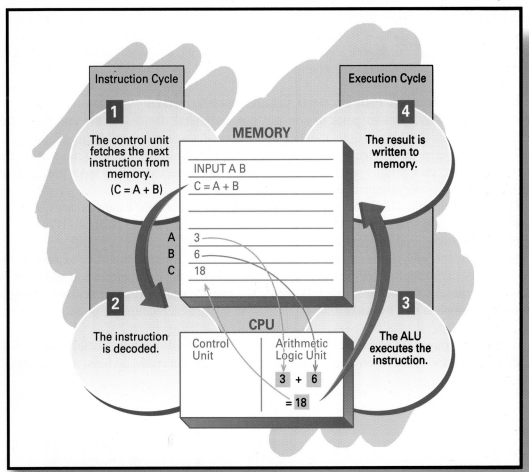

Instruction Cycle

1 The control unit fetches the next instruction from memory.
(C = A + B)

2 The instruction is decoded.

Execution Cycle

4 The result is written to memory.

3 The ALU executes the instruction.

MEMORY

INPUT A B
C = A + B

A   3
B   6
C   18

CPU

Control Unit

Arithmetic Logic Unit

3 + 6
= 18

READ-ONLY MEMORY

Another type of memory you will find on the motherboard is *ROM*, or *read-only memory*. ROM chips are found throughout a computer system. The computer manufacturer uses this type of chip to store specific instructions that are needed for the computer operations. This type of memory is nonvolatile. These instructions remain on the chip regardless if the power is turned on or off. The most common of these is the BIOS ROM. The computer uses instructions contained on this chip to boot or start the system when you turn on your computer. A computer can read from a ROM chip, but cannot write or store data on the chip.

 Did You Know?

Another type of memory is called cache memory. This very high-speed RAM is used to increase the speed of the processing cycle.

Basic Controllers

The motherboard also contains several controllers. A controller is a device that controls the transfer of data from the computer to a peripheral device and vice versa. Examples of common peripheral devices are keyboards, mouse, monitors, and printers. Controllers are generally stored on a single chip. When you purchase a computer, all the necessary controllers for the standard devices are contained on the motherboard. See Figure 2.7.

Serial and Parallel Ports and Expansion Slots

We use serial and parallel ports to connect our peripheral devices to the computer. Serial devices transmit data one *bit* at a time. Parallel devices transfer several bits at a time. A bit is a zero or one. Most computers have at least one parallel port and one serial port. You will most likely find a printer connected to your parallel ports and perhaps a modem connected to your serial port. A modem is a device that allows one computer to talk to another.

The Universal Serial Bus (USB) is a new standard that supports data transfer rates of up to 12 million bits per second. You can use a single USB port to connect up to 127 peripheral devices. USB is expected to replace serial and parallel ports.

Expansion slots are an opening on the motherboard where a circuit board or expansion board can be inserted. Let's suppose that you want to add pictures to your list of names and addresses. You need a scanner to scan the pictures. And you need some way to connect the scanner to the computer. You could accomplish this by adding an expansion board and then connecting the scanner to the board.

Or perhaps you would like to add more memory. Motherboards contain special expansion slots for additional memory. Expansion boards are also called expansion cards, add-ins, and add-ons. See Figure 2.8.

FIGURE 2.7
A close-up of a motherboard

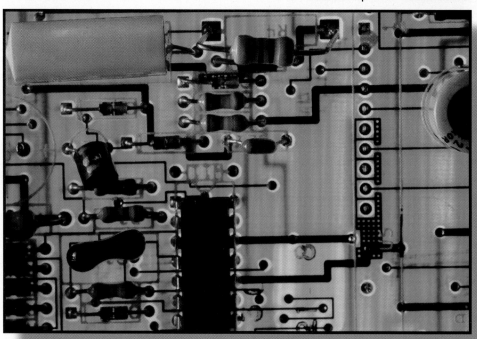

FIGURE 2.8
Expansion card

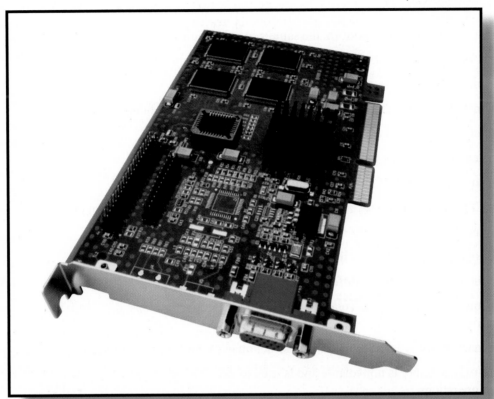

Data Representation

Earlier in this module, you read about binary and that a bit is either a zero or a one. You may wonder, though, just exactly how the computer determines what combination of zeros and ones represent the letter A or the number 1. It's really very simple. This is accomplished through standardized coding systems. The most popular system is called ASCII (pronounced as-kie) and stands for American Standard Code for Information Interchange. There are other standard codes, but ASCII is the most widely used. It is used by nearly every type and brand of microcomputer and by many large computers as well.

Eight bits or combinations of ones and zeros represent a letter such as A. Eight bits are called a *byte* or character. Each capital letter, lowercase letter, number, punctuation mark, and various symbols has its own unique combination of ones and zeros.

Another type of standard code is called or *Extended* Binary Coded Decimal Interchange Code, or EBCDIC (pronounced EB-si-dik). This code is mostly used in very large computers.

 Internet

Find out more about the ASCII standard by visiting the Webopedia Web site located at webopedia.internet.com/TERM/A /ASCII.html. Type the URL exactly as shown here.

Summary

- Just about all computers perform the same general options: input, process, output, and storage.

- Input, output, and processing devices grouped together represent a computer system.

- The motherboard is the center of all processing.

- The motherboard contains the CPU, memory, and basic controllers for the system.

- The motherboard also contains ports and expansion slots.

- The central processing unit is the brains of the computer.

- The computer is given instructions through computer programs.

- The CPU has two main sections—the arithmetic logic unit and the control unit.

- All calculations and comparisons take place in the ALU.

- The control unit coordinates the CPU activities.

- The motherboard contains different types of memory.

- Random access memory is volatile and is used to store instructions, data, and information temporarily.

- The machine cycle is made up of the instruction cycle and the execution cycle.

- Read-only memory is nonvolatile and is used to store permanent instructions needed for computer operations.

- A controller is used to control the transfer of data between the computer and peripheral devices.

- Peripheral devices are connected to the computer through serial and parallel ports.

- The Universal Serial Bus is a new standard expected to replace serial and parallel ports.

- Expansion boards are used to connect specialized peripheral devices or to add more memory to the computer.

- The ASCII code is a standard code used to represent the alphabet, numbers, symbols, and punctuation marks.

LESSON 2 REVIEW QUESTIONS

MULTIPLE CHOICE

1. Eight _____ make one character.
   - **A.** characters
   - **B.** bits
   - **C.** bytes
   - **D.** codes

2. The _____ contains the CPU, memory, and basic controllers.
   A. memory
   B. motherboard
   C. processor
   D. expansion slot

3. The _____ is considered the brains of the computer.
   A. program
   B. ALU
   C. CPU
   D. control unit

4. Random access memory is _____.
   A. permanent
   B. volatile
   C. nonvolatile
   D. the same as ROM

5. A printer would be considered a(n) _____.
   A. controller
   B. peripheral device
   C. input device
   D. USB

TRUE/FALSE

Circle the T if the statement is true. Circle F if it is false.

T F 1. You would most likely use a serial port to connect a modem to your computer.

T F 2. The ASCII code is the most widely-used standardized coding system.

T F 3. A bit has eight bytes.

T F 4. The two primary sections of the CPU are the ALU and the control unit.

T F 5. The computer only understands machine language.

SHORT ANSWER

1. You can think of RAM as _____-term memory.

2. The instruction cycle and the execution cycle create a _____ cycle.

3. The _____ the machine cycle, the faster your computer.

4. A _____ is a board that contains electronic components.

5. You would add memory to a computer by inserting it into a(n) _____ slot.

27

MATH/LANGUAGE ARTS/SCIENCE

Collect three or four computer ads from your local Sunday paper. Using either a spreadsheet program or paper and pencil, complete a comparison table. Include the following elements in your table: processor speed, amount of memory, number of expansion slots, and price. Based on your comparisons, write a short paragraph explaining which computer you would purchase and why.

SCIENCE/LANGUAGE ARTS

If possible, find a computer system with the case removed. Examine the motherboard and the components connected to the motherboard. Locate and count the number of available expansion slots. Locate the RAM chips. See if you can find the CPU. Can you see the chip itself? Create a drawing of the system and label as many of the components as you can.

SOCIAL STUDIES/LANGUAGE ARTS

Using the Internet or other resources, see what you can find about the history of computers. See if you can find the answers to the following questions: (1) What is the name of the first commercially available electronic digital computer? (2) In what year was the IBM PC first introduced? (3) What software sent Bill Gates on his way to becoming the richest man in the world? (4) In what year did Apple introduce the Macintosh computer? Use your word processing program to answer each of these questions and/or to provide some additional historical facts.

LANGUAGE ARTS/SCIENCE

Many people compare the computer to our brain. We input data into the computer, process the data, and then output it in the form of information. Consider how we function as a human—that we input through our five senses, process what we input by thinking about it, and then talk or perform some action as output. If we as humans can function like a computer, then what's so great about this technology and why do we need it? Write a paragraph or two explaining and contrasting how you function versus how the computer works. List advantages and disadvantages. Do you think there will ever be a computer that can rival the human brain? Explain your answer.

WEB PROJECT

Launch your Web browser and type in the following URL: www.AskJeeves.com.
When the Web site is displayed, ask Jeeves "Who invented the microprocessor?" and click **ASK**. Jeeves will provide several answers for you. Choose the one most appropriate and click **ASK**. This takes you to the Web site where you can find the answer to your question. Use your presentation systems program to create a presentation on what you found at this Web site. Include the name of and an overview of the person who developed the first transistor. Add two or three more slides to your presentation with information you find at this Web site. Share your presentation with your teacher and classmates.

TEAMWORK PROJECT

The manager at Vista Multimedia is ready to update the company computer system. The manager doesn't like to spend money. She wants to buy the cheapest system on the market. She has asked you and three of your fellow employees to do some research and make a recommendation on a best buy. Your team, however, thinks that the cheapest computer is not the best deal for the company. Your team's job is to convince the manager that she needs to invest in a more expensive system.

HOW DO I INPUT DATA AND OUTPUT AND STORE INFORMATION?

OBJECTIVES

When you complete this module, you will be able to:

- Identify and describe the most common input devices.

- Identify and describe the most common output devices.

- Identify and describe how input and output devices are connected to the computer.

- Identify and describe storage devices.

⏱ **Estimated Time: 1.5 hours**

VOCABULARY

Input devices
Keyboard
Monitors
Mouse
Optical storage devices
Output devices
Parallel port
Printers
Serial port
Voice recognition

We all can agree it is the computer that does all of the work of processing data! However, it needs help. Data must be entered into the computer. Once the data has been entered and processed, it has to be "presented" to the user. Special devices are used for these tasks. Such devices are called input and output devices.

When customers come into the video store to rent videos, they leave with the rented videos and a receipt. In order for the receipt to be printed, you enter the customer's information into the computer and the printer produces a receipt.

You used the keyboard or a scanner to enter the information or to input the data. The printer produced a copy of the transaction, or the output of the information.

Input devices enable you to input data and commands into the computer and ***output devices*** enable the computer to give you the results of the processed data.

Some devices perform both input and output functions. The modem is an example. When it is used for transmitting an e-mail message, it is an input device when the sender inputs the message to be sent to the receiver. The message received is the output.

Input Devices

The type of input device used is determined by the task to be completed. An input device can be as simple as the keyboard or as sophisticated as those used for specialized applications such as voice or retinal recognition devices.

Keyboard

The *keyboard* is the most common input device for entering numeric and alphabetic data. Therefore, if you are going to use the computer efficiently, it is very important that you learn to keyboard. *Keyboarding* means being able to type without having to look at the keys.

When you enter information into the computer at the video store, it is important to be able to enter the information in a reasonable amount of time. You would not want to have the customer standing around waiting too long.

The keyboard comes in many different sizes and shapes. The standard keyboard, similar to the typewriter keyboard, is divided into four sections: the typewriter keyboard, the function keys, the directional keys, and the numeric keypad. See Figure 3.1.

- The computer keyboard is much like the keyboard of a typewriter. They both have alphabetic and numeric keys; however, the computer keyboard has some additional keys called *modifier keys*. They are used in conjunction with other keys. These are the Shift, Ctrl (control), and Alt (alternate) keys. A letter or number must be depressed while the modifier key is held.

- The numeric keypad is located on the right side of the keyboard and looks like an adding machine. However, when you are using it as a calculator, be sure to depress the Num Lock key so the light above Num Lock is lit.

- The *function keys* (F1, F2, and so forth) are usually located at the top of the keyboard. These keys are used to give the computer commands. The function of each key varies with each software program. For example, F2 in Corel WordPerfect performs a different function than F2 in Microsoft Excel.

FIGURE 3.1

A typical computer keyboard divided into four sections: function keys, typewriter keyboard, numeric pad, and directional keys

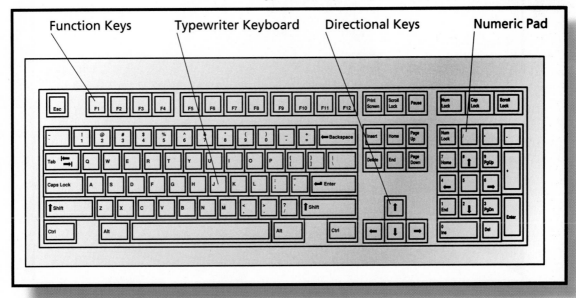

- The *arrow keys* allow you to move the position of the cursor on the screen.

- *Special-purpose keys* perform a specialized function. The Esc key's function depends on the program being used. Usually it will back you out of a command. The PRINT SCRN sends a copy of whatever is on the screen to the printer. The Scroll Lock key, which does not operate in all programs, usually controls the strolling of the cursor keys. The Num Lock key controls the use of the number keypad. Remember: In order for the keypad to operate as a calculator, the light on Num Lock must be lit. The Caps Lock key controls typing text in all capital letters.

Internet

Many companies specialize in developing ergonomic keyboards that minimize the stress caused by keying data for long periods of time. Use a search engine such as AskJeeves.com or Dogpile.com to locate several of these companies and see the types of products they produce.

- Some keyboards may have additional keys. Many keyboards are now ergonomic, which means they have been designed to fit the natural placement of your hands and should reduce your risk of repetitive motion injuries such a carpal tunnel syndrome. See Figure 3.2.

FIGURE 3.2
An example of a keyboard

Mouse

The *mouse* is a pointing device that rolls around on a flat surface and controls the *pointer* on the screen. The pointer is an on-screen arrow-shaped object used to select text and access menus. As you move the mouse, the "arrow" on the screen also moves.

The mouse fits conveniently in the palm of your hand. It has a ball located on the bottom that rolls around on a flat surface as the mouse is moved. Most of these devices have two buttons; however some have three buttons. You usually use the left button for most mouse operations. Once you place the on-screen pointer where you want it, depress a button on the mouse. This will cause some type of action to take place in the computer; the type of action depends on the program being used.

Everything that you do with the mouse will be done by these techniques:

■ *Pointing:* placing the on-screen pointer at a designated location

■ *Clicking:* pressing and releasing the mouse button

■ *Dragging:* pressing down the mouse button and dragging the mouse while continuing to hold down the button

■ *Double clicking:* pressing and releasing the mouse button twice in rapid succession

■ *Right clicking:* pressing the right mouse button. See Figure 3.3.

FIGURE 3.3
The mouse is used as a pointing device to select an option.

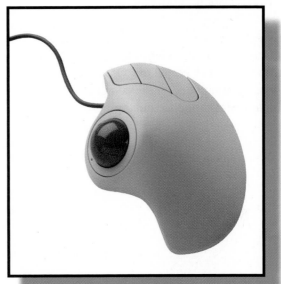

TECHNOLOGY CAREERS

PC SUPPORT SPECIALIST

The PC support specialist provides support for application software and related hardware via telephone and/or site visits to all workstation users.

As a PC support specialist you need to be knowledgeable about current software and have good oral communication and organizational skills. You will be required to interface with all departments within the company and users with various skill levels ranging from novice to expert. You must be willing to learn other areas of MIS (Management Information Systems) such as networking, printer maintenance, and e-mail.

A bachelor's degree is preferred for most of these jobs; however impressive experience is also accepted. Experience performing actual hands-on hardware and software upgrades is important. Depending on the size and location of the company, salaries can range from $28,000 to

Joystick

The *joystick* is also a pointing device. It consists of a plastic or metal rod mounted on a base. It can be moved in any direction. Some joysticks have switches or buttons that can input data in a on/off response. Joysticks are most often used for games. See Figure 3.4.

Trackball

The *trackball* is a pointing device that works like a mouse turned upside down; the ball is on top of the device. You use your thumb and fingers to operate the ball, thus controlling the arrow on the screen. See Figure 3.5.

Graphics Tablet

A *graphic tablet* is a flat drawing surface on which the user can draw figures or write something freehand. The tablet is connected to the computer. Once the drawing has been inputted to the computer, it can be manipulated like a regular graphic.

FIGURE 3.5
Trackball

FIGURE 3.4
Joystick

Touch Display Screen

The *touch display screen* has pictures or shapes. You use your fingers to "point" to the desired object to make a selection. These screens can be found in many public establishments such as banks, libraries, delivery services, and fast-food restaurants. These are very user-friendly input devices. See Figure 3.6.

Voice Recognition Devices

Voice recognition devices are used to "speak" commands into the computer and to enter text. These devices are usually microphones. The computers must have some type of voice recognition software installed on the computer. Directory assistance is also a type of voice recognition technology. Voice recognition technology has also enabled disabled persons to command wheelchairs and other objects that will make them more mobile. See Figure 3.7.

Scanners

Scanners are devices that can change images into codes for input to the computer. There are various sizes and types of scanners:

- *Image scanners* convert images into electronic form that can be stored into a computer's memory. The image can then be manipulated.

- *Bar code scanners* read bar lines that are printed on products (for example, in a grocery store or department store).

- *Magnetic scanners* read encoded information on the back of credit cards. The magnetic strip on the back of the cards contains the encoded user's account number. See Figure 3.8.

FIGURE 3.6
Touch screens are often used in retail stores where keyboards are impractical.

FIGURE 3.7
Speech recognition devices can be used by handicapped persons to command wheelchairs.

FIGURE 3.8
Optical character reading equipment is frequently
used in grocery stores to read the price on an item.

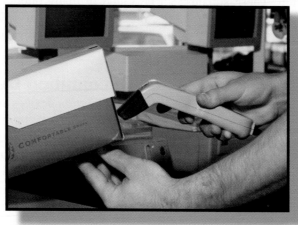

FIGURE 3.9
Digital camera store photographs that can
later be transferred to a computer system
and viewed on a monitor.

Video Input

Video input allows images generated with camcorders and VCRs to be transferred to the computer. Once input into the computer, the images can be viewed on the screen and even edited.

Digital Cameras

The pictures taken with a digital camera are stored in the camera's memory and can be transferred to the computer's memory. These pictures can be viewed quickly and any imperfections can be edited. See Figure 3.9.

 Did You Know?

You don't need a digital camera to have digital pictures. Your photo lab can deliver your photos to you via the Internet or on a disk in digital format.

Output Devices

Output devices display information. Examples of output are printed text, spoken words, music, pictures, or graphics. The most common output devices are monitors and printers.

Monitors

Monitors are called video display screens because images are displayed on the screen. They can be either monochromatic or color. A monochromatic (monochrome) monitor screen is a one-color display. It could be white, green, or amber. Color monitors display thousands of colors. Most computers today are color.

Factors that influence the quality of a monitor are screen size, resolution, and dot pitch. *Screen size* is the diagonal measurement in inches from one corner of the screen to the other. Common measurements for monitors are 15, 17, 19 and 21 inches. With large monitors you can make the objects on the screen appear larger, or you can fit more information on the screen. The larger screens are more expensive. Most computers are sold with 15–17-inch monitors. *Resolution* is the number of pixels or dots that a monitor can display. Most 15-inch monitors have pixel grids settings of 640 x 480, 800 x 600, and 1024 x 768. *Dot pitch* measures the distance between pixels. See Figure 3.10.

FIGURE 3.10
Monitors come in various sizes while notebook computers use flat-panel displays that are built into the lid.

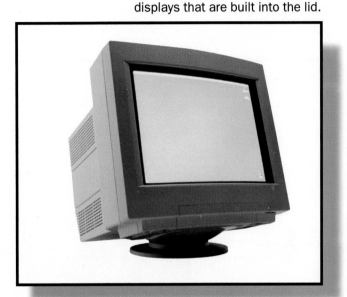

Printers

Printers are used to produce a paper or hard copy of the processing results. There are several types of printers with tremendous differences in speed, print quality, price, and special features.

When selecting a printer, consider the following features:

- **Speed:** Printer speed is measured in ppm, pages per minute. The number of pages a printer can print per minute varies for text and for graphics. Graphics print slower than regular text.

- **Print quality:** Print quality is measured in dots per inch, dpi. This refers to the resolution.

- **Price:** The price includes the original cost of the printer as well as what it costs to maintain the printer. A good-quality printer can be purchased very inexpensively; a high-output system can cost thousands of dollars. The ink cartridges and toners need to be replaced periodically.

The three most popular types of printers are laser, ink jet, and dot matrix. Printers are classified as either impact or nonimpact. *Impact printers* use a mechanism that actually strikes the paper to form images. Dot

Hot Tip

Downloading graphic and text files from the Internet is another form of computer input. Once you download file from the Internet, you can save it on your computer's hard drive or to a floppy disk if there is enough space to hold it.

matrix printers are impact printers. ***Nonimpact printers*** form characters without striking the paper. Laser printers and ink jet printers are examples of nonimpact printers.

LASER PRINTERS

Laser printers produce images using the same technology as copier machines. The image is made with a powder substance called toner. A laser printer produces high-quality output. The cost of a laser printer has come down substantially. Color laser printers are much more expensive, costing thousands of dollars. See Figure 3.11.

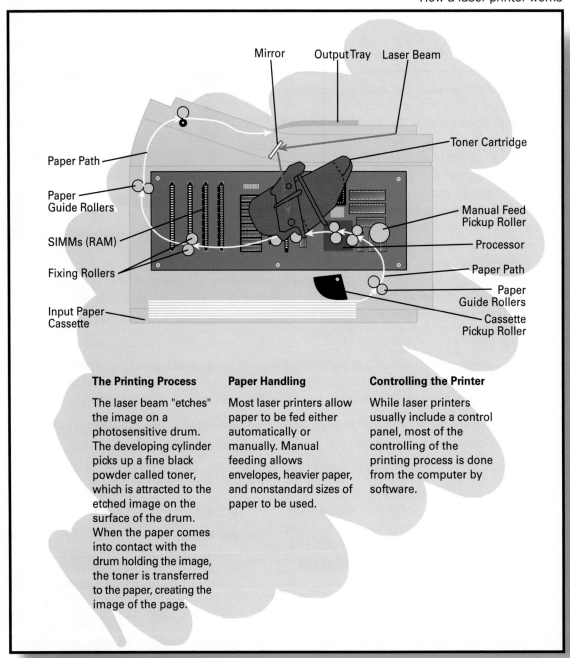

FIGURE 3.11
How a laser printer works

The Printing Process

The laser beam "etches" the image on a photosensitive drum. The developing cylinder picks up a fine black powder called toner, which is attracted to the etched image on the surface of the drum. When the paper comes into contact with the drum holding the image, the toner is transferred to the paper, creating the image of the page.

Paper Handling

Most laser printers allow paper to be fed either automatically or manually. Manual feeding allows envelopes, heavier paper, and nonstandard sizes of paper to be used.

Controlling the Printer

While laser printers usually include a control panel, most of the controlling of the printing process is done from the computer by software.

INK JET PRINTERS

The use of ink jet printers is a less expensive way to have color printing available. The color is sprayed onto the paper. The same process used in laser printers is used in ink jet printers; it just works slower. Unlike earlier versions of the ink jet printers, the new versions can use regular photocopy paper. Ink jet printers are also combined with other technologies to create complete "three-in-one" office machines. These machines combine printer, copier, and fax capabilities into one. See Figure 3.12.

FIGURE 3.12
How an inkjet printer works

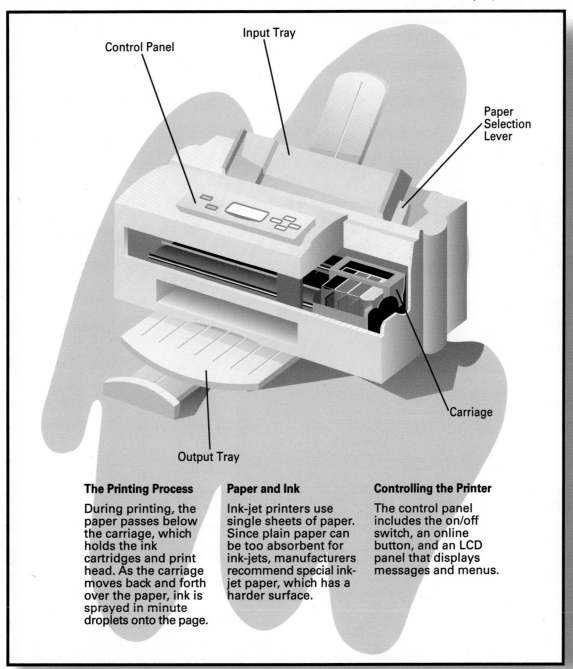

Control Panel

Input Tray

Paper Selection Lever

Carriage

Output Tray

The Printing Process

During printing, the paper passes below the carriage, which holds the ink cartridges and print head. As the carriage moves back and forth over the paper, ink is sprayed in minute droplets onto the page.

Paper and Ink

Ink-jet printers use single sheets of paper. Since plain paper can be too absorbent for ink-jets, manufacturers recommend special ink-jet paper, which has a harder surface.

Controlling the Printer

The control panel includes the on/off switch, an online button, and an LCD panel that displays messages and menus.

DOT MATRIX PRINTERS

Impact printers have been around for a long time. They print by transferring ink to the paper by striking a ribbon with pins. The higher the number of pins (DPI), the better the resolution or output. The mechanism that actually does the printing is called a ***printhead.*** The speed of the dot matrix printer is measured in characters per second (cps). See Figure 3.13.

FIGURE 3.13

Dot matrix printers are impact printers that are often used to print on multi-part paper. Tiny pins in the printhead tap the paper through a ribbon to form an image, which is made up of dots.

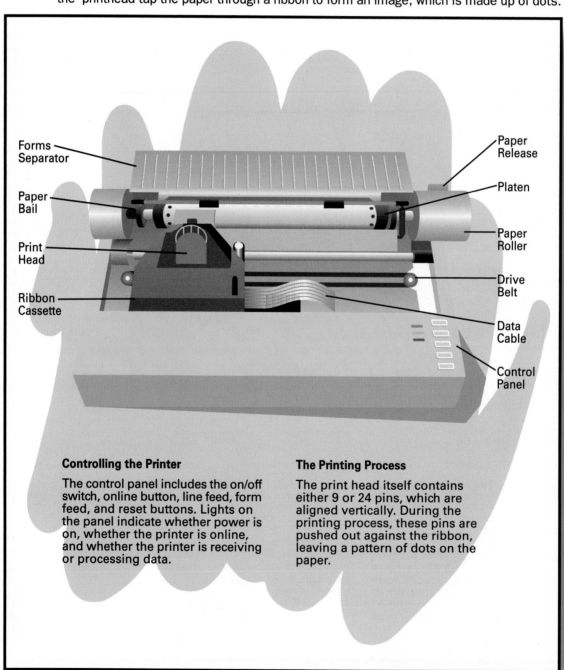

Controlling the Printer

The control panel includes the on/off switch, online button, line feed, form feed, and reset buttons. Lights on the panel indicate whether power is on, whether the printer is online, and whether the printer is receiving or processing data.

The Printing Process

The print head itself contains either 9 or 24 pins, which are aligned vertically. During the printing process, these pins are pushed out against the ribbon, leaving a pattern of dots on the paper.

Connecting Input/Output Devices to the Computer

Input and output (I/O devices) must be physically connected to the computer. There are two ways to connect these devices to a computer. You can plug the device into an existing socket or port located on the back of the computer, or you can install a circuit board with the port you need already included.

Serial and Parallel Ports

Computers can have several types of ports, including the following:

■ *Parallel ports* transmit data eight bits at a time.

■ *Serial ports* transmit one bit at a time. It is like a narrow one-lane road. A mouse, keyboard, and modem are connected in serial ports.

Special Ports

■ *SCSI* (pronounced "scuzzy") stands for small computer system interface. One SCSI port can provide connection for one or more peripheral devices; they allow many devices to use the same port.

■ *MIDI* (pronounced "middy") ports are used to connect computers to electronic instruments and recording devices.

■ *PC cards* are used to add memory and to connect peripheral devices to notebook computers. They act as the interface between the motherboard and the peripheral device. The use of expansion cards in notebook computers is impractical because of the size of the notebook computer. These slots allow for the attachment of printers, modems, hard disks, and CD-ROM drives.

■ *USB* ports can replace other types of ports such as serial and parallel ports, and and they can plug up to 127 devices.

Storage Devices

As data is entered into the computer and processed, it is stored in RAM. If you want to keep a permanent copy of the data, you must store it on some type of storage medium such as the following:

■ Floppy diskettes

■ Hard disks

■ CDs

■ Magnetic tape cartridges

■ WORM disks (Write once, read many)

■ Zip and Jaz diskettes

■ Super floppy

Storage devices are categorized by the method they use to store data. Magnetic storage devices use oxide-coated plastic storage media called mylar. As the disk rotates in the computer, an electromagnetic read/write head stores or retrieves data in circles called *tracks*. The number of tracks on a disk varies with the type of diskette. The tracks are numbered from the outside to the inside. As data is stored on the disk it is stored on a numbered track. Each track is labeled and the location is kept in a special log on the disk called a *file allocation table* (FAT).

The most common types of magnetic storage medium are floppy diskettes, hard drives, and magnetic tape.

Floppy Diskettes

Floppy diskettes, usually just called diskettes, are flat circles of iron oxide-coated plastic enclosed in a hard plastic case. Most floppy diskettes are 3¹/₂-inches, although you may see other sizes. They have a capacity to hold 1.44 MB or more of data. To protect unwanted data from being added to or removed from a diskette, write protection is provided. To write-protect a diskette, open the write protect window on the diskette. See Figure 3.14.

Hard Disk Drives

Hard disk drives are used to store data inside of the computer. They provide two advantages: speed and capacity. Accessing data is faster and the amount of data that can be stored is much larger than what can be stored on a floppy diskette. The size of the hard drive is measured in megabytes or gigabytes. See Figure 3.15.

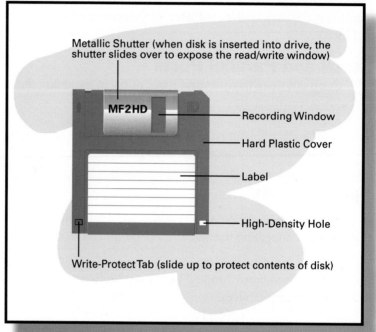

FIGURE 3.14
The parts of a diskette

Metallic Shutter (when disk is inserted into drive, the shutter slides over to expose the read/write window)

MF2HD

Recording Window

Hard Plastic Cover

Label

High-Density Hole

Write-Protect Tab (slide up to protect contents of disk)

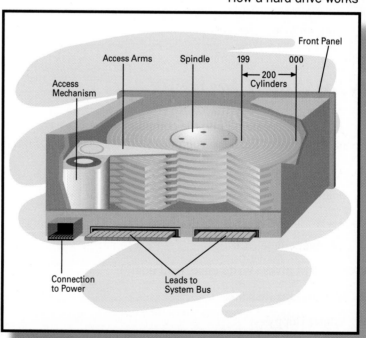

FIGURE 3.15
How a hard drive works

Front Panel

Access Arms   Spindle   199   000

← 200 →
Cylinders

Access Mechanism

Connection to Power

Leads to System Bus

Zip Drives and Jaz Drives

Zip drives and Jaz drives house disks that are capable of storing tremendous amounts of storage. Even though they are only the size of a 3-inch diskette, they can hold as much as 1 GB of data. The Zip drives are slower than the Jaz drives; they can hold as much as 70 floppy diskettes but are less expensive than the Jaz drive. The Jaz drive is much faster and can store up to 1 GB of data. See Figure 3.16.

Magnetic Tape Drives

Magnetic tape drives are used for making backup copies of large volumes of data. This is a very slow process and therefore not used for regularly saving data. The tape can be used to replace data that may have been lost on the hard drive.

Optical Storage Devices

Optical storage devices use laser technology to read and write data on silver platters.

CD-ROM

The *CD-ROM* (Compact Disk Read-Only Memory) can store up to 680 MB. This is the equivalent of about 450 floppy diskettes! You can only read data from the CD; you cannot store data on a CD unless you are using the new writable CDs.

FIGURE 3.16
Types of removable storage

ETHICS IN TECHNOLOGY

COMPUTER VIRUSES

The word "viruses" can put fear into anyone who uses the Internet or exchanges diskettes. How can such a small word cause such fear? It is because a virus can cause tremendous damage to your computer files!

A virus is simply a computer program that is intentionally written to attach itself to other programs or disk boot sectors and duplicates itself whenever those program are executed or the infected disks are accessed. A virus can wipe out all of the files that are on your computer.

Viruses can set on your computer for weeks or months and not cause any damage until a predetermined date or time code is activated. Not all viruses cause damage. Some of just pranks; maybe your desktop will display some silly message. Viruses are created by persons who are impressed with the power they possess because of their expertise in the area of computers and sometimes they create them just for fun.

To protect your computer from virus damage, install an anti-virus software program on your computer and keep it running at all times so that it can continuously scan for viruses.

WORM DISKS

WORM disks (Write Once Read Many) are optical disk storage devices that use laser beams and optical technology. They are usually used for permanently storing large volumes of data. The data is stored by making imprints into the surface of the disk that cannot be removed.

CD-R

CD-R (Recordable) drives make it possible for you to create your own CD-ROM disks that can actually be read by any CD-ROM drive. Once information has been written to this type of this, it cannot be changed.

PHOTOCD

The **PhotoCD** is used to store digitized photographic images on a CD. The photos stored on these disks can be uploaded into the computer and used in other documents.

DVD MEDIA

Full-length movies can be stored on the **DVD** (Digital Versatile Disk). It is the size of a regular CD and can be played in a regular CD. However, the DVD movie player can connect to your TV and play movies like a VCR.

Caring for Removable Storage Media

Removable storage media require special care if the data stored is to remain undamaged. Here are some safeguards that should be taken:

- Keep away from magnetic fields such as those contained in televisions and computer monitors.

- Avoid extreme temperatures.

- Never open the data shutter or attempt to disassemble a removable disk cartridge. Never touch the surface of the media itself.

- Remove media from drives and store them properly when not in use.

- Write-protect important data to prevent accidental erasure.

- When handling CD-ROMs and other optical discs, hold them at the edges.

- Never try to remove the media from a drive when the drive indicator light is on.

- Keep disks in a sturdy case when transporting.

Summary

- Input devices enable you to input data and commands into the computer.

- The most common input devices are the keyboard and mouse.

- The keyboard is divided into four sections: alphabetical keys, function keys, cursor keys, and the numeric keypad.

- Additional special-purpose keys perform specialized functions.

- The mouse is a pointing device used to input data.

- Other types of input devices include joysticks, track balls, graphic tablets, touch display screens, voice recognition devices, scanners, and electronic pens.

- Printers are used to produce a paper or hard copy of the processed result.

- Criteria for selecting a printer includes speed, print quality, and cost.

- Printers are classified as either impact or nonimpact.

- The most popular types of printers are laser, ink jet, and dot matrix.

- Input and output devices must be physically connected to the computer.

- There are two ways to connect I/O devices to a computer: Plug the device into a port in the back of the computer or install a circuit board with the needed port included.

- There are several types of ports: USB, SCSI, MIDI, parallel, and serial.

- To maintain a permanent copy of data, you must store it on some type of storage medium. These may include floppy diskettes, hard drives, CDs, magnetic tape cartridges, and WORM disks.

LESSON 3 REVIEW QUESTIONS

MULTIPLE CHOICE

1. Laser, ink jet, and dot matrix are types of _____.
   A. monitors
   B. printers
   C. storage devices
   D. input devices

2. Monitors and printers are types of _____.
   A. input devices
   B. output devices
   C. storage devices
   D. ports

3. All of the following are types of ports, *except* _____.
   A. MSO
   B. USB
   C. SCSI
   D. MIDI

4. Floppy diskettes are also called _____.
   A. diskettes
   B. hard drives
   C. CDs
   D. magnetic disks

5. All of the following are sections of the keyboard *except* _____.
   A. alphabetic keys
   B. function keys
   C. Esc key
   D. numeric keypad

TRUE/FALSE

Circle the T if the statement is true. Circle F if it is false.

T F 1. Modifier keys are used in conjunction with other keys.

T F 2. Input and output devices perform the same function.

T F 3. The mouse is a pointing device that rolls around on a flat surface and controls the pointer.

T F 4. Factors that influence the quality of a monitor are screen size, resolution, and dot pitch.

T F 5. PPM refers to the number of pages that a printer prints per minute.

SHORT ANSWER

1. A /An _____ is used to enter data into the computer.

2. _____ and _____ are the most popular output devices.

3. Input and output devices are connected to computers through _____.

4. The two types of ports are _____ and _____.

5. Hard disks and floppy diskettes are types of _____ mediums.

CROSS-CURRICULAR PROJECTS

MATH

Contact computer vendors, read computer magazines, research the Internet, and use any other resources to collect data concerning the prices of at least five storage devices. Find sales information for the same product from three vendors. Determine the average cost of each device. Prepare a chart like the one here to show your findings.

Storage Device	Capabilities	Vendor	Cost	Vendor	Cost	Vendor	Cost	Avg. Cost

SCIENCE

There are many styles of keyboards for computers. Many of the designs were developed to address various health issues related to keyboard use. Use appropriate research sources to locate information on various keyboard designs and report on the theory on which they are designed. You may also visit retail stores that sell computers to obtain information and sales documents. Prepare a written report of the information you locate.

SOCIAL STUDIES

Prepare a written report in table format of early storage media. Your table should have the columns shown here. Include at least five types of early storage media.

Type	Media	Capacity	Advantages	Disadvantages

LANGUAGE ARTS

Prepare a report describing several applications in which a user would need to use the Jaz or Zip drive to store data. Describe the application and explain why it would be necessary to use the Zip or Jaz drive. Also explore the alternatives to using these drives. You may find useful information at www.iomega.com.

WEB PROJECT

Christopher Sholes is given credit for inventing the first typewriter (keyboard). How did he design his keyboard? Why did he design it the way that he did? Who invented the one before his? Why was this person not given credit for inventing the first typewriter? Use a search engine on the Internet to answer these questions and to find other information concerning the early typewriter. Prepare a written report of your findings. The following keywords may be helpful in your search: *Christopher Sholes, typewriter,* and *keyboard.*

TEAM PROJECT

Your supervisor at the video store is interested in setting up a teleconference with several of the stores throughout the state. However, she would like to get more information on this capability. She has asked you and the assistant manager to research this technology for her and let her know the steps needed to set up such a conference. Research the Internet and any other materials to prepare a step-by-step guide for setting up a teleconference. Include an introduction that gives basic information about teleconferencing.

WHAT IS SOFTWARE?

OBJECTIVES

When you complete this module, you will be able to:

- Distinguish between software and hardware.

- Describe the difference between applications software and systems software.

- Describe the three categories of system programs.

- Describe operating systems for microcomputers.

- Describe network operating systems.

⏱ Estimated Time: 1.5 hours

VOCABULARY

Applications software
DOS
Graphical user interface (GUI)
Hardware
Network operating system
Operating systems
Software
Systems software

Over the last 50 years or so, computer technology has changed the world. Not so long ago, Vista Multimedia employees would not have used computers. The customers would not have ID cards that could be scanned. The accounting was done using ledgers.

When most of us think about computers, we think of hardware and how the hardware has changed—that computers have become smaller and faster. If we look at the history of computers, however, we find that the early computers were used for little more than high-speed calculators. This alone would not have had such a major influence on our culture and economy. The reason that computers have had such an impact is through the vision and desire of software developers. These software creators came up with hundreds of ideas and ways in which to use computers. They created programs that affect us in every aspect of our lives.

Hardware vs. Software

You have probably heard the words software and hardware many times. Sometimes it is difficult to distinguish between these two terms. Hardware refers to anything you can touch. This includes objects such as the keyboard, mouse, monitor, printer, chips, disks, disk drives, and CD recorders. You cannot touch software because it has no substance. Software is instructions issued to the computer so that specific tasks may be performed. Another word for software is program.

For example, a computer programmer may write a program that lets the user download music from the Internet. Or suppose the Vista Multimedia bookkeeper has a problem with his computer.

You might hear him say, "The problem lies in the software." This means there is a problem with the program or data, and not with the computer or hardware itself. He may also say, "It's a software problem." A good analogy here is a book. The book, including the pages and the ink, is the hardware. The words and ideas on the pages are the software. One has little value without the other. The same is true of computer software and hardware.

Types of Software

There are two basic types of computer software: ***applications software*** and ***systems software.*** Application software helps you perform a specific task. System software refers to the operating system and all utility programs that manage computer resources at a low level. Figuratively speaking, applications software sits on top of systems software. Without the operating system and system utilities, the computer cannot run any applications program.

Applications Software

Applications software is widely referred to as productivity software. Applications software is comprised of programs designed for an end user. Some of the more commonly used application programs are word processors, database systems, presentation systems, spreadsheet programs, and desktop publishing programs. Some other applications categories are as follows:

- Education, home, and personal software—reference, entertainment, personal finance, calendars, e-mail, browsers

- Multimedia software—authoring, animation, music, video and sound capturing and editing, virtual reality, Web site development

- Workgroup computing software—calendars and scheduling, e-mail, browsers, electronic conferencing, project management

FIGURE 4.1
Operating systems: an interface between users and computers

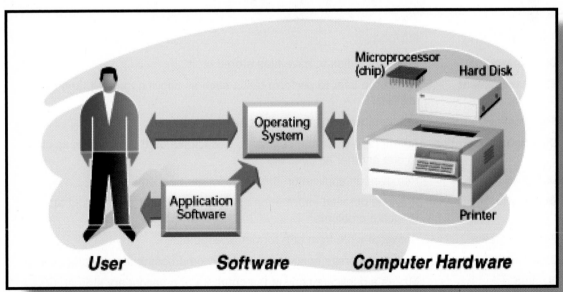

Systems Software

Systems software is a group of programs that coordinate and control the resources and operations of a computer system. Systems software enables the many components of the computer system to communicate. There are three categories of systems software: operating systems, utilities, and language translators.

OPERATING SYSTEMS

Operating systems provide an interface between the user or application program and the computer hardware. See Figure 4.1. There are many brands and versions of operating systems software. Each of these is designed to work with one or more particular processors. For example, an operating system like Windows is designed to work with a processor made by Intel. Many IBM PC compatible computers contain this brand of processor. Most Macintosh computers contain a processor manufactured by Motorola. The Windows operating system does not work with this Motorola processor.

UTILITIES

Utility programs help you perform housekeeping chores. You use these programs to complete specialized tasks related to managing the computer's resources, file management, and so forth. Some utility programs are part of the operating system, and others are self-contained programs. See Figure 4.2. Some examples of utility program functions are as follows:

- You format a disk—a disk formatting utility provides the instructions to the computer on how to do this.

- You copy a file from the hard drive to a floppy disk—the file management utility provides the instructions to the computer.

- Ms. Perez, Vista Multimedia manager, asks that you do a backup of the hard drive—you use the backup utility.

See Table 4.1 for a list and purpose of the most commonly used utilities.

TABLE 4.1

UTILITY PROGRAMS

Type of Utility	Purpose
Disk formatting	Prepares a disk to have files stored on it
File management	Allows the user to perform tasks such as copying, moving, and deleting files
File recovery	Attempts to recover a file that has been erased
Disk defragmentation	Attempts to place the segments of each file on the hard disk as close to one another as possible
Uninstall	Removes an application that is no longer needed
Diagnostic	Provides detailed information about the computer system and attempts to locate problems
File conversion	Converts a file from one format to another
Disk compression	Frees up storage space on a disk by compressing the existing files.
Backup	Makes a duplicate copy of the contents of a secondary storage device
Anti-virus	Protects the computer system from viruses

FIGURE 4.2
File conversion utility

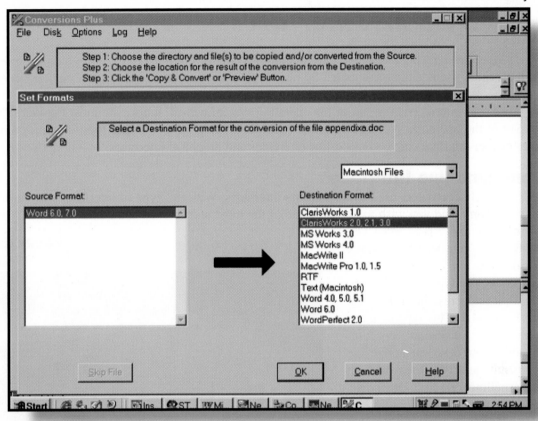

LANGUAGE TRANSLATORS

Language translators convert English-like software programs into machine language that the computer can understand. Vista Multimedia hires a programmer to write a software program to inventory all of the items in the store. The programmer writes the program statements using a programming language called Visual Basic. A program statement directs the computer to perform a specified action.

The computer, however, cannot read the Visual Basic programming statements because they are written in a language that we understand. This is where the language translator takes over. The translator changes each of the Visual Basic programming statements into machine language. A single statement in a high-level language can represent several machine-language instructions. Now the statements can be executed and the Vista Multimedia inventory can be processed.

Hot Tip

If you have a computer, you should have an emergency boot disk. Sooner or later, your computer may not boot from the hard drive. You can use your emergency boot disk to get your computer started. Each operating system has its own unique way of creating a boot disk. Check your operating system help files for information on how to create this disk. Then be sure to store it in an easy-to-find and safe place.

Microcomputer Operating Systems Interfaces

All computers, big and small, have operating systems. For most of us, however, the computer we most often use is a microcomputer. So our focus in this module is on microcomputer operating systems.

The user interface is the part of the operating system with which we are most familiar. This is the part of the operating system we interact with when using our computer. The two most common types of user interfaces are command-line interfaces and graphical interfaces.

Command-line Interfaces

All early computers used command-line interfaces. With this type of interface, you must type the exact command you wish to execute. One of the most widely used command-line interfaces for microcomputers is MS-DOS. Using DOS, you want to look at a list of files on your computer's hard drive. You type the DOS command dir and press the Enter key. See Figure 4.3. This type of interface is not considered very user friendly. You must memorize the commands and type them without any spelling errors. Otherwise, they do not work.

C:\APPROACH>dir

Volume in drive C has no label
Volume Serial Number is 1103-0776
Directory of C:\APPROACH

.   <DIR>   06-25-95   7:42p
..   <DIR>   06-25-95   7:42p
EXAMPLES   <DIR>   06-25-95   7:42p
TMPLATES   <DIR>   06-25-95   7:42p
ICONS   <DIR>   06-25-95   7:44p
IMGBMP   DIL   7,088 08-18-93   12:00a
IMGTGA   DIL   9,376 08-18-93   12:00a
IMGGIF   DIL   9,888 08-18-93   12:00a
README   WRI   9,984 08-18-93   12:00a
IMGPCX   DIL   15,920 08-18-93   12:00a
IMGEPSF   DIL   20,784 08-18-93   12:00a
IMGTIFF   DIL   38,496 08-18-93   12:00a
APPROACH HLP   215,152 08-18-93   12:00a
APPROACH EXE   1,205,504 08-18-93   12:00a
APPROACH V21   3 08-18-93   12:00a
       15 file(s)   1,532,195 bytes
                       139,026,432 bytes free

C:\APPROACH>

FIGURE 4.3
Command line interface

Graphical User Interfaces

As microcomputer technology developed, so did the operating system interface. The next step in this progression was menus. The user could choose commands from a list.

The big breakthrough in ease of use came with the development of *graphical user interfaces (GUIs)*. When the user turns on the computer and starts the operating system, a symbolic desktop is displayed. On this desktop are various objects, or icons. These graphical symbols represent files, disks, programs, and other objects. GUIs permit the user to manipulate these on-screen icons. Most people use a pointing device such as a mouse to click on the icons and execute the commands. See Figure 4.4.

FIGURE 4.4
Graphical user interface

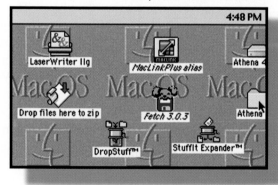

Microcomputer Operating Systems

There are several popular operating systems for microcomputers. If you are using a Macintosh or a Macintosh clone, you will most likely be using a version of the Mac OS.

If your computer is what is commonly referred to as a PC or an IBM PC compatible, you most likely are using one of these three operating systems:

- DOS

- A combination of DOS and Windows

- A stand-alone version of Windows

Internet

The history of Apple Computer and Steve Jobs and Steve Wozniak is a fascinating story. For an overview of this story and some interesting facts about the Macintosh operating system, check out the Web site at www.hypermall.com/History/ah0 1.html.

Did You Know?

Macintosh popularized the first graphical user interface; however, Apple did not invent the interface. Xerox Corporation developed the idea for a graphical user interface.

Mac OS

The Mac OS is used with Apple's Power Macintosh computers and Power Macintosh clones. The Macintosh was introduced in 1984. One of the main features of this new computer was a graphical user interface (GUI). The GUI was called the Finder and contained icons or symbols that represented documents, software, disks, and so forth. To activate the icon, the user clicked on it with a mouse. See Figure 4.5. This operating system was also the first OS to provide on-screen help or instructions.

FIGURE 4.5
Macintosh operating system

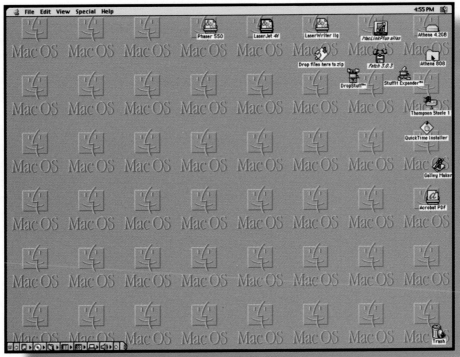

DOS

IBM introduced its first IBM PC in 1981. With the introduction of this new microcomputer came a new operating system (OS). This system was called DOS (Disk Operating System). IBM referred to this operating system as PC DOS. They licensed this software from a small start-up company called Microsoft. But as agreements go, Microsoft retained the rights to market its own version of the OS. Microsoft called their version MS-DOS. This OS was the catalyst that launched Microsoft into the multibillion dollar company it is today.

DOS is a character-based operating system. The user interacts with the system by typing in commands. DOS is a single-user or single-tasking operating system because the user can run only one program at a time.

Windows

In response to the competition from the Macintosh, Microsoft introduced its own GUI in 1987. This OS was called Windows.

■ The first versions of Windows contain a graphical shell and were called operating environments because they work in combination with DOS.

■ The different applications installed on a computer appeared as icons.

■ The user activates the icons by clicking on them with a mouse.

■ These early versions of Windows were consecutively numbered beginning with Windows 3.0, Windows 3.1, and so forth.

TECHNOLOGY CAREERS

SOFTWARE DEVELOPER

A software developer maintains and helps develop new application and operating systems programs. When you see a job listing for software developer, it could include many requirements.

A company may be looking for someone to develop software using a particular programming language such as Visual Basic, C, or C++. Or a company may be looking for someone to develop add-ons to operating systems programs. This could include enhancements to utility programs, updates to language translators, or new additions to the operating system itself. Many companies seek employees with skills in operating systems programs such as Unix and Windows NT.

If you go online and look for software developer jobs, you will find that many of them refer to Oracle, a large information technology software company. Oracle products support database technology, data design and modeling, Web applications, and much more.

There is a great variation in salaries and educational requirements. Salaries can range from $25,000 to $100,000 plus. Educational requirements range from some college to a bachelor's or master's degree or maybe even a Ph.D. Generally, but not always, the more education you have, the higher your starting salary. Most companies require some experience, but a few have entry-level positions.

54

Windows 95 was Microsoft's first true multitasking operating system. Multitasking allows a single user to work on two or more applications that reside in memory at the same time. Some advantages of Windows 95 include the following:

■ An improved graphical interface.

■ Programs run faster than with earlier Windows versions.

■ Includes support for networking, which allows a group of two more computers to be linked.

Internet

Want to learn more about Windows CE, Microsoft's operating system for small handheld devices? Access the Web site www.whatis.com; in the Quick Search text box, type Windows CE and click Go. You can also find additional information at www.microsoft.com/windowsce/.

■ Uses Plug and Play technology, the goal of which is to just plug in a new device and immediately be able to use it, without complicated setup maneuvers.

Windows 98 is easier to use than Windows 95 and has additional features. Some of these new features include the following:

■ Internet integration.

■ Windows Explorer has a Web browser look option.

■ Faster system startup and shutdown.

■ Support for the Universal Serial Bus that is used to easily add and remove devices on the computer.

Windows 2000 is an update to the Windows 98 and the Windows NT operating systems. See Figure 4.6. Some new features include the following:

■ Tools for Web site creation

■ Wizards that guide the user through various operations

■ Monitoring programs

Windows CE is a scaled-down Windows operating system. It is used on small handheld computers and wireless communication devices.

FIGURE 4.6
Windows 2000 operating system

Still another operating system is Unix. This operating system, developed by AT&T, is considered a portable operating system. This means it can run on just about any hardware platform. There are several variants of the language, such as Linux and IBM's AIX. See Figure 4.7.

FIGURE 4.7
Unix operating system

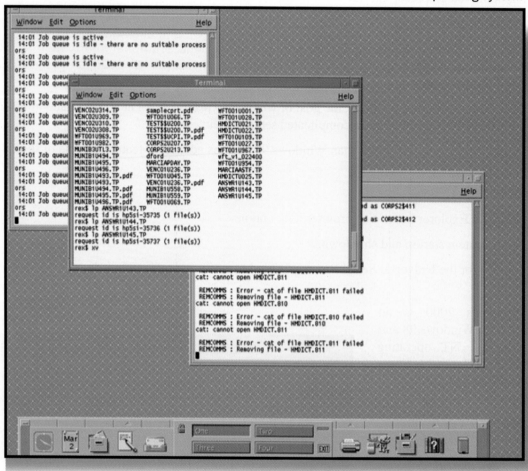

STEP-BY-STEP ▷ 4.1

When you start your computer, operating system commands are loaded into memory. Each operating system boots or starts the computer in its own individual way. Understanding the boot process is the key to diagnosing many computer start-up problems.

The Step-by-Step given in this example is based on the Windows OS system. Keep in mind, however, that the boot process is similar for all operating systems.

1. When you turn on the computer, the first thing that happens is POST, an acronym for Power-on Self Test. This is a series of diagnostic tests to check RAM and to verify that the keyboard and disk drives you may have are physically connected to the computer.

2. The BIOS (Basic Input Output System) searches for the boot record—first on drive A and then on drive C. The BIOS is built-in software that is normally placed on a ROM chip. It contains all of the code that controls the most common devices connected to your computer. This includes the monitor, keyboard, disk drives, and other components. This chip comes with your computer when you purchase it.

3. The boot record is loaded into RAM. The boot record contains several files. These files contain programming configuration instructions for hardware devices and software applications that you may have installed on your computer.

4. Next, the software drivers are loaded. Drivers are what enable you to use your printer, modem, scanner, or other devices. Generally when you add a new device to your system, you install drivers for that device.

5. Next to be loaded is the GUI or graphical user interface. In this instance, the GUI is Windows. When loading the GUI, the operating system reads the commands for your desktop configuration. It also loads whatever programs you have previously specified into the Windows Start-up Folder.

6. If everything goes as it should, the GUI displays and the computer is ready to use.

Network Operating Systems

Network operating systems allows a group of two or more microcomputers to be connected. There are several brands of network operating systems. Three of the most popular are as follows:

- Microsoft Windows NT
- Novell's Netware
- IBM's Warp Server

WHAT IS COMPUTER ETHICS?

Webster's Online Dictionary[1] offers the following definition of ethics:

(1)the discipline dealing with what is good and bad and with moral duty and obligation

(2)a: a set of moral principles or values, b: a theory or system of moral values <the present-day materialistic ethic>, c: plural but singular or plural in construction: the principles of conduct governing an individual or a group <professional ethics>, d: a guiding philosophy.

Ethical judgments are no different in the area of computing than they are in any other. The use of computers can raise many issues of privacy, copyright, theft, and power, to name just a few. In 1990 the Institute of Electrical and Electronics Engineers created the following code of ethics. Many businesses and organizations have adopted this code as their code. Remember that this is just a code—not a law. People choose to follow it voluntarily.

CODE OF ETHICS

We, the members of the IEEE, in recognition of the importance of our technologies affecting the quality of life throughout the world, and in accepting a personal obligation to our profession, its members, and the communities we serve, do hereby commit ourselves to the highest ethical and professional conduct and agree:

1. to accept responsibility in making engineering decisions consistent with the safety, health, and welfare of the public, and to disclose promptly factors that might endanger the public or the environment;

2. to avoid real or perceived conflicts of interest whenever possible, and to disclose them to affected parties when they do exist;

3. to be honest and realistic in stating claims or estimates based on available data;

4. to reject bribery in all its forms;

5. to improve the understanding of technology, its appropriate application, and potential consequences;

6. to maintain and improve our technical competence and to undertake technological tasks for others only if qualified by training or experience, or after full disclosure of pertinent limitations;

7. to seek, accept, and offer honest criticism of technical work, to acknowledge and correct errors, and to credit properly the contributions of others;

8. to treat fairly all persons regardless of such factors as race, religion, gender, disability, age, or national origin;

9. to avoid injuring others, their property, reputation, or employment by false or malicious action;

10. to assist colleagues and co-workers in their professional development and to support them in following this code of ethics.

[1] Webster's Online Dictionary: courses.ncsu.edu:8020/classes-a/computer_ethics/basics/principles/

Summary

- Hardware refers to anything you can touch.

- Software is instructions that tell the computer what to do.

- Software is also called a program.

- The two basic types of computer software are applications software and systems software.

- Applications software is also known as productivity software.

- Systems software coordinates and controls the resources and operations of a computer system.

- Three major categories of systems software are operating systems, utilities, and language translators.

- Operating systems provide an interface between the user and application program and the computer hardware.

- Utility programs help users complete specialized tasks such as file management.

- Language translators convert English-like software programs into machine language.

- A programmer uses a programming language to write program statements.

- All computers have operating systems.

- The user interface is the part of the operating system with which we are most familiar.

- The two most common user interfaces are command-line interfaces and graphical user interfaces.

- The Mac operating system is used with Apple's Power Macintosh computers and Power Macintosh clones.

- Icons are symbols that represent documents, software programs, disks, and so forth.

- DOS was introduced with the IBM PC in 1981 and is a character-based operating system.

- Microsoft introduced the first version of Windows in 1987; this was an operating environment.

- Windows 95 was Microsoft's first true multitasking operating system.

- Windows CE is a scaled-down Windows operating system used for small handheld computers.

- Unix is a portable operating system.

- Network operating systems allow a group of two or more microcomputers to be connected.

MULTIPLE CHOICE

1. Another word for software is _____.
   A. hardware
   B. program
   C. programming statement
   D. an interface

2. The two basic types of computer software are _____ and
   _____.
   A. program, applications
   B. productivity, applications
   C. applications, systems
   D. systems, networking systems

3. A group of programs that coordinate and control the resources of a computer system is called
   _____.
   A. systems software
   B. applications software
   C. language translator
   D. utility program

4. The _____ is the part of the operating system with which we are most
   familiar.
   A. formatting utility
   B. programming statement
   C. language translator
   D. user interface

5. DOS was first introduced with the _____.
   A. Apple Macintosh
   B. IBM PC
   C. Unix operating system
   D. Windows

TRUE/FALSE

Circle the T if the statement is true. Circle F if it is false.

T F 1. The first version of Windows was a true operating environment.

T F 2. DOS is a multitasking operating system.

T F 3. Apple Computer Company developed the GUI.

T F 4. Computer hardware is anything you can touch.

T F 5. There are five categories of systems software.

SHORT ANSWER

1. The second step in the progression of the operating system interface was

   _____.

2. Word processing is an example of _____ software.

3. Novell NetWare is an example of _____ system.

4. One of the main features of Apple's Power Macintosh was the _____ interface.

5. DOS is a _____-user operating system.

CROSS-CURRICULAR PROJECTS

MATH/LANGUAGE ARTS

To use a floppy disk, you must first format it. Use the Internet or other written resources and write step-by-step instructions on how to format a floppy disk. If you have a computer available, give your instructions to one of your classmates. Ask them to use your instructions and format a floppy disk. Were they able to follow the instructions easily? At the end of the formatting process, a summary displays telling you the number of available bytes on the disk. Include the name in your report. If there are any bad bytes in bad sections, include that information as well.

SCIENCE

Operating systems have come a long way over the last few years. They are much easier to user and support many more features. If you were going to design an operating system for computers for the year 2010, what features would you include? How would your operating system be different from those that are currently available? Use your word processing program to write a report or give an oral report to the class.

SOCIAL STUDIES/LANGUAGE ARTS

The more recent versions of operating systems include accessibility options for people with visual or hearing disabilities. Research the operating system on your computer and complete a report on the accessibility options.

LANGUAGE ARTS

You have been hired to create an icon to represent a new software program that has just been developed. This is an interactive encyclopedia. It also contains games to help reinforce the topics presented in the encyclopedia. Think about the icons on your computer's desktop or that you see in the figures throughout this chapter. Using graph paper or a computer drawing program, create an icon for this new interactive encyclopedia.

WEB PROJECT

Office 2000 is a popular applications suite of programs. For an online tutorial of some of the ways you can use Office 2000, go to www.actden.com/o2k/HTML/index_h.htm.

When you complete the tutorial, use your word processing program to write an overview of what you learned. Your report should be at least one page.

TEAM PROJECT

You and two team members have been given the responsibility for purchasing new computers for Vista Multimedia. One team member wants to purchase an Apple Macintosh with the Mac OS, another wants to purchase a PC with the latest version of the Windows OS, and the third wants to purchase a PC with the Unix operating system. The manager has requested that your team do some research and present her with a report so that she can make the best choice. Your report should include the positives and negatives for each of these operating systems.

How Do I Keyboard?

OBJECTIVES

When you complete this module, you will be able to:

- Identify the parts of the standard keyboard.
- Identify the home row keys.
- Identify the parts of the word processing screen.
- Identify correct typing techniques.
- Key (type) text without watching the keys
- Save, print, retrieve, spell check, and format files.

⏱ **Estimated Time: 1.5 hours**

VOCABULARY

Home row keys
Keyboarding
Menu bar
Ribbon
Ruler
Status bar
Text area
Title bar
Toolbar
Word wrap

A major part of your work at Vista Multimedia involves typing information into the computer. You enter information when customers rent videos and CDs as well as when you create letters and other documents for the store. Because of the amount of typing you need to do, it is important that you develop good keyboarding skills.

Some people think it is not necessary to have good typing skills. However, if you look at a computer, you will see that the keyboard is a major element of a computer system. See Figure 5.1.

True, it is not necessary to be a speed typist, but having adequate keyboarding skills will enable you to use the computer much more effectively to be more productive. The skill of typing, or *keyboarding*, as it is called today, is the ability to enter text by using the correct fingers without looking at the keys. This is also sometimes called touch typing.

Efficient keyboarding is essential for using application programs such as word processing, database, spreadsheet, desktop publishing, presentation, telecommunication, and other miscellaneous programs.

 **Hot Tip**

Christopher Sholes invented the first typewriter.

 Internet

Visit www.members.aol.com/typebar/collectible/gallery.htm to see pictures of early computers.

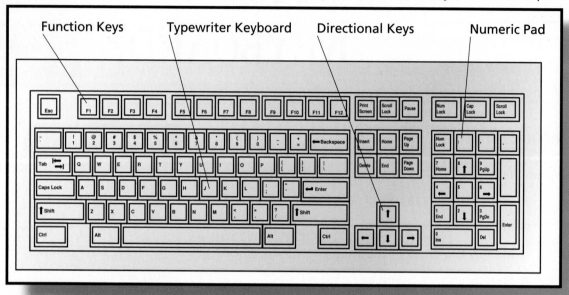

FIGURE 5.1

The computer keyboard is divided into four sections: function keys, typewriter keyboard, directional keys, and numeric pad.

Function Keys   Typewriter Keyboard   Directional Keys   Numeric Pad

First Things First

Let's get started on learning to keyboard properly. Mastering this skill will let you use your time on the computer concentrating on the application you are working on instead of searching for keys!

The Keyboard Layout

Refer to Figure 5.1 again. This is only one style of keyboard. There are many different styles. Your keyboard may look different. However, they all have the same basic parts.

Some keyboards are designed to relieve stress that can result from repeated and/or longtime use on a keyboard. These are called *ergonomic keyboards*. See Figure 5.2

- Alphanumeric keys: the parts of the keyboard that look like a typewriter. They are arranged the same way on all keyboards. This arrangement is sometimes called the *QWERTY* layout because the first six keys on the top row of letters are Q, W, E, R, T , and Y.

- *Modifier* keys: These keys are used in conjunction with other keys.

  - CTRL for control

  - ALT for alternate

  - SHIFT

- The numeric keypad is usually located on the right side of the keyboard. It looks like a calculator. The keys look like the ones on a calculator; however, if you look closely, you will see some additional symbols on the keys. These are used in various software programs.

- The function keys are usually located in a row at the top of the keyboard. You use these to give the computer commands. Each function key varies with the software being used.

Did You Know?

The arrangement of the keys on the first typewriter was alphabetical. Early typists used a two-finger technique to type called "hunt and peck." This arrangement of keys made typing very slow and was soon changed.

- The directional keys control the movement of the pointer on the screen. The cursor is also referred to as the insertion point.

- The special-purpose keys perform specialized functions.

  - Esc key: The function depends on the program. Usually used to "back up" one level in a multilevel environment, that is, back up one step in a multistep process.

  - Print Screen: Depressing this key sends a copy of your screen directly to the clipboard.

  - Scroll Lock: Despite the term, this key does not allow you to scroll documents necessarily. The way this key functions depends on the software being used.

  - Pause/break: In some software programs, this key can be used to stop a command in progress.

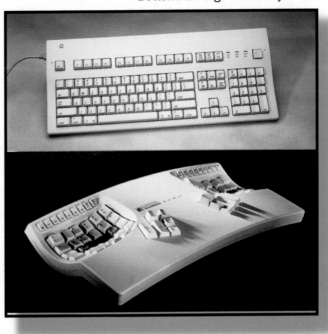

FIGURE 5.2
Top: a traditional keyboard;
Bottom: an ergonomic keyboard

The Computer Screen

Once you load the word processing program you are going to use to learn how to keyboard, a screen similar to Figure 5.3 will appear.

The information you see in this figure will assist you in learning to keyboard and preparing documents.

FIGURE 5.3
Word processor display

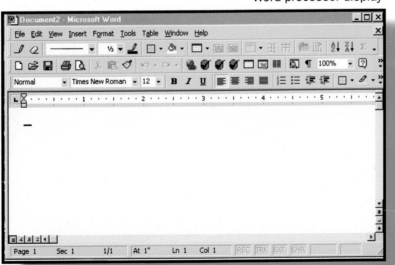

- **Document title:** You will give all of your documents a name. The name will appear in this area. This area is sometimes called the **Title Bar**.

- **Menu bar:** The commands you will use are displayed on this bar.

- **Standard toolbar:** Icons (little pictures) of commonly used commands are displayed on this bar.

- **Formatting toolbox** The icons in this area allow you to change the appearance of your document. It is sometimes called the Formatting toolbar.

- **Ruler:** The ruler is used to change paragraph indentations and margin settings and add tab settings.

- **Text area:** This is the area that contains the information you type. As you type in this area, the insertion point continues to move to the right.

- **Vertical scroll bar:** This bar is used to scroll through your document vertically.

- **Horizontal scroll bar:** This bar is used to scroll through your document horizontally.

- **Status bar:** This bar displays information about your document, including current page number, total pages in document, location of cursor, and the status of some of the specialized keys.

Your screen may look a little different. Different software programs have different screens. However, they are basically the same. One last point about the screen: As you type and the insertion point moves to the right, the text will drop down to the next line. This is called **word wrap**. The text will wrap around the right margin and continue on the next line. You do not need to press the Enter key to get to the next line. You will see this when you begin to type paragraphs.

Correct Typing Techniques

KEYSTROKING

Using the correct fingers to type is very important. Your hands should be placed in a curved position over the home row. The **home row** keys include a, s, d, f, j, k, l, and ;. These are called the home row because these are the keys from which all keystrokes are made. After the keystroke is made, the finger returns to the home row. See Figure 5.4.

FIGURE 5.4
Correct hand position on a keyboard

FIGURE 5.5
A student sitting correctly at a computer

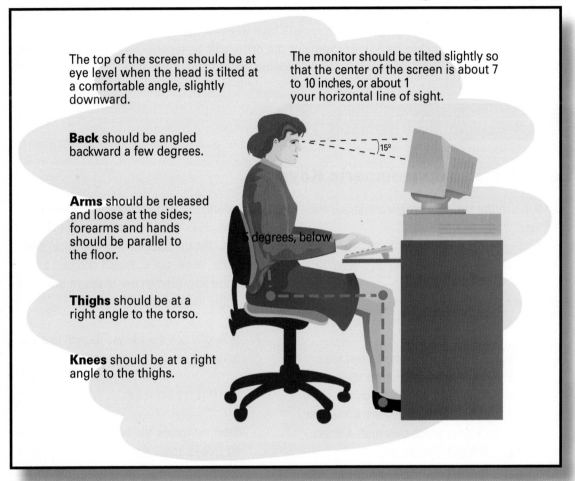

The top of the screen should be at eye level when the head is tilted at a comfortable angle, slightly downward.

The monitor should be tilted slightly so that the center of the screen is about 7 to 10 inches, or about 1 your horizontal line of sight.

Back should be angled backward a few degrees.

15º

Arms should be released and loose at the sides; forearms and hands should be parallel to the floor.

5 degrees, below

Thighs should be at a right angle to the torso.

Knees should be at a right angle to the thighs.

POSITION

The correct keyboarding position refers to your posture. Sit up straight and lean forward slightly from the waist. Keep your feet flat on the floor. Your body should be about a hand's length from the front of the keyboard and centered with the keyboard. Focus your eyes on the book or whatever you are typing unless you are composing at the keyboard; then keep your eyes on the computer screen. See Figure 5.5.

YOUR WORKSTATION

Your workstation, which includes your desk, chair, computer, printer, supplies, and reference materials, should always be organized. Place materials you will type on the right side of the computer and supplies on the left side. Keep any items you are not using off your desk.

Developing Beginning Keyboarding Skills

Developing keyboarding skill requires a lot of practice. The most important factor to master keyboarding is good technique. Speed and accuracy are built around good technique. However, at this point, you do not need to concern yourself with speed. If you concentrate on being accurate, the speed will come later.

6 7

The first part of learning to keyboard is learning to key the alphabetic keys. Your instructor may hang a large poster on the board that shows the correct finger position for reaching to other keys.

Learning to key all of the alphabetic keys will take weeks to learn. You will complete many, many drills to acquire the desired skills. Some of the drills will be repetitious—all right, maybe even boring. However, they are necessary in developing your keyboarding skill.

STEP-BY-STEP ▷ 5.1

Learning the Alphanumeric Keys

1. Launch the software program that you will use.

2. Be sure your workstation is organized.

3. Check your posture to be sure you are following the guidelines stated earlier.

4. Place your fingers on the home row keys. Be sure your fingers are curved so the tips of your fingers are resting on the home row keys. Your fingers are named for the home key on which they rest: A finger, S finger, D finger, and so on.

5. Depress the space bar to space between words. It is operated with the right thumb. Practice using the space bar. Tap the space bar once; tap it twice, tap it once, tap it twice, tap it once, tap it twice.

6. Depress the Enter key when you are ready to go down to the next line. This is called a **hard return**. To press the Enter key,

extend the Semi finger to the Enter key, and press lightly. Practice using the Enter key. Tap the space bar once, twice, once, twice, once, twice. Reach and press the Enter key. (Remember to return the Semi finger to the ; key.)

7. Now practice the f keys. You will use the following line:

fff fff ff ff f f ff ff f f

Type: fff (press the space bar once), type fff (press space bar once), type ff (press space bar once), type ff (press space bar once), type f (press the space bar once), type f (press space bar), type ff (space bar once), type ff (press space bar once), type f (press space bar once), type f (press the Enter key once).

8. Follow the same procedure in learning to type the remainder of the alphabetic keys.

Saving Your Practice Work

Once you have completed your practice, your instructor may want you to save your work on a diskette. Before you begin to save work, let's review some steps to take care of your diskettes.

■ Store your diskettes away from extreme temperatures.

■ Insert and eject diskettes carefully from the disk drive.

■ Never remove or insert a disk while the drive is running. Check for the light on the drive.

■ Make backup copies of your diskettes.

S TEP-BY-STEP ▷ 5.2

1. Click File on the menu bar. From the drop-down menu, click on Save As.

2. The Save As window will open. Be sure to select the appropriate drive on which to save your work. If you are saving your work on your own diskette, you will be using a floppy.

3. In the filename box at the left bottom, key in the name of the lesson or whatever name your instructor tells you to use.

4. Click the Save button.

5. You will be returned to the original screen where you were working. When you finish practicing, you need to exit from the software program.

6. Click on File on the menu bar. Click on Exit or Close at the bottom of the drop-down menu. You will now be returned to the computer's desktop.

After learning the alphabetic keys, you will learn to key the numeric keys and the symbols on the keyboard. You will use the same procedure to learn these keys.

Additional Concepts

Retrieving a File

Once a file has been saved, you can open that file to use it again to add additional information, to delete information, or just to read it. To open a file:

■ Click File on the menu bar.

■ Click Open on the drop-down menu.

■ Once the Open dialog box opens, be sure the drive where your file is located is displayed. This will probably be drive A. If it is not, change it so that drive A is displayed.

■ Click on the name of the file you want to open.

■ Click the Open button.

A copy of the file will appear on your screen.

Printing a File

You may be instructed to print your practice session. If you are:

■ Click File on the menu bar.

■ Click Print on the drop-down menu.

■ Once the Print dialog box opens, click the OK button. There are options in this window that you will learn to use later.

■ Once the file prints, you will be returned to the file on your screen.

69

Checking the Spelling in Your Document

If you make a spelling error as you are typing your document, the misspelled word will have a wavy red line under it. You can correct the error yourself or you can use the built-in spell checker.

If you want to correct the word yourself, use:

■ the Backspace key to delete text to the left of the insertion point.

> **Example: If the insertion point is in front of the "m" in computer and you depress the Backspace key, the "m" will be erased.**

■ the Delete key to delete text to the right of the insertion point.

> **Example: If the insertion point is behind the "m" in computer and you depress the Delete key, the "m" will be erased.**

The spell checker in your software will check your document for any misspelled words or words that it doesn't recognize. Many programs also include a grammar checker either with the speller checker or separately. To access the spell checker:

Click on Tools on the menu bar (or the spell checker icon on the toolbar).

The Speller dialog box will open. A word that the software does not recognize will be displayed. You have several options from which to choose. If the word is misspelled, click on the corrected word, and then click Change. If the word is not misspelled, click on Ignore. See Figure 5.6.

Even though your word processing software has a spell checker, it is still necessary to proofread your document carefully. It will not check for word usage such as their and there or cite, sight, and site.

FIGURE 5.6

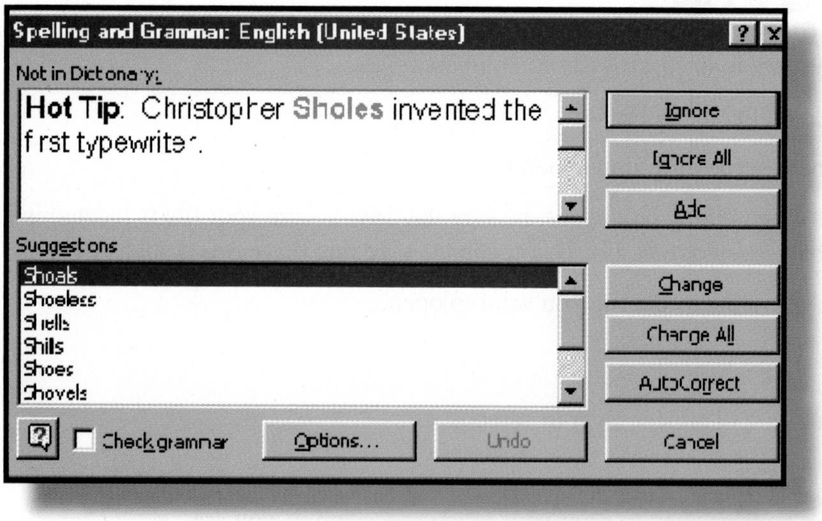

70

Formatting Your Documents

Once you have learned to keyboard, you will begin to type various types of documents like letters and reports. These documents will need to be formatted for margins, spacing, and so on. You may even want to change the style of the letters, the size of the letters, or bold or underline or italicize the text. All of these enhancements, and more, can be applied to your document. This is called *formatting* your document.

You can enter commands to format your document before you type the document or you can format your text after it has been typed. The commands for formatting documents are accessed through different commands in various software programs. However, the way that you format once the command has been selected is pretty much the same. Example: You have typed a report and now want to go back and format the title to be bold in a 14-point font.

STEP-BY-STEP ▷ **5.3**

1. Select the title by clicking on the first letter of the title, holding down the left mouse button and dragging to the end of the title.

2. Once the title is highlighted (selected), click on the Bold button on the formatting toolbar.

3. While the title is still highlighted, click on the Font Size button on the formatting toolbar and select 14 from the drop-down menu.

You can use keystrokes to access commands instead of the mouse.

TECHNOLOGY CAREERS

MANAGER OF INFORMATION SYSTEMS

The manager of information systems directs the operation of the computer system in an organization. He or she also provides the employees with any services they may need to perform their jobs.

An element of the manager's job is to keep abreast of new technology and evaluate it for possible use in the organization. Security of information is also a major responsibility.

The person in this position must have excellent communication skills because he or she has to work with both the users in the organization and senior administrators. Organizational skills are also very important.

A bachelor's degree in computer science or engineering is preferred. A master's degree in computer science would allow you the opportunity to advance quickly in the field of information systems. It is also helpful to have experience as a programmer, systems analyst, or project manager.

The salary range for this job is between $60,000 and $80,000. Of course, salary varies depending on location of position, size of organization, and experience level.

Using Your New Keyboarding Skill

Now that you have learned to keyboard efficiently, you are ready to produce a correctly formatted letter, saved it, and printed it. Use the letter in Figure 5.7.

FIGURE 5.7

Current Date

Ms. Lakita McDaniel
1106 College Drive
Cincinnati, OH 45226

Dear Ms. McDaniel

Our class has been studying various plays in our Theater class during this semester. Reading plays can sometimes transform you into a totally different person in a totally different place.

As wonderful as it is to read plays, it is even more exciting to actually see one on stage. Well, we have gotten permission and financial assistance from our principal to see the play Ragtime on the second Friday of next month at 2 p.m. at the Wilder Performing Arts Center.

The cost of the tickets has been taken care of by our principal. However, we do need you to send us signed permission for your child to attend the play with our class.   Your child will be bringing home a permission slip for you to sign. Please sign it promptly and return by the second Monday of next month.

We look forward to having your child on the field trip with us.

Sincerely

Mr. David Snead
Theater Teacher

cc

STEP-BY-STEP 5.4

1. Launch your word processing software.

2. Set your left and right margins for 1" inches.

3. Set your top margin at 2 inches.

4. Type the date and press the Enter key four times.

5. Type the inside address. Remember to press the Enter key at the end of each line. After you type the last line of the inside address, press the Enter key twice.

6. Type the salutation and press the Enter key twice.

7. Type the first paragraph. Remember that you don't press the Enter key until you complete the paragraph; then press it twice.

8. Type the second paragraph and press the Enter key twice.

9. Type the third paragraph and press the Enter key twice.

10. Type the complimentary close and press the Enter key four times.

11. Type the writer's name and press the Enter key once.

12. Type the writer's title and press the Enter key twice.

13. Type your initials in lowercase letters. Example: Carnell Cherry would type cc.

14. Save the letter on your disk with the filename Field Trip. Make sure the Save in box displays drive A.

15. Run the spell checker.

16. Print one copy of the letter.

17. Close the letter and exit from the software.

ETHICS IN TECHNOLOGY

PLAGIARISM

"Plagiarism is stealing a ride on someone else's train of thought."—Author unknown

This definition of plagiarism is very accurate. The basis of plagiarism involves using information as if it were your own.

Why is plagiarism illegal? Even though you may consider it as just taking words from someone, you are still taking something that belongs to someone else. It is his or her possession just like a person's car, house, and so on.

With widespread use of the Internet, incidents of plagiarism have risen at an astonishing rate because it is possible to find huge amounts of information with little effort. It does not take as much time to find information electronically as it does to go through volumes of books to find the same information. A research paper can easily be put together using the cut-and-paste function in your word processing program. We could say that it is just easier to find resources on the Net.

Easy it may be, but it is also illegal! It is a form of theft. You are taking the thoughts, words, and ideas of another person and using them as if they were your own. Paraphrasing someone else's thoughts is also a form of plagiarism unless you give the originator the credit for the work.

How can you avoid plagiarism? You must give credit whenever you use another person's thoughts, ideas, or opinions.

Summary

- Keyboarding is the ability to enter text by using the correct fingers and not watching your keys.

- Adequate typing skills will enable you to use a computer much more effectively.

- The standard keyboard is divided into six major sections and four additional keys:

  - Alphanumeric keys

  - Modifier keys

  - Numeric keypad

  - Function keys

  - Cursor movement keys

  - Special-purpose keys

  - Esc key

  - Print Screen key

  - Scroll Lock key

  - Pause key

- The computer screen contains features that will allow you to give commands to create a document.

- Most word processing programs have the word wrap feature. This means that instead of depressing the Enter key at the end of a line of a paragraph, you just continue to type and the text wraps around the right margin and goes down to the next line.

- All typing should begin from the home row. The home row consists of the following keys: A S D F J K L.

- Correct posture is very important in developing keyboarding skill.

- Your workstation should be kept neat and orderly.

- Learning to keyboard requires a lot of practice and patience.

- You should save your work often.

- You can retrieve files that have been saved.

- The spell checker checks the document for words it doesn't recognize. It gives you several options when words are displayed.

- Grammar checkers are also included in many word processing programs.

- You may enhance the appearance of your document by using any of the many formatting features available in the software.

- Formatting features may be applied before or after the text has been typed.

LESSON 5 REVIEW QUESTIONS

MULTIPLE CHOICE

1. Standard keyboards have the _____ layout.
   A. QWARTY
   B. QWERTY
   C. QWAZXY
   D. QWYTRE

2. _____ keys perform specialized functions.
   A. Shift keys
   B. Special-purpose keys
   C. Backspace keys
   D. Cursor keys

3. _____ bar displays information about document including current page number, total pages in document, location of cursor, and so on.
   A. Formatting toolbar
   B. Status bar
   C. Vertical scroll bar
   D. Horizontal scroll bar

4. The home row keys include _____.
   A. a, b, c, d, k, l, ;, '
   B. q, w, e, r, t, y
   C. a, s, d, f, j, k, l, ;
   D. y, r, t, q, k l, j

5. To save work on your diskette, the "Save in" box in the "Save As" dialog window should be _____.
   A. drive A
   B. drive B
   C. drive C
   D. drive D

TRUE/FALSE

Circle the T if the statement is true. Circle F if it is false.

T F 1. Keyboarding is also referred to as touch typing.

T F 2. Ergonomic keyboards relieve stress that can be incurred from repeated and/or longtime use on a keyboard.

T F 3. Christopher Sholes invented the first typewriter.

T F 4. Slouching down in the chair while keyboarding affects your keyboarding skill in a positive way.

T F 5. You press the space bar with the right pinky.

75

SHORT ANSWER

1. A _____ occurs when you press the Enter key to go down to the next line.

2. The _____ keys are usually located in a row at the top of the keyboard.

3. The correct keyboarding position refers to your _____.

4. The most important factor to master keyboarding is good _____.

5. If you concentrate in the beginning on being accurate, the _____ will come later.

CROSS-CURRICULAR PROJECTS

MATH

Most word processing programs have mathematical features built in. Use the software manual or the Help feature in your software to find out what formulas are available. Prepare a handout for your classmates describing what these formulas are, how to access them, and how to use them.

SCIENCE

Use the Internet and any other resources to locate information on El Niño. You are looking for information that will explain what it is and how it affects our weather. Write a one- to two-page report of your findings using your word processing software. Look up El Niño using a search engine.

SOCIAL STUDIES

Use the Internet and any other resources to locate information on how a bill becomes a law. Use a word processing report to list the steps involved in the lawmaking process. Use www.AskJeeves.com to find information for this project.

LANGUAGE ARTS

Use a word processing program to write a one-page summary of a movie you have seen recently or a book you have read for pleasure. Format the summary appropriately.

WEB PROJECT

www.AskJeeves.com to find information for this project.

LANGUAGE ARTS

TEAM PROJECT

Use a word processing program to write a one-page summary of a movie you have seen recently or a book you have read for pleasure. Format the summary appropriately.

Many word processing software programs have the capability to work with different languages. Access the Internet to identify several word processing programs that have this capability, and briefly describe how this feature is used. Print your report in English and two other languages of your choice.

Ms. Perez, your supervisor at the multimedia store, has asked you and the other part-time employee to design and type a form to be used to record videos that employees are allowed to check out free of charge. The form should include the name of the employee, the employee ID number, the title of the video, date checked out, due date, and date returned. Don't forget to give the form a title.

WHAT BASIC SKILLS DO I NEED TO USE THE COMPUTER?

OBJECTIVES

When you complete this module, you will be able to:

- Describe a graphical user interface.
- Start and shut down a graphical user interface.
- Open and close a window.
- Format a disk.
- Create files and folders.
- Start a program.
- Manage Windows.
- Manage files.
- Access Help

⏱ **Estimated Time: 1.5 hours**

VOCABULARY

Desktop
Finder
Folder
Formatting
Graphical User Interface (GUI)
Window
Windows

Several of the employees at Vista Multimedia have had limited experience with computers. In fact, a couple of them have only used a computer to play Hearts or other games. They know how to use the mouse, but that is just about all they know about the computer. Ms. Perez plans to set up a network in the near future and she would like all employees to have some degree of computer literacy. She has asked if you could help in this endeavor.

Overview of Graphical User Interface

Most of today's computers come with some type of GUI, an acronym for *Graphical User Interface*. This type of interface lets you interact with your computer using pictures and symbols as opposed to text. A well-designed graphical user interface makes a computer easier to use by freeing you from memorizing complicated text commands. Instead, you point and click with a mouse, or some other type of input device, to activate programs or commands.

A true graphical interface includes standard text and graphic formats. This makes it possible for the user to share data among different programs. For instance, you can create a chart in Excel and copy it into a PowerPoint document.

To work with a GUI, it is important to understand the associated terminology. Some of the more popular components are as follows:

- **Desktop:** The desktop is the first screen you see when the operating system is up and fully running. It is called the desktop because the icons symbolize real objects on a real desktop.

- **Icons:** A small picture that represents a file, commands, or some other computer function. You execute the associated command by clicking or double-clicking the icon.

- **Pointer:** An on-screen symbol that shows the current position of the mouse. It usually appears as an arrow or an I-beam pointer.

- **Pointing** *device*: A device, such as a mouse or trackball, that allows the users to select objects such as icons or text.

- **Menus:** A text interface that includes drop-down options; the user clicks on one of the choices to execute a command.

- **Scroll bar:** A horizontal or vertical bar that allows the user to control which part of a list or document is currently in the window 's frame. The scroll bar makes it easy to move to any part of a file.

- **Window:** Rectangular area of the screen; used to display a program, data, or other information. Windows can be resized and moved around the screen.

Important note: Windows is the operating system for the PC. A *window* is an object within both the Macintosh and Windows operating systems. Both Macintosh and Windows operating commands are covered in this module.

Despite the convenience of these GUI features, it is still necessary to use a keyboard for many programs. For instance, trying to enter a document in a word processor with a mouse would be impossible.

Starting and Shutting Down the GUI

To start a graphical user interface is as simple as turning on your computer. When you turn on the computer, it first performs a self-test. Next, it loads the system software. Once the computer is up and going, you're looking at the desktop. The two most popular GUIs are the Macintosh OS and Windows. The program that displays the Macintosh desktop is called Finder. There is no comparable name in Windows; it is simply called the desktop. See Figures 6.1 and 6.2.

Desktop

The desktop contains windows and icons. It is a representation of how people work at a desk. Think about how you work at your desk. You look at and read documents or files, you move the documents around, put them in folders, and store and retrieve them from a file drawer. The computer desktop works in a similar way. You have documents that you can read. You can store those documents in folders and retrieve those documents from folders. These documents and folders are represented by icons. These activities may seem very basic, but they are an essential part of any job. They help you stay organized.

 Did You Know?

The first graphical user interface was designed by Xerox Corporation's Palo Alto Research Center in the 1970s. It was not, however, until the 1980s and the development of the Apple Macintosh that graphical user interfaces became popular.

79

FIGURE 6.1
Windows desktop

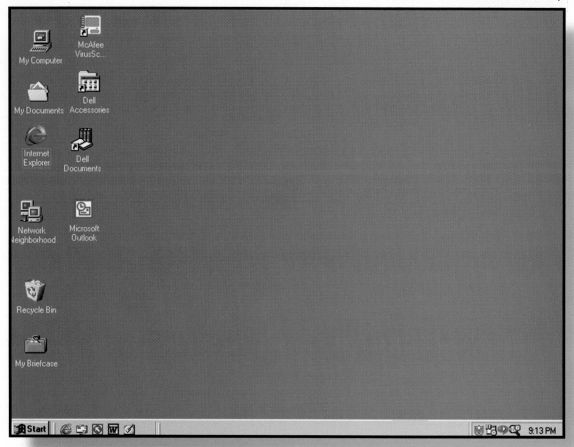

Shutting Down the System

If you are using Windows, point to Start and select ***Shut Down***. When the Shut Down Windows dialog box displays, select Shut down and click OK. If you are using a Macintosh, point to the Special menu option to display the drop-down menu. Select Shut Down.

Opening a Window

To open a window means to double-click an icon. This executes a command and opens a window on the desktop. It is easy to open and close windows and to move windows from one place to another on the screen. One of the windows you may want to view often is the Trash (Macintosh) or Recycle Bin (Windows).

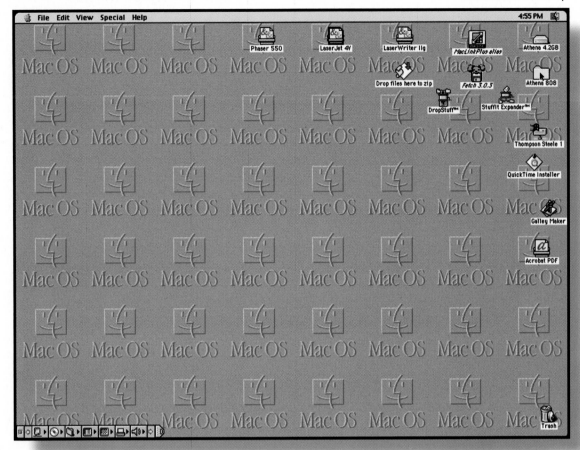

S TEP-BY-STEP ▷ 6.1

If necessary, start your computer.

1. Point to the Trash or Recycle Bin icon and double-click the mouse. This executes the program and opens a new window. Is there anything in the trash? If so, it is either represented by icons or by text. Notice that the window contains a title bar. This title bar contains lines

(Macintosh) or is highlighted (Windows), indicating the window is the active window. See Figures 6.3 and 6.4.

2. Close the window by pointing to the File menu option and selecting **Close**.

Closing a Window

To close a window within Windows, on the File menu, click *Close*. Or click the Close button [X] in the upper-right corner. To close a window within the Macintosh environment, on the File menu, click *Close Window*. Or make the window active and press Command + W.

FIGURE 6.3
Windows Recycle Bin window

FIGURE 6.4
Macintosh Trash window

Formatting a Disk

If you want to save your work on a floppy disk, you must first format the disk. A floppy disk is a portable storage medium. This means you can store data on the disk and take it with you from computer to computer. A floppy disk is a type of magnetic media. It uses magnetic patterns to store data on the disk's surface.

When you purchase a new floppy disk, chances are it is not formatted, although you can purchase preformatted disks. **Formatting** is the process of preparing the disk so that you can write data to and read data from the disk. When a disk is formatted, it is organized into tracks and sectors. A sec-

82

tor is pie shaped and can hold 512 bytes of data. A track is a narrow band that forms a full circle on the surface of the disk.

Sometimes when you format a disk, you may receive a message that the disk has a bad sector. This doesn't necessarily mean the entire surface of the disk is bad—just a small portion. However, it is generally best to discard the disk if you have one with a bad sector. There may be occasions when you store data on a disk and find a sector becomes damaged. If so, you may be able to recover the data with special utility programs.

If you have a floppy disk with a lot of data you would like to discard, you can just reformat the disk. Keep in mind that when you format a disk, any data contained on that disk is erased. See Figure 6.5.

Did You Know?

Formatting a disk does not erase the data on the disk. It only erases the address tables. Unless you write something else to the disk, you can probably recover your files. There are special operating commands that can help you recover your data. If this doesn't work, there are utility programs available for purchase. Most of the time, You can retrieve your data with one of these programs.

FIGURE 6.5
Formatting a disk

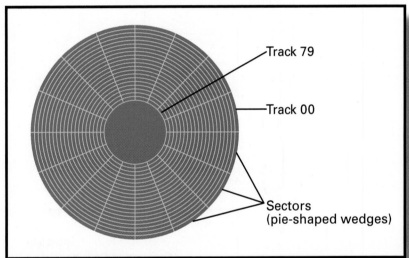

Track 79

Track 00

Sectors (pie-shaped wedges)

STEP-BY-STEP ▷ 6.2

To format a new floppy disk with Windows:

1. Insert the floppy disk into the drive.

2. On the desktop, double-click the My Computer icon to open the window.

3. Single-click the Floppy disk (A:) icon to select it.

4. Move the mouse pointer over the selected icon and right-click to display the Shortcut menu.

5. Select Format to display the Format dialog box.

6. Under File Type, select **Full.**

7. Click Start to begin formatting your disk. The line at the bottom of the dialog box indicates the format progress. See Figure 6.6.

(continued on next page)

7. When your disk is formatted, check to make sure there are no bad sectors.

8. Click the Close button to close the Format Results dialog box. See Figure 6.7.

FIGURE 6.6
Format Dialog Box

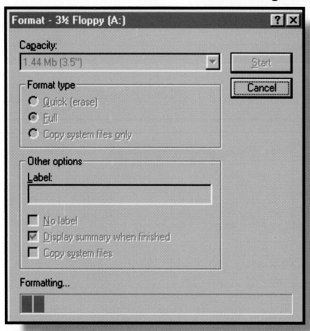

FIGURE 6.7
Formatting Results Dialog Box

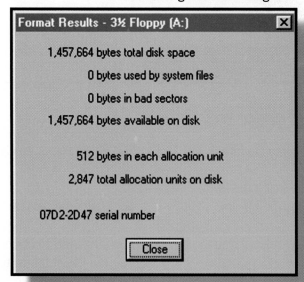

To eject a disk from a Windows computer, press the eject button on the floppy disk drive.

S TEP-BY-STEP ▷ 6.3

To format a new floppy disk with the Macintosh:

1. Insert the disk into the drive. A prompt is displayed asking if you want to initialize the disk.

2. In the Format drop-down list, choose Format.

3. Click Initialize and then click Continue.

To eject the disk, drag the floppy disk icon to the Trash icon. The disk icon is removed from the desktop and the floppy disk is automatically ejected. The disk content is not erased.

Here are some floppy disk precautions:

■ Do not expose disks to magnetic fields such as monitors, calculators, telephones, and so forth.

■ Do not drink, eat, or smoke near a disk.

■ Do not expose disks to extreme temperatures.

■ Do not place heavy objects on the disk.

■ Do not touch the flexible plastic part of the disk.

 Internet

If you're looking for links to Macintosh tutorials, including Hypercard, try the MacInstruct site at www.macinstruct.com/tutorials/index.html.

Files and Folders

When you start using a computer you will quickly accumulate a large number of files. These files can quickly become unmanageable. One of the best ways to organize your files is to do what you would do with paper files—create folders. Folders are represented by icons that look like a traditional manila folder.

The following Step-by-Step instructions are for creating a folder on a floppy disk. Most of the time you would probably not create too many folders on a floppy disk. However, for illustration purposes, we use the floppy disk.

S TEP-BY-STEP ▷ 6.4

Create a Folder—Windows:

1. Insert a formatted floppy disk into drive A.

2. On the desktop, double-click the My Computer icon to open the window.

3. Double-click the Floppy disk (A:) icon to open the window.

4. On the file menu, point to New and select Folder. The new folder appears, displaying a temporary name [New Folder].

5. Type a name for the new folder, such as **Assignments.**

6. Press [Enter].

In Windows, to delete a folder—select the folder, move the mouse pointer over the selected folder, and right-click. Select Delete from the Shortcut menu. In response to the Confirm Folder Delete dialog box, click Yes. Or click the folder, hold down the mouse button, and drag the folder to the Recycle Bin.

S TEP-BY-STEP ▷ 6.5

Create a Folder—Macintosh:

1. Insert the formatted floppy disk into the drive. The floppy disk icon appears on the disk.

2. Double-click the floppy disk icon.

3. On the File menu, select New Folder. A folder icon is displayed and the name "untitled folder" is selected.

4. Type a new name, such as **Assignments**.

To delete a folder from a Macintosh desktop, select the folder, hold down the mouse button, and drag the folder to the Trash icon. The folder and its contents are deleted.

Hot Tip

You can even create folders within folders. These are called subfolders. For example, you may have a folder called Science, and within your Science folder, have two subfolders—one called Project 1 and another called Project 2.

Starting a Program

Almost everything you do within a GUI environment requires working with windows and icons. Windows contain the programs you run and the data with which you are working. To get a better overview of how to manage windows, we will start a program. For Windows, we use an application called WordPad.

S TEP-BY-STEP ▷ 6.6

1. Click the Start button.

2. Point to Programs, then Accessories, and then click WordPad. See Figure 6.8.

3. Type a sentence or two about your favorite school subject.

4. On the File menu, click Save.

5. When the Save As dialog box displays, click the Save in drop-down arrow and select floppy disk drive A. The contents of

your disk in drive A displays.

6. Double-click the Assignments folder; this opens the folder so you can store your data within the folder.

7. In the File name text box, type Science.

8. In the Save as type text box, click the drop-down arrow and select Text document. See Figure 6-9.

9. Click OK to save your file.

FIGURE 6.8
Starting WordPad

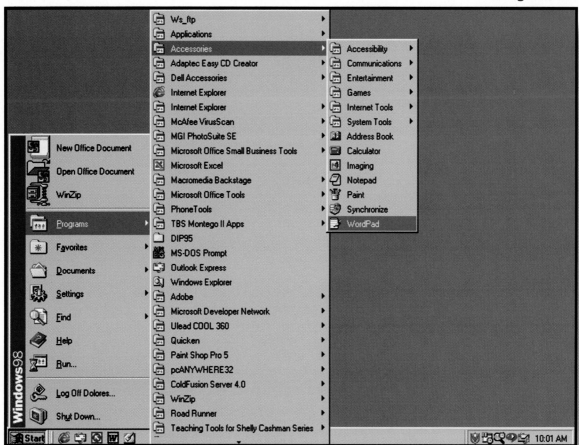

FIGURE 6.9
Wordpad Save as dialog box

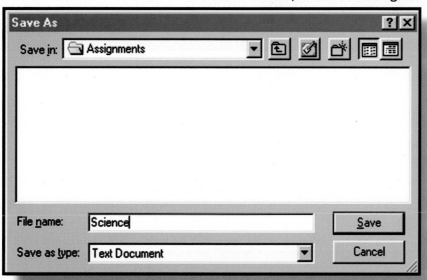

FIGURE 6.10
WordPad Window showing parts of the window

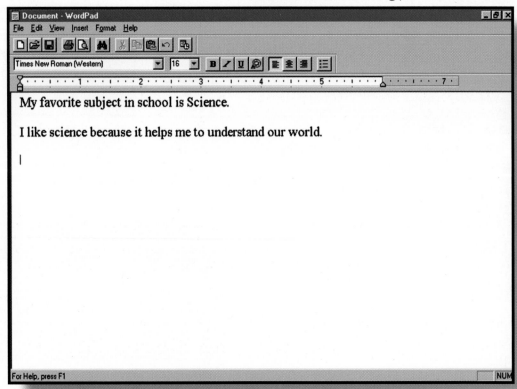

FIGURE 6.11
Macintosh window showing parts of the window

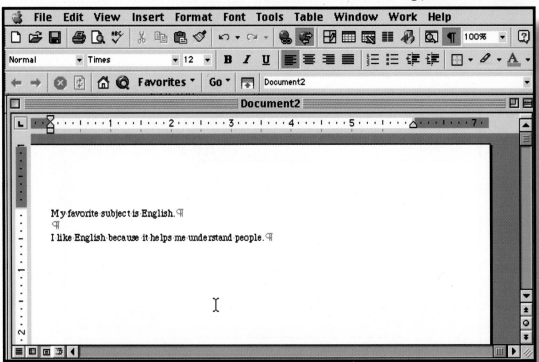

Exploring a Window

A window contains many parts. In our illustration, we point out the various parts of a window. See Figures 6.10 and 6.11. To help you manage the desktop effectively, you have the following options you can use to manipulate windows:

Maximize: Move the mouse pointer over the Maximize button and click the button. The window fills the full screen. Notice that the shape of the Maximize button changes and now becomes the Restore button. See Figure 6.12.

■ *Restore:* Move the mouse pointer over the Restore button and click the button. The window returns to its previous size. See Figure 6.12.

■ *Minimize:* Move the mouse pointer over the Minimize button and click the button. The window disappears from the screen and is displayed as a button on the task bar. See Figure 6.13.

FIGURE 6.12
Maximize button/Restore button

FIGURE 6.13
WordPad displayed as button on Taskbar

■ *Move:* If you don't like where the window is located on the screen, just move it. Move the mouse point over the title bar. Hold down the button and drag the window to its new location.

■ *Resize:* You can easily change the size of a window. Move the mouse pointer over an edge of the window; hold down the button and drag to make the window smaller or larger. You can change both the width and height of a window at the same time by dragging a corner.

Within the Macintosh environment, you have two different options to resize windows. The first is the *Size Box*. This box is located in the lower-right corner of the window. Just drag the box to make the window larger or smaller. When you drag the box, an outline follows the mouse pointer.

FIGURE 6.14
Macintosh Size and Zoom boxes

When you release the mouse button, the window becomes the new size.

The second option is the *Zoom Box*. This feature functions like a switch. When you click it, the window reduces or enlarges. When you click it again, the window returns to its previous size. See Figure 6.14.

Hot Tip

If you have used the Minimize button to reduce an application to a button on the toolbar, and you want to close the application window, you have two choices. First, you can click on the button to open the window and then click the Close button; or, you can move the mouse pointer over the button and right click. Choose Close from the Shortcut menu.

89

Switching Between Windows

Another advantage of working with a GUI is that you can have many windows open at one time. For instance, suppose you want to open a paint program and a word processing program and switch back and forth between the two. This is very easy to do.

Internet

For a history of the graphical user interface, visit the Apple Museum Web site at www.apple-museum.seastar.net/sections/gui.html.

S TEP-BY-STEP ▷ 6.7

1. Click the Start button.

2. Point to Programs, then Accessories, and then click Paint. You now have two programs open on the desktop—WordPad and Paint.

3. To move the window you want to work with to the front, move the mouse pointer over its taskbar button and click the button. See Figure 6.15.

This example illustrates only two open programs. However, you can have as many open programs as the memory in your computer will support. You can also have more than one instance of the same program open; that is, you can have two or more WordPad windows open, and so forth.

FIGURE 6.15
Two open windows

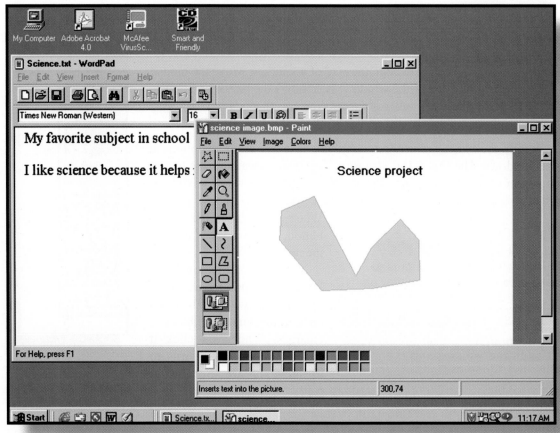

Managing Files

You can move a file or copy a file from one folder to another or from one disk to another. You cannot, however, have more than one file in a folder with the same name.

Moving a File

When you move a file, it is copied to a new location. Then the version in the original location is erased. You will find this feature very useful if you want to organize or reorganize files by moving them into folders.

STEP-BY-STEP ▷ 6.8

1. Click the Start button.

2. Point to Programs, then Windows Explorer.

3. Locate, point to, and select the file you want to move.

4. Move the mouse pointer over the selected file name and right-click to display the

shortcut menu. Click Cut. See Figure 6.16.

5. Locate and select the destination folder.

6. Move the mouse pointer over the selected folder and right-click to display the shortcut menu. Click Paste to move your file into the destination folder.

To move a file within the Macintosh environment, drag the file from one location to another on the same disk.

FIGURE 6.16
Moving a file

Copying a File

When you copy a file, you create an exact duplicate of your original file. For example, you may want to transfer a copy from your hard drive at home to a floppy so you can transport it to a computer at school. Or you may want to share a copy of a file with a friend. With one exception, you use the same basic procedure to copy a file as you do to move a file.

STEP-BY-STEP ▷ 6.9

1. Click the Start button.

2. Point to Programs, then Windows Explorer.

3. Locate, point to, and select the file you want to copy.

4. Move the mouse pointer over the selected file name and right-click to display the shortcut menu. Click Copy. See Figure 6.17.

5. Locate and select the destination folder.

6. Move the mouse pointer over the selected folder and right-click to display the shortcut menu.

7. Click Paste to copy your file into the destination folder.

To copy a file within the Macintosh environment, drag a file from one disk to another. If you want to make a copy of the file on the same disk, but in a different folder, hold down the Option key as you drag the file.

FIGURE 6.17
Copying a file

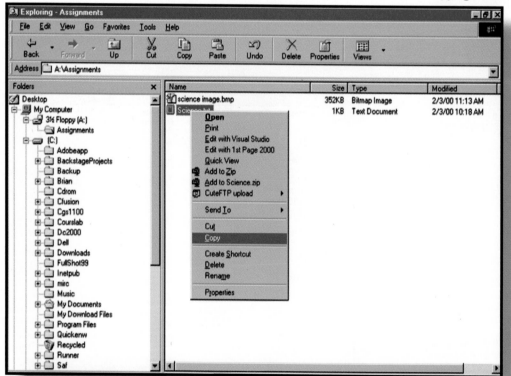

Deleting a File

To delete a file within Windows, select the file, right-click to display the shortcut menu, and select Delete. To delete a file within the Macintosh environment, drag the file icon to the Trash.

When you delete a file, it is removed from the list of available files. It is sent to the Recycle Bin (Windows) or Trash (Macintosh). What if you discover you have deleted the wrong file or need to retrieve a deleted file? This is easy as long as you have not emptied the "trash." Simply open the Recycle Bin or Trash, locate and click the file name, right-click, and select Restore.

Views

Windows offers several options that control how file folders and file names are displayed in a window. Depending on the task and your goal, you can choose the option to best meet your objectives.

- *Large icons:* A large icon and title for each file displays and provides a visual clue to the type of file and the file contents.

- *Small icons:* Small icons provide basically the same information as large icons—they're just smaller. Small icons are generally arranged horizontally across the screen.

- *List:* Provides a list of all files and folders. Displays small icons and the name; generally in a vertical arrangement.

- *Details*: With details, you get much more information than you do with the other view types. Detail shows the file icon, the file name, the file size, the associated application, and the date and time the file was created or last modified.

S TEP-BY-STEP ▷ 6.10

1. Click the Start button.

2. Point to Programs and click Windows Explorer. Most likely when this window open, the view will be large icons. See Figure 6.18.

(continued on next page)

FIGURE 6.18
Windows Explorer – large icon view

3. On the View menu, click Small Icons. The display now shows a horizontal arrangements of folders and files represented by icons and titles.

4. On the View menu, click List. The display now shows a vertical arrangement of folders and files represented by icons and titles.

5. On the View menu, click Details. The display now shows a detailed list of each folder, including name, size, type, and date and time created or last modified. See Figure 6.19.

FIGURE 6.19
Windows Explorer – details view

If you're working with a Macintosh computer, you can use the Finder View menu to view the list of files. On the View menu, select By_Icon to view the full size icon or select By_Small Icon to see many files at one time. Or you can select By_Name to obtain additional information, such as the time and date the file was created or last updated.

Sorting

To help you more easily locate files and folders, you can also sort the items displayed in a window. For example, you're looking for a file, but you can't remember the name. However, you know you created the file within the last few days. Your best option is to sort by date. You can also sort by name, size, and type. To sort by any of these four options, just click the column name. See Figure 6.20.

You can also sort files within the Macintosh environment. You can sort on the name or you can sort on the date and time the file was created.

Selecting Files

You've already learned how to copy and/or delete a single file. But what if you have a group of files you would like to delete? It could be a time-consuming chore if you had to do these one by one. You can, however, easily select a group of files. The files can be next to each other or they can be separate.

FIGURE 6.20
Windows Explorer – Files sorted by type

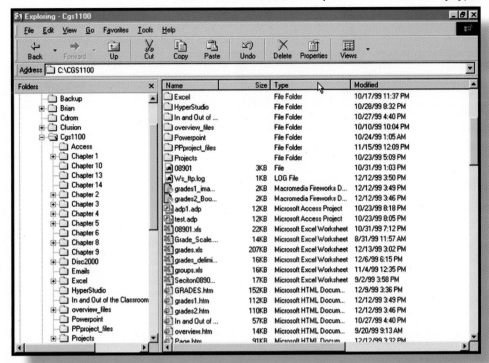

Within the Windows desktop, to select a group of adjacent files, click the first file to select it. Then hold down the Shift key and select the last file in the list. See Figure 6.21.

FIGURE 6.21
Adjacent selected files

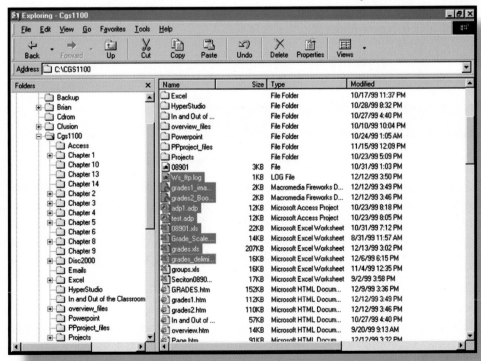

To select a group of nonadjacent files, select the first file, hold down the Control [CTRL] key, and click on the remaining file names you want to select. See Figure 6.22.

FIGURE 6.22
Non-adjacent selected files

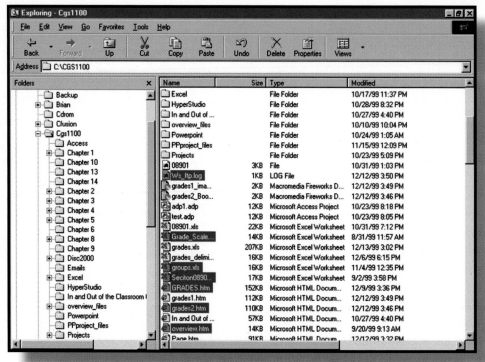

After you select the files, move the mouse pointer over any of the selected file names, right-click to display the context menu, and then choose Delete or Copy.

If you're using a Macintosh, hold down the Shift key as you select the files. Then drag the entire group of files to a new folder in one single step.

TECHNOLOGY CAREERS

PROJECT MANAGEMENT

Project Management is one of the components that a System Analyst might find in a job description. However, because the job of a system analyst can sometimes be so detailed, many companies are hiring a project manager to work with the analyst and other team members.

This could cover a wide array of projects—from Web site development to implementing an entire new computer system. The responsibilities of the project manager would be to manage, guide, keep everyone on task, and coach the team.

People who work in this profession need strong leadership abilities and good organizational skills. Many people use a software program called Project Management to help them with this job.

Educational requirements vary depending on the company and job requirements—some employers may require a two-year degree whereas others require a master's degree. Likewise, salary levels also vary—anywhere from $22,000 to $35,000 for entry level.

Getting Help

Both the Macintosh and Windows programs offer Help. If you are using Windows, on the File menu, click Help. If you are using a Macintosh computer, use the Apple Guide Help Balloons feature.

 **Hot Tip**

For the Macintosh computer, Apple Guide provides a reference system that you can use to learn more about the computer and applications. This guide can lead you step-by-step through tasks such as formatting a disk, creating a folder, and so forth.

ETHICS IN TECHNOLOGY

SPAM

If you use the Internet a lot and if you have an e-mail account, you have most likely encountered SPAM. Some people define SPAM as junk mail or junk newsgroup postings. However, real SPAM is unsolicited e-mail advertising or advertising posted to a newsgroup.

The first thing that you must be aware of is that if you sign Web site guest books, post to newsgroups, or request information from a Web site, you are leaving information about yourself. This information can be collected by various software programs, and your e-mail address added to a list that can be sold over and over again.

You will not be able to avoid all SPAM, but there are some ways in which you can eliminate some of this unwanted advertising.

■ If you post to newsgroups, go through the Web site www.dejanews.com; this site provides you with a special e-mail account so that your "real" e-mail address is not recorded.

■ If you sign a guest book, don't use your real e-mail address. Instead, use another one that you can check at your leisure. There are many places on the Internet that provide free e-mail.

■ Most sites post their privacy policy regarding selling of e-mail addresses. Read this policy before you fill out all of those online form.

Summary

■ Most of today's computer come with some type of graphical user interface.

■ A graphic interface includes standard text and graphics.

■ Some of the components of a GUI are the desktop, icons, pointer, pointing device, menus, scroll bar, and window.

■ A window is an object within both the Macintosh and Windows operating systems.

■ The desktop is a representation of how people work at a desk and contains windows and icons.

■ Double-click an icon to open a window.

- Close a window in Windows by clicking the Close button and by selecting Close Window from the File menu in the Macintosh environment.

- Formatting is the process of preparing a disk so you can write data to and read data from the disk.

- If you have a disk with a bad sector, it is better not to use the disk.

- Use folders to organize your files.

- Delete folders and files in both Windows and Macintosh by dragging to the Trash or Recycle Bin.

- With a window, you can move it, resize it, maximize it, minimize it, or restore it to its original size.

- You can have several windows and/or programs open at one time.

- You can move a file or copy a file from one folder to another.

- When you move a file, it is moved to a new location.

- When you copy a file, you create a duplicate of your original file in another location.

- When viewing file and file folders, you can view these as large icons, small icons, a list, or details.

- You can sort files and folders by date, name, size, and type.

- You can select and copy a group of adjacent or a group of nonadjacent files and folders.

- You can select and move a group of adjacent or a group of nonadjacent files and folders.

- To get help within Windows, select Help from the File menu.

- Use the Apple Guide Help Balloons feature to get help on the Macintosh.

LESSON 6 REVIEW QUESTIONS

MULTIPLE CHOICE

Circle the best answer to each of the following statements.

1. The _____ is the first screen you see after the operating system is loaded.
   A. WordPad
   B. menu options
   C. desktop
   D. format

2. To keep your files organized, you would create _____.
   A. menus
   B. icons
   C. folders
   D. desktops

3. Graphical representations of files and programs are called _____.
   A. icons
   B. menus
   C. pictures
   D. scroll bars

4. To move a window, move the pointer over the _____ press down the button, and drag.
   A. scroll bar
   B. icon
   C. desktop
   D. title bar

5. When you create a duplicate of a file, you are _____ the file.
   A. moving
   B. copying
   C. deleting
   D. executing

TRUE/FALSE

Circle the T if the statement is true. Circle F if it is false.

T F 1. Within both the Macintosh and Windows environments, you can only copy files, not move them.

T F 2. You can only open one window at a time.

T F 3. When viewing files as large icons, you can see the date and time the file was created and/or modified.

T F 4. To more easily locate a particular file, you can use the Sort option.

T F 5. To select a group of adjacent files, select the first file and then hold down the Shift key and select the last file in the group.

SHORT ANSWER

1. A small picture that represents a file or program is called a(n) _____.

2. _____ provide drop-down options from which to choose commands.

3. The program that displays the Macintosh desktop is called _____.

4. A disk must be _____ before you can use it.

5. When you change the size or a window, you are _____ it.

CROSS-CURRICULAR PROJECTS

MATH

When you format a floppy disk, it is formatted with sectors and tracks. Do some research, either on the Internet or from reference books, and determine the total number of bytes or characters you can store on the floppy disk you are using. Then convert that into bits.

SCIENCE/LANGUAGE ARTS

Examine the desktop of the computer you are using and write a report on the various elements on the desktop. Describe the system you are using and then describe what you think is the best operating system—a visual system with icons or a text-based system.

SOCIAL STUDIES

In social studies, you often learn about working as together as a group. Now think about putting groups of files into folders. Are there any similarities between this and people working together as groups? Any differences?

LANGUAGE ARTS

Your rich grandmother has told you she will buy you any type of computer you want. Describe for your grandmother what type of computer you would like to have and why. Explain to her about the desktop and why you would choose this type of desktop.

WEB PROJECT

At www.microsoft.com/education/tutorial/classroom/win98/default.asp, you can find a Windows tutorial. Complete this tutorial and submit the results to your teacher.

TEAM PROJECT

Ms. Perez is encouraged by all of the information and knowledge you have about using a computer. She would like you and another Vista Multimedia employee to put together the outline for a training program for the other employees. Create an outline for a training program. Include all the main elements that you think are necessary for someone to be an effective computer user. Write a short description of your plan and present it to the class.

How Do I Use Word Processing Software?

OBJECTIVES

When you complete this module, you will be able to:

- Identify the components of the Word window.
- Select commands using menus and toolbars.
- Create and edit a document.
- Apply character, paragraph, and document formatting.
- Correct spelling and grammar errors in a document.
- Save and print a document.
- Identify advanced features of word processing software.

⏱ **Estimated Time: 1.5 hours**

VOCABULARY

Cursor
Editing
Formatting
Grammar checker
Spell checker
Templates
Thesaurus
Word processing
Word wrap
WYSIWYG

Ms. Perez, your supervisor at Vista Multimedia, has asked you to type a letter to one of the customers who won the drawing for two free video rentals. She would like the letter to look very professional. She has given you the draft of the letter. See Figure 7.1.

You are taking a word processing class at school and are very excited about being able to use your new skills. Word processing software makes preparing professional-looking documents a very easy task. Let's see what you can do!

What Is Word Processing Software?

It would be almost impossible to spend a day in a business office, a school, a hospital, or even a home without seeing a word processing program in use. Most people have had some experience with word processing. For many, word processing is the sole application for which they use the computer.

Word processing software is one of the most common applications for computers today. It provides the capability to handle text, which makes it easy to create (and modify) all kinds of documents from simple one-page documents to multipage reports, to flyers, to brochures, to books.

FIGURE 7.1

January 15, 200

Mrs. Elizabeth Stevenson
1204 Drumcastle Court
Chesapeake, Virginia 23320

Dear Mrs. Stevenson

Congratulations! You are the winner of this month's drawing. Your name was drawn from more than 1,000 entries.

As the winner, you will receive two free movie rentals of your choice. Just think, you get to see two exciting, entertaining movies absolutely free.

You may come into the store anytime within thirty days of the date of this letter to make your selection. Bring this letter in with you. This is our way of saying thanks for your patronage. Enjoy your movies.

Sincerely

Ms. Perez
Store Manager

xx

 Did You Know?

Sometimes word processing is referred to as computerized typing.

Most word processing programs share the same basic features, although the way you access these commands may differ. Some of these commands include Open, Close, Save, Save As, Print, Cut, Copy, Paste, and Speller. They also contain a menu structure, graphic tool bars with icons representing most common commands, and scroll bars or some other mechanism for allowing you to move around in documents.

The Word Processing Screen

Once you open a word processing program, the main editing window is displayed on your screen. The following list describes the tools available in the word processing program. See Figure 7.2.

■ **Title bar** displays the name of the software program and displays the name of the document on which you are working after you have saved and named the document.

■ **Menu bar** contains commands needed to operate the word processing software.

■ **Toolbars** contain icons from which the most frequently used commands may be quickly chosen. For example, if you wanted to print your document, you could click on the picture of the printer on the tool bar and your document would go to the printer to be printed.

■ **Ruler** shows you the positioning of text, tabs, margins, and any other elements across the page.

■ **Document area** is where you actually type and see your document.

■ **Scroll bars** allow you to scroll through a document that is too large to fit in the document area.

■ **Status bar** across the bottom of the window contains information related to your position in the document, the page count, and the status of keyboard keys.

FIGURE 7.2
The word processing screen

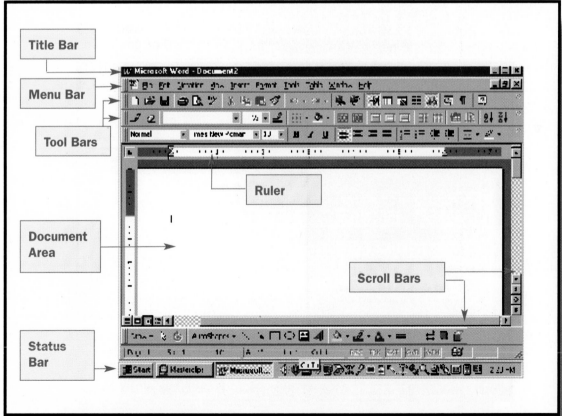

MENU OPTIONS

Most word processing programs are menu driven. This characteristic or environment makes the programs easy to use. Many word processing programs have many of the same menus. Once you click on (select) a menu item from the menu bar, a drop-down menu appears. Figure 7.3 shows a sample of a drop-down menu.

The following list describes some of the most common menu options:

- The *file menu* is usually the first selection and offers options common to most word processors.

    - To open a file that has been saved, select *Open* from the drop-down menu.

    - As you are typing a new document, it is stored into RAM until you select the *Save* option from the file menu, indicating that you want to save it permanently on either the hard drive or a floppy diskette.

    - If you want to save this same document again using a different name, select *Save As* from the File menu.

- The *Print* option sends your document to the printer.

- The *Page Setup* option allows you to set margins, select orientation, determine paper size, and so on.

- The *Print Preview* option allows you to see a full-page view of your document before printing.

- Near the bottom of the File menu is the *Exit* or *Quit* option. This tells the program that you are done. It will also prompt you to save any unsaved work before you quit the program.

FIGURE 7.3
Drop down menu

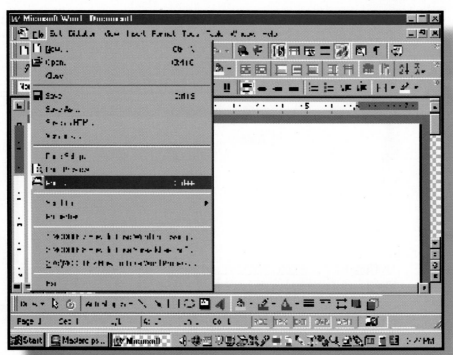

Entering Text

When you start the word processing program, a blank screen appears with a blinking line in the upper left corner. This line is called the ***insertion point.*** It is indicating that it is ready for you to begin typing. As you type text, the insertion point advances across the screen, showing you where the next character will be placed. See Figure 7.4.

When you type a short line such as a date or the salutation in a letter, you will need to press the Enter key to move to the next line. If you continue to type, as your text reaches the right edge of the screen, the cursor automatically moves down to the next line; you do not have to press the Enter key to get down to the next line. This feature is called ***word wrap***. The text automatically wraps around the right margin and continues onto the next line. The only time you need to press the Enter key is at the end of a paragraph or at the end of a short line.

FIGURE 7.4
Insertion point (top) and typing a line of text (bottom)

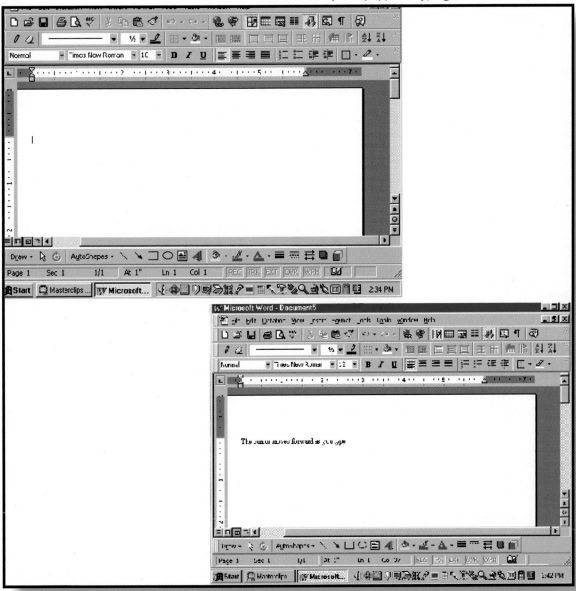

When word processing software is capable of showing the document on the screen the same way it will look when printed, it is said to have WYSIWYG capability. *WYSIWYG* stands for "What You See Is What You Get." The formatting commands such as bold, underline, and italics are visible. A WYSIWYG environment also makes it easy to select or highlight blocks of text.

Editing Text

Probably the greatest advantage of word processing software is the capability to change text without retyping the entire page or document. Changing an existing document is called *editing* the document. The insertion pointer can be moved to any position in a document in order to make corrections or to insert text. It is moved with either the directional keyboard control keys (the cursor keys) or the mouse.

There are several simple methods for correcting text quickly:

■ The *Backspace key:* The backspace key deletes text to the left of the insertion point. Each time you press the Backspace key, a character of text or blank space is deleted.

> **Example: If your insertion point is behind the "r" in Computerl and you press the Backspace key, the "r" will be deleted.**

■ The *Delete key:* The delete key deletes text to the right. Each time you depress the Delete key, characters in front of the insertion point are deleted.

> **Example: If your insertion point is in front of the "p" in Comlputer and you press the Delete key, the "p" will be deleted.**

■ *Overtype key:* Most word processing software is in the Insert Mode by default. This means that wherever you place the insertion pointer, the text that you type enters at that point and the text to the right of the insertion point moves to the right. Pressing the Overtype key allows the new text to overwrite the existing text. In other words, the old text disappears and the new text takes its place.

■ *Autocorrect:* Many of the latest word processing programs have a feature called Autocorrect. Preselected errors automatically correct themselves. These would be words that are commonly misspelled. You may customize this feature to include words that you may misspell often.

> **Example: If you accidentally typed "teh" instead of "the," the software automatically makes the correction for you.**

SELECTING TEXT

When you are editing a document, you must indicate which text you want to change. You do this by *selecting* the text you want to edit. When you select a block of text, it becomes highlighted indicating that it has been selected. To select a block of text, you can use the mouse or keyboard or both. With the mouse you would click at the beginning of the text you want to change and drag it to the end of the text you want changed. Once you have selected the text you want to change, you can choose the command you want, such as bold or underline. See Figure 7.5.

If you have selected a block of text and decide that you do not want to change it in any way, you can deselect the block of text. Click the mouse anywhere on the screen or press any arrow key.

A block of text can also be copied, cut, and pasted. If you want to repeat pasting a block of text to another portion of the document or even into another document, you would select the block of text and click the *Copy* icon. You will not see anything happen on the screen. A copy of the blocked text is placed in a special part of memory called the clipboard.

FIGURE 7.5
Text that has been selected

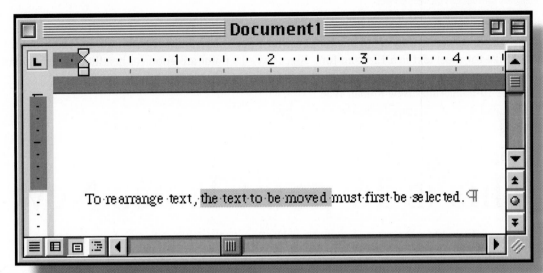

Using the ***Cut*** command works the same way, except the text is deleted from the document and placed in memory. Once you have decided where you want the block of text to be inserted, place the insertion point at that location and click the ***Paste*** icon. It will copy the contents of the clipboard into the document.

FORMATTING TEXT

Another advantage of the word processing software program is the ability to control the formatting:

- the appearance of the text

- the layout of the text

- other objects on the page

- spacing

- margins

- indentations

- alignments

You can format characters, paragraphs, or the entire document.

CHARACTER FORMATTING

You can change the way a character or letter looks like by changing the ***font style***. Fonts have names such as Times New Roman, Tekton, and Helvetica.

This is Times New Roman	This is Helvetica
This is Tekton	*This is Kaufman*

Fonts are either ***serif*** or ***sans serif*** fonts. Serif fonts have little lines at the ends of the strokes of the letter. Sans serif fonts do not have these. Many people use serif fonts for the body of text because the little lines make it easier to follow the line of writing, and use sans serif fonts for headings.

107

| Times New Roman is a serif font. | Helvetica is a sans serif font. |

The size of fonts is measured in **points**. Seventy-two points equal one inch. However, sizes vary from one font to the next; 10 point in one font may be bigger in 12 point of another font. The most common font size for most text is a 12-point font. Sizes over 18 point are good for headlines and banners.

This is 10-point Times New Roman Type

This is 12-point Times New Roman Type

This is 14-point Times New Roman Type

This is 18-point Times New Roman Type

This is 36-point Times New

You can also add attributes such as bold, underline, italics, and color to characters.

| You can **bold** your text. | You can <u>underline</u> your text. |
| You can type your text in *italics*. | You can outline your text. |

All of these formats are found in the Format menu. After accessing the Format Menu, click on Font. See Figure 7.6.

FIGURE 7.6
Examples of font, size, and style options

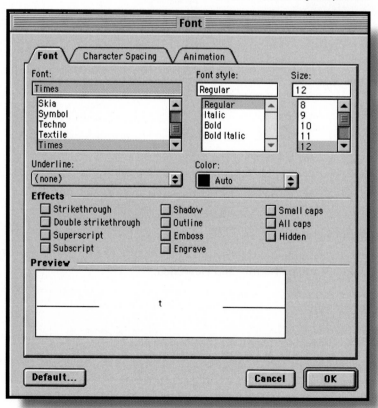

PARAGRAPH AND LINE FORMATTING

Most documents are organized into paragraphs. In word processing, a paragraph is defined by the pressing of the Enter key. You can control the line spacing inside the paragraph and the justification of the paragraph.

 **Hot Tip**

You can access all of these commands by selecting their icons on the formatting toolbar.

■ Line spacing can be set at single, double, triple, or some other setting.

Example of single spaced text.

Word processing software is one of the most common applications for computers today.

Example of double-spaced text.

Word processing software is one of the most common

applications for computers today.

■ Justification (alignment) can be set to left, right, center, or justify.

Left justified text.

Right justified text.

Centered text

Full justified text is aligned at the right and left margins. Columns in newspapers are justified so that all complete lines end directly under each other.

DOCUMENT FORMATTING

You can also format your document so that all pages have the same formatting.

Margins are the white space around the edge of the page where the text ends. The margins "frame" the document. The margins can be adjusted to be wider or smaller. Each margin, top, bottom, left, and right, can be changed individually.

Page size can be selected based on the size of paper you will use for your document. The standard size for a page is 8-1/2 x 11 inches. You can also format your page to print in portrait or landscape orientation. Portrait orientation prints with paper lengthwise (8-1/2 x 11 inch) and landscape prints with paper widthwise (11 x 8-1/2).

Portrait Orientation

Portrait Orientation

Headers and *footers* are special areas at the top of the page and at the bottom of the page, respectively. You enter information in the header or footer and this text is printed on every page.

Examples of other document formatting features include:

- page numbers
- footnotes
- columns

Proofreading the Document

SPELL CHECKERS

Word processing software has a tool to detect mistakes in documents and suggest corrections or improvements. This feature is available through spell checkers. The spell checker checks each word of the document against a dictionary of known words. If it finds a word that it does not recognize because it is not in its dictionary, it displays the word. The word may be displayed as a different color or with a wavy red line under it.

Once it displays a word, it asks you what to do. Options are to correct the word, ignore the word, or add the word to the dictionary. It may also give suggestions for correct spelling. Figure 7.7 displays the spell checker screen.

FIGURE 7.7
Spell checker

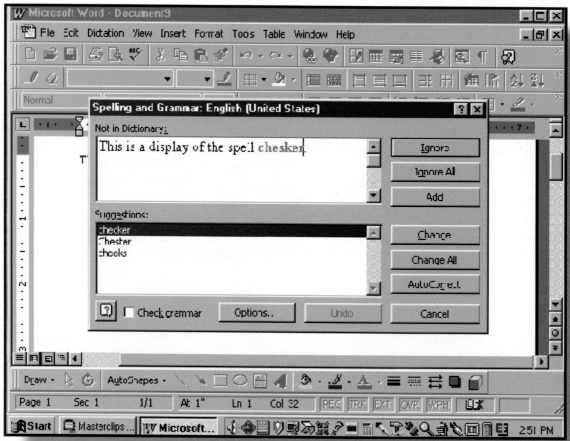

Be aware that even though the spell checker may display a word as misspelled, it is not necessarily misspelled. It is just not in the software's dictionary. Examples of this would be proper names, It is very important that you proofread the document very carefully.

Most spell checkers can display a word count, or the number of words in a document. This is handy when you have to write a 500-word paper and want to be able to know when you have typed 500 words!

THESAURUS

A *thesaurus* is a list of synonyms that assist you in using different words in a document. To use this tool, select the word that you want to replace, and start the Thesaurus. Once you see the list of available words, give careful thought to your selection. Be sure to select the most appropriate word for the content of your document. See Figure 7.8.

FIGURE 7.8
The Thesaurus screen

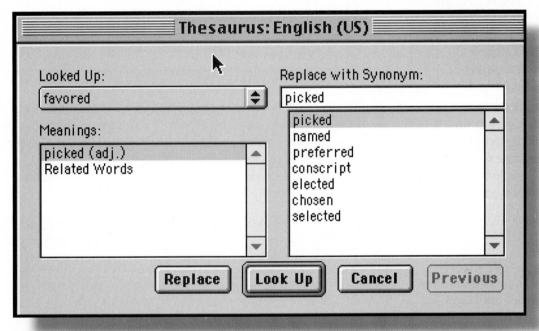

GRAMMAR CHECKERS

The grammar checker evaluates each sentence in the document and points out grammatical errors like subject and verb agreement, sentence fragments, sentence structure, sentence length, and punctuation. The checker offers advice on how to reword the sentence.

 **Hot Tip**

The grammar checker may be included with the speller checker command in some word processing software programs.

SAVING A DOCUMENT

In order to maintain a permanent copy of your document, you will need to *save* it on your hard drive or on a floppy *diskette*. As you are creating and editing your document, it is always a good idea to save your work often. Don't wait until you have completed the entire document. Something may happen to your computer (like the power going off, the computer freezing, printer hanging up) that may cause you to lose your work.

111

When you save a document, you can use the Save command or the Save As command under the File menu. The Save command allows you to save the file under the current file name (the name that was given when the file was saved the first time) and the Save As command allows you to save the same document under a different name.

When you save a document, you indicate where you want to store the document. This includes drive and folder name. Next, you need to give the document a name. See Figure 7.9.

Printing a Document

As you key a document, you see a "soft copy" on the screen. If you want a hard copy of the document, you need to *print* the document. The print command is under the File menu. There are several options available including the number of copies to print, the exact pages to print, and which printer to use. See Figure 7.10.

The quality of the printing of documents depends on the type of printer used to print the documents. Documents may also be "printed" electronically. They may also be attached to e-mail messages.

FIGURE 7.9
Save As window

FIGURE 7.10
Print window

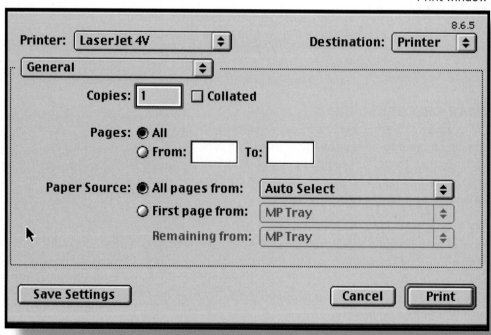

Closing a Document and Exiting the Software

CLOSING A DOCUMENT

Once you have completed working on a document, you need to close it. When you close a document, you remove it from the screen. Before you close the document, be sure you have saved it. However, if you have not saved it, you will be prompted to save it. Use the Close option in the File menu to close your document.

EXITING THE SOFTWARE

After you have finished typing, saving, and printing your documents, you are ready to exit or quit the software program. To exit the program, select the Exit option from the File menu.

 Hot Tip

If you are going to exit from the software program after closing the current document, you can bypass the close option and select the Exit option from the File menu. You will be prompted to save the document, and both the file and the program will be closed.

Other Features of Word Processing Software

Mail Merge

If you need to send the same letter to 25 club members, you can use the mail merge command. You start by preparing a form letter and a data file that will contain information for each individual who is to receive a copy of the letter. Next, you merge these two files. A personalized letter will be prepared for each club member! You can even use the mail merge command to prepare the envelopes or labels.

Templates

Templates are predesigned documents that are already formatted. Most word processing programs have templates for letters, reports, newsletters, memos, and faxes. To use a template, you only need to insert your text in the appropriate places. Templates save you formatting time, especially for those types of documents you use over and over. You can also create your own templates.

Graphics

You can spruce up your document by adding photos, drawings, or clip art to your documents. Many software programs come with graphics that can be used in your documents. Once you have selected a graphic and inserted it into your document, you can move and size it; you can also control the alignment of text around the graphic.

Web Page Documents

Web page documents are documents located on the Internet. These "pages" must contain HTML (Hypertext Markup Language) codes. Documents created in word processing programs can be converted into Web pages that contain HTML codes.

 Did You Know?

If you save a document as HTML or a web page, be sure to view it in your browser.

113

Preparing a Letter

Now you are ready to prepare the letter for the drawing winner. Follow the steps here to create a professional-looking letter. Refer to Figure 7.1 on page 102.

S TEP-BY-STEP ▷ 7.1

1. Start your word processing program.

2. Access the menu option to change your left and right margins to 1 inch.

3. Change your font style to a serif font of your choice. Use a font size between 10 and 12. You want the font to be large enough to read easily.

4. Press the Enter key six times so you will begin about 2 inches from the top of the page.

5. Begin typing the letter in the appropriate format.

6. Save the letter on your diskette. Use the filename Drawing Letter.

7. Edit the document to bold the word "Congratulations" in the first paragraph and add italics to "two free movie rentals" in the second paragraph.

8. Proofread the letter very carefully. Run the spell checker.

9. Print the letter on the store's letterhead.

10. Close the letter and exit from the word processing program.

Ms. Perez will be very impressed with the professional-looking letter you just prepared using word processing software!

TECHNOLOGY CAREERS

WORD PROCESSING OPERATOR

The word processing operator performs a variety of routine word processing tasks to produce various printed materials such as manuscripts, correspondence, labels, reports, lists, statistical information, tables, and other printed materials from rough draft and/or machine dictation.

Duties and responsibilities are usually routine. They are accomplished by following established work methods and procedures. Maintaining disk/mainframe filing systems including cataloging, coding, and filing documents and instructions for future use is also part of the word processing operator's job description.

A high school diploma or an associate's degree is usually required for this position along with one year of word processing experience. Keyboarding skill of 50 words per minute is also usually required. The salary for this position ranges between $20,000 and $25,000, depending on experience and size and location of company.

ETHICS IN TECHNOLOGY

DIGITAL SIGNATURES

It is possible to send an e-mail message disguised as someone else. Sometimes that can be a security problem. A security device that guards against this type of computer crime and protects e-mail messages is called a digital signature.

A digital signature consists of several lines of code that appears at the end of the e-mail message. It guarantees that the message was originated by the person who signed the message, that it has not been forged, and that the message has not been altered in any way in transmission or by anyone else in an attempt to change the message.

Summary

- Word processing software is used to create documents such as letters, memos, brochures, and reports.

- Commands for using the features of a word processing program are selected from menus.

- Tool bars contain icons that represent commonly used commands.

- Formatting features may be added to characters, paragraphs, or the entire document.

- Word processing software allows for easy formatting and modification of documents by selecting blocks of text and applying changes such as cutting, copying, and pasting or adding attributes such as bold, underline, or italics.

- WYSIWYG means "What You See Is What You Get" and refers to the ability of the word processing software to display text on the screen as it will appear on the page.

- The speller checker checks the document for misspelled words, and the grammar checker checks the document for grammatical correctness. The thesaurus assists with using different words in a document by suggesting synonyms.

- Documents should be saved to disk often. When saving a document, you must give it a name and indicate where it is to be stored.

- Hard copies of documents are generated through printers. Documents may also be transmitted electronically.

- Some special features of word processing equipment include mail merge, templates, graphics, and Web page.

- For more information on this topic, you can complete Mission Plan 6: Wonder Words on the "Computer Concepts: Systems, Applications, and Design" CD. Check with your instructor for further instructions.

MULTIPLE CHOICE

1. The _____ is used to access commands.
   A. menu bar
   B. title bar
   C. scroll bar
   D. status bar

2. The _____ is used to make corrections.
   A. CTRL key
   B. Backspace key
   C. Enter key
   D. ALT key

3. Times New Roman, Arial, and Technical are types of _____.
   A. templates
   B. commands
   C. font styles
   D. formatting

4. Font size is measured in points: _____ points equal one inch.
   A. 12
   B. 24
   C. 36
   D. 72

5. The thesaurus identifies _____ to be used in a document.
   A. antonyms
   B. homonyms
   C. synonyms
   D. proper names

TRUE/FALSE

Circle the T if the statement is true. Circle F if it is false.

T F 1. Word processing software is used for calculation applications.

T F 2. Editing documents mean making changes to existing text.

T F 3. Documents typed lengthwise are in landscape orientation.

T F 4. The spell checker corrects all errors in a document.

T F 5. The computer automatically saves a document.

SHORT ANSWER

1. All documents should be _____ to a disk if you want to keep a permanent copy.

2. _____ means "what you see is what you get."

3. The _____ command inserts copied or cut text at the insertion point.

4. A _____ is a predesigned format for documents.

5. The _____ feature automatically corrects certain errors in a document.

CROSS-CURRICULAR PROJECTS

MATH

Word processing programs have the capability to perform various mathematical operations using mathematical symbols. Check your software's manual or use the Help feature to identify which symbols are available and how to access them.

Prepare a table consisting of the symbol, the meaning of the symbol, and how to access it. The title of your report will be "Mathematical Symbols in Word Processing Software."

SCIENCE

Use the table feature of your word processing software to prepare and print the following Electron table on page 118. Use the Help feature to find out how to use the Table feature if necessary.

SOCIAL STUDIES

Many people think that their individual vote decides who wins a presidential election. This is not true. The Electoral College determines the winner. Using the Internet and other resource options, find information about the Electoral College. Explain its origin, its function, and how it operates. Use word processing software to write a report on your findings. You may decide on the setup of your findings.

LANGUAGE ARTS

Most word processing programs have features that are especially useful to writers such as Strikethrough. Use the software's manual, the Internet, brochures, and any other resource to identify other features that are useful to writers. Prepare a report that includes the name and description of each feature. The title of your report will be "Writers' Aids in Word Processing Software."

WEB PROJECT

Launch your Web browser and search for information about word processing capabilities in foreign languages. List several word processing programs that have this capability. Describe how these capabilities are used. Use the following keywords with your favorite search engines: word processing features and word processing foreign languages.

TEAM PROJECT

Ms. Perez at the video store would like to see how the store could take advantage of templates that are available in their word processing program. She would like to see actual samples with the store's information included.

Because there are quite a few templates available in the software, you have asked the other part-time employee to assist you. After viewing the templates available, decide on three each that would be appropriate for the store, and complete with the store's information.

See the CD-ROM "Computer Concepts: Systems, Applications, and Design" for more information on this subject or careers in this area. Use Mission #6—Wonder Words.

TABLE 7.1

ELECTRON TABLE

GP	AN	AS	K	L	M	V
1	1	H	1	–	–	±
18	2	He	2	–	–	0
1	3	Li	2	1	–	+1
2	4	Be	2	2	–	+2
13	5	B	2	3	–	+3
14	6	C	2	4	–	±4
15	7	N	2	5	–	-3 +5
16	8	O	2	6	–	-2
17	9	F	2	7	–	-1
18	10	Ne	2	8	–	0
1	11	Na	2	8	1	+1
2	12	Mg	2	8	2	+2
13	13	Al	2	8	3	+3
14	14	Si	2	8	4	±4
15	15	P	2	8	5	-3 +5
16	16	S	2	8	6	-2
17	17	Cl	2	8	7	-1
18	18	Ar	2	8	8	0

HOW DO I USE SPREADSHEET SOFTWARE?

LESSON 8

OBJECTIVES

When you complete this module, you will be able to:

■ Understand the purpose and function of a spreadsheet.

■ Identify the major parts of a spreadsheet window.

■ Enter labels, values, formulas, and functions into a spreadsheet.

■ Create graphs.

■ Save and print a spreadsheet.

■ Format data in a spreadsheet.

■ Perform what-if statements.

🕐 **Estimated Time: 1.5 hours**

VOCABULARY

Cell
Column
Formula
Formula View
Function
Label
Row
Spreadsheet
Value
What-if-analysis

Many small businesses, like Vista Multimedia, use spreadsheet software programs for various activities that require calculation such as their payroll. Preparing the payroll using a spreadsheet is a very easy task to perform. Once the hours worked and wage and deduction information have been entered, it's just a matter of minutes before the entire staff's pay can be determined.

Ms. Perez completes the payroll for the video store. However, she has never taken the time to graph the information. She also has never tried to use the "what-if" function. She's been thinking about giving a small bonus to those employees who work more hours than their usual 20. The store has been very busy and she wants to show her appreciation for those who helped out by working extra hours. The what-if function will allow her to determine this information quickly.

In addition to preparing the payroll with the regular information, she has decided to try these two functions on this week's payroll.

What Is the Purpose of Spreadsheets?

Spreadsheet software is simply a row and column arrangement of data used to enter, calculate, manipulate, and analyze numbers. Spreadsheets are used to prepare budgets, financial statements, and inventory management. They are also used to make forecasts and to assist in making decisions.

Once information has been entered into a spreadsheet, it can be calculated easily. It can be formatted in various ways. It can even be presented in a graph. But the best feature of all is that information can be changed and the spreadsheet will automatically recalculate itself!

The Anatomy of a Spreadsheet

A spreadsheet form looks much like a page from a journal; it is a grid with columns and rows. This grid is often called a worksheet. The terms worksheet and spreadsheet are used interchangeably. The columns are identified by letters in the alphabet, and the rows are identified by numbers. The point at which a column and a row intersects or meets is called a *cell.* This intersection or cell has a name that is represented by the column letter and the row number. Example: The first cell in a worksheet is cell A1. It is located in column A and on row 1. The *active cell* is the cell in which you are currently working. It will have a black border around it. In the diagram here, cell C4 is the active cell. See Figure 8.1.

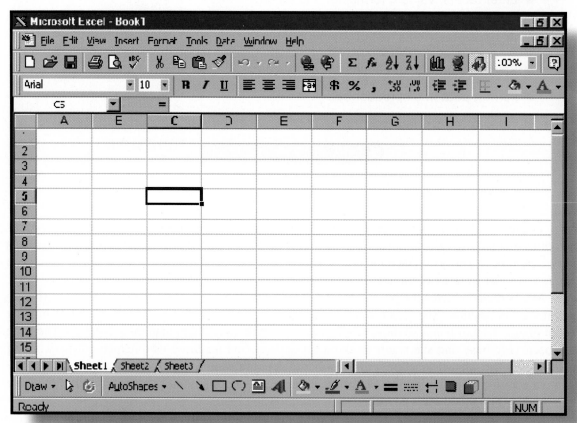

FIGURE 8.1
Database cells

You would think only 26 columns would be available in a spreadsheet because there are only 26 letters in the English alphabet. Spreadsheet developers decided to use two letters for the additional columns, much like we use two digits to indicate numbers above 9. The 27th cell is AA, then AB, and AC, and so on, until IV, which is the last column. It is column 256. Rows are numbered 1 to 65,536. Here is a display of a spreadsheet screen. See Figure 8.2.

FIGURE 8.2
The anatomy of the spreadsheet window

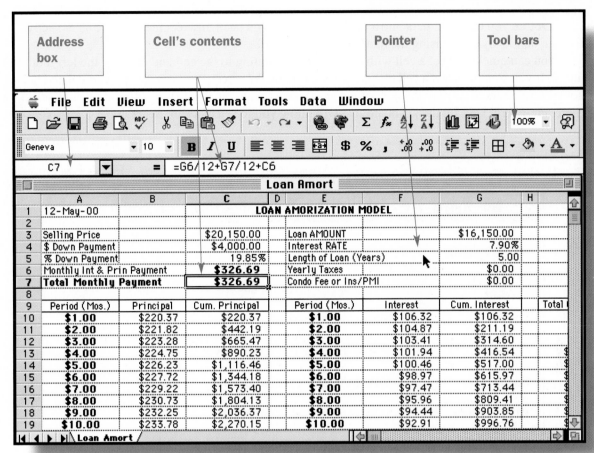

Toolbars allow you to organize the commands in the software program. The menu bar located at the top of the screen contains menu items such as File, Edit, View, Insert, and so on.

- The standard toolbar has icons for commands that are used frequently.

- The formatting toolbar has icons that are used frequently for formatting the appearance of the spreadsheet.

The formula bar displays the content of the active cell. A cell's contents is the text, numbers, or formulas you have entered into the cell. The address box displays the cell reference for the active cell. The pointer is the indicator that moves on your spreadsheet as you move the mouse. The shape of the pointer changes depending on the task you are performing.

 Did You Know?

Spreadsheets can be used to prepare budgets, maintain inventories, prepare payrolls, and maintain students' grades.

Moving Around in a Spreadsheet

Before you can enter data into a cell or edit a cell, you need to select that cell to make it active. You can do this by either using the mouse or the keyboard.

You can quickly select a cell with the mouse by pointing to the cell and clicking the left mouse button. If you want to select a cell that is not currently on the screen, you can use the vertical and horizontal scroll bars to display the area of the spreadsheet that contains the cell(s) you want to select. There are several keys on the keyboard that will allow you to select a cell. See Table 8.1.

TABLE 8.1

KEYSTROKES AND ACTIONS

KEYSTROKE	ACTION
← ↑ ↓ →	Moves up, down, left, right one cell
PgUp	Moves the active cell up one full screen
PgDn	Moves the active cell down one full screen
Home	Moves the active cell to Column A of the current row
CTRL + Home	Moves the active cell to cell A1
F5 (Function Key)	Opens Go To dialog box, in which you enter cell address of cell you want to make the active cell

ETHICS IN TECHNOLOGY

PHYSICAL SECURITY

With all the concern about major computer crime, the subject of internal security may be overlooked. It is usually fairly easy for someone unauthorized to access systems by simply going to a valid user's desk.

Machines and consoles should be kept in a secure place. Only a limited number of persons should have access. A list of persons with keys (access) should be kept up to date. Some organizations actually have security guards to monitor computer rooms and to control entry.

Remember that limited access means less opportunity for computer equipment and/or data to be stolen. That is why no alternative methods for getting into a computer room should be available. This includes hidden spare keys in an unsecured place.

Some organizations have taken computer security an extra step by securing equipment physically to desks and tables. This may seem like overkill, but you should protect your investment and your data by whatever means necessary.

Entering Data into a Spreadsheet

The data entered into a spreadsheet will be one of three types. It will be a label, a value, or a formula. A *label* is alphabetical text, a *value* is a number, and a *formula* is a statement that performs a calculation. A *function* is a built-in formula that is a shortcut for common calculations such as addition and average. Each type of data in the spreadsheet program has a particular use and is handled in a unique way. Examine the following diagrams for entering labels, values, and formulas and functions.

Now that we have gone over the basics of a spreadsheet, let's enter the information for the part-time payroll.

STEP-BY-STEP ▷ 8.1

Use the information in the table provided to enter the labels and values into the spreadsheet.

Vista Multimedia
Part-time Employees
Payroll

Week Ending January 29, 200-

Employee	MON	TUES	WED	THURS	FRI	SAT	Total Hours	Pay Rate	Gross Pay	Deductions	Net Pay
Regatti, S.	4	4	4	4		4		6.55			
McDavis, R.	4		4	2	4	3.5		5.35			
Tyler, C.	3	3		3	4	4		6.55			
Rodiquez, A		3.5	3	6	4	4		5.5			
Cornfeld, B.	4	2	5		5.5	5.5		5.75			

1. Click in cell A1 and type *Vista Multimedia*. Press the **Enter** key. You will notice that Vista Multimedia aligns at the left of the cell. Click in cell A2 (if you are not there) and type *Part-time Employees*; depress **Enter** key. Continue until you have typed the entire spreadsheet. You will notice that the numbers (values) align on the right side of the cells.

   If you make an error in keying information into a cell before you depress the **Enter** key, just press the **Backspace** key to delete it. If you want to key the text over,

   depress the Esc key. If you have already pressed the Enter key, select the cell that contains the error you want to correct. It will be displayed on the formula bar. You may click on the text here and make whatever corrections you need to.

2. Enter a formula to calculate the total number of hours worked during the week for all part-time employees. Place the cell pointer in the cell that will hold the result of the formula/function, H9. You will

   (continued on next page)

notice that the function appears on the formula bar. Whenever you enter a formula, you must inform the program that you are entering a formula and not a label. You do this by keying the equal sign (=). To key a formula, you combine numbers, cell references, arithmetic operators, and/or functions. The arithmetic operators indicate the desired arithmetic operations. These include addition (+), subtraction (-), multiplication (*), and division (/). Before you key a formula, be sure you have selected the cell in which you want the result of the formula to appear. After typing the function, depress the Enter key, click on the ✔, or use one of the directional keys. (The deduction is 18% of Gross Pay.) See Figure 8.3.

The formula could have been typed as =b9+c9+d9+e9+f9+g9. However, using the SUM function saves typing time. So instead of keying each cell, we used one of the many built-in formulas, called **functions.** To use the function to add a range of cells, we would just key =sum(b9:g9). The range of cells we want to add, sometimes referred to as an **argument**, is keyed inside parentheses with the first cell of the range, a colon (:), and the last cell of the range. A **range** of cells is a group of cells closely situated. Some of the functions are very simple, like SUM; others are more complex like PMT. Table 8.2 shows a list of commonly used functions.

FIGURE 8.3
Entering a formula

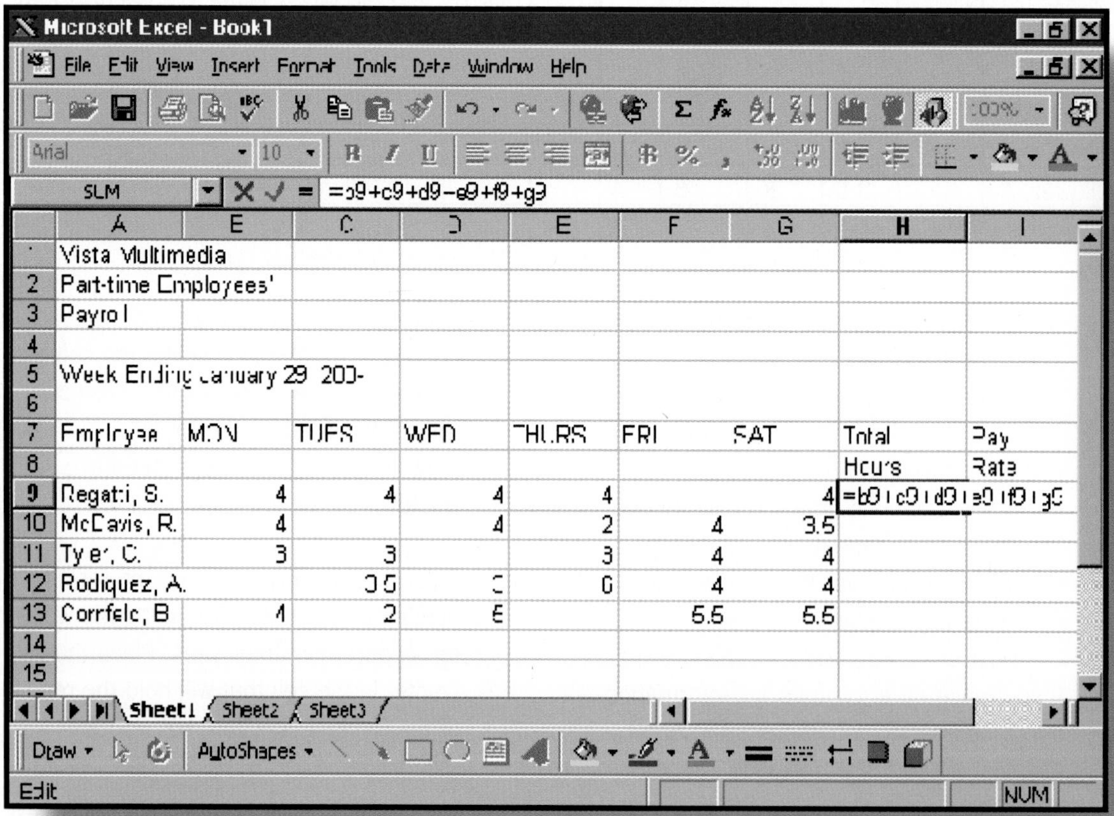

	A	B	C	D	E	F	G	H	I
1	Vista Multimedia								
2	Part-time Employees'								
3	Payroll								
4									
5	Week Ending January 29 200-								
6									
7	Employee	MON	TUES	WED	THURS	FRI	SAT	Total	Pay
8								Hours	Rate
9	Regatti, S.	4	4	4	4		4	=b9+c9+d9+e9+f9+g9	
10	McDavis, R.	4		4	2	4	3.5		
11	Tyer, C.	3	3		3	4	4		
12	Rodiquez, A.		3.5	3	6	4	4		
13	Corrfelc, B	4	2	6		5.5	5.5		
14									
15									

TABLE 8.2

FUNCTIONS

Function Name	Description
AVERAGE	Average of arguments.
COUNT	Counts the number of cells in a range.
IF	Specifies a logical test to perform; then performs one action if test result is true and another if it is not true.
MAX	Maximum value of range of cells.
MIN	Minimum value of range of cells.
ROUND	Rounds a number to a specified number of digits.
SUM	Totals a range of cells.

3. Calculate the remaining columns. The formulas for the next columns will be the same as the formula we entered for the first column. We can key it again for these columns or we can copy the formula into the other cells. We are going to use the copy-and-paste method to copy the formula.

   ■ Select cell H9 by clicking it. This cell contains the formula you want to copy.

   ■ Click Edit on the menu bar; click the Copy option to copy the contents of cell H9.

   ■ Select the cells you want to copy the formula into by clicking the first one (H10) and dragging the mouse down until all cells are selected through H13.

   ■ Click Edit on the menu bar again; now click the Paste option to paste the formula into the four selected cells. See Figure 8.4.

4. When you copy formulas from one cell to another, the cell references or addresses automatically adjust to the new location(s). Click in cell H9. Now click in cell H10; you see that the cell references have changed from the original formula keyed for the first column to cell H9. Your software does this automatically. This type of cell referencing, cell references or cell names that change when copied, is called relative cell referencing.

(continued on next page)

 Hot Tip

A very useful feature of spreadsheet software is the macro, a recorded series of keystrokes that will be replayed later. For example, all of the keystrokes necessary to copy a formula from one cell to the cell below it might be recorded as a macro.

125

Sometimes cells that are copied need to remain the same. These cell references are called absolute cell references, cells that do not change regardless of where they are copied. To designate a cell as an absolute cell, key a $ in front of the letter and behind the letter, for example, h9.

5. Save the spreadsheet. You should save your spreadsheet often. You do not want to lose any of the work you have completed.

   ■ Click File on the menu bar.

   ■ Click Save As. Once the Save As windows opens, be sure to select the location of your diskette; which will probably be 3-1/2 Floppy (A).

   ■ In the Filename box, key the name of your spreadsheet. Let's name this one PT Payroll 1/29.

6. Print your spreadsheet. Once you have completed your spreadsheet, you may print it. Click File on the menu bar. Click Print from the drop-down menu. Once the Print dialog window opens, adjust any settings you desire and then click OK.

FIGURE 8.4
Calculating the remaining columns

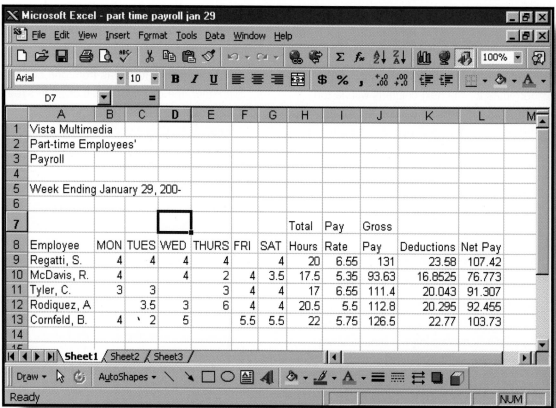

	A	B	C	D	E	F	G	H	I	J	K	L	M
1	Vista Multimedia												
2	Part-time Employees'												
3	Payroll												
4													
5	Week Ending January 29, 200-												
6													
7								Total	Pay	Gross			
8	Employee	MON	TUES	WED	THURS	FRI	SAT	Hours	Rate	Pay	Deductions	Net Pay	
9	Regatti, S.	4	4	4	4		4	20	6.55	131	23.58	107.42	
10	McDavis, R.	4		4	2	4	3.5	17.5	5.35	93.63	16.8525	76.773	
11	Tyler, C.	3	3		3	4	4	17	6.55	111.4	20.043	91.307	
12	Rodiquez, A		3.5	3	6	4	4	20.5	5.5	112.8	20.295	92.455	
13	Cornfeld, B.	4	2	5		5.5	5.5	22	5.75	126.5	22.77	103.73	
14													

Additional Features

Several features increase the efficiency and effectiveness of a spreadsheet. These include inserting and deleting rows and columns, changing column widths, formatting cells as well as the entire spreadsheet, hiding cells, spell checking, and displaying spreadsheet data in graph and chart formats. Spreadsheets can also be linked and inserted into other documents.

- *Changing the column* width is one way to improve the appearance of the spreadsheet. There are several methods to adjust the column width including using the Format option or clicking on the line between two column headings and dragging to the desired width.

- The process of *inserting rows and columns* into a spreadsheet is done in a similar way. You select the number of rows or columns you want to insert and then click on the Insert command on the menu bar. The adjacent rows or columns position themselves appropriately.

- The process of *deleting rows and columns* from a spreadsheet is done similarly to inserting, only you select Delete from the Insert on the menu bar.

 Did You Know?

You can insert a spreadsheet into a letter and if you make changes to the spreadsheet in the letter, it will also make changes in the original spreadsheet.

- To *format cells* in a spreadsheet, select the cells you want to format and click on the formatting you want. These may include Bold, Alignment, Italics, Underline, Font Size, Borders, and so on.

- You may choose to *print your spreadsheet* sideways on the paper (landscape orientation); centered vertically and/or horizontally on the page; printed with gridlines, or any other formatting that would affect your entire spreadsheet. This can be done by choosing the Page Setup command in the File menu. You may even print your spreadsheet with the formulas showing instead of the result of the formulas. This is called the *Formula View*.

TECHNOLOGY CAREERS

DIRECTOR, INFORMATION TECHNOLOGY

The director of information technology is an administrator who is responsible for planning, promoting, and supporting information technologies within an organization. These technologies include computing, networking, and telecommunications.

By planning, organizing, directing, and supervising all information technology activities. the director ensures that all users are able to apply technologies in performing their daily tasks

The director of information technology should be knowledgeable about principles, practices, and techniques for operating microcomputers as well as large-scale, high-volume data processing operations and principles, practices of personnel management, and budget development and administration.

A bachelor's degree in business administration, computer science, or a closely related field is usually required. However, a master's degree is preferred. Many firms require significant experience including experience at a management level.

The salary for this position ranges between $45,000 and $55,000 a year depending on experience and the size and location of the company.

- Many spreadsheet programs allow you to *hide data* in a spreadsheet from printing or displaying. The feature is useful when you don't want someone else to see certain data that is in a spreadsheet or if you do not want to print certain data. You can also unhide this data so it will be available for printing and displaying.

- You may use the *spell check feature* to check your spreadsheet for misspelled words.

- Spreadsheets can be *integrated into document*s created in other programs such as word processing.

STEP-BY-STEP ▷ 8.2

1. Use the following formatting tools to improve the appearance of the part-time spreadsheet. Widen the columns as needed, add $ to total row and Net Pay column, and center the headings over the columns and boldface them. See Figure 8.5.

2. Graphing the contents of a spreadsheet provides a visual view of the contents.

Many spreadsheet programs can use the data in a spreadsheet to create many different kinds of graphs: bar, line, stacked, pie, and so on. Use the procedure outlined here to create a pie graph of the payroll spreadsheet:

3. Select the range of cells to be graphed. Chose the New Graph command from the

FIGURE 8.5
Changing the format

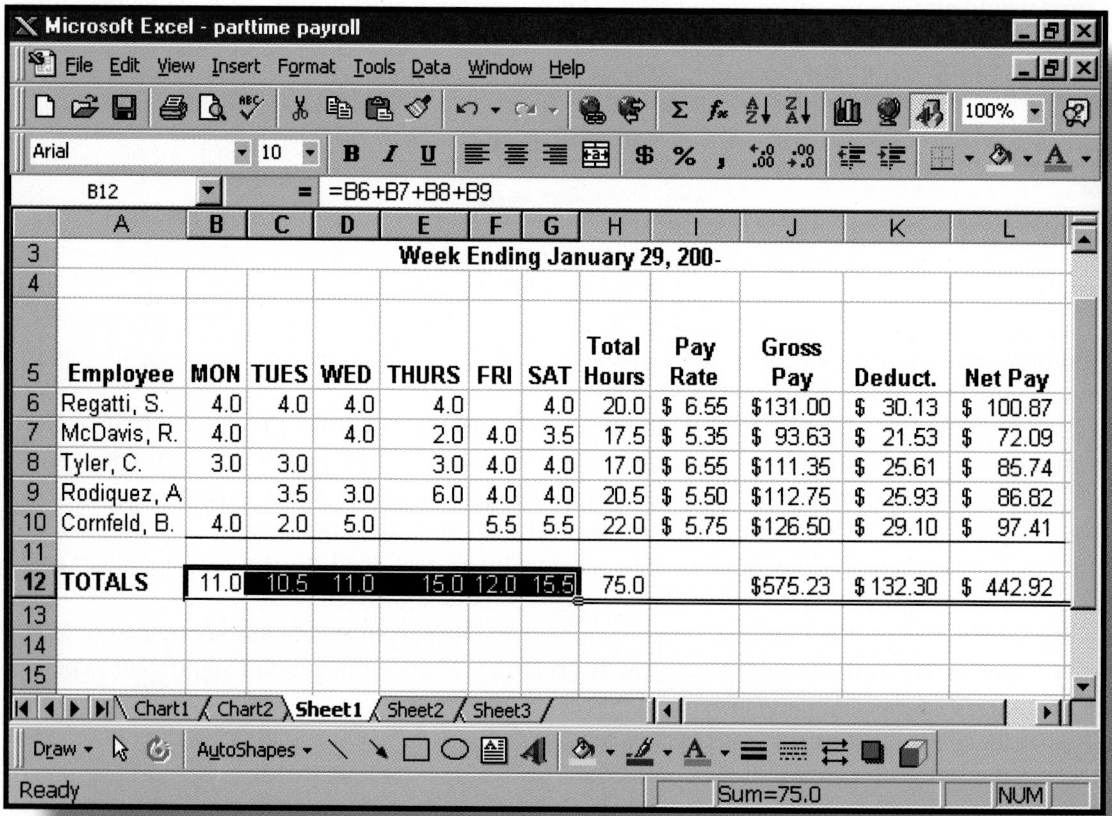

Microsoft Excel - parttime payroll

File Edit View Insert Format Tools Data Window Help

Arial 10 B I U

B12 = =B6+B7+B8+B9

	A	B	C	D	E	F	G	H	I	J	K	L
3					Week Ending January 29, 200-							
4												
5	Employee	MON	TUES	WED	THURS	FRI	SAT	Total Hours	Pay Rate	Gross Pay	Deduct.	Net Pay
6	Regatti, S.	4.0	4.0	4.0	4.0		4.0	20.0	$ 6.55	$131.00	$ 30.13	$ 100.87
7	McDavis, R.	4.0		4.0	2.0	4.0	3.5	17.5	$ 5.35	$ 93.63	$ 21.53	$ 72.09
8	Tyler, C.	3.0	3.0		3.0	4.0	4.0	17.0	$ 6.55	$111.35	$ 25.61	$ 85.74
9	Rodiquez, A		3.5	3.0	6.0	4.0	4.0	20.5	$ 5.50	$112.75	$ 25.93	$ 86.82
10	Cornfeld, B.	4.0	2.0	5.0		5.5	5.5	22.0	$ 5.75	$126.50	$ 29.10	$ 97.41
11												
12	TOTALS	11.0	10.5	11.0	15.0	12.0	15.5	75.0		$575.23	$ 132.30	$ 442.92
13												
14												
15												

Chart1 Chart2 **Sheet1** Sheet2 Sheet3

Draw AutoShapes

Ready Sum=75.0 NUM

appropriate menu. (There may be an icon on the toolbar for this command.) You may be asked for a name for your graph.

4. Select the type of graph you want. Remember, we are creating a pie graph.

5. Choose the Data Labels command (or similar command) from the appropriate menu and provide any additional information requested.

6. Prepare a pie chart of the spreadsheet that shows the number of hours worked by each employee. See Figure 8.6.

FIGURE 8.6
Pie graph of spreadsheet

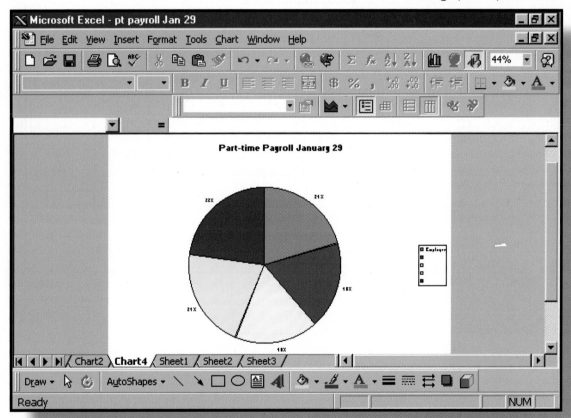

Using a Spreadsheet

Once spreadsheets have been developed, the information can be analyzed so you can use it to make decisions, make changes, forecast for the future, or whatever you need the information to do. One commonly used feature is the ***what-if analysis.*** It is the process of using a spreadsheet to test different scenarios or to apply a certain condition if a certain condition exists. The IF function is used to perform this task.

An example would be to give employees who worked more than 20 hours a week a bonus of 2% of their gross pay. Those who did not work more than 20 hours would not get the bonus. The bonus formula would be keyed as "if(h9>20,(j9*2%),0. Insert a column between Deduct. and Net Pay with the heading "Bonus." The amount of the bonus should be entered in this space. See Figure 8.7.

FIGURE 8.7
Bonus row and amount entered

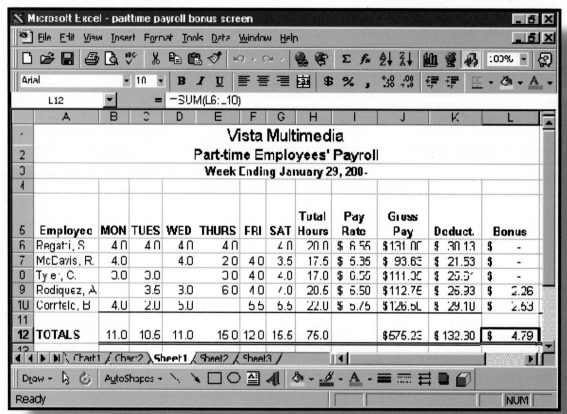

Summary

- The purpose of spreadsheet software is to enter, calculate, manipulate, and analyze numbers.

- The major part of a spreadsheet window consists of the toolbars.

- Columns are identified by letters. There are 256 columns in a spreadsheet.

- Rows are identified by numbers. There are 65,536 rows in a spreadsheet.

- The point at which a column and a row intersects is a cell.

- A cell that has been selected (highlighted or outlined with a black border) is referred to as an active cell.

- A range of cells is a group of closely situated cells.

- Cells containing alphabetic information are referred to as labels, and cells containing numeric information that can be calculated are referred to as values.

■ A formula is a statement that performs a calculation. All formulas begin with the equal sign.

■ A function is a built-in formula that is a shortcut for common calculations such as addition and averages.

■ Formulas may be copied to other cells by using several methods such as the copy-and-paste method.

■ New rows and columns may be added to an existing spreadsheet; likewise, unwanted rows and columns can be deleted.

■ Formatting attributes can be added to a spreadsheet to improve its appearance.

■ Selected data in a spreadsheet can be hidden so it will not be displayed or printed.

■ A relative cell reference refers to cells that change when they are copied into other cells.

■ An absolute cell reference does not change regardless of where it is copied.

■ A spreadsheet should be saved often so that commands and formats entered are not lost.

■ The contents of a spreadsheet can be displayed in chart or graph formats.

■ Spreadsheets can be integrated into other program documents such as a word processing document.

■ Spreadsheet programs have many features available to make spreadsheets more efficient and attractive.

For more information on this topic, complete Mission Plan 7: Know the Score on the "Computer Concepts: Systems, Applications, and Design" CD. See your instructor for further instructions.

LESSON 8 REVIEW QUESTIONS

MULTIPLE CHOICE

1. The point at which a column and a row intersects is called a/an _____.
   A. cell
   B. pointer
   C. value
   D. label

2. There are _____ columns in a spreadsheet.
   A. 65,536
   B. 26
   C. 256
   D. 2,182

3. The formula is keyed in the _____.
   A. standard toolbar
   B. formula bar
   C. menu bar
   D. formatting toolbar

4. Pie, bar, stacked, and line are examples of types of _____.
   A. spreadsheets
   B. cells
   C. formulas
   D. graphs

5. The _____ is used to select cells.
   A. pointer
   B. cell
   C. toolbar
   D. name box

6. Labels, values, formulas, and functions are types of _____ that can be entered into a spreadsheet.
   A. fonts
   B. data
   C. formats
   D. headings

TRUE/FALSE

Circle the T if the statement is true. Circle F if it is false.

T F 1. A spreadsheet program can be used to type letters.

T F 2. A spreadsheet is also referred to as a worksheet.

T F 3. The point at which a column and row intersects is a cell.

T F 4. Spreadsheets can also be printed in graph format.

T F 5. You can move around in a spreadsheet by using keys on the keyboard.

SHORT ANSWER

1. A cell address consists of a _____ letter and a _____ number.

2. Four types of data entered into a spreadsheet are _____, _____, _____, and _____.

3. To identify a cell as absolute, type a _____ before and after the letter in the cell address.

4. The point at which a column and row meets is called a _____.

5. All formulas should begin with a/an _____.

CROSS-CURRICULAR PROJECTS

MATH

During the past five years the cost of cars has increased quite drastically. Research the cost of at least five cars that were on the market five years ago and are still on the market today. Find the cost of those cars five years ago and their cost today. Record the information into a spreadsheet. Calculate the amount of increase in price for each car. Also create a graph showing the percentage of increase for each car. The URL for most cars is www., the name of the car, and .com. For example, the URL for Lexus is www.lexus.com.

SCIENCE

Create a spreadsheet to record the freezing point of the following solutions, and then generate a bar graph showing the information.

Solution	Freezing Point
Salt	-2
Sugar	0
Distilled water	2
Calcium	-6

SOCIAL STUDIES

Use the Internet and other resources to find information concerning population figures in the five largest cities in your state for the past 10 years. Record the information in a spreadsheet. Calculate the increase/decrease in population. Calculate the percentage of increase/decrease.

LANGUAGE ARTS

The students in your class have had a reading contest during this past year. Create a spreadsheet to enter the information concerning the number of books read by each member in the class who participated. Use the information provided for your spreadsheet. Create formulas to determine the total number of books read by boys; the total number of books read by girls, and the total number of books read. Also determine the percentage of books read by boys and the percentage read by the girls.

READING CONTEST

Student	1st Semester	2nd Semester	Total	% Read
Girls				
Name				
Name				
Name				
Total				
Boys				
Name				
Name				
Name				
Total				
Grand Total				

WEB PROJECT

Access the Internet, and use your search engine to find information about spreadsheet template files that can be used for spreadsheet applications. Identify the template file(s) found, and describe how it/they can be used with a spreadsheet program. Use terms such as spreadsheet, template, files, and so on, to help narrow your search.

TEAM PROJECT

Many spreadsheet programs have templates available that would make using them even more efficient. Your supervisor has asked you and one other employee to identify spreadsheet templates that would increase the efficiency of the video store. You are to identify the templates and give a description of each.

See the CD-ROM "Computer Concepts: Systems, Applications, and Design" for more information on this subject or careers in this area. Use Mission #7 - Know the Score.

HOW DO I USE DATABASE SOFTWARE?

OBJECTIVES

When you complete this module, you will be able to:

- Define the purpose of a database.

- Give examples of uses of databases.

- Identify and define the components of a database.

- Plan and design a database.

- Enter records into a table.

- Modify a table structure.

- Perform queries.

- Sort tables.

- Modify data in a table.

- Create and use forms and reports.

⏱ **Estimated Time: 1.5 hours**

VOCABULARY

Database
Field
Form
Primary key
Query
Record
Report
Table
Updating

Since you have been working at the Multimedia store, you have purchased many CDs. The fact that you receive a 20% employee discount has made it possible for you to buy more CDs than you normally do. And you get to save even more when the CDs are also on sale. Because you have so many more now than before, you would like to organize them so you will know exactly what you have. You would like to be able to answer the following questions: How many CDs do I have? How much money do I have invested in my collection? When did I purchase them? All of these applications are possible if you enter the information about your collection into a database software program. A database program will allow you to do all of the above and much more. A database program is often referred to as a database management system, or DBMS.

What Is Database Software?

A *database* is a collection of related data. Database software is used to enter, store, maintain, and retrieve data into useful information. Individuals at home can also use a DBMS (database management

135

system) to maintain address lists of friends and business contacts, to maintain a property inventory, or to maintain membership lists for organizations to which they belong. Businesses use database software to maintain customer files, inventory files, and personnel files. The files in a database can also be used to merge with other documents such as letters and sets of labels (such as address labels).

Did You Know?

Some popular examples of databases include libraries, the telephone directory, encyclopedias, and even the almanac!

Creating a Database

Before you actually begin to design and develop your database, you must do some planning. You need to answer questions such as what information to include and how the information will be used. Once you have made these decisions, you are ready to create your database.

Database Structure

Let's look at the structure of a database for organizing your CD collection:

- A *field* is an individual piece or item of information. Examples of fields would be the title of the CD, the artist, the year recorded, the date purchased, and the cost.

- A *record* is a collection of fields. Each CD would be a record and would contain all the fields identified.

- A *table* is a group of records. In some database programs, a group of records is called a file.

FIGURE 9.1
Database structure

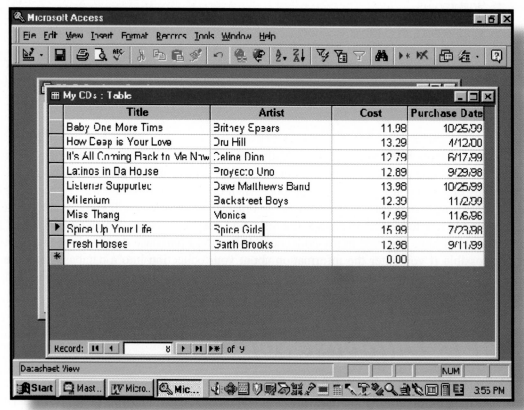

Before entering data into a database program, its structure must be created. But once this has been completed and saved, you can begin to enter the information about each CD. Once you have entered the information for all of your CDs, you can get a printout of your database. See Figure 9.1.

Now you are ready to organize and arrange the data in your table to really make it useful to you. When you purchase new CDs, you can add the information to the table, you can print sorted lists, and you can even print labels to attach to your CD cases.

STEP-BY-STEP ▷ 9.1

1. Launch the database software program that your instructor tells you to launch and click on the appropriate tools to create the database file. You will enter the filename CD Collection in the appropriate space when asked.

2. Create a table structure. Before you can enter data into a table, the table structure must be designed and created. Designing the structure includes naming the fields you will use, specifying the size of the field, and identifying what type of data will be stored in each field. You must also define one of your fields as a primary key. A **primary key** uniquely identifies a field for each record. The information in this field will only appear for one record. Example: Only one person would have the

same account number or the same identification number. See Figure 9.2.

- Field names should be short and descriptive. Most software programs allow many more spaces than a field name needs to be.

- The size of a field is determined by the number of spaces required for the data that will fill a particular field. Example: If LastName is a field, the field size could be 15. (Most last names are 15 letters or less.) Some fields do not require you to indicate the field size. These fields, Date/Time, Logical, and so on, have predefined field sizes.

- Each field must be identified by the type of information that will be entered. Field types include text, numeric, date/time, logical, memo, and currency. These may have different names depending on the database software

(continued on next page)

Hot Tip

The primary key must never be blank.

FIGURE 9.2
Field names

Field Name	Data Type	Field Size	Description
Title	Text	25	Primary key
Artist	Text	25	
Recording Date	Date/Time	—	
Cost	Numeric	3	
Purchase Date	Date/Time	—	

program you are using. There may also be additional types. Some programs will allow you to indicate additional formatting features.

3. After you have created the table structure, you will name and save it. See Figure 9.3.

FIGURE 9.3
Naming a table structure

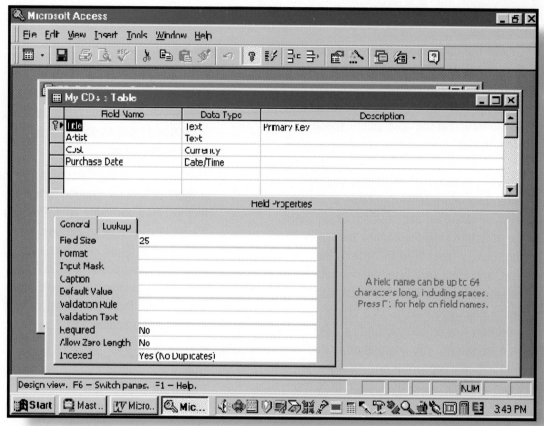

Entering Data into a Table

Once you have created the table structure, you are ready to enter records. This information may be entered differently depending on the specific database software program you are using. Basically you will have a screen that displays the field names you have identified. You will enter the information for each record. See Figure 9.4.

Once you have entered the records into the table, you can print a copy of all of the records. You can also sort the table by either of the fields in the table. When sorting records, you must decide if you want to sort in ascending or descending order. An *ascending sort* arranges records in alphabetical or numerical order according to the field sorted. A *descending sort* arranges records in the opposite alphabetical or numerical order, that is, from Z to A or 9 to 0.

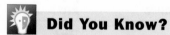 **Did You Know?**

As an alternate to using the data entry form to enter data into your table, you can enter data in the table view also.

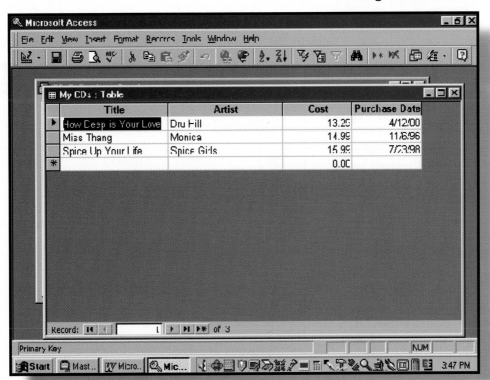

ETHICS IN TECHNOLOGY

PRIVACY: JUNK E-MAIL

How many times have you received e-mail messages from unknown persons or organizations? Such messages are referred to as junk e-mail. It is much like junk mail you receive through the postal service: solicitations to purchase something. The difference between the two, however, is that many times the electronic junk mail contains obscene materials.

Junk e-mailers use two methods: spamming and spoofing. In spamming, the sender sends hundreds of thousands of e-mail messages at the same time to persons across a wide geographic location. They are able to use unique ways to get e-mail addresses. Some purchase authentic mailing lists; some purchase hacked mailing lists. They hope the more their so-called ads are seen, the greater the possibility of sales.

Spoofing enables junk e-mailers to hide their identity from the recipient. This makes it difficult to stop the excessive messages because the recipient does not know who is sending the messages.

You may ask how do all these people get your e-mail address. Your e-mail is not private. It does not have the security of first-class mail. Whenever you enter personal information on the Internet, you make it possible for others to locate information about you.

There are ways for you to protect yourself when sending e-mail messages. The most effective method is encryption software. It scrambles letters according to a mathematical formula, and the person receiving the message uses the same formula to unscramble the letters and read your message. Pretty Good Privacy is free encryption software. You obtain a copy of it at www.ifi.uio.no/pgp.

139

Querying a Database

A *query* is a question you ask about the data stored in a database. Querying a database means to search a database for specific records that meet a given criteria. Example: You want to see a list of all of the CDs that you purchased in January 1999. You may have a printout with all of the fields in the table displayed or may choose exactly which fields you want displayed with this information.

You will need to use a comparison operator to match the range of information in your fields. For example, one data item can be equal to another, not equal to another, greater than another, greater than or equal to another, less than another, or less than or equal to another. You may also combine some of the operators. Some database programs may use additional operators. See Table 9.1.

TABLE 9.1

COMPARISON OPERATOR

Operator	Meaning
=	Equal to
>	Greater than
>=	Greater than or equal to
<	Less than
<=	Less than or equal to
<>	Not equal to
Between and And	Includes a range

When you perform a query, you select the field you want to query and type in the criteria for which field you want to query. Example: If you want a list of all CDs that cost $13 or more, you would select COST as the field to be queried and key in ">12." See Figure 9.5.

Modifying the Table Structure

The structure of the database table may be modified. If you decide that you want to add a field or delete a field, you may do so. You can also change the field type, the field size, or any of the attributes you assigned originally. Open the original table structure, make any changes you need to make, and save the changes. Let's add a field to our table that will indicate whether the artist is male or female.

STEP-BY-STEP ▷ 9.2

1. Open the original structure.

2. Add a field named "Sex" as the last field.

3. Enter the following information: Data type is text and field size is 1. You will enter M for males and F for females.

4. Save changes by clicking on the Save icon or Save on the File menu.

FIGURE 9.5
Database query

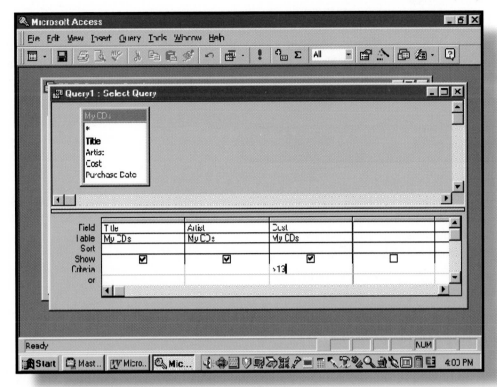

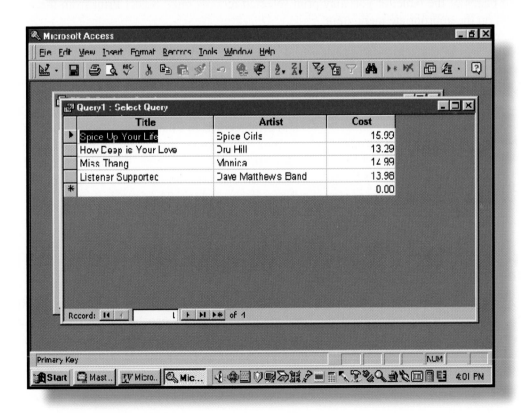

Updating a Database

Updating a database is the process of adding, changing, and deleting records in a table to keep them current and accurate. When you delete a record from a table, all of the information entered in that record is permanently deleted. You may also select a record and make any necessary changes in the field values. You recently purchased two additional CDs. Enter the information for these two CDs in your database.

STEP-BY-STEP ▷ 9.3

1. Open the CD Collection table.

2. Add the information for your two new CDs at the bottom of the last entries made.

3. Save the table with the new entries. Click on the Save icon or on Save on the File menu.

Printing a Database

The records in a database may be printed in various forms. You can print the entire table, selected pages of the table, or you may print selected records only. Select Print from the File menu and click on the appropriate menu item.

Creating and Using Forms

Hot Tip

In some database software programs, the same form used to define the database fields can be used as a form to enter or edit data.

A form is an object you use to maintain, view, and print records in a database. Although this can be performed using other functions of the software, forms allow the user to customize the appearance of the form. The form can even be formatted attractively to include the company 's logo. The form is used to input data for one record at a time. See Figure 9.6.

Creating and Using a Report

An important feature of database management software is the ability to generate sophisticated reports that contain the contents of the database. These reports can be used to summarize data, pulling out only what is needed. The formatting, such as headings, spacing, and graphics, can be decided by the user. Once the report has been generated, you can decide which records you want included in the report, you can sort the report, and you can even insert a picture in the report. See Figure 9.7.

FIGURE 9.6
Input data one record at a time

FIGURE 9.7
Creating a report

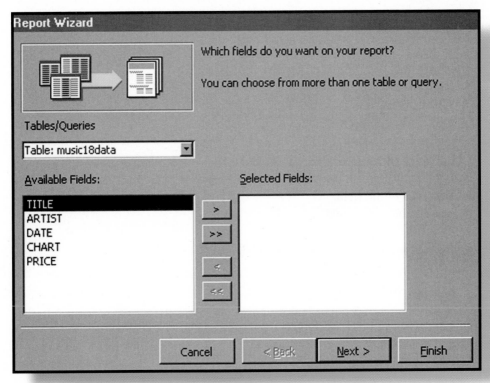

Summary

- Databases allow for organizing, storing, maintaining, retrieving, and sorting data.

- The components of a database are fields, records, and tables.

- The database structure is designed and created first.

- The fields to be used in a table are identified in the structure. Any special attributes including field data type and size are also included in the structure.

- Once the table structure has been created, records may be added to the table.

- The structure may be modified to include any necessary changes.

- Data in a table may be sorted in ascending or descending order.

- Specific records may be selected based on a given criteria. This process is called a query.

- Forms are used to display the data of one record. Forms may be formatted in customized formats.

- A report is a formatted display (printed or on screen) of the contents of a table in a database.

LESSON 9 REVIEW QUESTIONS

MULTIPLE CHOICE

Write the letter of the correct answer for each question in the space provided.

1. To perform a query to select a greater than criteria, use the following comparison operator: _____.
    - **A.** <
    - **B.** =
    - **C.** >
    - **D.** >=

2. The size of a field is determined by _____.
    - **A.** the number of spaces required for the data that will fill the field.
    - **B.** the number of fields in the table.
    - **C.** the data type of the field.
    - **D.** the description of the field.

3. The _____ uniquely identifies a field.
    - **A.** foreign key
    - **B.** primary key
    - **C.** memo field
    - **D.** Esc key

4. _____ are not prepared with a database management program.
   A. Membership rosters
   B. Customer accounts
   C. Monthly budgets
   D. Resumes

5. A _____ is a group of records.
   A. field
   B. table
   C. database
   D. file

6. To arrange the data in your database, you can _____ it.
   A. filter
   B. type
   C. align
   D. sort

TRUE/FALSE

Circle the T if the statement is true. Circle F if it is false.

T F 1. The foreign key uniquely identifies a record in a table.

T F 2. Updating a database is the process of adding, changing, and deleting records in a table to keep them current and accurate.

T F 3. Designing the table structure includes naming the fields, identifying the data type, choosing the size, and writing the description.

T F 4. It is better if field names are long and descriptive.

T F 5. Data in a table may be sorted in ascending and descending order.

SHORT ANSWER

1. A _____ is an organized collection of data.

2. A _____ is a group of fields.

3. Perform a _____ when you want to display specific records and fields.

4. The _____ feature of a database program allows you to generate printouts formatted with headings and other user-defined features.

5. Text, numeric, date, and memo are examples of _____.

CROSS-CURRICULAR PROJECTS

MATH

Assume you are the treasurer of your math club. It is your responsibility to maintain records on members' names, addresses, phone numbers, original membership date, and date of dues payment. Create a database to contain this information.

Make up information for this database. Create the database structure based on the information above. Enter at least 12 members into your database. Enter dues having been paid for all but two members. Once you have entered the records:

■ Print the entire database sorted by members' last name.

■ Print a list of all members who have paid dues.

■ Delete two members from the database.

■ Create a report showing all members with names and telephone numbers.

SCIENCE

There have been quite a few hurricanes in certain parts of the country in recent years. Some of these hurricanes have been very costly in lives and dollars. Use the Internet to locate information on hurricanes during the past ten years. Use your favorite search engine and the keyword hurricanes.

Create a database file containing the following information: name, year, state, classification, dollar damages, and lost lives. After entering the information in the database, print the entire file sorted by hurricane name, and again by the year of the hurricane. Answer the following questions using data from your database: (1) Which state had the most hurricanes during the ten-year period? (2) Which hurricane caused the most financial damage?

SOCIAL STUDIES

Use the Internet and other resources to find information on at least 15 inventors. Use your search engine with the keyword inventions. You can also visit www.AskJeeves.com for the information.

Create a database to store the information you find. You will need the inventor's first name and last name, gender, nationality, invention, year of invention, and brief description if necessary. Once you have entered the data, print a copy of the entire file. Use the query feature to organize and print your data in various ways. For example, print a query of all inventions made by women; print a query of all inventions that were made during a certain year.

LANGUAGE ARTS

Your instructor will give you a list of writers. Use the Internet and any other resources to find additional information on the writers such as birthdate, place of birth, sex, type of writing, most recent book, publication date, and theme of book. Create a database containing these authors' information. Print the entire file sorted by authors' last name. Prepare additional printouts by performing queries requesting various scenarios such as a printout of female authors.

WEB PROJECT

Use the Internet to obtain information on different database programs. There are various types of database software programs on the market. Some of them have many of the same applications; many have different applications. You are especially looking for a description of the applications that are available with the software.

TEAM PROJECT

Your store manager, Ms. Perez, has asked you and the other part-time employees to work together to design a report format for displaying videos whose shelf lives have expired and are for sale at a reduced rate. The report should have an appropriate title and headings over columns (fields). You do not need to print the report from the database. She just wants to see what the format would look like.

See the CD-ROM "Computer Concepts: Systems, Applications, and Design" for more information on this subject or careers in this area. Use Mission #11 - Data Control.

How Do I Use Presentation Graphics Software?

OBJECTIVES

When you complete this module, you will be able to:

- Describe presentation graphics software.
- Explain the advantage of using visuals.
- Create a presentation.
- Work in different views.
- Add design.
- Add charts and WordArt.
- Add transitions and animations.
- Print a presentation.
- Describe effective presentation rules.
- Identify some presentation tips and hints.

⏱ Estimated Time: 1.5 hours

VOCABULARY

Animation
Audience handouts
Design templates
Electronic presentation
Presentation graphics program
Transitions

Have you given a report in front of a class recently? Or have you listened to a report by a class-mate or a lecture by your teacher? If so, you may have noticed that no matter how interesting the subject matter or how dynamic the speaker, it's still hard to keep everyone's attention. One atten-tion-holding technique is to include visuals, such as those in a presentation graphics program. This is not the total answer to the problem, but this software application will help. If you have a flair for graphics, there's almost no limit to what you can do.

Using Visuals in a Presentation

Ms. Perez, Vista Multimedia store manager, is giving a presentation tomorrow on a new in-store feature. She has purchased special equipment for creating a Digital Versatile Disk (DVD). The general public can rent the equipment and create a DVD. The president and other officers of Vista Multimedia are eager to learn about the project.

Ms. Perez is anxious about the presentation and asks you for advice. You suggest that she use a *presentations graphics program*. You explain to her that she can use this software to create a sequence of ideas and pictures that support her presentation. Equipment requirements for the presentation include a portable projector and computer—all of which she has available. See Figure 10.1.

FIGURE 10.1
A presentation using a projector and presentation graphics

Overview

Presentation graphics programs are used in business and education. Using this software, a computer, and a projector for an on-screen or *electronic presentation* allows the presenter to bring together and present a variety of special effects and features. Presentation graphics program are excellent for creating on-screen shows, but that's not their only output option. Other options include the following:

 **Hot Tip**

We are witnessing many new happenings and innovations with presentation graphics software. Accountants, engineers, teachers, and other professionals all use this software. However, one of the most dramatic and unique uses of this software is by attorneys in courtrooms.

■ Self-running presentation: You participate in a science fair. You can set up a self-running presentation illustrating your project. When the presentation is completed, it automatically restarts.

■ Online meetings: Use a program like Microsoft's NetMeeting and share a presentation in real time (occurring immediately) with classmates at a neighboring school or in a neighboring country.

■ Presentation broadcasting: Use the Web to broadcast your presentation to classmates all over the world.

■ Web presentation: Create your presentation, save it as a Web or HTML document, and upload it onto your school's Web site.

- Overhead transparencies: For those presenters who don't have access to a computer and projector, you can create and print either black and white or color transparencies. Use plastic transparency acetate sheets and print directly to your printer.

- 35mm slides: Some schools may not have computers and projectors in every classroom, but most schools have slide projectors available. Use PowerPoint to save each screen as a separate slide. Then have these converted to 33mm slides.

- Audience handouts: Use handouts to support your presentation. These smaller versions of your slides can be printed two, three, six, or nine to a page.

Several software companies produce presentation graphics programs. Some of the more popular of these include the following:

- Microsoft PowerPoint—both Macintosh and Windows versions

- Corel Presentations

- Lotus Freelance

Creating a Presentation

Ms. Perez is impressed with your presentation graphics knowledge. In fact, she is so impressed that she has asked you to help her create the DVD presentation for the big meeting next week. Most presentation programs contain the same features. In the following Step-by-Step, instructions are generic, but screen captures are from Microsoft's PowerPoint 2000 presentation program.

STEP-BY-STEP ▷ 10.1

FIGURE 10.2
New dialog box

1. Launch your presentation graphics program. The New dialog box displays. See Figure 10.2.

2. Click the Blank Presentation option button and then click OK. The New Slide dialog box displays.

3. From this dialog box, you can select an AutoLayout format for your slide. Most of these presentation offers several different layout options.

4. The highlighted layout is for a title slide. See Figure 10.3. Notice that the name of

150

the slide is given in the lower right corner.
Click OK to display the slide.

4. Click in the Click to add title box. Type
   Vista Multimedia.

FIGURE 10.3
AutoLayout dialog box

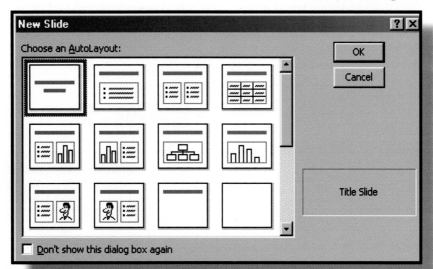

5. Click in the Click to add subtitle box. Type
   DVD Creation Project. See Figure 10.4.

6. On the Insert menu, click New Slide. The
   AutoLayout dialog box displays.

(continued on next page)

FIGURE 10.4
Presentation slide

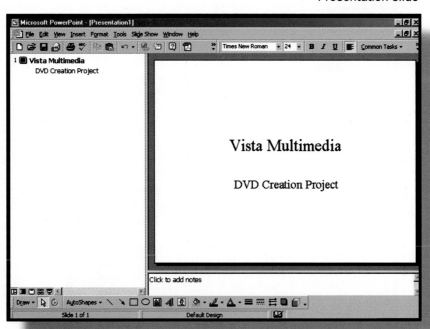

151

7. Click the Text and ClipArt layout. Click OK. The new slide is added to your presentation.

8. Click in the Click to add title box and type Status of DVD Creation Project.

9. Click in the Click to add text box. Type the following:

   On time [Enter]

   Profitable [Enter]

   Popular [Enter]

10. Double-click the icon to add clip art to display the Clip Gallery.

11. In the Search for Clips text box, type CD and press [Enter] to display a variety of CD pictures. See Figure 10.5.

12. Select a graphic that you like and click Insert. Your selected graphic is inserted into the presentation.

13. On the Standard toolbar, click the Save button. Give your presentation a name and click the Save button.

Internet

Need a quick guide to preparing presentations? Check out www.mhhe.com/socscience/comm/lucas/student/birdsell/birdsell12.htm. You can find lots of tips and hints that will help make you a better presenter.

FIGURE 10.5
Clip Art Gallery

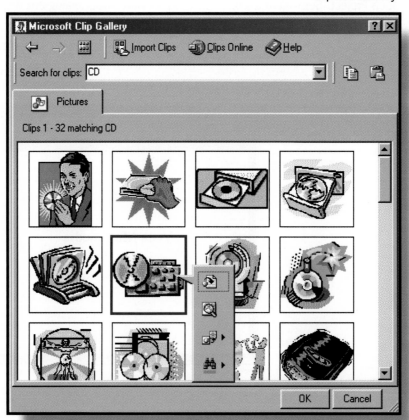

Working in Different Views

Presentation software graphic programs come with different views to help you while you are creating a presentation. The two main views are normal view and slide sorter view. You can easily switch between views by clicking the appropriate buttons. See Figure 10.6.

- Normal view: contains three panes—the outline pane, the slide pane, and the notes pane. These panes let you work on all parts of your presentation from one screen. Adjust the size of the different panes by dragging the pane borders. Normal view was shown earlier in Figure 10.3.

- Outline view: shows an outline of the presentation's text. Use this view to organize and develop the content of your presentation.

- Slide sorter view: displays thumbnails or miniature images of all slides in your presentation. Use this view to add transitions and animations and to add, delete, and move slides. See Figure 10.7.

- Slide view: displays a full screen image of your slide.

- Slide show: view your presentation as you will present it to your audience.

FIGURE 10.6
View buttons

FIGURE 10.7
Slide Sorter view

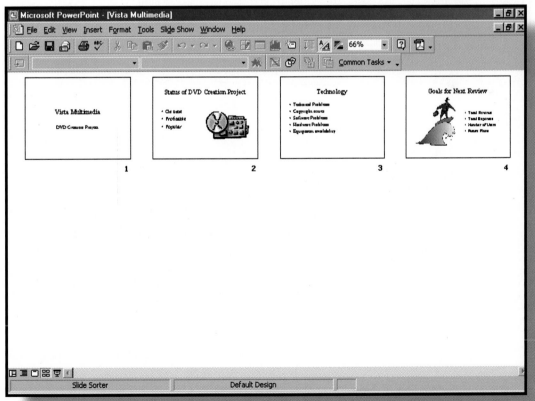

153

Adding a Chart to your Presentation

Another popular feature of presentation software is charts. Charts help us to visualize statistical information and to simplify complex sets of data. Ms. Perez can use a chart in her presentation to show the projected growth for her DVD project over the next three years.

S TEP-BY-STEP ▷ 10.2

1. On the Insert menu, click New slide to display the New Slide dialog box.

2. Scroll down and locate the Text and Chart layout. Click this layout to select it and then click OK to insert the slide into the presentation.

3. Click in the Click to add title box and type Projected Growth.

4. Double-click the chart icon to display the datasheet.

5. Select and delete all of the data in the datasheet. See Figures 10.8 and 10.9.

FIGURE 10.8
Datasheet with data selected

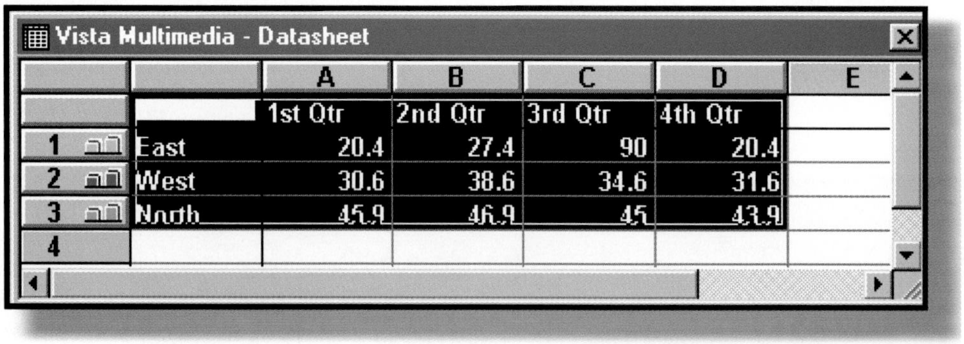

		A	B	C	D	E
		1st Qtr	2nd Qtr	3rd Qtr	4th Qtr	
1	East	20.4	27.4	90	20.4	
2	West	30.6	38.6	34.6	31.6	
3	North	45.9	46.9	45	43.9	
4						

Vista Multimedia - Datasheet

FIGURE 10.9
Datasheet with data deleted

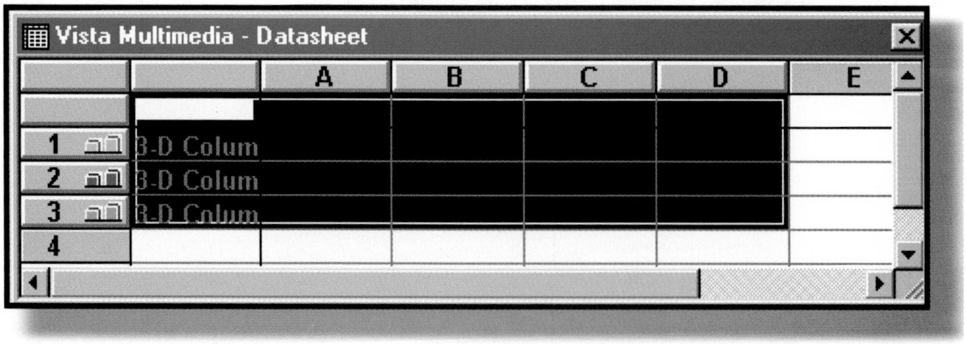

		A	B	C	D	E
1	3-D Colum					
2	3-D Colum					
3	3-D Colum					
4						

Vista Multimedia - Datasheet

6. Click in the first cell in column A and type Year 1. Type Year 2 under B and Year 3 under C.

7. In the cell under Year 1, type 12; under Year 2, type 18; under Year 3, type 22.

Notice to the right of the 1 that it says 3-D column. PowerPoint has several different types of charts. In this instance, we'll use a pie chart.

8. On the Chart menu, click Chart Type to

154

display the Chart Type dialog box. See Figure 10.10.

9. Click Pie to display the chart pie subtype. Select a subtype of your choice and click OK.

10. Click the X in the upper right corner of the Datasheet to close the datasheet and to view your newly created chart. See Figure 10.11.

11. Click the Save button.

 Did You Know?

Most people read from left to right. Put the most important information in the upper left corner and least important information in the lower right corner.

FIGURE 10.10
Chart Type dialog box

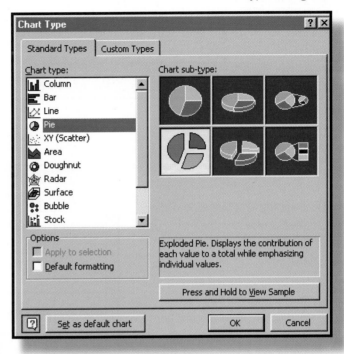

FIGURE 10.11
Slide with chart

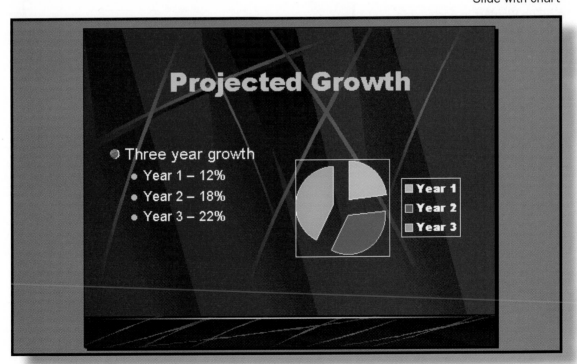

Adding WordArt to a Presentation

After viewing the slide show, both you and Ms. Perez agree that Slide No. 3 could use a little more pizzazz. You suggest that perhaps some special text effects may be just what the slide needs. You can do this through a special feature called WordArt or TextArt. To accomplish the bullet points Ms. Perez listed on this slide will take support. This is the word you add to the slide.

STEP-BY-STEP ▷ 10.3

1. On the Drawing toolbar, click Insert WordArt. See Figure 10.-12.

2. Click the WordArt style of your choice and then click OK to display the Edit WordArt text box.

3. In the Edit WordArt Text dialog box, type the text you want to format, select any other options you want, and then click OK. See Figure 10.13.

4. The WordArt is pasted into your slide. See Figure 10.14.

FIGURE 10.12
WordArt Gallery

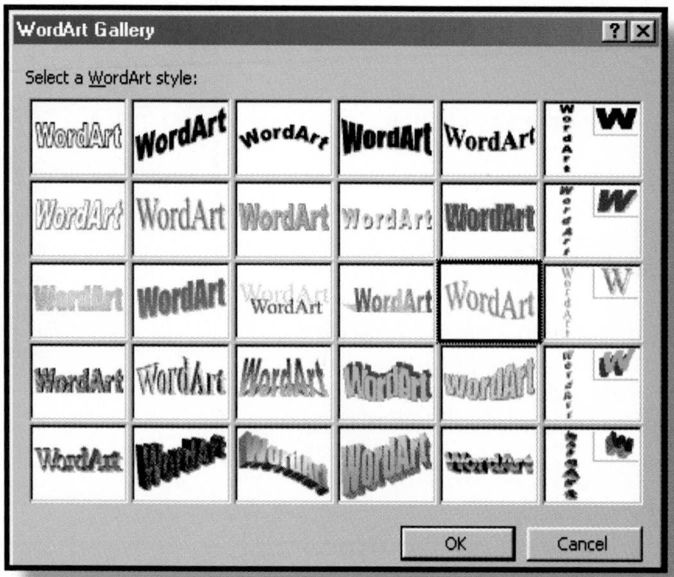

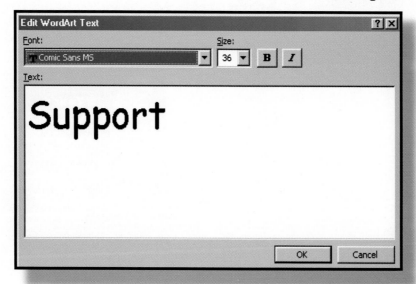

FIGURE 10.13
Edit WordArt Text dialog box

FIGURE 10.14
Slide No. 3 with WordArt added

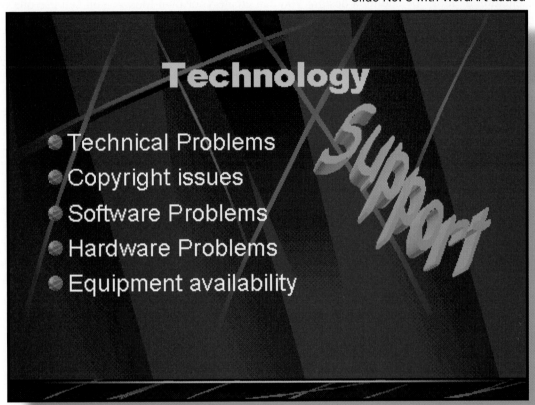

WordArt is an *object*, which means you can click it to select it, move it, and resize it. You can also add or change effects to the text by using the tools on the WordArt and Drawing toolbars. See Figure 10.15.

5. On the Standard toolbar, click Save.

 Hot Tip

When creating a presentation, use one concept per slide; font size should be a minimum of 24 points.

FIGURE 10.15
Drawing Toolbar

Adding Design to a Presentation

Ms. Perez likes the presentation, but finds it rather bland. You suggest that she could give the presentation a "look" by adding a design. You can create your own look or you can use one of the professionally designed looks that come with most presentation graphics programs.

The **design templates** contain color schemes with custom formatting and styled fonts, all designed to create a special look. **Transitions** and **animation** can make the presentation more entertaining. Transitions are special effects that display when you move from slide to slide, and animations are special visual or sound effects that you can add to text or to an object.

STEP-BY-STEP ▷ 10.4

1. To add a design template, on the Format menu select Apply Design Template to display the Apply Design Template dialog box. Ms. Perez likes a design called Network Blitz. Click Apply to apply the design to all slides. See Figure 10.17.

2. The next step is to add transitions and animations. To do this you must be in either Slide or Slide Sorter View. Click the Slide Sorter View button in the lower left corner of the screen. Notice that Slide 1 is highlighted or selected. See Figure 10.18.

FIGURE 10.17
Selecting a design

FIGURE 10.18
Slide sorter view with design

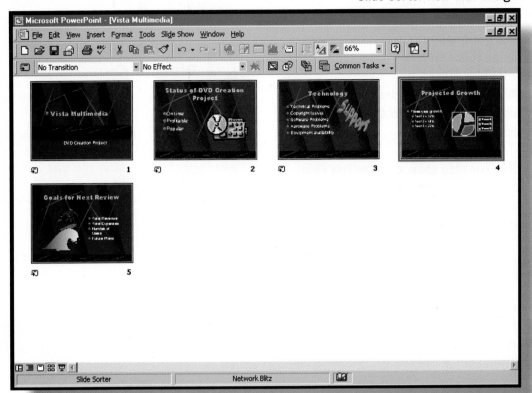

3. To add a transition, in the Transition box, click the drop-down arrow and select the transition you want. See Figure 10.19. You can apply the same transition to all slides or select a different transition for each slide.

4. Click Slide 2 to select it. Notice that this slide has three bullet points. By adding animation, you can click the mouse button to control the display of the bullets during

(continued on next page)

FIGURE 10.19
Selecting a transition

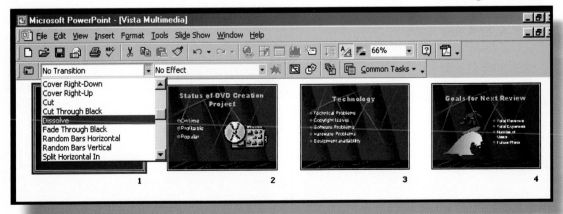

your presentation. You can have them come in one at a time.

5. Click the drop-down arrow to the right of No Effect and select an effect you like.

6. Click the rest of the slides one by one and add transitions and animations to each slide.

7. View your slide show. Click the first slide to select it, and then click Slide Show View. Click the mouse button to move from slide to slide.

8. On the Standard toolbar, click the Save button.

 Did You Know?

On the Web, you can send graphical greeting cards to all of your friends. Some of the cards even contain music and animation. Categories range from birthdays to congratulations to whatever special occasion you can imagine. Check out www.bluemountain.com and greetings. msn.com for just a couple of free online sites.

Printing Your Presentation

Most presentation programs provide many print options. For example, you can print your entire presentation—the slides, outline, notes, and audience handouts—in color, grayscale, or pure black and white. You can also print specific slides, handouts, notes pages, or outline pages. In this instance, you print a handout for your audience.

STEP-BY-STEP ▷ 10.5

1. On the File menu, click Print to display the Print dialog box.

2. In the lower left corner, click the Print what: drop-down arrow and select Handouts. To the right under Handouts, notice that the number defaulted to 6 per page. You can easily change this to 2, 3, 4, or 9. See Figure 10.20.

3. Click Print to print your handout.

FIGURE 10.20
Print dialog box with Handouts selected

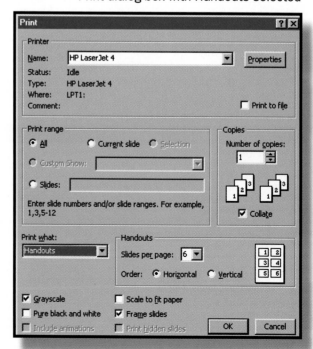

Preparing an Effective Presentation

You can use presentation tools can be used to make any presentation more effective and interesting. However, beware! Presentation programs contain so many features and so many options, it is difficult to not get carried away. The first-time user tends to add distracting sounds, animations, and excessive clip art to each slide. Some general presentation rules to consider are as follows:

- Keep it simple—this includes words and images.

- Use words or phrases—no sentences and no fine detail.

- Don't clutter the slide—leave a lot of white (blank) space.

- Be consistent—use the same design template, the same font, and so forth, on all of your slides.

- Project an image—use visuals to clarify or emphasize a point, to add variety, and to change focus.

- Organize the information—it should be easy to follow such as in an outline format.

- Create high contrast between the background and the text.

- Use color wisely.

TECHNOLOGY CAREERS

PRESENTATION EXPERT

Presentations are an organization's most direct communication effort. Many times, a presentation can make or break a sale or prevent a company from landing that big contract. As more and more employees are using computers and presentation graphics programs, companies are beginning to realize the importance of this media.

A growing trend in large companies is to hire a presentation expert to oversee the creation and delivery of presentations within the organization. Depending on the size of the company and the number of presentations required, this person might work alone or work as part of a media department. The media department generally functions as a service bureau for the rest of the company. The presentation manager may also be responsible for design. They must keep updated and be aware of technological advances in the areas of multimedia. This position will most likely require additional education such as workshops, conferences, and classes.

Many large companies may have a set of master slides and templates. All employees are expected to use these standards. The presentation manager may be reponsible for creating these masters and templates and may even be responsible for teaching the physical presentation delivery skills and/or either coach frequent speakers.

Since there are no certifications or degrees for presentation managers, many people employed in this field have graphics design and/or Web design backgrounds. They may or may not have a four-year degree. It is not unusual to find someone with a community college two-year degree in design or someone with design certifications employed for this type of job.

Salaries are varied and can range from as little as $20,000 to as much as $80,000 or more.

A popular rule used by many designers is the rule of thirds. You divide your screen into thirds, both horizontally and vertically, and place your images one third of the way in. For example, the following table shows a screen divided into thirds, horizontally and vertically. Place the images at points where the lines intersect. See Figure 10.21.

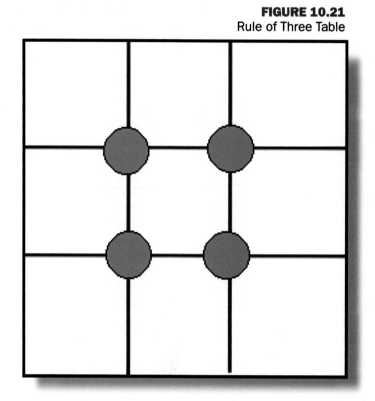

FIGURE 10.21
Rule of Three Table

Delivering a Presentation

The TV show 60 Minutes did a survey on people's worst fears and found that number one is public speaking. Most of us, however, will at one time or another find ourselves in a position where we must talk to a group or give an oral presentation. Professional organizations like Toastmasters and companies such as Dale Carnegie work with and train people in presentation skills. Even with training, most of us will not become professional speakers overnight. But there are some special techniques you can use. If you practice and use some of the following suggestions, you may find that you actually enjoy public speaking.

■ Plan—know the purpose of your presentation, plan your content, and know your audience.

■ Prepare—have an attention-getting opener, be positive, and develop a memorable closing.

■ Outline your main points—outlining helps you stay focused, but don't be afraid to skip some points or move ahead if that's what your audience wants.

■ Talking—don't talk too slow or too fast; watch your audience and take your cue from them.

■ Present—make eye contact, be natural and sincere; involve your audience.

■ Questions—be sure to leave time at the end of your presentation to answer questions.

ETHICS IN TECHNOLOGY

COPYRIGHT ISSUES

The Internet and electronic media have made a major impact on copyright issues throughout the world. With one click of a mouse, anyone with an Internet connection can distribute copyrighted property to millions of Internet users. And, many people feel that if it's on the Internet that it is fair game.

When people hear the word copyright, they tend to think of traditional media such as books, magazines, and so forth. Copyright applies to much more—it can include artwork, musical recordings, computer programs, videotapes, movies, maps, graphs, databases and many other original creations. Copyright law would seem to be an simple one to enforce. However, the copyright law also grants a right of "fair use" to the public. This is where the confusion comes in—no one can agree on what's fair.

To evaluate the issue of "fair use," the law includes four aspects: (1) the purpose of the use, including a non-profit educational purpose; (2) the nature of the copyrighted work; (3) the amount of the copying; and (4) the effect of the copying on the potential value of the original work.

One major issue of digital copyright is the future of music on the Internet. MP3, which is the technical abbreviation for a method of compressing audio files into digital format, allows users to download songs from the Internet to play back via their own computers or on Walkman-like players. Protections schemes are being developed in an effort to prevent copyright theft. An example of a protection scheme is that the music would expire after a certain date. However, many people point to the unsuccessful implementation of protection schemes for software some years back. These schemes did not work and it is doubtful if they will work for music.

Summary

- With presentations graphic software you can create a presentation to illustrate a sequence of ideas.

- Use presentation graphics software for on-screen shows, self-running presentations, online meetings, presentation broadcasting, Web presentation, overhead transparencies, audience handouts, and 35mm slides.

- Some of the more popular presentation graphics programs are Microsoft PowerPoint, Corel Presentation, and Lotus Freelance.

- Presentation graphics programs come equipped with different views to help you while you are creating a presentation. These views include normal, outline, slide sorter, slide view, and slide show.

- Presentation graphics programs come with a collection of professionally designed templates.

- The addition of transitions and animation can make your presentation more entertaining.

- You use WordArt or TextArt to create special text effects.

- When creating a presentation, do not use a feature unless it adds to the presentation.

- Some general presentation rules to consider are these: Keep it simple, use words or phrases, don't clutter, be consistent, project an image, organize the information, use contrast between the text and background, and use text wisely.

■ When doing page or screen layout, many designers use the rule of thirds.

■ Some techniques to help you give a better presentation include planning, preparing, outlining, talking at a moderate speech, natural presence, and leaving time for questions.

LESSON 10 REVIEW QUESTIONS

MULTIPLE CHOICE

1. With a presentations graphics software program, you can _____.
   A. create slides
   B. create handouts
   C. create overhead transparencies
   D. all of the above

2. Online meetings are conducted in _____.
   A. real time
   B. late time
   C. after 12 noon
   D. before 12 noon

3. Using a presentation program in normal view, the screen is divided into _____ panes
   A. one
   B. two
   C. three
   D. four

4. _____ are special effects that display when you move from slide to slide.
   A. Animations
   B. Programs
   C. Formats
   D. Transitions

5. A tool for creating special text effects is called _____.
   A. animation
   B. WordArt
   C. shadowing
   D. AutoShapes

TRUE/FALSE

Circle the T if the statement is true. Circle F if it is false.

T F 1. One presentation attention-holding technique is the use of visuals.

T F 2. Each slide in your presentation should contain a lot of detail.

T F   3. You should rarely use visuals in your presentation.

T F   4. Outline view shows an outline of the presentation's text.

T F   5. The only output option for presentation graphics programs is on-screen shows.

SHORT ANSWER

1. When in _____ view, image thumbnails are displays.

2. _____ are special visual or sound effects that you can add to text or to an object.

3. To present an on-screen presentation, you need the software, a computer, and a _____.

4. A _____ presentation is one that automatically restarts.

5. You can put your presentation on the Web if you save it as a Web or _____ document.

CROSS-CURRICULAR PROJECTS

MATH

One of the most popular features of presentation graphics program is charts or graphs. Look for some real-life statistical information. Check newspapers, sports data, magazines, and so on. Using this statistical information and using a presentation graphics program, create a two- or three-slide presentation. If a presentation program is not available, use paper and colored pens or pencils to create your chart.

SCIENCE

Your instructor will assign you a special science project. Complete the project and then report to the class on your findings. Use a presentation graphics program to support your report. Include at least five slides with transitions and animations. Print handouts for the other students in your class.

SOCIAL STUDIES/LANGUAGE ARTS

This activity involves observation, role playing, and presentation to the class. Visit the mall and sit on a bench for about 30 minutes. Pretend you are someone else—a person from the past. Observe the different people in the mall and make notes on how you think your historical person might react to these people. Present your findings in a presentation to your class. See if you can find a picture of the person you were pretending to be and include it in your presentation.

LANGUAGE ARTS

Your instructor will share with the class several common items that you see every day. Choose an item and examine it carefully. Think of other ways, in addition to its intended purpose, in which it can be used. Create a presentation illustrating some of your ideas. Be sure to use lots of graphics and visual clues.

WEB PROJECT

Located at members.xoom.com/PMartin/hammurabicodeoflaw.htm is a Web site on Hammurabi, the Priest King. Click the Some of the Problems Hammurabi Faced link and read about one or two of these problems. Determine what you would do if you were Hammurabi. Then read the information on how Hammurabi actually solved the situation. Create a presentation about the Web site. Include a slide on each of the problems, with your solution and Hammurabi's solution. The class votes on the best solution.

TEAM PROJECT

Your teacher will provide each team with a survey topic related to Vista Multimedia. Design and record it on a survey form. Collect and analyze the data. Use presentation graphics software to present your findings to the class. Included in your presentation should be an overview of your survey and information on your analyzed data. Display the results in a chart.

HOW DO I USE DESKTOP PUBLISHING SOFTWARE?

OBJECTIVES

When you complete this module, you will be able to:

- Define desktop publishing.

- Identify the stages in desktop publishing.

- Identify layout and design techniques.

- Identify the parts of a font and select appropriate fonts.

- Insert graphics into documents.

- Create an effective publication.

⏱ **Estimated Time: 1.5 hours**

VOCABULARY

Balance
Coherence
Desktop publishing
Focus
Font
Layout and design
Templates
Thumbnail sketch
Typeface
Wizards

Vista Multimedia is having a sale on discontinued CDs and videos! Hundreds will be sold at great savings. Ms. Perez, your supervisor, has asked you to prepare a flyer. She had thought about sending the job out to a printing company, but she heard you talking about preparing flyers in one of the classes you are taking at school. After discussing this with her, you assured her that the flyer will look very professional when you are finished with it. It will even have color because the store has a color printer. See Figure 11.1.

What Is Desktop Publishing?

Desktop publishing is the process of producing professional-looking documents such as flyers, brochures, reports, newsletters, and pamphlets using a desktop personal computer and a color printer. Years ago, the preparation of these documents involved many participants including a copywriter, an editor, a designer, a typesetter, and a paste-up artist. Today, the tasks performed by these persons have merged and can be completed by one person.

The advantages of desktop publishing over traditional publishing include (1) substantial savings in production costs, (2) time saved in sending copy and proofs back and forth between the printer and the author, (3) greater author control of the entire production process, and (4) WYSIWYG capability, which means "What You See Is What You Get." This capability allows you to see on the screen how the publication will look.

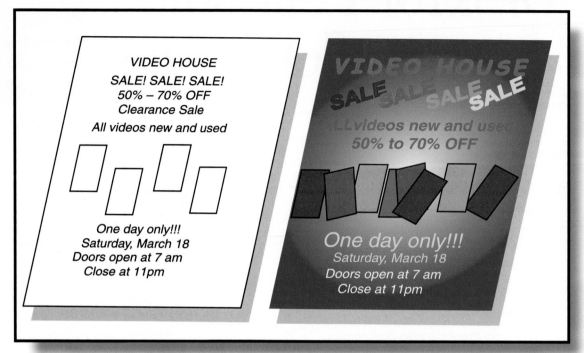

Before the mid-1980s, publishing meant taking your work to a professional typesetter. Three inventions changed this:

- In 1984 the Apple Macintosh was introduced. It used pictures and the mouse to communicate.

- In 1985 the first laser printer was invented. The LaserWriter, as it was called, could deliver professional output at a cost the general public could afford.

- A dedicated desktop publishing software program was developed. This program is PageMaker.

So now almost anyone can be a publisher. There are several types of desktop publishing software. Some are called dedicated desktop publishing software. These are page layout or composition software programs. Another type is word processing software with desktop publishing capabilities. In addition to the software, a good understanding of design theory is invaluable. Although many of the software programs are very sophisticated, the user must be familiar with page layout and design, the use of graphics, as well as have some degree of creativity.

 Did You Know?

Many individuals have gone into business for themselves providing desktop publishing services.

Stages in the Desktop Publishing Process

In order to produce our sales flyer, two steps must be followed: planning the publication and creating the content. Careful thought must be given to the purpose of the publication, the audience that the publication is being designed for, as well as how the final document will look.

Planning

Planning is the most important stage. The flyer must contain all the information prospective customers will need to make the decision to purchase products.

- Identify the purpose of the publication.

- Identify the audience.

- What format should be used to deliver the message?

- What response do you want from your audience?

Creating the Content

The content must be exact. It must say what we want to say and in a way that will appeal to prospective customers. It must be visually attractive.

- Decide what information needs to be included.

- Prepare a thumbnail sketch, a rough draft drawing used to explore layout options of a document you are creating.

- Follow appropriate design guidelines.

- Create focus, the element that pulls the reader's eye to it. This can be a graphic or large headlines or titles.

- Create balance by distributing the weight of various elements. This includes graphics, text, or lines.

- Maintain simplicity. The simpler the design, the more likely the reader will understand the publication's message.

- Create coherence. Documents, especially multipage documents, should follow a consistent format.

- Use white space appropriately. Do not fill every inch of space with text, graphics, and other elements. See Figure 11.2.

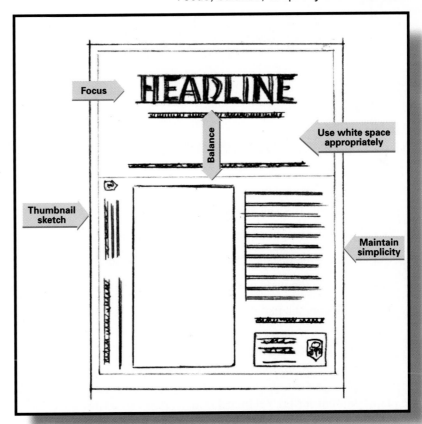

FIGURE 11.2
Focus, balance, simplicity and coherence

Layout and Design

The microcomputer and desktop publishing software alone will not ensure a well-designed publication. A very important element in the desktop publishing process is layout and design, the way graphics and text are used to produce a quality document.

Using Text

The text used in a document is very important. The content of the document sometimes will influence the text style that is used. A *font* is a typeface, size, and style, such as Times New Roman 12-point bold. A *typeface* is a set of characters with a common design and shape. Typefaces can add mood or "feeling" to a document. An elementary school teacher may use comical or childish typeface to create a flyer about an upcoming fair at the school, a hostess may use an elegant typeface to create invitations to a dinner party, and so on.

Typefaces have characteristics that distinguish them from each other. However, they all have characteristics in common. These are shown in the display here. See Figure 11.3.

FIGURE 11.3
Anatomy of a typeface

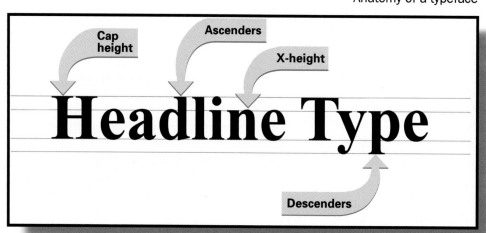

Each typeface rests on an imaginary baseline located at the bottom of the typeface.

- X-height is the height of the main body of the lowercase character.

- Cap height is the distance between the baseline and the top of the capital letters.

- Ascenders are the parts of the lowercase characters above the x-height.

- Descenders are the parts of the lowercase characters that extend below the base line.

Types of Typefaces

Serif typefaces are fonts in which the letters have small strokes at the end. Times New Roman is an example of a serif typeface. *Sans serif* typefaces are those fonts in which the ends of the letters are plain (without serifs). Technical is an example of a sans serif typeface. Ornamental typefaces are those font types used for special effects and headlines. EngrvrsOldEng is an example of an ornamental typeface.

The font size determines how large or how small the font will appear when printed. The standard measurement unit is the *point,* approximately 1/72 of an inch. The higher the point size, the larger the font. However, a 14 point in one typeface may not be the same size as a 14 point in another. A popular size for text in the body of a document is 12 points. Attributes like bold, italic, and color can also be added to any font. See Figure 11.4.

FIGURE 11.4
Font sizes

Times New Roman is a serif font. This is font size 10.

Palatino is a serif font. This is font size 14.

Helvetica Bold is a sans serif font. This is font size 16.

Avant Garde is a sans serif font. This is font size 18.

Isadora is a decorative font. This is font size 20.

Tekton is a sans serif font, point size 24.

To select various fonts and font sizes, click Fonts on the Format command on the menu bar. You may also select attributes to enhance the font. See Figure 11.5.

FIGURE 11.5
Font attributes

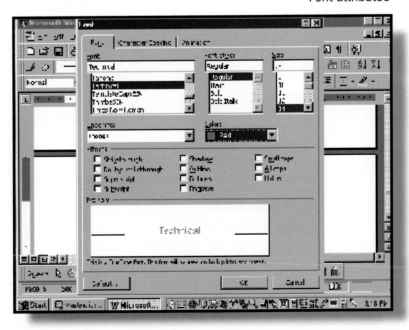

Using Graphics

Graphics are used to add focus, interest, and excitement to a publication. To be used effectively; they should relate to the subject of the document.

Word processing software programs come with a fairly adequate number of graphic images. These are sometimes referred to as clip art. In addition to using the graphics included in the software, pictures that were scanned may also be used. Additional graphics can be purchased and installed on the computer.

Scanners are used often in desktop publishing. Scanners are used to make digital copies of pictures so they can be used in preparing publications. Pictures taken with digital cameras are also a good source of graphics for your publication.

STEP-BY-STEP ▷ 11.1

To insert a graphic into a document:

1. Click the Insert command from the menu bar. From there, you click Picture, then Clip Art if you are using clip art provided with the software. If you are using a graphic other than one provided with the software, click on From File and indicate the graphic's location. See Figure 11.6.

2. Once a graphic has been inserted into the document, it can be cropped, rotated, sized, or moved.

- Cropping a graphic means cutting out a part of the graphic that you do not want to use.

- Rotating a graphic means changing the direction of the graphic.

- Sizing a graphic means changing the size of the graphic.

- Moving a graphic means changing the location of the graphic on the page.

FIGURE 11.6
Selecting a graphic

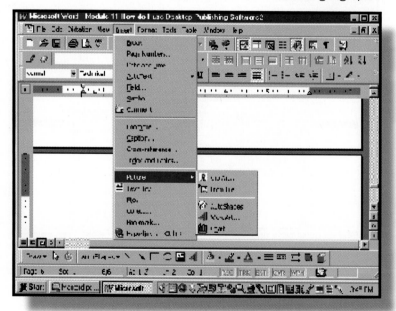

Using WordArt

Some word processing software programs have a feature that changes normal text into graphic objects. These can be used for headlines. This feature may have a different name in different programs. It is called WordArt in Microsoft Word and Textart in Corel WordPerfect. See Figure 11.7.

FIGURE 11.7
Word or text art

TECHNOLOGY CAREERS

DESKTOP PUBLISHER/GRAPHIC DESIGNER

What is a desktop publisher? It is anyone whose job or business involves using desktop publishing systems to produce documents. A desktop publisher is most often referred to as a graphic designer.

Graphic designers use visual media to convey a message. They create art for corporations, stores, publishing houses and advertising agencies. They use the computer for designing, sketching, and manipulating images.

Graphic designers still create flyers, brochures, newsletters, and pamphlets; however, their work has expanded to include three-dimensional work such as graphics for screen displays such as television and World Wide Web pages. Graphic designers also work on the design and layout of magazines, newspapers, and other print publications.

The likely employers for a graphic designer would be advertising agencies, design firms, and commercial art houses. Still others are employed by manufacturing firms, retail and department stores. They can also work for themselves deciding on their own set of clients who contract their services. This is called freelancing.

Graphic designers usually maintain a portfolio of their work to demonstrate their abilities. A bachelor's degree in fine art, graphic design or visual communications is helpful. Many companies require demonstrated skill in scanning and image correction, the ability to manage multiple simultaneous projects, and demonstrated experience using HTML to develop pages.

Entry level graphic designers earn between $21,000 and $24,000 annually. Experienced designers can earn much more; up to approximately $55,000, depending on location, level of experience and type of work.

Using Color

Color can be used to organize ideas and highlight important facts, create focus, and add emphasis. You can add color to your text, lines, borders, symbols, bullets, and even shapes. You can even change the color of some graphics. If you do not have access to a color printer, you can print your document on color paper. Choose a color that complements the contents of the document if possible. When using color, keep these guidelines in mind:

- Use color sparingly—less is best. Use only two or three colors per page.

- Use color to communicate, not to decorate!

- Color can be used to identify a consistent element.

- Do not let color overpower the words!

- Light-colored text is difficult to read. Black is best.

Using Lines

Lines can be used in a document to create a focal point, to add emphasis, separate columns, or add visual impact. Both horizontal and vertical lines can be created. Lines can be created in various lengths, thicknesses, and shadings. See Figure 11.8.

FIGURE 11.8
Looking at lines

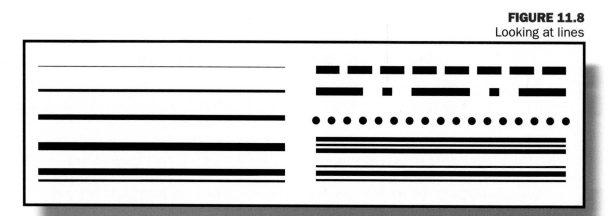

Using Other Elements

Other elements available to enhance documents include page borders, color, drawing objects, watermarks, and even text boxes.

Many word processing software programs have features that assist in the creation of documents. These are wizards and templates. **Wizards** walk you through a series of steps in completing a document. You respond to questions as you supply information related to the document you are creating. **Templates** are predesigned documents that already have formatting for margins, tabs, fonts, and some objects included. They save time in creating basic documents such as letters, memos, and reports.

S TEP-BY-STEP ▷ 11.2

We are ready to begin to create our sales flyer. Before we begin using the computer, we need to create a thumbnail sketch of how the flyer might look. We will Include at least one graphic, use various font sizes, and use a border. Once the thumbnail is completed, we are ready to begin your flyer. See Fig. 11.9.

1. Launch your word processing or desktop publishing program.

2. Set the document's margins at 1 inch.

3. Type the text for the flyer. Use font types, sizes, and color that will add to the appearance and message of your flyer. You may center each line of text.

4. Insert an appropriate clip art in the flyer— a computer or maybe a picture of a meeting. You may need to size and place the graphic appropriately on the page.

5. Place a border around the page.

6. Save the flyer.

7. Print the flyer.

FIGURE 11.9
From thumbnail to finished flyer

HERITAGE HIGH SCHOOL
Future Business Leaders
of America
BUSINESS MEETING

Wednesday, February 12
1:20p.m. in Room B12
Business of importance
to be discussed.

ETHICS IN TECHNOLOGY

HACKER/PIRATES

The most popular definition of a computer hacker is a person who has gained unauthorized access to computer systems. Hackers are part of the computer underground that engages in illicit and/or illegal behavior. Modern hackers are skilled at invading computer systems and concealing the fact that they had been there. They range from being teenagers to computer professionals.

Hacking activity falls into four categories: searching for systems, attempting to gain entry into unauthorized systems, exploring systems, and bragging about getting into systems.

A software pirate is a person who copies and distributes commercial; software in violation of copyright laws. A pirate is very organized and uses the Internet for distribution of this illegal software.

175

Desktop Publishing Tips

Here are some guidelines that will help you to design and create professional-looking documents.

- Collect ideas.

- Use no more than two typefaces per page. Use a serif typeface for the body of the document and a sans serif typeface for the headings.

Hot Tip

Desktop publishing publications can be converted to contain HTML codes so that they can be linked to the Internet.

- Use plenty of white space so the pages do not look overcrowded.

- Use good contrast between the background and the text that appears on it.

- Keep the design simple so the reader gets the message immediately. Limit the number of objects on a page.

- Make the design consistent within a multipage publication.

Summary

- Desktop publishing is the process of producing professional-looking documents such as flyers, brochures, reports, newsletters, and pamphlets.

- The advantages of desktop publishing over traditional publishing include savings in production costs, time saved, greater control, and WYSIWYG.

- The two stages in the desktop publishing process are planning and creating the content.

- Follow these guidelines in designing the publication:

    - Focus

    - Balance

    - Coherence

    - Appropriate white space

- Layout and design refer to the way graphics and text are used to produce a quality document.

- The text, font style, font size, and font face used in a document is very important.

    - Serif fonts have small strokes at the end of the letters.

    - Sans serif fonts do not have small strokes at the end of letters.

    - Font size is measured in points. Seventy-two points equal 1 inch.

- Graphics are used to add focus, interest, and excitement to a publication.

- Color can be used to organize ideas and highlight important facts, create focus, and add emphasis.

- Lines can be used in a document to create a focal point, to add emphasis, separate columns, or add visual impact.

- Other elements available in most desktop publishing software include wizards and templates.

LESSON 11 REVIEW QUESTIONS

MULTIPLE CHOICE

1. To save time in creating basic documents, _____ may be used.
   A. thumbnail sketches
   B. fonts
   C. templates
   D. DTP

2. In terms of font size, _____ points equal to 1 inch.
   A. 36
   B. 24
   C. 18
   D. 72

3. The invention of the _____ computer was the beginning of desktop publishing.
   A. IBM Selectric
   B. Windows 95
   C. Apple Macintosh
   D. Gateway

4. _____ is the element that pulls the reader's eye to it.
   A. Coherence
   B. Consistency
   C. Balance
   D. Focus

5. _____ is/are used to add focus, interest and excitement to a publication.
   A. Color
   B. WordArt
   C. Lines
   D. Graphics

TRUE/FALSE

Circle the T if the statement is true. Circle F if it is false.

T F 1. Apple Macintosh computer was introduced in 1984. This was the beginning of desktop publishing.

T F 2. Planning is the first step in designing and creating a professional-looking document.

T F 3. Serif fonts have small strokes at the end of each part of the letter.

T F 4. Graphics downloaded from the Internet may be inserted into a document.

T F 5. color in a document will make the document more effective.

SHORT ANSWER

1. _____ is the first step in the desktop publishing process.

2. The ability to see on the screen how the document will look when printed is called _____.

3. A _____ is a rough draft drawing used to explore layout options of a document you are creating.

4. A _____ is a set of characters with a common design and shape.

5. _____ are used to add focus, interest, and excitement to a publication.

CROSS-CURRICULAR PROJECTS

MATH

Seldom are the measurements used in desktop publishing and typesetting in inches. The most popular measurement is points. Use the Internet and any other resources to identify other measures used for desktop publishing and typesetting. Create a flyer that will display each measurement, convert it to inches, and give a brief description. Use the keywords desktop publishing and desktop publishing measurements with your favorite search engine such as www.AskJeeves, www.mamma.com, or www.dogpile.com.

SCIENCE

Use the Internet to locate information on the first typewriter. Look for specifics on the design of the keyboard, how it was supposed to work, reactions and responses to this new tool (during that time). Design and prepare a flyer announcing this new phenomenon using the desktop publishing features of your word processing software or your dedicated desktop publishing software. Hint: Christopher Sholes invented the typewriter. Use the following keywords with search engines: early typewriters, typewriters, Christopher Sholes, and typewriter keyboards.

SOCIAL STUDIES

Research the Internet and other sources to find information on a place you would like to visit. Gather all the important information you would need to make a decision to visit this place and create a travel brochure. List exciting places to see, historical information, tourist attractions, and any other information you think would enhance your brochure.

LANGUAGE ARTS

Select a book that you have read in class, and design and create a new cover for the book. Use the desktop publishing features of your software program.

WEB PROJECT

Even though word processing programs offer excellent features for creating desktop publications, a dedicated desktop publishing program is the best choice for professional-quality typesetting and page layout. Use the Internet to identify dedicated desktop publishing programs. Prepare a flyer describing these programs with information concerning the name of the software, outstanding features, cost, and hardware requirements. You may use the following search words: desktop publishing, dedicated desktop publishing software.

TEAM PROJECT

The store manager has asked you and the other part-time employees to work together to develop a brochure on the services and products that Vista Multimedia offers. You are to work together to develop the brochure: development, writing, editing of the text, page layout, and any graphics that will be incorporated. You will need to sign individual assignments.

See the CD-ROM "Computer Concepts: Systems, Applications, and Design" for more information on this subject or careers in this area. Use Mission #8—Publishing Power.

WHAT IS A NETWORK?

OBJECTIVES

When you complete this module, you will be able to:

- Describe a network.

- Explain the benefits of a network.

- List and describe the types of networks.

- List and describe communications media.

- Describe communications hardware.

- Describe communications software.

- Describe the different network topologies.

- Describe network architecture.

- Describe network protocols.

🕑 **Estimated Time: 1.5 hours**

VOCABULARY

Communications channel
Data communications
Local area network
Modem
Network
Network operating systems software
Site license
Topology
Transmission media
Wide area network

As companies grow and purchase more computers, they often find it advantageous to connect those computers through a network. This allows users to share software applications and to share hardware devices such as printers, scanners, and so forth. Because Vista Multimedia now has 12 computers in the local store, Ms. Perez feels it's time to investigate networking options. She has assigned you this task. Your job is to learn about networking basics and then to report your findings to Ms. Perez.

Introducing Networks

When most people think of networks, they envision something fairly complicated. At the lowest level, networks are not that complex. In fact, a *network* is simply a group of two or more computers linked together. As the size of a network increases and more and more devices are added, the installation and management does become more technical. Even so, the concept of networking and the terminology remains basically the same regardless of size.

In this module we discuss *local area networks (LANs)* and *wide area networks (WANs)*. The primary difference between the two is that a LAN is generally confined to a limited geographical area, whereas a WAN covers a large geographical area. Most WANs are made up of several connected LANs.

Most organizations today rely on computers and the data stored on the computer. Many times they find they need to transmit that data from one location to another. The transmission of data from one location to another is known as *data communications*. To transmit that data requires the following components:

- A sending device, which is generally a computer

- A communications device, such as a *modem*, that converts the computer signal into signals supported by the communications channel

- A communications channel or path, such as telephone lines or cable, over which the signals are sent

- A receiving device that accepts the incoming signal, which is generally a computer

- Communications software

See Figure 12.1.

FIGURE 12.1
Communications components

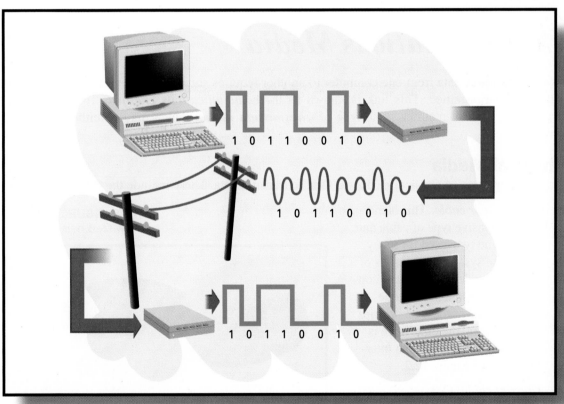

Most networks have at least one server and many clients. A server is a computer that manages network resources, and a client is a computer on the network that relies on the server for resources.

Network Benefits

To consider the topic of network benefits, you might first think about the biggest network of all, the Internet. Think about some of the changes that have occurred in our society because of the Internet. Perhaps the most profound of all of these changes is electronic mail. A network provides almost instant communication and e-mail messages are delivered almost immediately. Other benefits include the following:

■ *Information sharing:* Authorized users can use other computers on the network to access and share information and data. This could include special group projects, databases, and so forth.

■ *Hardware sharing:* No longer is it necessary to purchase a printer or a scanner or other frequently used peripherals for each computer. Instead, one device connected to a network can serve the needs of many users.

■ *Software sharing:* Instead of purchasing and installing a software program on every single computer, it can be installed on just the server. All of the users can then access the program from one central location. This also saves companies money because they purchase a site license for the number of users. This is much less expensive than purchasing individual software packages.

■ *Collaborative environment:* Enables users to work together on group projects by combining the power and capabilities of diverse equipment.

Communications Media

To transfer data from one computer to another requires some type of link through which the data can be transmitted. This link is known as the *communications channel.* To send the data through the channel requires some type of *transmission media,* which may be either physical or wireless.

Physical Media

Several types of physical media are used to transmit data. These include the following:

■ *Twisted-pair cable:* This is the least expensive type of cable and is the same type used for many telephone systems. It consists of two independently insulated copper wires twisted around one another. One of the wires carries the signal and the other wire is grounded to absorb signal interference. See Figure 12.2.

FIGURE 12.2
Twisted pair cable

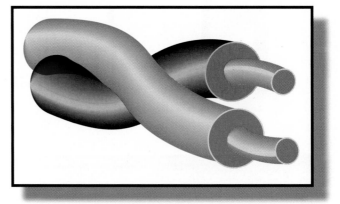

■ *Coaxial cable:* Coaxial cabling is the primary type of cabling used by the cable television industry and it is also widely used for computer networks. Because the cable is heavily shielded, it is much less prone to interference than twisted-pair cable. However, it is more expensive than twisted-pair. See Figure 12.3.

FIGURE 12.3
Coaxial cable

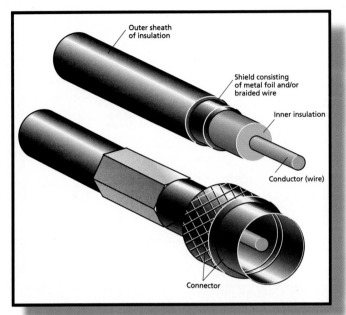

Outer sheath
of insulation

Shield consisting
of metal foil and/or
braided wire

Inner insulation

Conductor (wire)

Connector

FIGURE 12.4
Fiber-optic cable

■ *Fiber optic cable:* Fiber optic cable is made from thin, flexible glass tubing. Fiber optics has several advantages over traditional metal communications line. The bandwidth is much greater, so it can carry more data; it is much lighter than metal wires, and is much less susceptible to interference. The main disadvantage of fiber optics is that it is fragile and expensive. See Figure 12.4.

 Internet

To view some illustrations and examples of coaxial cable, visit the Astrolab located at www.astrolab.com/cable.htm.

TECHNOLOGY CAREERS

NETWORK ADMINISTRATORS

One of today's fastest growing career fields is for network administrators. When you think about networks and the function they play in today's society, you might think this type of career is logical and organized. This is not so; in fact, it is just about anything but organized. Just about every day is different with new and evolving problems. Technology changes, new hardware, and new software are all elements that add to this job.

To become a network administrator doesn't necessarily mean that you need to have a four-year degree. Many of today's network administrators have only a two-year degree and some not even that. What most of them do have, however, are certifications. These are network courses for which they have enrolled and passed required test. Two of the most popular of these types of certification are the Microsoft Certified Systems Engineer (MCSE) and the Novell Certified Systems Engineer (CSE). People with these certifications and a little bit of experience can expect starting salaries in the range of $25,000 to $40,000 a year.

Wireless Media

Just like physical media, several wireless options are also available:

- **_Radio signals:_** Transmissions using radio signals require line of sight; that is, the signal travels in a straight line from one source to the other. For radio transmission, you need a transmitter to send the signal and a receiver to accept the signal.

- **_Microwaves:_** A microwave signal is sent through space in the form of electromagnetic waves. Just like radio signals, they must also be sent in straight lines from one microwave station to another. To avoid interference, most microwave stations are built on mountaintops or placed on the top of large buildings. See Figure 12.5.

- **_Satellites:_** Communication satellites are placed in orbit 22,300 feet above the surface of the earth. This allows the satellite to maintain a constant position above one point on the earth's surface by rotating at the same speed of the earth. The satellite contains equipment that receives the transmission, amplifies it, and sends it back to earth. See Figure 12.6.

The type of communications media an organization may select to use within a network is determined by several different factors: the type of network, the size of the network, and the cost.

FIGURE 12.5
Microwave tower

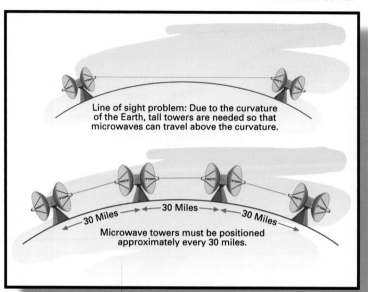

Line of sight problem: Due to the curvature of the Earth, tall towers are needed so that microwaves can travel above the curvature.

30 Miles → ← 30 Miles → ← 30 Miles →

Microwave towers must be positioned approximately every 30 miles.

 Did You Know?

Telephone companies are continually replacing traditional telephone lines with fiber optic cables. In the future, almost all communications will use fiber optics.

FIGURE 12.6
Satellites

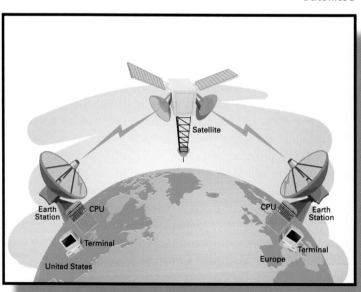

Satellite

Earth Station | CPU | CPU | Earth Station

Terminal

Terminal

United States

Europe

Network Hardware

Most networks consist of a network server and computer clients. In addition to the server and the client, there are two other categories of network hardware: communication devices and devices that connect the network cabling and amplify the signal.

Communications Hardware

Communications hardware devices facilitate the transmitting and receiving of data. When we think about communications hardware, the first thing that generally comes to mind is the desktop computer and modem. However, all types of other devices send and receive data. Some examples are large computers such as supercomputers, mainframe computers, and minicomputers; handheld and laptop computers; and even fax machines and digital cameras. Two of the more commonly used transmitting devices for personal use are as follows:

■ *Modem:* The word MODEM is an acronym for modulate-demodulate, which means to convert analog signals to digital and vice versa. This device enables a computer to transmit data over telephone lines. Computer information is stored digitally, whereas information sent over telephone lines is transmitted in the form of analog waves. Both the sending and receiving users must have a modem. See Figure 12.7.

■ *Cable modem:* A cable modem uses coaxial cable to send and receive data. This is the same type of cable used for cable TV. The bandwidth, which determines the amount of data that can be sent at one time, is much greater with a cable modem. A cable modem can be connected directly to your computer or connected to a set-top box used with your television. With a set-top box, you can access and surf the Web from your TV.

FIGURE 12.7
Computer with modem attached

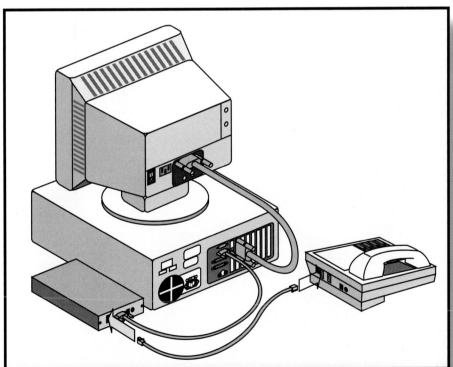

Network Transmission Hardware

Modems work well for personal computers and a small one- or two-person office. However, when it comes to transmitting data across LANs and WANs, the devices are considerably different. Some of the more widely used of these devices are as follows:

■ *Network interface cards (NICs):* This is an add-on card for either a desktop PC or a laptop computer. Each computer on a network must have a NIC. This card enables and controls the sending and receiving of data between the PCs in a LAN.

■ *Hub:* You may have heard the word hub applied to airports. Travelers make connections through various hubs to go from one location to another. In data transmission, a hub works similarly. It is a hub or junction where data arrives from one or more directions and is forwarded out in one or more other directions. Hubs contain ports for connecting computers and other devices. The number of ports on the hub determines the number of computers that can be connected to a hub. See Figure 12.8.

■ *Bridge:* A bridge is a special computer that connects one LAN to another LAN. Both networks must use the same protocol, or set of rules. Think about the bridge as a device that determines if your message is going to the LAN within your school or to the high school across the street.

■ *Gateway:* A gateway is a combination of software and hardware that links two different types of networks that use different protocols. For instance, gateways between electronic mail systems permit users on different systems to exchange messages.

FIGURE 12.8
Computers connected to a hub

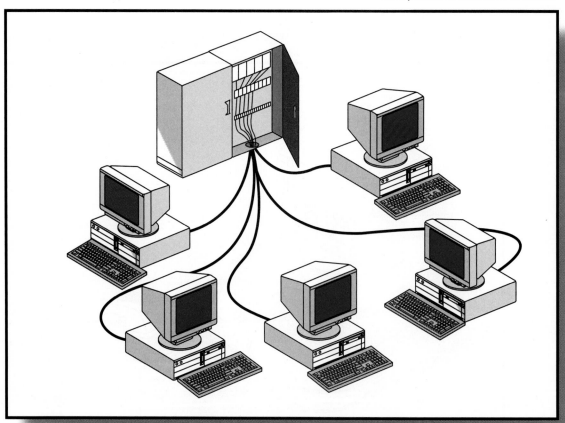

■ *Router:* A router is like a traffic policeman—this intelligent device directs network traffic. When you send data through a network, it is divided into small packets. All packets don't travel the same route; instead one may go one in one direction and another in a different direction. When the packets reach their final destination, they are reassembled into the original message. A router connects multiple networks and determines the fastest available path to send these packets of data on their way to their correct destination. And, just like our traffic policeman, in the event of a partial network failure, the router can redirect the traffic over alternate paths.

Internet

For a complete glossary and definitions of networking terminology, visit the Novell network Web site located at www.novell.com/documentation/lg/nw5/docui/index.html#/usreflib/glossenu/data/glossenu.html. A second network glossary is located at www.datacom.textron.com/training/glossary.html.

Types of Networks

Many types of networks exist, but the most common types are *local area networks (LANs)* and *wide area networks (WANs)*. As explained earlier, a LAN is generally confined to a limited geographical area and a WAN covers a wide geographical area.

Local Area Networks

Most LANs connect personal computers, workstations, and other devices such as printers, scanners, or other devices. There are two popular types of LANs—client/server and peer-to-peer. The basic difference is how the data and information is stored.

■ *Client/server network:* This is a type of architecture in which one or more computers on the network acts as a *server*. The server manages network resources. Depending on the size of the network, there may be several different servers. For instance, there may be a print server to

ETHICS IN TECHNOLOGY

COMPUTER SECURITY

Computer security violation is one of the biggest problems with computer networks. People who break into computer systems are called hackers. The reasons for why they do this are many and varied. Some of the more common reasons are as follows:

■ Theft of services: For instance, AOL, Prodigy, and other password protected services charge a fee for usage. A hacker finds a way to bypass the password and uses the service without paying for it.

■ Steal information: A hacker may hack a system to steal credit card numbers, test data, or even national security data. The right kind of information can bring some big money.

■ Hatred and vengeance: Many people have groups or companies that they don't like. They may hack into their system to destroy files or to steal information to sell to other opposing groups.

■ For the thrill of it: Some hackers break into sites just to see if they can do it. The thrill is in breaking the code.

manage the printing and a database server to manage a large database. In most instances, the server(s) is a high-speed computer with lots of storage space. The network operating system software and network versions of software applications are stored on the server. All of the other computers on the network are called clients. They share the server resources. See Figure 12.9.

Peer-to-peer: In this type of architecture, all of the computers on a network are equal. There is no computer designated as the server. People on the network each determines what files on their computer they will share with others on the network. This type of network is much easier to set up and manage. Many small offices uses peer to peer. See Figure 12.10.

Wide Area Networks

A WAN covers a large geographical network. This area may be a large as a state or a country or even the world, since the largest WAN is the Internet. Most WANs consist of two or more LANs and are connected by routers. Communications channels can include telephone systems, satellites, microwaves, or any combination of these.

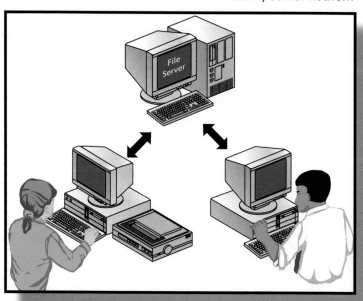

FIGURE 12.9
Client/server network

FIGURE 12.10
Peer-to-peer network

 Hot Tip

From a market that barely exists today, a leading research firm predicts that the U.S. home networking market will reach $1.4 billion in the next 2 to 3 years. This is over a 600 percent increase in the growth of this market.

Network Topologies

Networks can be designed using a variety of configurations. These configurations are referred to as topologies. A ***topology*** is simply the geometric arrangement of how the network is set up and connected. There are three basic topologies.

■ ***Bus topology:*** Within this type of topology, all devices are connected to and share a master cable. This master cable is called the bus or backbone. There is no one host computer. Data can be transmitted in both directions, from one device to another. This type of network is relatively easy to install and inexpensive. See Figure 12.11.

FIGURE 12.11
Bus topology

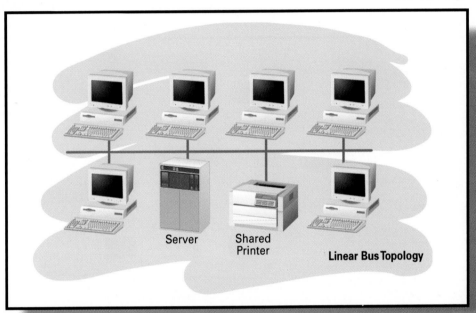

Server   Shared Printer   **Linear Bus Topology**

FIGURE 12.12
Ring topology

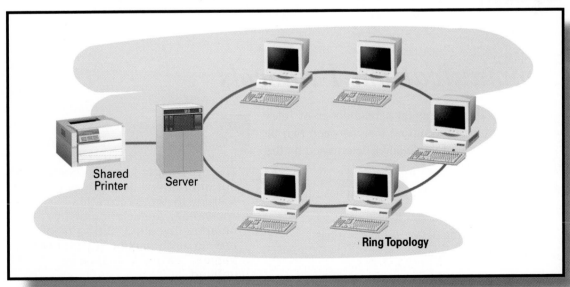

Shared Printer   Server   **Ring Topology**

- ***Ring topology:*** A ring topology is somewhat similar to a bus. However, the devices are connected in a circle instead of a line. Each computer within the circle is connected to an adjoining devices on either side. Data travels from device to device around the ring. This type of topology is more difficult to install and manage and more expensive. However, it does provide for faster transmission speeds and can span large distances. See Figure 12.12.

- ***Star topology:*** Within a star topology, all devices are connected to a central hub or computer. All data that transfer from one computer to another must pass through the hub. Star networks are relatively easy to install and manage, but bottlenecks can occur because all data must pass through the hub. This type of network requires more cabling than the other types. See Figure 12.13.

These topologies can also be mixed or combined to perform hybrid topologies.

FIGURE 12.13
Star topology

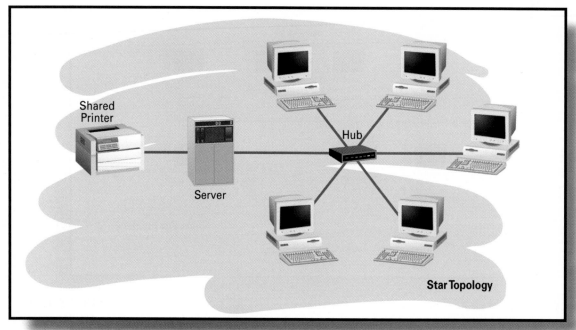

Star Topology

Communications Protocols

A protocol is simply an agreed on set of rules and procedures for transmitting data between two or more devices. Some of the features determined by the protocol are as follows:

- How the sending device indicates it has finished sending the message.

- How the receiving device indicates it has received the message.

- The type of error checking to be used.

 Hot Tip

Looking for that perfect career? Then you might want to check out Information Technology (IT). A study by the Information Technology Association of America reveals 346,000 IT jobs are currently vacant in U.S. companies, leaving 1 in 10 jobs unfilled.

190

Many protocols have been developed over the years. However, within networking and LANs, the two most widely used protocols are Ethernet and token ring. On the Internet, the major protocol is TCP/IP.

Internet

For those students interested in networking as a career and would like to have a more detailed introduction to the topic, you can find an excellent primer located at www.novell.com/catalog/primer.html.

- **Ethernet:** The *Ethernet* protocol was the first approved industry standard protocol. It is one of the most popular LAN protocols. Ethernet is based on the bus topology, but can work with the star topology as well. It supports data transfer rates of up to 10 megabits per second (Mbps). There are two new Ethernet versions. The first is called Fast Ethernet and supports data transfer rates of 100 Mbps. The second is called Gigabit Ethernet and supports data transfer rates of 1,000 megabits, or 1 gigabit, per second.

- **Token ring:** The second most widely used LAN protocol is called *token ring*. Within this type of network, all of the computers are arranged in a circle. A token, which is a special signal, travels around the ring. To send a message, a computer on the ring catches the token, attaches a message to it, and then lets it continue to travel around the network.

- **TCP/IP:** TCP/IP is the acronym for Transmission Control Protocol/Internet Protocol. This protocol is used by both LANs and WANs and has been adopted as a standard to connect hosts on the Internet. Even network operating systems, such as Microsoft NT or Novell Netware, support TCP/IP.

Network Operating Systems Software

All computers require an operating system. The operating system, among other functions, manages the computer's resources. Some of the operating systems with which you may be familiar are Windows, Mac OS, and UNIX.

Two types of operating systems are necessary in computer networking. The first is the desktop operating system, such as Windows or Mac OS. The second is the networking operating system. Some desktop operating systems, such as Windows, UNIX, and the Mac OS, have built-in networking functions. These functions work adequately within a very limited environment. To really utilize a network, however, full function network operating systems (NOS) software is required.

Network operating systems run on the server and provide features such as administration, file, print, communications, security, database, management, and other services to personal computer clients.

Summary

- A network is a group of two or more computers linked together.
- A local area network is generally confined to a limited geographical area.
- A wide area network is made up of several connected local area networks.
- Data communications is the transmission of data from one location to another.
- The Internet is the biggest network of all.

- You can use a network for information sharing, hardware sharing, software sharing, and as a collaborative environment.

- The link through which data is transmitted is the communications channel.

- Transmission media can be either physical or wireless.

- Physical media includes twisted-pair cable, coaxial cable, and fiber optic cable.

- Wireless media includes radio signals, microwaves, and satellites.

- Most networks consist of a network server and computer clients.

- A modem is a type of communications device.

- Network interface cards enables the sending and receiving of data between the PCs in a LAN.

- A hub is a device that controls the incoming and forwarding of data.

- A bridge connects one LAN to another.

- A gateway links two different types of networks.

- A router directs the Internet or LAN traffic.

- The two popular types of LANs are the client/server network and peer to peer.

- Network topologies include bus, ring, and star.

- A protocol is an agreed on set of rules and procedures for transmitting data between two or more devices.

- The Ethernet protocol is one of the most popular LAN protocols.

- Token ring is the second most widely used LAN protocol.

- TCP/IP is a protocol used by both LANs and WANs to connect to the Internet.

- All computers require an operating system.

- Networks require network operating systems.

LESSON 12 REVIEW QUESTIONS

MULTIPLE CHOICE

1. A _____ is confined to a limited geographical area.
   - **A.** wide area network
   - **B.** local area network
   - **C.** tiny area network
   - **D.** metropolitan area network

2. The least expensive type of physical communications media is _____.
   - **A.** twisted-pair cable
   - **B.** fiber optics cable
   - **C.** coaxial cable
   - **D.** radio signals

3. A _____ changes analog signals to digital signals and digital signals to analog.
   A. satellite
   B. NIC
   C. bridge
   D. modem

4. A _____ is a combination of software and hardware that links two different types of networks.
   A. hub
   B. bridge
   C. gateway
   D. router

5. A geometric arrangement of a network is called a _____.
   A. bridge
   B. WAN
   C. LAN
   D. topology

TRUE/FALSE

Circle the T if the statement is true. Circle F if it is false.

T F   1. Within a bus topology, all devices are connected to a master cable.

T F   2. A protocol is a type of topology.

T F   3. Token ring is the most widely used LAN protocol.

T F   4. Satellites orbit the earth.

T F   5. Software sharing is one of the benefits of networking.

SHORT ANSWER

1. The least expensive type of cable is _____.

2. _____ signals must be sent in straight lines.

3. Fiber optic cable is made from _____.

4. An add-on card that allows a computer to connect to a network is called a _____.

5. The _____ protocol was the first approved industry standard protocol.

CROSS-CURRICULAR PROJECTS

MATH

Keep a record of the different types of data communications devices you use in a day or week. For instance, did you use the telephone, the computer, a fax machine, and so forth? Create a graph illustrating your data.

SCIENCE/LANGUAGE ARTS

Your teacher has assigned you a science project. You are to work with several of your classmates. However, it is difficult for everyone to get together at the same time. Write a paper, giving a short overview of the science project you have been assigned and an explanation of how using a computer network would help your group accomplish its goal.

SOCIAL STUDIES

As a result of computers and networks, more and more people are working from home. These people are called telecommuters. Prepare a paper describing some jobs you think people could do at home. Then add two paragraphs: one on the advantages of working at home and a second on the disadvantages of working at home.

LANGUAGE ARTS

The goal for this project is to describe an existing network. Interview someone at your school, a family member , or a neighbor who works with a network. Find out what kind of network he or she uses and for what purposes. Prepare a presentation and share it with your class.

WEB PROJECT

Two of the most popular networking operating systems are Microsoft NT and Novell Netware. Search the Web for information on both of these network operating systems. Prepare a report and chart comparing the features of these two NOSs.

TEAM PROJECT

Ms. Perez is very pleased with the research you have completed on networking. She would now like for you and two or three of your teammates to put together a proposal for a network for Vista Multimedia. Ms. Perez has asked that you determine the type of network, what devices should be on the network, what network operating system to use, and what communications media to use. She has requested a brief description of why you selected each item.

WHAT IS THE INTERNET?

OBJECTIVES

When you complete this module, you will be able to:

- When you complete this module, you will be able to:

- Explain the origin of the Internet.

- Explain how to connect to the Internet.

- Explain how the Internet works.

- List the major features of the Internet and explain what they do.

⏱ **Estimated Time: 1.5 hours**

VOCABULARY

Domain name
Electronic mail
File transfer protocol (FTP)
Hypertext markup language (HTML)
Newsgroup
Protocols
Search engine
URL
USENET
World Wide Web

Ms. Perez is interested in learning more about the Internet and how she can use it to promote Vista Multimedia. She has asked you to explain how the Internet can help her personally and within the business. You first tell her that the Internet is all about information. You explain to her that each day millions of people "surf" the information superhighway. The "information highway" refers to the Internet. It is compared to a highway system because it functions much like a network of interstate highways. People use the Internet to research information, to shop, to go to school, to communicate with family and friends, to read the daily paper, to make airplane reservations, and so forth. They use the Internet at work and at home. Anyone with access to the Internet can connect with and communicate with anyone else in the world.

Evolution of the Internet

Even though no one person or organization can claim credit for the Internet, we can trace its early origins to the 1960s and the U.S. Department of Defense. The birth of the Internet is closely tied to a networking project started by a governmental division called the Advanced Research Projects Agency (ARPA). The goal was to create a network that would allow scientists to share information on military and scientific research.

The original name for the Internet was ARPANET. In 1969 ARPANET was a wide area network with four main host node computers. A host node is any computer directly connected to the network. These computers were located at the University of California at Santa Barbara, the University of California at Los Angeles, the Stanford Research Institute, and the University of Utah.

Over the next several years, the Internet grew steadily but quietly. Some interesting details are as follows:

■ The addition of e-mail in 1972 spurred some growth.

■ By 1989 more than 100,000 host computers were linked to ARPANET.

■ In 1990 ARPANET ceased to exist, but few noticed because its functions continued.

■ The real growth began when the World Wide Web came into being in 1992.

■ The thousands of interconnected networks were called an Inter-Net-Network and became known as the Internet, or a network of networks.

■ In 1993 the world's first browser, Mosaic, was released. A browser is a graphical interface for the Internet. Mosaic made it so easy to access the Internet that there was a 340% growth rate in this one year.

■ The Internet is still growing at an unprecedented rate.

Accessing the INTERNET—Dial in or Direct Connection

Before you can even begin to surf the Net you have to be connected. If you connect to the Internet from your school, you are probably connecting through a local area network (LAN). You connect to the Internet using a network interface card (NIC). This is a special card inside your computer that allows the computer to be networked. A direct connection is made from the local area network to a high-speed connection line, most likely leased from the local telephone company. See Figure 13.1.

For the home user, the most common type of Internet connection is with a modem and a telephone line. Signals transmitted across a normal telephone line are analog or continuous. A modem is a device that converts the computer's digital signal into an analog signal, therefore allowing data to be sent from one computer to another. See Figure 13.2.

FIGURE 13.1
Ways to access the Internet

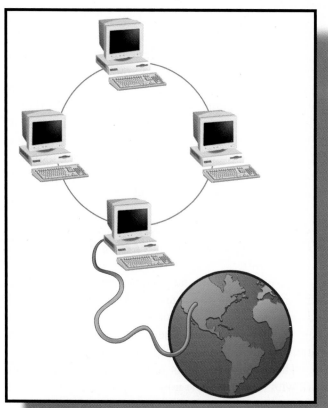

Getting connected to the Internet is fairly simple, but there are a few steps you need to take:

- **Step 1:** Locate an Internet service provider (ISP) or an online service. There are thousands of Internet service providers. Most are small local companies. Their service is primarily an Internet connection. Online services are large national and international companies. Four of the largest online services are America Online, Prodigy, CompuServe, and MSN. Generally, the local ISP is less expensive, but many people use the online services because of the additional information and services they offer.

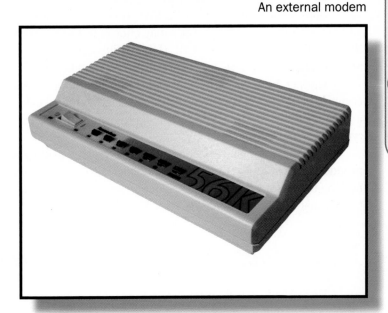

FIGURE 13.2
An external modem

- **Step 2:** Once you find an ISP, you must install some type of telecommunications software. This software enables your computer to connect to another computer. Most likely your ISP or online service company will provide this software.

- **Step 3:** You will need to install a software application called a Web browser in order to surf the Web. The Web is one component of the Internet (see later in this chapter). Two of the most popular browsers are Netscape's Navigator and Microsoft's Internet Explorer.

You've contracted with your ISP and you've installed your software. It's now time to connect to the Internet. This is the easy part. You give instructions to your computer to dial a local telephone number. This number connects you to your ISP's computer, which in turn connects you to the Internet. You're online with the world. See Figure 13.3.

FIGURE 13.3
Modem and telephone connection

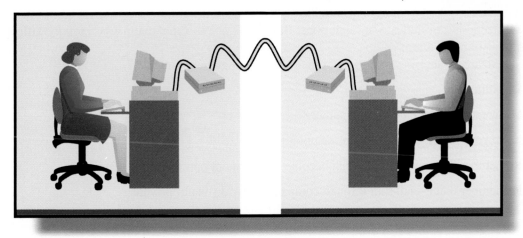

Other Types of Connections

Many people are happy with their Internet telephone connection, but some want more speed and are willing to pay for it. They may choose to use high-speed digital lines such ISDN (Integrated Services Digital Network) or DSL (Digital Subscriber Lines). With ISDN and DSL, special hardware allows data transmission at far greater speeds than the standard phone wiring.

Another high-speed option is the cable modem. This type of modem also connects to your computer, but it uses a network interface card such as what you use at your school. Instead of using a telephone line as a transmission media to connect to the ISP, coaxial cable is used. This is the same type of cable used for cable TV.

Finally, a third way to connect to the Internet is using your television and WebTV. Most WebTV products consist of a set-top box that connects to your telephone line and television. It makes a connection to the Internet via your telephone service and then converts the downloaded Web pages to a format that can be displayed on your TV.

How does the Internet Work?

First of all, the Internet is transitory, ever changing, reshaping, and remolding itself. It is a loose association of thousands of networks and millions of computers across the world that all work together to share information. The beauty of this network of networks is that all brands, models, and makes of computers can communicate with each other. This is called interoperability.

So how do we communicate across the Internet? Think about our postal service. If you want to send someone a letter anywhere in the world, you can do that—as long as you know the address. The Internet works in a similar fashion. From your computer, you can connect with any other networked computer anywhere in the world—as long as you know the address.

ETHICS IN TECHNOLOGY

ELECTRONIC MAIL: RULES OF ETIQUETTE

Electronic mail (e-mail) is the most popular feature on the Internet today. It is easy to understand and simple to use. It is also easy to abuse and easy to give someone the wrong impression of what you are trying to say.

When we communicate face to face with someone, our visual cues indicate much of what we are trying to express. We smile, cry, wrinkle our nose. If we are communicating via telephone, our voice inflections can indicate our emotions. But this is not so for e-mail. It is a totally different communications medium.

There are no set rules, but some of the following may help you with your e-mail:

- Be polite.

- Limit each message to a single subject.

- Keep your message short and to the point.

- Remember that your message can become a permanent part of someone's records.

- Remember that e-mail sent through company networks is not private.

FIGURE 13.4
Data travels the Internet

Computers on the Internet communicate with each other using a set of protocols known as TCP/IP, or Transmission Control Protocol and Internet Protocol. A protocol is a standard format for transferring data between two devices. TCP/IP is the agreed on international standard for transmitting data. It is considered the language of the Internet. The TCP protocol enables two host computers to establish a connection and exchange data. A host computer is simply a computer that you access remotely. The IP protocol works with the addressing scheme. It allows you to enter an address and sends it to another computer; from there the TCP protocol takes over. Returning to our postal service analogy, this is similar to what happens when you take a letter to the post office. You deliver the letter to the post office and then the post office takes over. See Figure 13.4.

Postal addresses usually contain numbers and street names. Likewise, when we access another computer on the Internet, we are accessing it via a number. However, we don't have to remember or type in that number. Instead we can type in the *domain name*. The domain name identifies a site on the Internet. An example of a domain name is www.microsoft.com. If we want to access the Microsoft Corporation's computers that are connected to the Internet, we start our browser and type the domain name.

 Did You Know?

Did you know that a new culture has developed around the Internet? The original use of the Internet was primarily to exchange research ideas. That is no longer true of today's Internet. The Internet is having an enormous impact on society all over the world.

Major Features of the Internet

So far in this module, we've discussed the Internet. The Internet, however, is made up of many services. Some of the more popular of these services include the World Wide Web, e-mail, chat, mailing lists, FTP, and Newsgroups.

The World Wide Web

Many people use the terms *World Wide Web*, or Web for short, and Internet interchangeably. In reality, they're actually two different things. The Web is a subset or an application that makes use of the Internet. The Internet can exist without the Web, but the Web cannot exist without the Internet. The Web actually began in March 1989 when Tim Berners-Lee, who works with a European organization known as Cern, wrote a small computer program for his own personal use. This text-based program permitted pages to be linked through a formatting process known as *Hypertext Markup Language* (HTML). Clicking a linked word transfers you from one computer to another. You do not have to type the Web site address. This was a step forward, but it is not the catalyst that made the Web what it is today.

Internet

There are hundreds or even thousands of online tutorials to help you become more familiar with Internet features. One of the better tutorials is called Beginners Central. You can find this tutorial located at <u>www.northernwebs.com/bc/</u>. Topics covered include learning while you surf, offline operations and file downloading, configuring e-mail and news readers, FTP, and myths of the Internet.

FIGURE 13.5
Mosaic Web Site

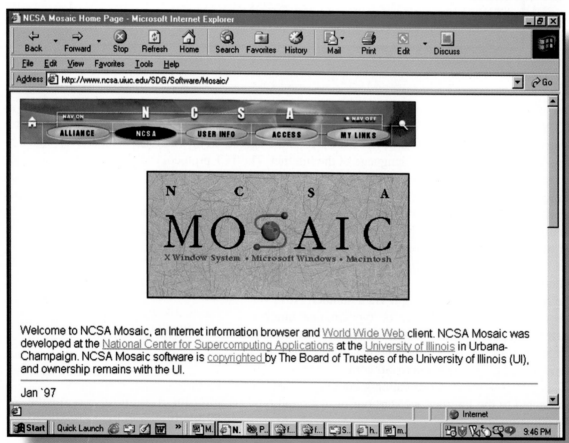

FIGURE 13.6
Hamsterdance

Lesson 13 What is the Internet?

The number of people using the Web greatly increased in 1993. This increase occurred when Marc Andreessen, working for the National Center for Supercomputing Applications at the University of Illinois, released Mosaic. Mosaic was the first graphical browser. See Figure 13.5.

In 1994 Andreessen co-founded Netscape Communications. With the introduction of Mosaic and the Web browsers that followed, the Web became a communications tool for a much wider audience. Currently, two of the most popular Web browsers are Internet Explorer and Netscape Navigator. As a result of these enhancements, the Web is one of the most popular services available on the Internet.

WEB PROTOCOLS—HTTP

The Web has its own underlying protocols. One protocol is known as HTTP, or *hypertext transfer protocol.* This protocol, or standard, defines how messages are formatted and transmitted. You can send and receive Web pages over the Internet because Web servers and browsers both understand HTTP. For instance, when you enter a Web site address in your browser, this sends an HTTP command to the Web Server to tell it to locate and transmit the requested Web page. A Web server is a computer that contains Web pages. By installing special software, any computer can become a Web server. Every Web server has its own IP address and most have a *domain name*. The domain name identifies the IP address.

The Web site address is commonly referred to as the *URL*, or *Universal Resource Locator*. Every Web page on the Internet has its own unique address. The first part of the address indicates what protocol to use, and the second part specifies the IP address or the domain name where the resource is located. For example, in the URL www.hamsterdance.com, the http protocol indicates this is a Web page and the domain name is hamsterdance. See Figure 13.6. The .com at the end of the name indicates that this is a commercial organization or business. See Table 13.1 for other domain abbreviations.

TABLE 13.1

DOMAIN ABBREVIATIONS

Domain Abbreviation	Type of Organization
edu	Educational institutions
com	Commercial businesses, companies, and organizations
gov	Government institutions, such as the IRS
mil	Military organizations, such as the army
net	Network provider org Nonprofit organization

Hot Tip

Have you ever had a burning desire to know just exactly how something works? For instance, have you wondered how a cell phone works? Or what happens to your body when you drink all of that caffeine? Or how nuclear energy works? Or what the name WD-40 stands for? You can find the answers to all of these questions at www.howstuffworks.com/.

WEB PROTOCOLS—HTML

A second protocol or standard that controls how the World Wide Web works is **HTML**, or **hypertext markup** language. This protocol determines how Web pages are formatted and displayed and allows the users to exchange text, images, sound, video, and multimedia files. Hypertext is a link to another location. The location can be within the same document, in another document on the same Web server, or on a Web server on the other side of the world. You click on the link and are transported to the location.

A Web page is nothing more than an ordinary text page coded with HTML markup tags and then displayed within a browser. Markup tags consist of set text commands that are interpreted by the browser. Different browsers may format and display the HTML markup tags differently. Altogether, three items determine the look of a Web page:

- The type and version of the browser displaying the Web page.

- The actual HTML markup tags used to code the page.

- The user's monitor and monitor resolution.

Many markup tags can be used within a document. However, all Web pages have a minimum basic requirement. See Figure 13.7.

FIGURE 13.7
Required HTML tags

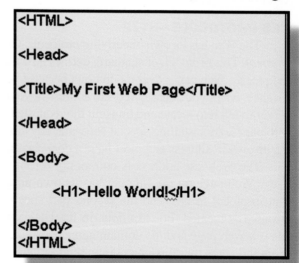

Electronic Mail

Another popular service on the Internet is *electronic mail*, or e-mail. In its simplest form, e-mail is an electronic message sent from one computer to another. Anyone with an e-mail account can send a message to anyone else who has an e-mail account. In addition to sending a message, you can include attachments such as pictures or documents. You can also forward messages to other people who have e-mail accounts.

When you send postal mail to someone, you must know the address. The same thing is true for e-mail. An e-mail address consists of three parts:

- The user name of the individual

- The "@" symbol

- The user's domain name

For instance, Mary Smith's e-mail address could be msmith@AOL.com.

To send an e-mail, you must have an e-mail program. This is generally supplied by your ISP. Many different e-mail programs are available. The following example illustrates how to send an e-mail message. The program shown in the figures is Microsoft's Outlook Express. It may not be identical to yours, but it should be similar.

> **Internet**
>
> How about an interactive tutorial that presents information about the Internet? You can find one free at www.sierramm.com/smp-net.html. Notice the FTP option.

STEP-BY-STEP ▷ 13.1

1. On your Browser toolbar, click Mail. This displays a menu. Select New Message to display the New Message window. See Figure 13.8.

2. Notice that within the window are several text areas into which you can enter information. See Figure 13.9.

3. Your first step is to indicate to whom are you are sending the message. Notice in our example that we are sending a message to the president of the United States.

4. If you would like to send someone a copy of the e-mail, include their name in the Cc: text box. In our example, we are sending a copy to the vice president.

5. Next, enter the subject. It is always very important to enter a subject. This helps the e-mail recipient quickly scan the list of e-mails. Always try to create single-subject messages when possible.

6. Enter the text of the message. Keep your message short and to the point. Try to avoid emotion if possible.

7. Identify yourself as the sender of the message.

FIGURE 13.8
New Message menu option

FIGURE 13.9
E-mail message

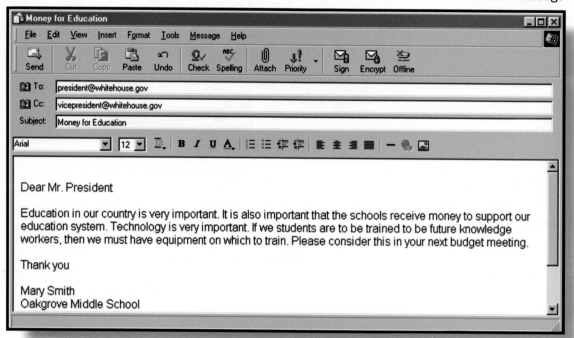

When your message is completed, click the Send button to transmit the message.

One of the best ways to learn how to use a mail program effectively is to experiment with it. Try sending messages to yourself to verify that it is working.

Chat Rooms

You can call someone through the Internet and "talk" to them the way you do on the phone, only you are writing and reading on your computer rather than talking and listening with a phone in your hand. You are using the computer to create real-time communication between yourself and another user or a group of users. To participate in a chat, you enter a virtual chat room. Once a chat has been initiated, users enter text by typing on the keyboard, and the message appears on the monitor of the other participants.

TECHNOLOGY CAREERS

WEB DEVELOPER

A Web developer can wear many hats. With the ever-expanding and changing Internet, skill requirements can change daily.

As a Web developer, you will need some technical skills including programming. Some of the more common programming languages are C++, Java, and CGI.. You will need a strong background in database development. Oracle and SQL are two of the most widely used database interfaces. Some other requirements may include using Active Server Pages, JavaScript, and Perl.

Employment opportunities in this field are increasing each day as more and more companies develop a Web presence. Depending on the size and location of the company, salaries can range from $25,000 to more than $100,000 a year. Education requirements vary—from certifications with only a high school diploma to a master's degree in information technology.

FIGURE 13.10
Internet relay chat

Lesson ⑬ What is the Internet?

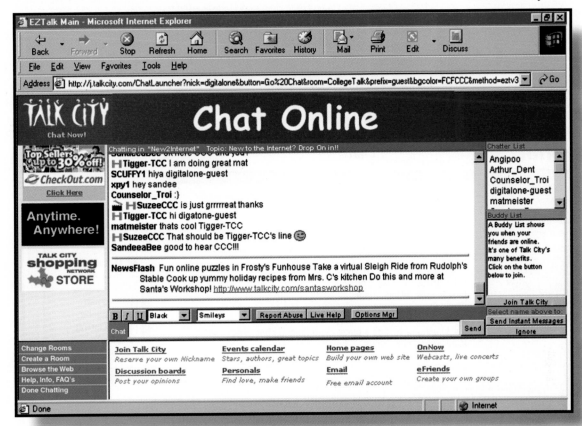

Internet Relay Chat (IRC), a text-based chat developed by Jarkko Oikarinen in 1988, was the first of the chat forums. It gained popularity in January 1991 as a result of the Baghdad bombings. Until recently it was the only available option for real-time discussion. See Figure 13.10. Even though it is still one of the most widely used chat forums on the Internet today, now many other options are available. Some of these options include the following:

- Web chat: There are several Web chat variations, but many of these can incorporate graphics, audio, and video; some of these are hosted by *search engine* sites such as Yahoo, Snap, and Excite. A search engine is another Internet tool to help you locate information on the Internet.

- Proprietary chat: This type of chat requires that you download and install software from a company; you can then use their server or use IRC. Microsoft Chat, AOL, and Prodigy are examples of proprietary chat. See Figure 13.11.

- Buddy lists: One of the new communication options is the buddy list; with this program you can specify your list of friends and even tell when they are online. Two of the more popular of these are ICQ and AOL Messenger.

 Did You Know?

Did you know there are Web sites where you can "Ask an expert" an educational question you may have—from the arts to law to health? One of the more popular educational "Ask an Expert" Web sites is located at www.askanexpert.com/. At this Web site, you can communicate with professionals such as astronauts, a fireplace expert, a nanny expert, and a public relations expert—just to name a few.

FIGURE 13.11
Microsoft Chat

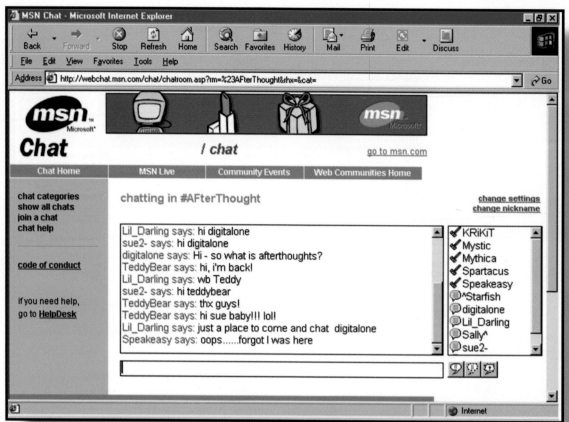

- Virtual worlds: In a virtual world, you can chat, explore, and communicate with others that are part of the world. You are represented by an avatar, which is a virtual character. Depending on the virtual world, the character may be humanoid or it could be an animated character or object. In some virtual worlds, you can even create your own character. As this character, you can move, talk, and pick up objects. Some virtual worlds, such as The Palace, are communication tools for social interaction. See Figure 13.12.

Mailing Lists

A mailing list is a group of people with a shared interest. Their e-mail addresses are collected into a group, and this group is identified by a single name. Whenever you send a message, everyone on the list receives a copy. There are mailing lists for every imaginable topic. You can subscribe to a mailing list just as you would subscribe to a magazine. A list owner is the person who manages the list.

Hot Tip

Interested in going to high school online? In Florida, you can do just that. The online high school started in 1996. Thousands of students are now attending the online high school. Students attending the online school can earn a high school diploma. There is no tuition charge for students living in Florida. You can visit the Florida High School Web site at www.fhs.net/. Or check out a list of other virtual high schools at www.vhs. ucsc.edu/vhs/cases-tudies.htm.

FIGURE 13.12
The Palace Virtual World

Lesson 13 What is the Internet?

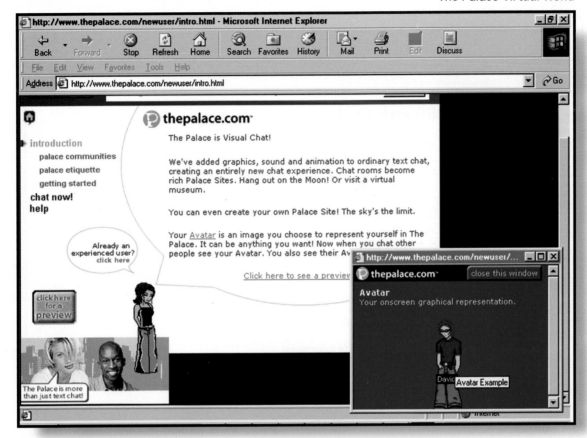

MAILING LISTS FEATURES

There are several variations of mailing lists, such as the following:

- Announcements are one type of mailing list. For example, you could subscribe to the IBM mailing list and receive announcements of new products.

- A discussion list is another type of list. Members use this type of list to ask questions and share information on a particular topic. For instance, let's assume you belong to a mailing list for word processing. You want to include a special feature within your document, but you're not sure how to do this. You can send your question to the list members. Most likely, if the list is an active list, you will receive several responses to your question.

- Some lists are public lists and some are closed or private lists. With a public list, anyone can subscribe. A private list limits subscribers to members of a particular organization or group. For example, you could have a private list for students within your class.

- Some mailing lists have a summary or digest version. Instead of receiving each individual message posted to the list, the list manager or list owner groups the postings. Generally this is for a designated time period, such as a day or a week. Then the postings are sent as a batch to all subscribers.

Internet

Like to play games? If so, you can play all types of games online—from board games to role-playing games. Check out the GameCenter Web site at www.gamecenter.com/Features/Exclusives/Online/.

FIGURE 13.13
Mailing lists with 10,000 or more subscribers

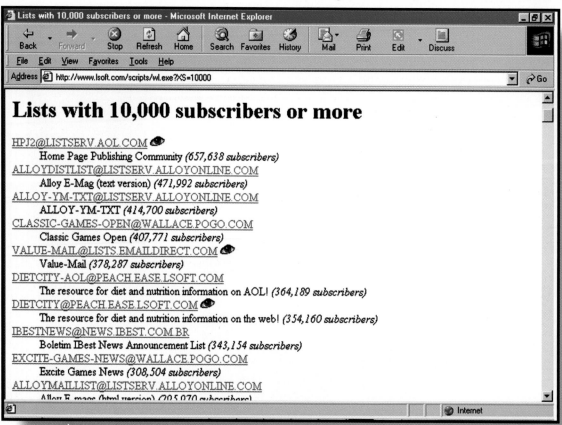

Before you start subscribing to mailing lists, do your homework. Many of these lists produce a huge volume of e-mail messages. You could end up receiving hundreds or even thousands of messages a day. See Figure 13.13.

Newsgroups

A *newsgroup* is a discussion forum or a type of bulletin board. Each "board" is dedicated to discussion on a particular topic. The difference between a newsgroup and a mailing list is that with a newsgroup you can select the topics you want to read. These messages are stored on a news server, which is a computer that contains the necessary newsgroup software.

A worldwide network of computers called USENET facilitates the transmission of messages among the news servers. The news servers utilize the Network News Transport Protocol (NNTP) to connect with other USENET news servers. This protocol also makes it possible to distribute messages to anyone using a newsreader. See Figure 13.14.

FIGURE 13.14
Newsgroups

To find groups and participate in discussions that interest you, you need a newsreader. This software enables you to read messages and to post your message to a newsgroup. Many e-mail programs contain a newsreader. If your e-mail program does not contain a newsreader or you want one with more features, many are available for download through the Internet.

There are over 50,000 different newsgroups, and the number is increasing each day. These newsgroups are easy to navigate because they are organized by subject into hierarchies. There are eight major subject headings. See Table 13.2. Each subject hierarchy is broken down into subcategories and there are hundreds of alternative hierarchies.

TABLE 13.2

USENET HIERARCHIES

Hierarchy Abbreviation	Description	Example
comp	Computer science and computer-related topics	comp.infosystems
humanities	Fine arts, literature discussions	humanities, classics
misc	Anything that doesn't fit within the other categories	misc.jobs
news	USENET information	news.announce
rec	Recreational topics	rec.music.info
talk	Discussions and debates on controversial subjects	talk.environment
sci	Scientific discussions and research	sci.energy
soc	Social issues	soc.culture

File Transfer Protocol

At one time or another, you may have been on the Internet and tried to access a special feature such as an audio file. You receive a message that a plug-in is required. A plug-in is an add-on software application that adds a specific feature to your Web browser or other programs. You click on a link and the plug-in is downloaded or transmitted to your computer. You most likely have just used *File Transfer Protocol* (FTP). This is an Internet standard that allows users to download and upload files to and from other computers on the Internet.

Many FTP servers are connected to the Internet. Some of these require user IDs and passwords. Others permit anonymous FTP access. This means that anyone can upload and download files from the server. The files on the server can be any type of file. Some examples are software updates for your printer, a revised instruction manual, or a new program that is being tested.

Many people use FTP servers to store compressed or zipped files that they want to share with someone

 Internet

Need some help with public speaking? This Web site has public speaking presentation tips. Check it out at www.home-businessmag.com/artapril/speaking.htm.

else. Using a compression program reduces the size of a file so it can be downloaded and/or uploaded more quickly. For this type of activity, it is generally easier to use a stand-alone application program. One of the more popular stand-alone programs is WS_FTP. This program is free to students and educational institutions. See Figure 13.15. The remote computer to which you are transferring a file must also have FTP available.

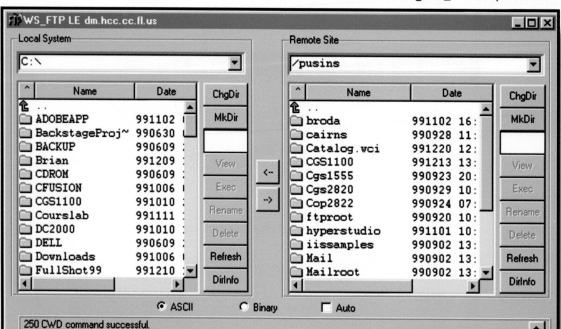

FIGURE 13.15
Using WS_FTP to upload a file

Summary

- No one person or organization can claim credit for the Internet.

- Origins of the Internet can be traced to the U.S. Department of Defense.

- The original name for the Internet was ARPANET.

- Mosaic was the Internet's first graphical interface.

- To connect to the Internet from school, you probably have a direct connection via a local area network and a network interface card.

- For the home user, the most common type of Internet connection is with a modem and telephone line.

- To connect to the Internet, you need an Internet connection, telecommunications software, and a browser.

- Other types of Internet connections include ISDN, DSL, cable modem, and WebTV.

- Interoperability means that all brands, models, and makes of computers can communicate with each other.

- A protocol is a standard format for transferring data between two devices.

- TCP/IP is the agreed on international standard for transmitting data.

- The domain name identifies a site on the Internet.

- The Internet is made up of many services.

- The Web is an application that makes use of the Internet.

- Web pages can be linked through hypertext.

- Microsoft's Internet Explorer and Netscape's Navigator are two of the most popular Web browsers.

- The HTTP protocol defines how Web messages are formatted and transmitted.

- The Web site addressed is referred to as the URL, or Universal Resource Locator.

- Every Web page on the Internet has its own unique address.

- HTML is another protocol that controls how Web pages are formatted and displayed.

- A Web page is coded with HTML markup tags.

- Electronic mail is another popular Internet service.

- You can have real-time communications through chat.

- There are several chat options, including IRC, Web chat, proprietary chat, buddy lists, and virtual worlds.

- A mailing list is a group of people with a shared interest. Their e-mail addresses are collected into a group.

- A list owner manages a mailing list.

- Some types of mailing lists include announcements, discussions, public and private lists, and digest versions.

- Newsgroups are discussion forums.

- You must have a newsreader to participate in a newsgroup.

- File transfer protocol is used to upload and download files.

MULTIPLE CHOICE

1. A _____ is any computer directly connected to a network.
   A. newsreader
   B. host node
   C. domain name
   D. URL

2. The process of all makes and models of computers being able to communicate with each other is called _____.
   A. services
   B. ISDN
   C. interoperability
   D. Internetwork

3. The first graphical browser was named _____.
   A. Internet Explorer
   B. Navigator
   C. Avatar
   D. Mosaic

4. If you wanted to send someone a message on the Internet, you would use _____.
   A. e-mail
   B. newsreader
   C. chat room
   D. list manager

5. A virtual world is a type of _____ program.
   A. e-mail
   B. chat
   C. newsgroup
   D. FTP

TRUE/FALSE

Circle the T if the statement is true. Circle F if it is false.

T F 1. IRC is a text-based chat program.

T F 2. A list owner manages virtual worlds.

T F 3. ISDN is a high-speed connection to the Internet.

T F 4. You must use a modem to communicate over a regular telephone line.

T F 5. TCP/IP is called the language of the Internet.

SHORT ANSWER

1. An e-mail address consists of _____ parts.

2 An announcement list is a type of _____ list.

3. The original name for the Internet was _____.

4. _____ software enables your computer to connect to another computer.

5. A _____ modem uses coaxial cable.

CROSS-CURRICULAR PROJECTS

MATH

Use the following table to create a graph regarding the growth of e-mail. If you have access to a spreadsheet program, enter the data and then create your graph from that data. Please note that the numbers in this table are estimates only.

SCIENCE

Visit the National Zoo at www.si.edu/natzoo/. Tour the Web site. Use your word processing software and write a summary of this Web site. Include the following topics: (1) information on the Web Cams and what animals you could view; (2) description of the elephant demo; and (3) description of the audio tours. What is your overall opinion about this site?

SOCIAL STUDIES/LANGUAGE ARTS

Do you think the government will ever be able to regulate the Internet? That is, will any agency ever be able to control and limit what someone puts online? Use your word processing program and write a page on your thoughts on this issue.

LANGUAGE ARTS/MATH

In this module, several Internet features were described. Which one of these features would you most likely use and why? List each of the features and use a ranking scale of 1 to 5 (1 means you probably never use this feature and 5 that you would definitely use it). Prepare a report to share with the class on your rankings. Explain why you ranked each feature as you did.

WEB PROJECT

Internet etiquette was discussed briefly in the Ethics feature. It is a very important topic for someone who uses the Internet for e-mail, newsgroups, and other Internet features. Do an Internet search and see what additional information you can find on Internet etiquette. Prepare a report for your class. If available, use a presentation program to deliver your report. Here are some URLs to get you started:

www.iwillfollow.com/email.htm
www.dtcc.edu/cs/rfc1855.html
www.albion.com/netiquette/
www.fau.edu/netiquette/netiquette.html

TEAM PROJECT

Ms. Perez is impressed with your knowledge of the Internet. She has asked you to coordinate a project with two other Vista Multimedia employees. There is no Internet connection at Vista Multimedia. Ms. Perez wants to convince the company president that an Internet connection could be a vital enhancement for the store. Your goal is to create a persuasive presentation for Ms. Perez that she can present to the company president.

WHAT BASIC SKILLS DO I NEED TO USE THE INTERNET?

LESSON

14

OBJECTIVES

When you complete this module, you will be able to:

- Describe a browser.

- Understand browser terminology.

- Understand how to use a browser to surf the Internet.

- Understand and use browser features.

- Understand e-mail features.

- Use e-mail features.

⏱ **Estimated Time: 1.5 hours**

VOCABULARY

Address bar
Address book
Bookmark
Browser
Electronic mail
History
Home page
Hypertext Markup Language
Toolbar
Universal Resource Locator
Web server

Since you have recently introduced Ms. Perez to the wonders of the Internet, she thinks it would be very helpful if you would show the other Vista Multimedia employees some of its benefits. You suggest to Ms. Perez that a workshop would be the easiest and best way to do this. She agrees, and you plan the workshop for next week. The topics you plan to cover are how to use the browser and how to use e-mail features.

What Is a Browser?

A *browser* is the software program that you use to retrieve documents from the World Wide Web (WWW or Web) and to display them in a readable format. The Web is the graphical portion of the Internet. The browser functions as an interface between you and the Internet. Using a browser, you can display both text and images. Newer versions of most browsers can also support multimedia information, including sound and video.

The browser sends a message to the *Web server* to retrieve your requested Web page. Then the browser renders the HTML code to display the page. HTML, or *Hypertext Markup Language*, is the language used to create documents for the WWW. You navigate through the Web by using your mouse to point and click on hyperlinked words and images.

Currently, the two most popular browsers are Microsoft Internet Explorer and Netscape Communicator. See Figures 14.1 and 14.2.

FIGURE 14.1
Internet Explorer

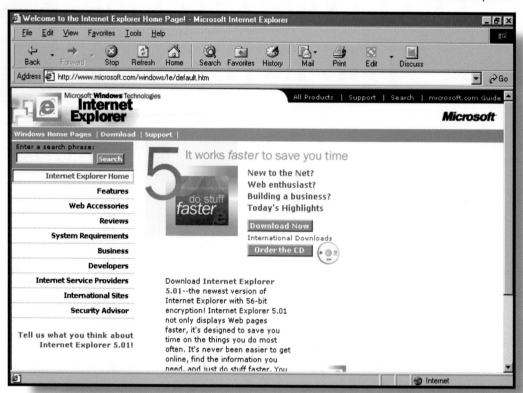

FIGURE 14.2
Netscape Communicator

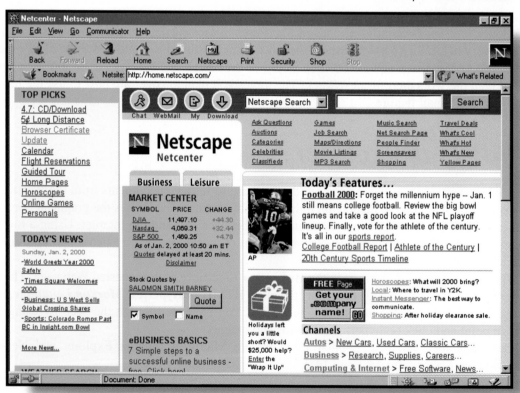

Both these browsers have very similar features, but the menu options to select these features may be somewhat different. The major differences between the two browsers are primarily within some special built-in tools. These tools include programs for mail, chat, viewing and listening to multimedia, and so forth.

Browser Terminology

Understanding browser terminology is the key to using a browser effectively. See Figure 14.3. Table 14.1 contains a definition of each part of the screen.

Internet

Welcome to BrowserWatch, the leading site for information about browsers, plug-ins, and ActiveX controls. We offer breaking news in the browser and plug-ins industry, as well as one of the most complete lists on development of different plug-ins and browsers. A quick check allows you to find the plug-ins or browsers you want quickly and effortlessly: browser-watch.internet.com/

FIGURE 14.3
Browser Window Terminology

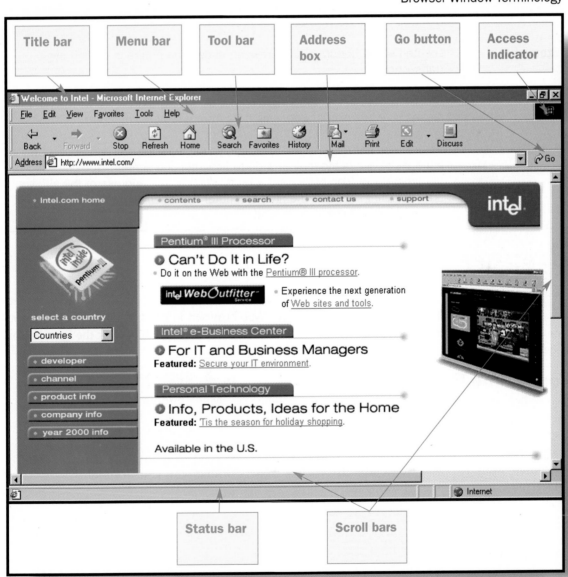

TABLE 14.1

BROWSER TERMINOLOGY DEFINITIO

Feature	Definitions
Title bar	The bar on top of the window that contains the name of the document.
Menu bar	A horizontal menu that appears on top of a window; provides a selection of options related to the Web page.
Toolbar	Icons for single-click access to most commonly used menu commands.
Address bar	Contains the URL, or address, of the active Web page; also where you type the location for the Web page you want to visit.
Go button	Connects you to address displayed in the Address bar. Document Window Displays the active Web page.
Status bar	Located at the bottom of the browser; shows the progress of Web page transactions.
Access indicator	A small picture in the upper right corner of the browser; when animated, it means your browser is accessing data from a remote computer.
Scroll bars	Vertical and horizontal scroll bars; lets you scroll vertically and horizontally if the Web page is too long or wide to fit within one screen. You can watch the progress of Web page transactions, such as the address of the site you are contacting, whether the host computer has been contacted, and the size of the files to be downloaded.

Browser Basics

In this module it is assumed you have an Internet connection—either dial-in or direct connection. To connect to the Internet, you first launch your Web browser. In most instances, you can double-click the browser icon located on your desktop. If the icon is not available, click the Start button, select programs, and then choose the browser name.

Your Home Page

When your browser is installed, a default home page is selected. The home page is the first page that's displayed when you launch your browser. You can easily change your home page. Most people choose a home page they want to view frequently. To change your default page, complete the following activity:

Did You Know?

Many people create a custom home page. If you have access to the Internet and can upload your own Web page, you may want to create a page with hyperlinks you visit frequently.

STEP-BY-STEP ▷ 14.1

Internet Explorer

1. Go to the page you want to appear when you first start your browser.

2. On the Tools menu, click Internet Options.

3. Click the General tab.

4. In the home page area, click Use Current.

STEP-BY-STEP ▷ 14.2

Step-by-Step (Communicator)

1. Go to the page you want to appear when you first start your browser.

2. From the Edit menu, select Preferences.

3. Select the Communicator category.

4. Click Use Current Page.

The Address Bar

The address bar (Internet Explorer) or location bar (Communicator) is located near the top of the browser window. This bar contains the address of the current page. This address is called the Universal Resource Locator (URL). The URL tells the browser where to locate the page. A unique URL identifies each Web page.

If you want to visit a specific Web site, you need to know the address. This address or location bar is also where you type the address of the Web site you wish to visit. In Internet Explorer, the Go button is located to the immediate right. After you type in the URL, you can click this button rather than pressing Enter. Communicator's button to the right of the bar takes you to related Web sites.

Both browsers have some automated features related to the address or location bar. These features may be similar, but not necessarily identical.

■ AutoComplete: Keeps track of and provides a list of sites you have already visited or fills out forms automatically.

■ AutoCorrect: Corrects typos as you type, especially those errors made on common URL conventions, such as http:// or www.

■ AutoSearch: Helps you to find a Web page quickly and easily by giving you Web search results when you type part of a URL in the address bar.

 Hot Tip

If you have one or more Web pages you access frequently, you may want to create a shortcut. You can store the shortcut on the desktop. To create a desktop shortcut, complete the following activity:

■ Go to the Web page for which you want to create the shortcut for.

■ Position your mouse anywhere on the Web page, except over an image.

■ Right-click your mouse button to display a pop-up menu.

■ Select **Create Shortcut** in the pop-up menu to display a confirmation window.

■ Click **OK** to accept the setting. The shortcut appears on your desktop.

219

FIGURE 14.4
Internet Explorer Address list

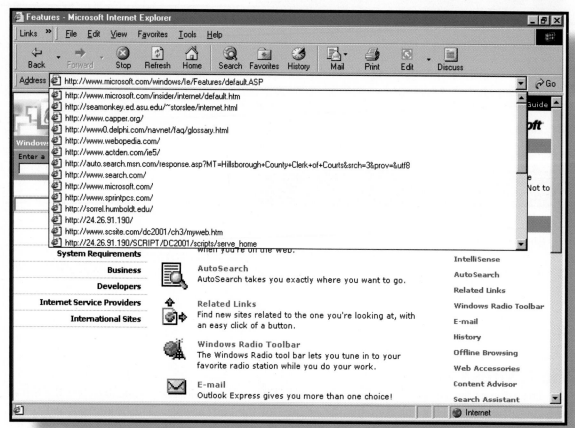

- Address List: Helps you by remembering the URLs you type; click the Address List arrow to view these. See Figure 14.4.

Toolbar and Menu Bar

The row of buttons at the top of your browser is known as the Toolbar. The toolbars for Communicator and Explorer differ slightly. See Figures 14.5 and 14.6.

- Back: Returns you to the previous page.

- Forward: Returns you to the page you viewed before clicking the Back button.

- Home: Takes you to your home page.

- Refresh or Reload: Refreshes or reloads the current Web page.

- Stop: Stops the current page from loading.

- Print: Prints the current document.

- Search: Connects you to the Microsoft or Netscape Internet search sites.

- Favorites or Bookmarks: Opens the Favorites or Bookmarks bar where you can store shortcuts to your most frequently visited Web sites.

- History: Opens the History bar, displaying a record of all the sites you have visited in the last 20 days. See Figure 14.7. In Communicator, click the Communicator button, point to Tools, and click History.

FIGURE 14.5
Internet Explorer Toolbar

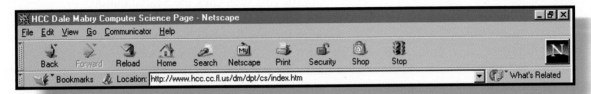

FIGURE 14.6
Communicator Toolbar

FIGURE 14.7
Internet Explorer History List

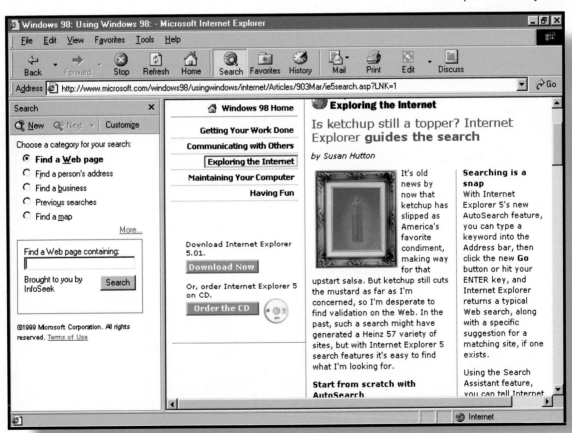

Searching

Both Communicator and Internet Explorer have a special search feature that makes it easy for you to quickly locate your desired information. Internet Explorer calls this AutoSearch, and Communicator calls it Internet Keywords. Just type a common term in the address or location bar and press the Enter key. For example, you're saving your money for that new Honda Accord, and you would like to have some additional information. Launch your browser, type Honda Accord, press Enter, and both Communicator and Internet Explorer take you to the Honda Web site.

Hot Tip

When surfing the Web at one time or another, you are probably going to receive a "401—Unauthorized" message. This means you're trying to access a Web site that's protected.

If the AutoSearch or Internet Keywords doesn't work for you, then click the Search button.

Clicking the Communicator Search button takes you to the Net Search page where you can search with several different search services. Simply choose a service, type the words you're looking for in the text box, and click the button to get a list of matching sites. See Figure 14.8.

Clicking the Internet Explorer Search button opens the Search bar and the Search Assistant. This is a separate frame on the left side of the window. You can choose the type of information you want, including a Web page, a person's e-mail address, a business, a map, and previous searches. The Search Assistant chooses a search service that specializes in the type of search you select. For instance, you select map, type in Tampa, FL, and click Search. A map of Tampa, FL, is displayed in the right frame. See Figure 14.9.

FIGURE 14.8
Communicator's Net Search site

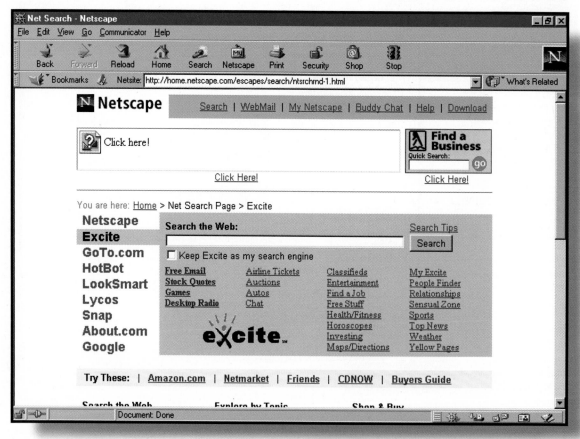

FIGURE 14.9
Results of search for map of Tampa, FL

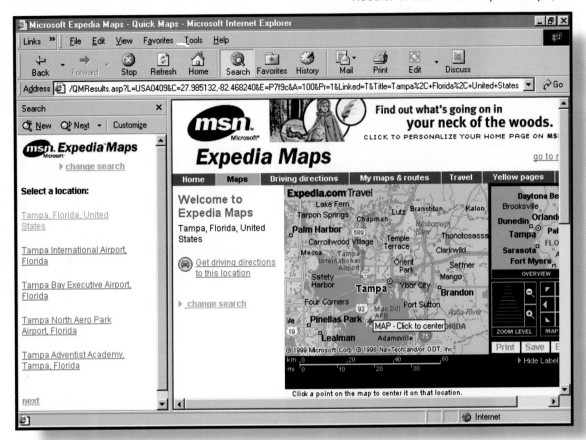

History

The Back and Forward buttons take you to sites you have visited in your current session. But what if you want to go back to that Web page you found last week and can't remember the URL? Then the History button is for you.

INTERNET EXPLORER

In Internet Explorer, the History bar opens in the left frame and displays a record of all the sites you have visited in the last 20 days. See Figure 14.10. The number of days (20) is the default. However, you can change the number of days through the Tools menu.

To make it easier to find the site you are searching for, you can sort the list in several ways:

- By date

- By site

- By most visited

- By order visited today

- You can also search the list for a keyword in a site name.

 **Hot Tip**

Another common error message you may receiving when surfing the Internet is "404—Not found." This indicates that the server hosting the site can't find the HTML document. This could mean several things: You may have mistyped the URL, the Web page doesn't exist anymore, or the Web page has moved. When this happens, try going up one level by deleting the last part of the URL to the nearest slash. This will give you an indication if the Web site still exists. If this doesn't work, you can try one more procedure. Delete the last slash and type .html or .htm.

223

FIGURE 14.10
Internet Explorer History Bar

To clear the History list, click Tools, point to Internet Options, select the General tab, and click the Clear History button.

COMMUNICATOR

To locate History in Communicator, on the File menu, click Communicator, point to Tools, and select History. In Communicator, you can search by title, location, first visited, last visited, and number of visits.

Favorites and Bookmarks

The Web has so much to offer that it's very likely you are going to find some sites you really like and wish to return to often. It's easy to keep these sites just a mouse click away by adding them to your Favorites (Internet Explorer) or Bookmark (Communicator) list.

To add a site to your list of sites:

- Go to the site you want to add.

- For Internet Explorer, on the Favorites menu, click Add to Favorites. For Communicator, click Bookmarks, and choose Add Bookmark.

- To revisit any of the Favorites or Bookmarks, just click the Favorites or Bookmarks button, and then select the shortcut to the site.

As your list begins to grow, you can organize it by creating folders. You can organize by topics in much the same way you would organize files in a file drawer.

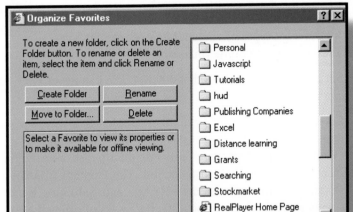

STEP-BY-STEP ⟹ 14.3

To create a folder in Internet Explorer:

1. On the Favorites menu, click Organize Favorites.

2. The Organize Favorites dialog box displays. See Figure 14.11.

3. Click Create Folder, type a name for the folder, and then press Enter.

FIGURE 14.11
Internet Explorer Organize Favorites

STEP-BY-STEP ⟹ 14.4

To create a folder in Communicator:

1. Click Bookmarks and choose Edit Bookmark to display the Bookmark page.

2. Click the item just above where you want to add a folder. See Figure 14.12.

3. On the File menu, choose New Folder.

4. Type a name for the folder and a description if you choose.

5. Click OK.

FIGURE 14.12
Communicator Organize Bookmarks

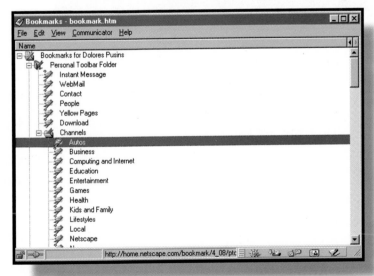

Controlling Access

The Content Advisor in Internet Explorer and NetWatch in Communicator provide some control over what content can be viewed on the Internet. With these two tools, you can:

- Control access to settings through a password.

- View and adjust the ratings settings to reflect what you think is appropriate content.

- Adjust what types of content other people can view with or without your permission.

- Set up a list of Web sites that other people can never view and a list of Web sites other people can always view.

- Set up a list of Web sites that other people can always view, regardless of how the sites' contents are rated.

Web site publishers voluntarily rate their pages. The Internet rating standard is known as PICS: Platform for Internet Content Selection. The Content Advisor and NetWatch use two independent PICS-compliant ratings systems—RSACi and SafeSurf. Each system uses a different method to describe in as much detail as possible the levels of offensive content on Web pages.

Internet

The University of Albany features several Internet tutorials, research guides, and links and hints on how to use Netscape Navigator and Communicator. You can find this Web site at www.albany.edu/library/internet/.

Cleanup Time

When you explore the Web, your browser keeps a record of the sites you visit. The pages are stored in temporary folders on your hard drive in your disk cache (pronounced cash). This process enables you to view the saved pages offline or without being connected to the Internet.

If you are surfing the Web and return to a cached Web page, that page will load faster because it is loading from cache. Sometimes this can be a problem because the page may have changed since you were last at the site. We discussed the Refresh and/or Reload buttons earlier in the module. Clicking the Refresh or Reload button will load the current page from the server. Another option is to change the "Checking for newer versions of stored pages" setting.

S TEP-BY-STEP ▷ 14.4

In Internet Explorer:

1. On the Menu Bar, click Tools, then Internet Options to display the Internet Options dialog box. See Figure 14.13.

2. Click the General tab.

3. Click the Settings button.

4. You have four options:

   - Every visit to the page

   - Every time you start Internet Explorer

   - Automatically

   - Never

5. Select the option best for you and your individual requirements. The first option can considerably slow down browsing time between pages. "Never" provides the fastest browsing time.

6. Click OK and then OK again to return to Internet Explorer.

FIGURE 14.13
Internet Options dialog box

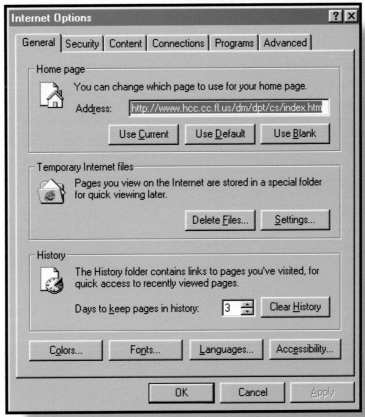

 ETHICS IN TECHNOLOGY

INTERNET SECURITY

If you've surfed the Internet recently, you know you can purchase just about any item you want—from a Mercedes Benz to Uncle Bill's Jam and Jellies. You can have the items shipped to you and pay for it when it arrives or you can use a credit card. The question is how safe you feel about transmitting credit card and other financial information over the Internet.

When you provide your credit card number, it travels through several computers before it reaches its final destination. To ensure that your credit card number is not easily stolen, companies use a technology called encryption. This encryption software acts similarly to the cable converter box on your television. The data is scrambled with a secret code so no one can interpret it while it is being transmitted. When the data reaches its destination, the same software unscrambles the information.

Not all Web sites use security measures. One way to identify a secure site is to check the status bar at the bottom of your Web browser. There you will see a small icon—usually a lock. When the lock is closed, it indicates the site is using security technology.

In Communicator:

1. On the Menu Bar, click **Edit** and then click **Preferences**. This displays the Preferences dialog box. See Figure 14.14.

2. Open the Advanced **category** and then click **Cache**.

3. You have three options:

   ■ Once per session

   ■ Every time

   ■ Never

4. Select the option best for you and your individual requirements. "Every time" is the slowest and "Never" is the fastest. Keep in mind, however, that with Never, the page may be out of date. Even so, you can click the Reload button to access the latest version.

5. Click **OK** to return to Communicator.

FIGURE 14.14
Preferences dialog box

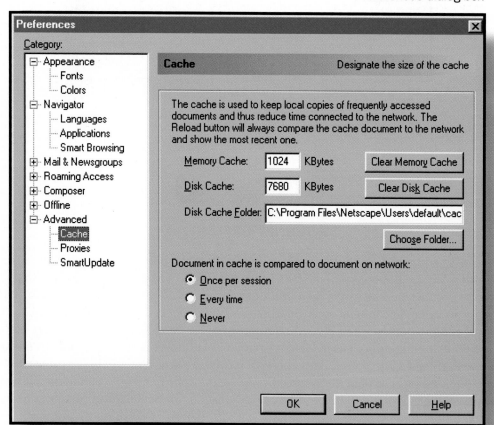

FIGURE 14.15
Settings dialog box

As you browse the Internet, your disk cache can fill up. When this happens, pages do not load as quickly. You can speed things up by cleaning the cache. When you do this, you delete all of the Web pages stored in cache.

■ To empty the cache in Internet Explorer, on the Tools menu, click **Internet Options**. Click the **General** tab. In the Temporary Internet Files area, click **Delete Files** and then click **OK**.

■ To empty the cache in Communicator, on the Menu Bar, click **Edit** and then click **Preferences**. Click **Advanced** and then **Cache**. Click the **Clear Memory Cache** button and then click **OK**.

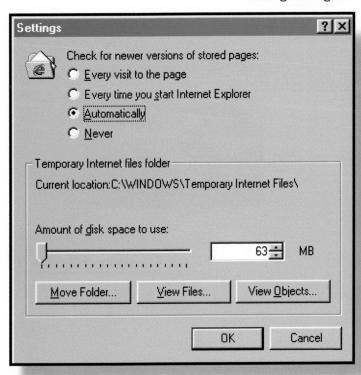

You just learned that deleting the files in cache could speed up your browsing. However, what if you don't want to delete these files? There is also another way you can increase browsing speed. You may have noticed in Figures 14.13 and 14.14 the option for increasing the amount of disk space. If you have a large hard drive with plenty of extra space, you may prefer to increase the amount of cache disk space. This will also increase your browsing speed. See Figure 14.15.

Copy and Save Text, Web Pages, and Images

As you view pages on the Web, you'll find a lot of things you'd like to save so that you can refer to them later. You can use both Internet Explorer and Communicator to save a complete Web page or any part of a web page. This includes text, images, or hyperlinks.

Using Communicator

To copy and save text:

■ Use your mouse to select the text.

■ On the Edit menu, select **Copy**.

■ Paste the text into a Word document or other file.

To copy and save a hyperlink (URL) from a Web page:

■ Use your mouse and right-click the link to display the pop-up menu.

FIGURE 14.16
Communicator with pop-up menu

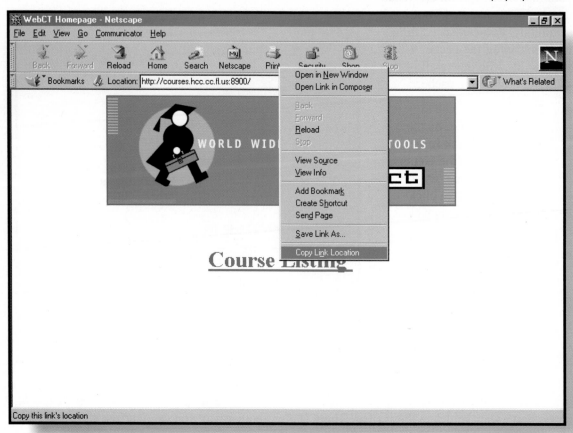

- From the pop-up menu, select **Copy Link Location** to copy the link's URL into the computer's memory. See Figure 14.16.

- Paste the link into another document or into the browser's location bar.

  To save an entire Web page:

- On the File menu, click **Save As** to display the Save As dialog box.

- Select the folder into which you want to save the Web page.

- Type a name for the Web page.

- Click Save.

  When you use Communicator to save a Web page, the images are not saved with the page. You must save each image separately.

  To save an image:

- Right-click the image to display a pop-up menu.

- Select **Save Image As** to display the Save As dialog box.

- Select the folder into which you want to save the image.

- Type the name for the image.

- Click Save.

230

Using Internet Explorer

To copy and save text:

- Use your mouse to select the text.

- On the Edit menu, select **Copy**.

- Paste the text into a Word document or other file.

    To copy and save a hyperlink (URL) from a Web page:

- Use your mouse and right-click the link to display the pop-up menu.

- From the pop-up menu, select **Save Target As** to copy the link's URL into the computer's memory.

- Paste the link into another document or into the browser's address bar.

    To save an entire Web page:

- On the File menu, click **Save As** to display the Save Web Page dialog box.

- Select the folder into which you want to save the image.

- In the File name box, type a name for the page.

- In the Save as type box, select **Web Page, complete**. This option saves all of the files needed to display this page in its original format. This includes images and any other Web page elements.

TECHNOLOGY CAREERS

PREPARING FOR THE JOB INTERVIEW

You have made it to the first step in the process of getting that new career opportunity. You have that first interview. So how do you prepare?

You can never be sure what questions your potential employer might ask. You can, however, prepare for some of the more obvious questions. These might include the following:

- Are you generally on time?

- How do you work under pressure?

- What are your plans five years from now?

- Do you plan to go to college?

- Tell me about some of the things you are learning in school.

Most people are nervous when being interviewed. There is no way that you are going to totally eliminate being nervous, but prepare with a positive attitude. Try to imagine what the interview might be like and rehearse in your mind. Or, better yet, find a classmate to play the role of the potential interviewer.

To save an image:

- Right-click the image to display a pop-up menu.

- Select **Save Picture As** to display the Save Picture dialog box.

- Select the folder into which you want to save the image.

- Type the name for the image.

- Click Save.

  If you need a printed copy of a Web page; just click the **Print** button.

Download and Install a Program

As you browse the Internet, you will eventually come across a program you want to *download*. To download means to transfer from the Web server to your computer. The program could be a plug-in or enhancement for your browser, a utility program to help you better manage your computer system, a shareware game, and so forth.

To download a program:

STEP-BY-STEP ▷ 14.6

1. Create a separate folder on your hard drive for your downloaded programs.

2. Go to the Web site where the program is located.

3. Follow the site's particular download instructions. This will vary from site to site, but most sites have some type of Download Now button. Click that button. The File Download dialog box appears. See Figure 14.17.

FIGURE 14.17
File Download dialog box

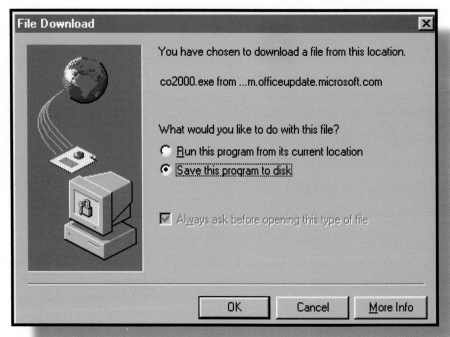

4. Click the option button to the left of Save this program to disk.

5. Click **OK** to display the Save As dialog box.

6. Select the directory on your computer where you want to store the downloaded program. See Figure 14.18.

7. Click **Save** to start the downloading process.

FIGURE 14.18
Save as dialog box

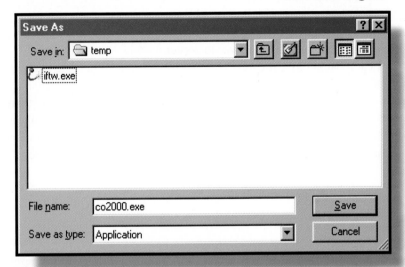

8. A downloading box displays; estimated download time and transfer rate are displayed. Now you wait while the download takes place. When the download is completed, click OK. See Figure 14.19.

9. Next, you need to install the program.

10. Using Windows Explorer, locate the file you downloaded and double-click the file name. Follow the installation instructions as provided by the program.

FIGURE 14.19
Downloading box

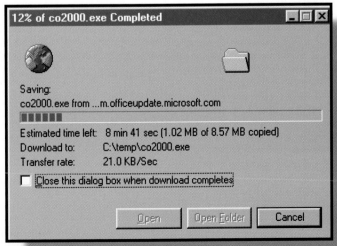

E-Mail

E-mail, or *electronic mail,* is one of the most popular services on the Internet. You can use e-mail to stay in touch with your family and friends, conduct business, and send attachments such as text and image files. You can even check your e-mail when you're on vacation or a business trip.

E-mail is not that different from regular mail. Actually, it's very similar. You have a message, an address, and a carrier that figures out to get it from one location to another. Most of the time, e-mail travels much faster than regular mail (sometimes referred to as "snail mail"). When you send someone an e-mail message, it is broken down into small chunks called packets. These packets travel independently from server to server.

 Did You Know?

You can use a Web page image as desktop wallpaper. Just right-click the image on the Web page, and then click **Set as Wallpaper**.

You might think of each packet as a separate page within a letter. When the packets reach their final destination, they are recombined into their original format. This process enables the message to travel much faster. In fact, some messages can travel thousands of miles in less than a minute.

Both Internet Explorer and Communicator come with a built-in e-mail program. Outlook Express is the name of Internet Explorer's program. See Figure 14.20. Communicator's e-mail program is called Messenger. See Figure 14.21. Both programs have similar features.

FIGURE 14.20
Outlook Express

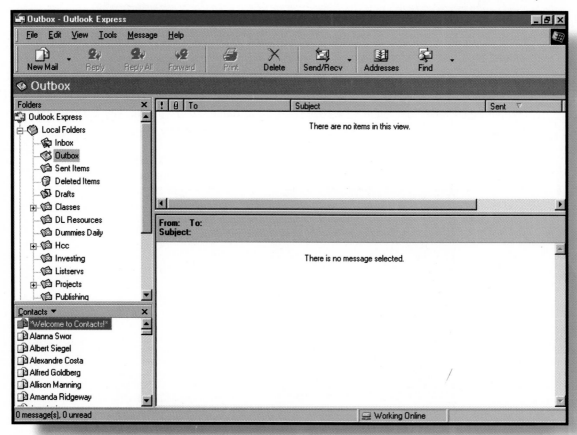

FIGURE 14.21
Messenger

Sending and Receiving Messages

The main purpose of e-mail, of course, is to send and receive e-mail messages. You can send a message to one person or to several people. You can send copies of messages and even apply stationery as a background for your message. You can send copies of files as attachments.

S TEP-BY-STEP ▷ 14.7

This example uses Outlook Express:

1. On the toolbar, click the **New Mail** button.

2. In the *To* box, type the e-mail name of the recipient. If there is more than one recipient, separate each name with a comma or semicolon. To add e-mail names from the address book, click the book icon in the New Message window next to *To* or *Cc*.

3. In the Subject box, type a subject for your message.

4. Type your message.

5. Click the **Send** button. If you are connected to the Internet, the message is sent automatically. Otherwise, it is stored in the Outbox until you connect.

You can even apply stationery to your e-mail message. Use one of the stationery selections that comes with Outlook Express or use your own design. See Figure 14.22.

FIGURE 14.22
E-mail message with stationery

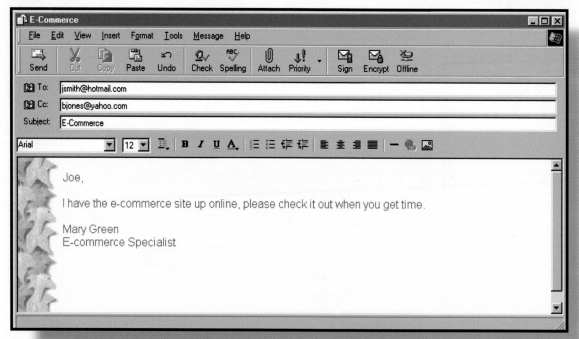

Address Book

Use the *address book* to keep a list of your contacts. There are several ways in which you can add a contact to your address book:

■ Type the name and other information.

■ Add names automatically from e-mail messages.

■ Import an address book from another program.

■ Find people and businesses on the Internet.

■ Important a vCard (virtual business card) that you receive as part of an e-mail message.

E-Mail Organization

When you receive an e-mail message, it is automatically placed in the Inbox. You can, however, create other folders or subfolders within existing folders. You can create folders for topics, for people, for businesses, and so forth.

To create folders:

S TEP-BY-STEP ▷ 14.8

1. On the File menu, point to **Folders** and click **New Folder** to display the Create New Folder dialog box.

2. In the **Name** box, type a name for your new folder.

3. Select the location for the new folder. See Figure 14.23.

4. Click **OK** to create your folder.

Groups

Do you have a list of people to whom you frequently send the same e-mail messages? If so, make your life easier by creating Groups. Then all you have to do is type the Group name in the To box.

To create a group:

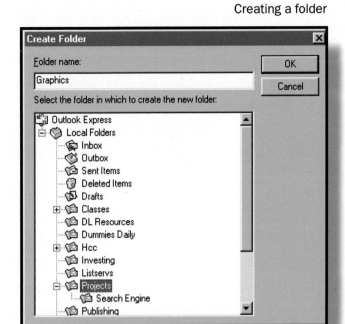

FIGURE 14.23
Creating a folder

S TEP-BY-STEP ▷ 14.9

1. Click the **Addresses** button to display the Address Book.

2. In the Address Book, click **New** and select **New Group** to display the Properties dialog box.

3. In the Group Name box, type the name of the group.

4. Select the names of the Group members. See Figure 14.24.

5. Click **OK** to save your new group.

FIGURE 14.24
Creating a Group

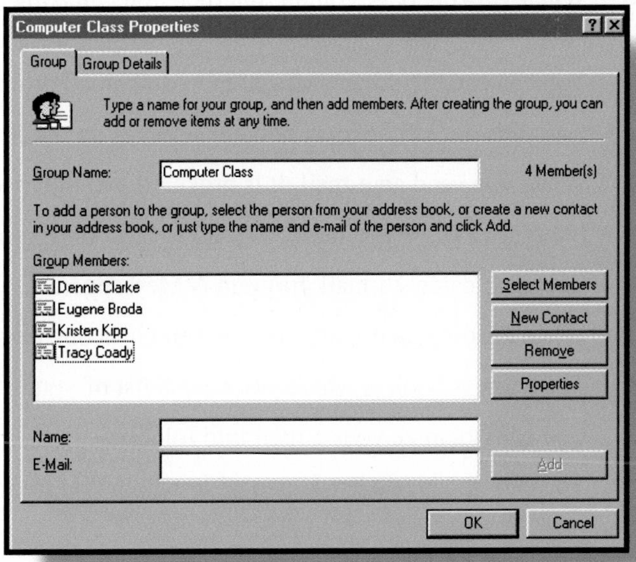

Summary

- A browser is a software program you use to retrieve documents from the WWW.

- The two most popular browsers are Microsoft's Internet Explorer and Netscape's Communicator.

- Your home page is the first page that's displayed when you launch your browser.

- Internet Explorer's address bar and Communicator's location bar are located near the top of the browser window.

- The address of a Web site is called the Universal Resource Locator.

- Both Internet Explorer and Communicator contain automated features related to the address or location bar.

- The row of buttons at the top of the browser is the toolbar.

- AutoSearch and Internet Keywords are a special search feature to help you locate the appropriate Web site quickly.

- Both Communicator and Internet Explorer contain Search buttons and offer search assistance.

- The History features keeps tracks of sites you have visited previously.

- For sites you will return to often, you can add them to your Favorites and Bookmarks.

- You can organize your e-mail into folders.

- The Content Advisor and NetWatch provide some control over what content can be viewed on the Internet.

- A record of Web sites you have visited is stored in cache.

- Clicking the Refresh or Reload button loads the current page from the server.

- You can increase the amount of your cache disk space.

- When viewing pages on the Internet, you can copy and save text, hyperlinks, images, and entire Web pages.

- You can use the download option to download programs.

- E-mail is one of the most popular services on the Internet.

- When you send an e-mail, it is broken down into packets.

- Internet Explorer's e-mail program is Outlook Express.

- Communicator's e-mail program is Messenger.

- When sending an e-mail, you can send it to one person or several people at one time.

- The address book is where you keep a list of your e-mail contacts.

- You can organize your e-mail into folders.

- You can organize a list of people to whom you frequently send e-mail into a group.

LESSON 14 REVIEW QUESTIONS

MULTIPLE CHOICE

1. A software program used to retrieve documents from the WWW is called a

   _____.
   A. packet
   B. home page
   C. browser
   D. Web server

2. A URL is _____.
   A. the Web site address
   B. same as the location bar
   C. same as the address bar
   D. toolbar

3. To display a record of sites you have previously visited, use the _____
   feature.
   A. bookmark
   B. favorites
   C. URL
   D. history

4. To save an image from a Web page document to your computer, _____.
   A. move the mouse pointer over the image and left-click.
   B. move the mouse pointer over the image and right-click.
   C. double-click the image
   D. select the image

5. When e-mail messages are sent over the Internet, they are broken down into

   _____.
   A. pieces
   B. packets
   C. messages
   D. contacts

TRUE/FALSE

Circle the T if the statement is true. Circle F if it is false.

T F 1. The home page is the first page that's displayed when you launch your browser.

T F 2. Use Internet keywords to locate information quickly.

T F 3. The Favorites list and History list are identical features.

T F 4. There is no way in which you can control the content that someone can display.

T F 5. You can view saved pages offline.

SHORT ANSWER

1. In e-mail, use the _____ to keep a list of contacts.

2. A virtual business card is also known as a _____.

3. You can apply _____ as a background for your e-mail messages.

4. When using the browser, click _____ or _____ to view the latest version of a Web page.

5. The language used to create documents on the WWW is called _____.

CROSS-CURRICULAR PROJECTS

MATH

If you have gone shopping with your parents or a friend to buy carpet or other floor coverings, you know that first you must determine how large the area it be covered is. To discover a simple and easy way to do this, visit the Smile Web site located at www.iit.edu/~smile/ma9706.html. Complete the exercise at this site, and then sit back and congratulate yourself on a job well done.

SCIENCE/MATH/LANGUAGE ARTS

The World Weather Watch is an interactive cross-curricular Internet project. To participate in the project, you collect weather data once a week for a specified time period. Your class can register to participate in the project or you can just post your data and use it for comparison discussions. The Web site is located at http://youth.net/weather/welcome.html.

SOCIAL STUDIES/LANGUAGE ARTS

Visit Friends of the Desert located at www.eduplace.com/ss/act/unity.html. This activity provides instructions on how you and your fellow classmates can hold a conference. Through the conference, you learn how cooperation might solve a problem that affects Africa. A list of what you need and procedures on what to do are listed at this Web site.

LANGUAGE ARTS/MATH

Access Microsoft's Encarta Learning zone at learn.msn.com/default.asp. Click the Homework Help resources link. Click one of the links that is related to one of your classes. Prepare a report on what you learned and how this link helped you. Present this to the class.

240

WEB PROJECT

At the Web site of Sierra Multimedia Productions, located at www.sierramm.com/smpnet.html, you will find a free Windows-based presentation called Interactive Guide to the Internet. Information at the Web site indicates that "This minicourse on how to use the Internet runs on the user's desktop as a stand-alone application and is aimed at beginners." Launch your browser and locate this Web site. Download this presentation and install it on your computer.

TEAM PROJECT

Ms. Perez would like for all Vista multimedia employees to have e-mail accounts. She has discovered several online sites where one can establish a free e-mail account. The URLs for some of these are as follows:

www.hotmail.com
www.usa.net
www.yahoo.com
www.myownemail.com

Ms. Perez would like for you and two of your fellow employees to investigate the Web sites listed here and any other free e-mail sites you can locate. She would then like for you to prepare a report on which e-mail program is the best and why it is the best.

HOW DO I DO RESEARCH ON THE INTERNET?

LESSON

15

OBJECTIVES

When you complete this module, you will be able to:

- List some reasons for searching the Internet .

- Describe different search approaches.

- Define a search engine.

- Explain how search engines work.

- Describe how search engines search.

- Identify some of the more popular search engines.

- List some of the specialty search engines.

- Describe the subject directory search approach.

- Describe some search tips and tricks.

⏱ Estimated Time: 1.5 hours

VOCABULARY

Boolean logic
Hits
Hyperlinks
Keywords
Math symbols
Related search
Search engine
Spider
Subject directories
Wildcard character

Ms. Perez needs some information for a report she is preparing for Vista Multimedia. She has already spent countless hours at the library and has searched through several reference books. However, she has not been able to locate some of the facts she needs for her proposal. You suggest to her that she may be able to find everything she needs on the Internet.

The Internet contains a wealth of information. In fact, you can find information on just about any topic you can imagine. The problem is that the Internet contains so much information, it can be difficult to locate just what you need. You suggest to Ms. Perez that certain techniques will help her locate information. If she masters some of these skills, she will probably be more successful in finding what she needs.

The Key to a Successful Search

We live in the information age, and information continues to grow at an ever-spiraling rate. To conduct an effective online search on a particular topic can be a real challenge. One can easily be overwhelmed by the overabundance of raw data. With the right tools, however, the task becomes easier. One key to a successful Internet search is an understanding of the many tools available. Certain tools are more suitable for some purposes than others.

When searching online, there are two basic tools that you can use for finding information: search engines and subject directories. You use a search engine to search for keywords. You use a directory to find specialized topics. The primary difference between these two search tools is that people assemble directories and search engines are automated. Search engines are discussed in the first part of this module, and an overview of directories is contained in the second part.

Why Search the Internet?

Y̲ou might ask yourself, "Why would I want to search the Internet? What's out there that can help me?" Reasons why people search the Internet are many. The following are just a few examples:

■ You need to do some research for that paper due in your science class next week.

■ Your grandfather is losing his hearing and has asked you to help him find some information on hearing aids.

■ Your next-door neighbor is an attorney and needs some information for a court case.

■ You plan to take a trip to Mexico this summer and would like to get information on some of the best places to stay.

As you can see from these illustrations, there can be hundreds of reasons why you might want to conduct an Internet search. See Figure 15.1.

FIGURE 15.1
Searching the Internet

 Did You Know?

No single Web tool indexes or organizes the whole Web. When using an online search tool, you are searching and viewing data extracted from the Web. This data has been placed into the search engine's database. It is the database that is searched—not the Web itself. This is one of the reasons why you get different results when you use different search engines.

Introducing Search Engines

A *search engine* is a software program. There are hundreds of search engines throughout the Internet. Each search engine may work a little differently, but most of them have some common search features. For example, all search engines support keyword searches. Although keyword searches may not be the most effective way to search, this is the search method most individuals use.

 Did You Know?

If you're using Web sources for your research paper, you need to give credit for the sources. You can find information on citing Internet sources at www.lib.berkeley.edu/Teaching Lib/Guides/Internet/MLAStyleSh eet.html.

Some search engines support an additional enhancement called concept-based searching. The search engine tries to determine what you mean and returns *hits* on Web sites that relate to the keywords. Hits are the number of returns or Web sites based on your keywords. If you search for "video games," the search engine may also return hits on sites that contain Nintendo and Playstation. One of the best known search engines using concept-based searching is Excite. Its search engine uses ICE (intelligent concept extraction) to learn about word relationships.

Another feature supported by some search engines is stemming. When you search for a word, the search engine also includes the "stem" of the word. For example, you enter the search word "play," and you may also get back results for plays, playing, and player.

Keyword Searches

Keyword searches let you search for keywords within a Web document. The Web page author can specify these keywords using meta tags within the Web page document. Meta tags are special tags embedded within the Web page document. They do not affect how the page displays. Many search engines use these tags to create the index. For example, if your Web site is about Nintendo 64, your Meta tag may look something like this:

<meta name="keywords" content="Nintendo 64, Mario, James Bond, Donkey Kong">

ETHICS IN TECHNOLOGY

SPAMMING

You may have heard of spam. No—it's not the luncheon meat that comes in a can. We're talking about Internet spam. Internet spam has several definitions. It is defined as electronic junk mail or junk newsgroup postings, or even unsolicited e-mail. This unsolicited e-mail is most likely some type of advertising or get-rich scheme, similar to the junk mail you or your family receive almost every day. With traditional junk mail, however, the people who send the mail pay a fee to distribute their materials.

Spam, in contrast, is similar to receiving a postage-due letter. Even though you don't pay the postage as it arrives in your electronic mailbox, you are still paying for it indirectly. The charges are in the form of disk space, connect time, or even long-distance Net connections.

Spam is not illegal yet, but several groups are trying to stop it. Several states are attempting to pass laws banning the sending of unsolicited e-mail. If you would like more information about spam and what is happening, you can find it on the Internet. One site is located at spam.abuse.net/ and a second Web site with links to several other antispam sites is located at spam.abuse.net/others/sites.html.

What if the Web page author doesn't specify meta tags? Then the search engine evaluates the document and indexes "significant" words. Depending on the search engine, significant words may be those words mentioned at the beginning of a document or words that are repeated several times throughout the document.

To search using keywords, the process is as follows:

■ You launch your Web browser and go to a search engine Web site.

■ You submit an online form to the search engine. This form contains your *keywords*. These key-words describe the information you are trying to locate.

■ The search engine matches as many keywords as possible by searching its own database. A database is a collection of organized information.

■ The search engine then returns a *hyperlink* list of Web site addresses where the keywords are found. You click the hyperlinks to view the Web sites.

■ If you are unable to find the information for which you are searching within these hyperlinked sites, you can revise your keywords and submit a new request.

Your question may then be, "How does a search engine find all of those links or how does it work?" You can even use the Internet to answer that question. In this instance, let's use the words *search engine* as the keywords. One popular search engine is AskJeeves. This search engine uses a natural language software feature. You ask your question in plain English. Jeeves compares your question to its database of questions and answers.

STEP-BY-STEP ▷ 15.1

1. Launch your browser and type the URL www.AskJeeves.com.

2. Type your question *How does a search*

engine work? and click the **Ask** button. See Figure 15.2.

(continued on next page)

FIGURE 15.2
Asking AskJeeves a question

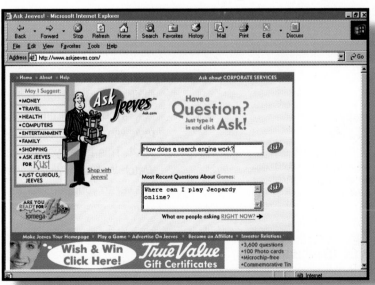

3. Within a few seconds AskJeeves responds to your question based on its internal knowledge base of millions of questions. See Figure 15.3. The screen is divided into two frames. AskJeeves provide links from its own database in the top frame and provides additional Web resources in the bottom frame. You can click on any of the links to go immediately to that page.

FIGURE 15.3
AskJeeves response to the question

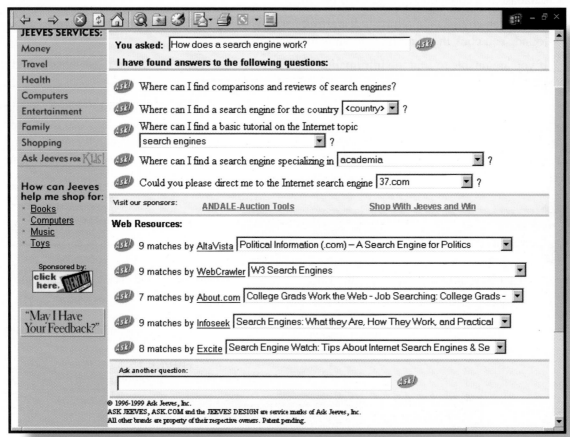

4. Click the **Ask** button to the left of the first link "Where can I find comparisons and reviews of search engines?" See Figure 15.4. This takes you to the Search Engine Watch Web site, where you can find the answer to your question.

Internet

Meta search engines sends your search simultaneously to several individual search engines and their databases of Web pages. Find out about meta search engines, how they work, and their limitations at www.lib.berkeley.edu/TeachingLib/Guides/Internet/MetaSearch.html.

FIGURE 15.4
Search Engine Watch Web site

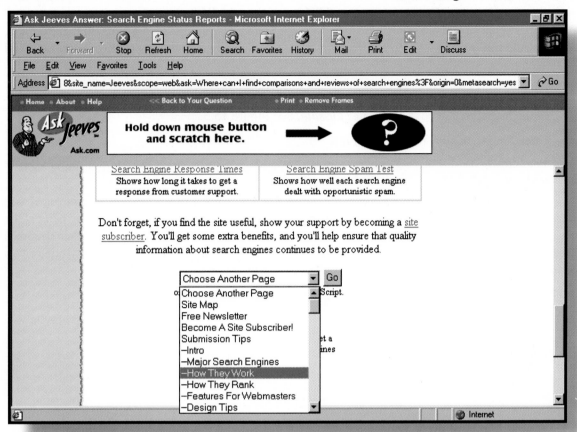

So what is the answer the question "How does a search engine find all of those Web sites?" To answer the question requires an overview of the search engine's three main parts:

■ The search engine program or software itself is the main component. This program searches through the millions of records stored in its database.

■ The second part is a *spider*, or crawler. The spider is a search engine robot that searches the Internet for the keywords. It feeds the pages it finds to the search engine. It is called a spider because it crawls the Web continually, examining Web sites and finding and looking for links. Every month or so, it may return to a previous Web site to look for changes.

■ The third part of the search engine is the index or indexer. When the spider finds a page, it submits it to the index. Once a Web page is indexed, it then becomes available to anyone using that search engine.

■ Some search engines claim to index all words, even the articles "a," "an," and "the." Other search engines index all words, except articles and stop words such as "www," "but," "or," "nor," "for," "so," or "yet." Some of the search engines index all words without reference to capitalization. Other engines differentiate uppercase from lowercase.

 Did You Know?

Some search engines such as AltaVista can translate your search results into another language.

When you use a keyword search, you may find that the number of hits you receive are in the thousands or even millions. Recall that hits are the number of returns on your keywords. Each hit is linked to the **Universal Resource Locator** (URL), which is the Web site address.

Let's suppose you are going to use the Internet to purchase some video games. In this example, you execute the search on video games using Infoseek, one of the Internet's more popular keyword search engines.

■ Launch your browser and type the URL www.infoseek.com.

■ In the Search box type *video games for sale*. See Figure 15.5.

■ Click Find to display the results of hits.

■ The hits are displayed—42,434,007 matches. There is also a short paragraph describing each URL. See Figure 15.6.

As you can see from this example, the number of hits is a bit overwhelming. However, if you examine the page a little more closely you will discover that each hit has a relevant percentage assigned, beginning with 100%. As you move down the list of hits, the relevant number becomes less. This indicates that the site does not contain all of the search words or contains only one or two instances of the keywords. At this point, you have several options:

■ You can click on any of the links and review the information at that site.

■ You can redefine your keywords.

■ You can use another search engine.

FIGURE 15.5
Searching for Video Games for Sale

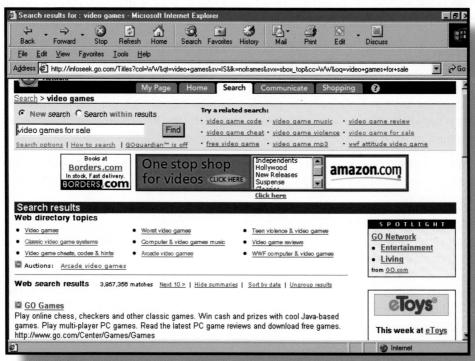

FIGURE 15.6
InfoSeek Video Games Hits

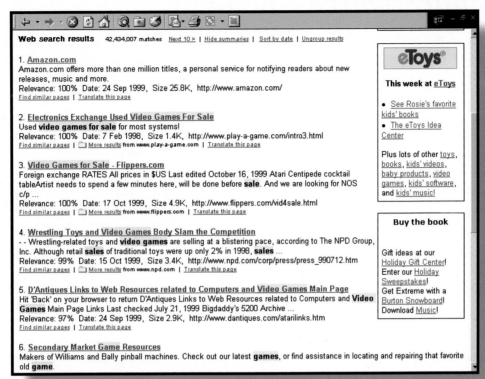

Many times option 3 is your best choice. It is impossible for any one search engine to index every page on the Web. Also each search engine has its own personal algorithm that it uses to index Web sites. An algorithm is a formula or set of steps for solving a particular problem. Therefore, using a different engine may provide a totally different list of hits. There are many popular search engine sites, and you may need to try several before you find the information you are seeking. See Table 15.1 for a list of some of the search engines.

TABLE 15.1

SOME POPULAR GENERAL SEARCH ENGINES

Search Engine Name	Description	Case Sensitive
Northern Light at www.northernlight.com	250 million pages plus; also articles from journals and business news sources	Ignores uppercase
Fast Search at www.alltheweb.com	Large and fast search engine; excellent ranking of Web sites	No
Alta Vista at www.altavista.com	General database; supports advanced searches	Yes
Google at www.google.com	General database; excellent ranking of Web sites	No

Specialty Search Engines

So far in this module, we've looked at general ***search engines***. However, there are many specialized search engines on the Internet. These search engines are sometimes called category-oriented search tools. They generally focus on a particular topic. If you know you are looking for information in a particular format, your best bet is to search a site that specializes in indexing and retrieving that information. Here are some examples:

- You're looking up a former classmate or a long-lost cousin; try the Switchboard Web site at www.switchboard.com or Yahoo's people search at people.yahoo.com.

- You want to download a shareware game called Renegade Racers; try the Shareware Web site at www.shareware.com.

- You want to do a little online jewelry shopping; try Catalog City at www.catalogcity.com or Bottom Dollar at www.bottomdollar.com.

- Perhaps you're a sports fan and want to find out about the latest happenings in the wrestling word; try Sports Search at www.sportsearch.com.

- Are you thinking about your future and what careers options you may have? Try CareerPath at www.careerpath.com to find a database of over 250,000 jobs.

> **Hot Tip**
>
> Some search engines automatically include plurals; others do not. To be on the safe side, include the plural. For example, if you're searching for squirrels, use keywords such as *squirrel* or *squirrels*.

FIGURE 15.7
Beaucomp Web site

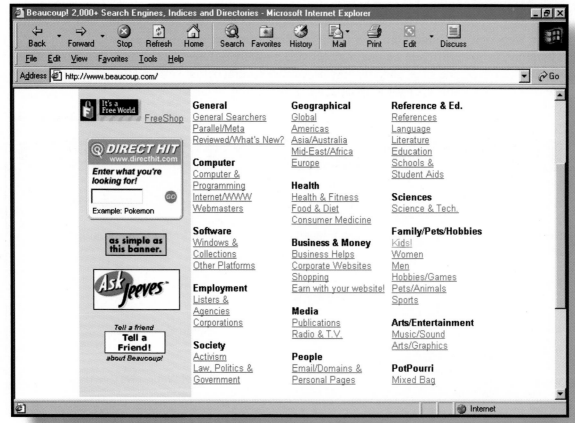

250

These are just a few examples of the many hundreds of specialty Web sites. If you are looking for a particular information source, but not sure where to look, try the Beaucoup Web site at www.beaucoup.com. This site contains links to more than 3,000 specialty search engines. See Figure 15.7. For a super search, you can also enter keywords at this site and search 10 different search engines at one time.

Another Web site similar to Beaucomp is the All-In-One-Search-Page. This site, located at www.allone-search.com, boasts "Over 500 of the Internet's best search engines, databases, indexes, and directories in a single site."

Multimedia Search Engines

Are you interested in finding graphics, video clips, animation, and even MP3 music files? Then a multimedia search engine is probably the best way to go. For music and MP3, you might want to try the Lycos search engine at mp3.lycos.com/, www.savvysearch.com/, or www.audiofind.com. MP3 is a file format that allows audio compression at near-CD quality. See Figure 15.8.

Corbis at www.corbis.com/ boasts of "The world's largest collection of fine art and photography." AltaVista at www.altavista.com has a special tab for images, audio, and video. Or try the Ditto, the visual search engine, at www.ditto.com to search for pictures, photographs, and artwork.

> **Internet**
>
> For education purposes, one of the best subject guides is the WWW Virtual Library. The VL is the oldest subject directory on the Web. This site is considered to have the highest quality guides to particular sections of the Internet. You can find the Virtual Library at www. vlib.org/.

FIGURE 15.8
AudioFind Web site

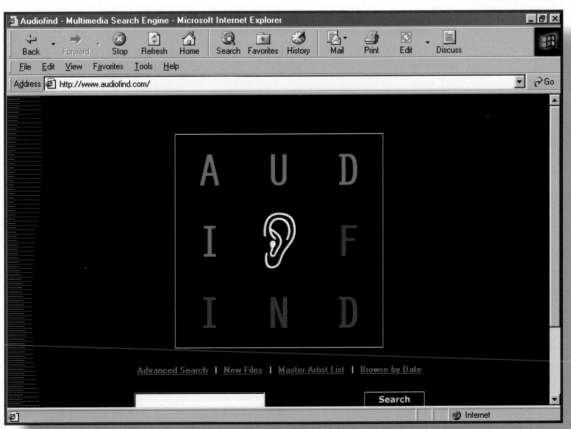

TABLE 15.2

SOME POPULAR SPECIALTY SEARCH ENGINES

Maps and Travel Information	People and Companies	Companies and Careers	World Data
Microsoft's www.expedia.com	People finder at www.peoplesite.com/ indexstart.html	Occupational Outlook Handbook at www.stats. bls.gov/ocohome.htm	World Health Organization at www.who.int/
MapQuest at www.mapquest.com	Yellow Pages Search Power at www.yellow.com/	America's Job Bank at www.ajb.dni.us/	CIA World Factbook at www.odci.gov/cia/publica-tions/factbook/
World Wide Rooms Online at www.irsus.com/ rooms.htm	Toll free numbers at 206.129.166.101/ 800.html	Monster Job bank at www.monster.com	World Bank at www. worldbank.org/
Great Outdoors at www.gorp.com/	Canada Yellow Pages at www.canadayellow-pages.com/	Career Resource Center at www.careers.org/	World Data Center at www.ngdc.noaa.gov/ wdc/wdcmain.html

Meta-Search Engines

Have you searched and searched for the right information—going from search engine to search engine? If so, then you might want to try a meta-search engine. This type of search engine searches several major engines at one time. They do not have their own database. Instead, they act as a middle person. They send the query to major search engines and then return the results or hits. Meta-search engines generally work best with simple searches. Two popular meta-search engines are Dogpile at www.dogpile.com and MetaCrawler at www.metacrawler.com.

TECHNOLOGY CAREERS

PROGRAMMER

A programmer is, of course, a person who writes computer programs. Software is another word for programs. A program is a list of instructions that tells the computer what to do. Without programs or software, computers are useless.

There are many programming languages – probably a hundred or more. Some of the more popular programming languages are Fortran, COBOL, C, C++, Visual Basic, and Java. Many times programmers do not create code from "scratch." Their job is to maintain or update existing code.

Another type of programmer is an applications programmer. This programmer works mostly with database or Internet applications.

Job demand is very high for programmers, with some entry-level positions starting at as much as $50 per hour.

Education requirements run from high school to two-year college degrees to bachelor's or master's degrees. This variation in education depends on the company and requirements of the job.

Subject Directory Searching

Earlier in this module we indicated that the primary difference between a search engine and a directory is that people assemble directories. Subject experts carefully check the Web sites to make sure they meet a particular set of standards. Then the URL for the Web site is added to the database.

Most *subject directories* are organized by subject categories, with a collection of links to Internet resources. These resources are arranged by subject and then displayed in a series of menus. To access a particular topic, you start from the top and "drill down" through the different levels—going from the general to the specific. This is similar to a traditional card catalog or the telephone yellow pages.

Let's say that your art teacher has asked you to prepare a report on ancient Greek sculpture. You can use a search engine and keywords to try to locate information, or you can use a subject directory search tool. One of the better educational directory Web sites is the Encyclopedia Britannica, located at www.britannica.com/bcom/. See Figure 15.9.

Hot Tip

Have you been given a research assignment, but had trouble coming up with a topic? Check out vweb.sau.edu/ bestinfo/ for a list of "hot paper topics."

FIGURE 15.9
Britannica Web site

1. Launch your Web browser and type the URL www.britannica.com/bcom/. This takes you to the Britannica Web site. Notice that the subject directories are listed on the left side of the page.

2. Move the mouse point over "Arts" to display a cascading menu. Click "The Web's Best sites . . ." This drills down one level. See Figure 15.10.

FIGURE 15.10
Britannica Web site – first level

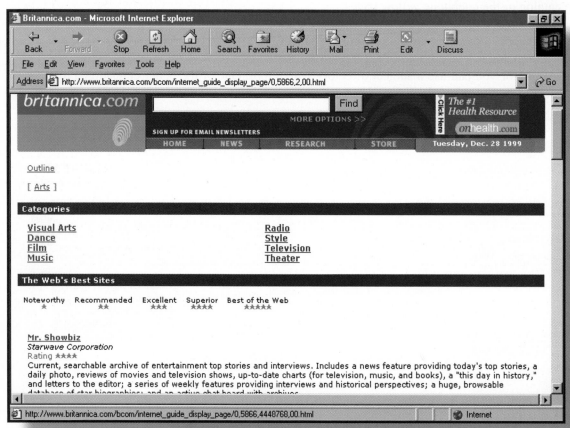

3. Now displayed is a list of art categories. Below the list of categories is a list of topics and links to general art Web sites. Notice that each of these is rated—from one to five stars. See Figure 15.11. Remember that you are looking for sculpture information, so click "Visual Arts."

4. Notice that at this third level the category list is quite extensive and it all relates to visual arts. Notice also that "Sculpture" is listed. See Figure 15.12. Click "Sculpture."

(continued on next page)

STEP-BY-STEP 15.2 CONTINUED

FIGURE 15.11
Britannica Web site – second level

FIGURE 15.12
Britannica Web site – third level

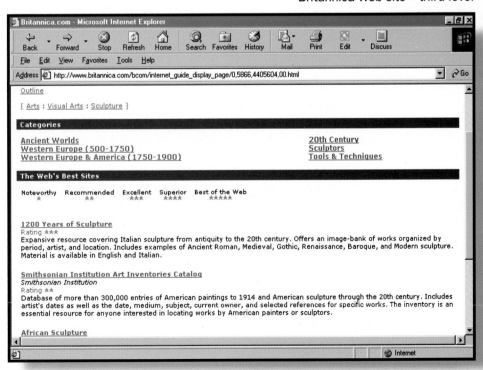

5. You have moved down to the fourth level where all of the categories relate to sculpture. The first category on the list is Ancient Worlds—click that category to move down to the fifth level.

6. At the fifth level, you find that Greece is one of your category selections. Click "Greece" to move to the sixth level.

7. You've finally reached your goal. At this level are a dozen or more links that will take you directly to Web sites devoted to Greek sculpture. See Figure 15.13. Just think how much you are going to impress your teacher!

FIGURE 15.13
Britannica Web site – sixth level

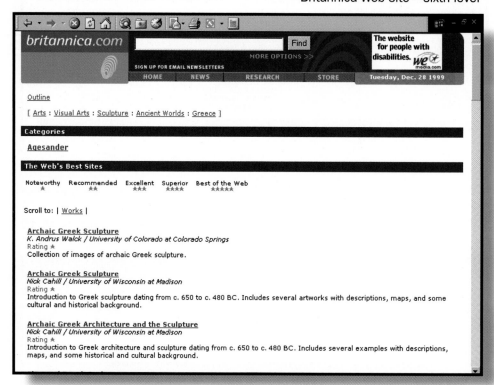

As you can see from this step-by-step exercise, drilling down through a subject directory is a more guided approach than entering keywords into a search engine. Additional benefits of directories are as follows:

■ They are easy to use.

■ You're not searching the entire Web.

■ The Web sites have been handpicked and evaluated.

■ Most links include some type of description.

■ They produce better quality hits on searches for common items.
See Table 15.3 for a list of some other popular subject directories.

256

TABLE 15.3

How Do I Do Research on the Internet? Lesson 15

SOME POPULAR SUBJECT DIRECTORIES		
Directory Name	**Description**	**Phrase Searching**
The Librarian's Index at www.lii.org	High quality; compiled by public librarians	No
Yahoo at www.yahoo.com	Biggest and most famous subject director	Yes—use " "
Galaxy at www.galaxy.com	Good annotations; good quality	No

Tools and Techniques for Searching the Web

As the Internet continues to expand and more and more pages are added, effective searching requires new approaches and strategies. Remember that the more specific your search, the more likely you will find what you want. Tell the search engine precisely what it is you're searching for. To find relevant information, you must use a variety of tools and techniques.

Phrase Searching

If you want to search for words that must appear next to each other, than phrase searching is your best choice. A phrase is entered using double quotation marks and only matches those words that appear adjacent to each other and in the order in which you specify.

If you are searching for more than one phrase, you can separate multiple phrases or proper names with a comma. For example, if you were searching for baseball cards, enter the phrase "baseball cards" in double quotes. The results will contain Web sites with the words "baseball cards" adjacent to each other. Without the quotes, the search engine would find Web pages that contain the words baseball and cards anywhere within each page. To find Mickey Mantle baseball cards, you would enter "baseball cards", "Mickey Mantle." It is always a good idea to capitalize proper nouns because some search engines distinguish between upper- and lowercase letters. On the other hand, if you capitalize a common noun such as Bread, you will get fewer returns than if you typed in *bread*.

Search Engine Math

You can use ***math symbols*** to enter a formula to filter out unwanted listings. For example:

■ Put a plus sign (+) before words that must appear (also called an inclusion operator).

■ Put a minus sign (-) before words that you do not want to appear (also called an exclusion operator).

■ Words without qualifiers need not appear, but are still involved in sorting your search.

You're making cookies for the homeroom party and would like to try some new recipes. Your search words are +cookie+recipes. Only pages that contained both words would appear in your results. Now let's suppose that you want recipes for chocolate cookies. Your search words are +cookie+recipe+chocolate. This would display pages with all three words.

To take this a step further, you don't like coconut. So you don't want any recipes that contain the word *coconut*. You will find that the minus (-) symbol is helpful for reducing the number of unre-

257

lated results. You would write your search phrase as +cookie+recipe+chocolate-coconut. This tells the search engine to find pages that contain cookie, recipe, and chocolate and then to remove any pages that contain the word coconut. To extend this idea and to get chocolate cookie recipes without coconut and honey, your search phrase would be +cookie+recipe+chocolate-coconut-honey. Simply begin subtracting terms you know are not of interest, and you should get better results. You will find that almost all of the major search engines support search engine math. You can also use math symbols with most directories.

Boolean Searching

Recall that when you search for a topic on the Internet, you are not going from server to server and viewing documents on that server. Instead you are searching databases. **Boolean logic** is another way that you can search databases. This works on a similar principle as search engine math, but has a little more power. Boolean logic consists of three logical operators:

- AND

- NOT

- OR

Returning to our cookie example, you're interested in a relationship between cookies and recipes. So you may search for "cookies AND recipes." The more terms you combine with AND, the fewer returns you will receive. Or you want chocolate cookie recipes without coconut. You would search for "cookies AND recipes AND chocolate NOT coconut."

OR logic is most commonly used to search for similar terms or concepts. For example, you search for "cookies AND recipes OR chocolate" to retrieve results containing one term or the other or both. The

FIGURE 15.14
HotBot's advanced search form

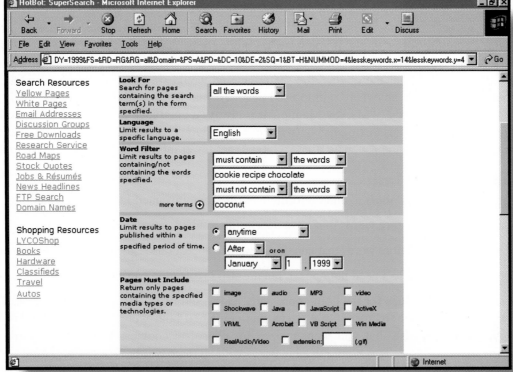

more terms you combine in a search with OR logic, the more results you will receive from your search.

The power of the Boolean search comes from the use of multiple parameters, which is not possible with the math symbols. For instance, you can create a search on "cookies AND recipes NOT (coconut OR honey OR spinach)."

Some search engines assist you with your logical search through the use of forms. For example, clicking on the HotBot search engine's Advanced Search tab brings up a form. Using this form, you can specify the language, words, and phrases to include and to omit, and even specify a time period. See Figure 15.14. Keep in mind that some search engines do not support Boolean logic.

Wildcard Searching

The * symbol, or asterisk, is considered a ***wildcard character***. If you don't know the spelling of a word or you want to search plurals or variations of a word, use the wildcard character. For example, you want to search for "baseball cards and Nolan Ryan," but you're not sure how to spell Nolan. You can construct you search using a wildcard—"baseball cards" and "N* Ryan." Some search engines only permit the * at the end of the word; with others you can put the * at the end or beginning. Some search engines do not support wildcard searches.

Title Searching

When a Web page author creates a Web page, the Web page generally contains a HTML title. The title is entered between title tags, such as

<Title>Learn the Net: An Internet Guide and Tutorial</Title>

When you go to a Web site, the title is what appears on the title bar at the top of the Web page. See Figure 15.15.

FIGURE 15.15
Learn the Net—Title Bar example

259

Many of the major search engines allow you to search within the HTML document for the title of a Web page. If you did a title search for "Internet Tutorial," then most likely one of your results or hits would be the page shown in Figure 15.16. Not all search engines support title searches.

Other Search Features

Another feature provided by several search engines is a related search. These are preprogrammed queries or questions suggested by the search engine. A related search can dramatically improve your odds of finding the information you are seeking. Several search engines offer this feature, although they may use different terminology. You may see terms such as "similar pages," "related pages," or "more pages like this." WebCrawler uses "similar pages." All of these terms basically mean the same thing. See Figure 15.16.

As you learn more about Internet searching, keep in mind that there is no single organization indexing the Internet the way the Library of Congress catalogs books. So how many ways to search are out there? There are dozens of primary search engines and hundreds of specialty search engines. And new ones are added continually. It's almost like looking for the needle in the haystack. However, with a little effort, you will probably find that special Web page which contains the information for which you are searching.

FIGURE 15.16
WebCrawler uses the term "Similar Pages."

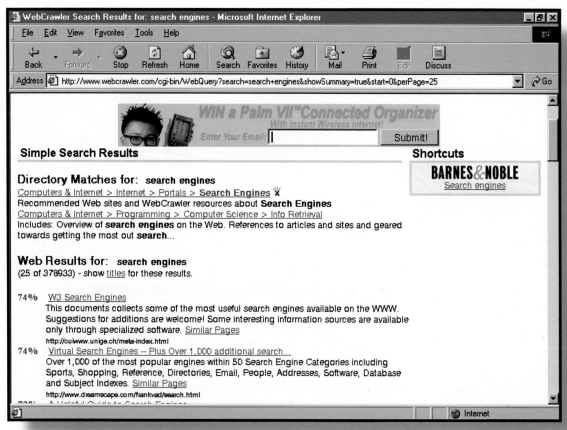

Summary

- Two basic tools you can use for finding information are search engines and directories.

- People assemble directories, and search engines are automated.

- A search engine is a software program.

- Most search engines support keyword searches.

- Concept-based searching occurs when the search engine returns hits that relate to keywords.

- Stemming relates to the search engine finding variations of the word.

- Meta tags are special tags embedded in a Web page; many search engines use the tags to create their index.

- Keywords describe the information you are trying to locate.

- Search engines contain a database of organized information.

- Some search engines use natural language.

- A search engine has three main parts: the search engine software, a robot that searches for keywords, and an index.

- Stop words such as www, but, or, and so forth, are not indexed by many search engines.

- The URL is the same as the Web site address.

- A relevant percentage indicates how close a site matches keywords.

- A search engine uses an algorithm to index Web sites.

- Specialized search engines focus on a particular topic.

- Multimedia search engines focus on video, animation, graphics, and music.

- Subject directories are organized by subject categories.

- Subject experts check the Web sites that are part of the subject directories' database.

- Use double quotation marks around a set of words for phrase searching.

- Use the plus and minus sign for inclusion and exclusion of words within a search.

- Boolean search contains the three logical operators OR, AND, and NOT.

- The * symbol is used for wildcard searching.

- Some search engines support title searching.

- A related search is a preprogrammed question suggested by the search engine.

- No single organization indexes the Internet.

MULTIPLE CHOICE

1. There are _____ basic tools that you can use for finding information on the Internet.
   A. one
   B. two
   C. three
   D. four

2. _____ occurs when the search engine includes other variations of the keyword.
   A. Concepts
   B. Stemming
   C. Meta tags
   D. Natural language

3. The _____ is a search engine robot that roams the Internet looking for keywords.
   A. Index
   B. searcher
   C. spider
   D. wart hog

4. The _____ indicates the Web site address.
   A. search box
   B. hits
   C. indexer
   D. URL

5. If you were looking for video and music resources, you might use a _____ search engine.
   A. multimedia
   B. sports
   C. phrase
   D. spider

TRUE/FALSE

Circle the T if the statement is true. Circle F if it is false.

T   F   1.   It is easy to find information on the Internet.

T   F   2.   Keywords describe the information you are trying to locate.

T   F   3.   The lower the relevant percentage, the more likely your search terms are included.

T   F   4.   The Britannica Web site is a search engine.

T   F   5.   Boolean searches and math symbol searches are identical.

SHORT ANSWER

1. The _____ is a symbol for a wildcard character.

2. A preprogrammed query is a _____.

3. Web pages for _____ directories are reviewed by people.

4. The AskJeeves search engine uses _____ language.

5. A Web author uses _____ to specify keywords within a Web page document.

CROSS-CURRICULAR PROJECTS

MATH

1. Use search engine math and create searches for the following:

    (a) Include carnivals and circuses in Canada, but not in Vancouver.

    (b) Include skateboards and roller blades in Florida.

2. Create searches for (a) and (b) using Boolean logic.

SCIENCE

Your teacher has assigned you a research project. You are to select a type of insect and provide information about the life and habits of the insect. Create a Search Strategy form that your fellow classmates can use to search the Internet. Within the form, list possible search tools and ways in which to search. Include the URLs for any suggested search engines or directory Web sites.

SOCIAL STUDIES/SCIENCE

One infamous question that most of us have heard throughout our lives is "Why did the chicken cross the road?" Use the search engine AskJeeves located at www.AskJeeves.com to find the answer to this question. How many links did you find? Prepare a report on your findings and present it to your class.

LANGUAGE ARTS

Create a Boolean search on your favorite search engine to locate information about your two favorite bands. Create a one-page report. Include within the report what search engine you used and why, how many sites you found, and how you were able to narrow the search.

Your teacher has asked you to prepare a presentation on the history of McDonald's. Use the search techniques that you think are best to find information for your presentation. Be sure to include at least one reference to McDonald's french fries.

TEAM PROJECT

Ms. Perez would like more information on MP3. Downloading and selling music from the Internet could be a possible enhancement for Vista Multimedia. Ms. Perez would like to have a detailed description of how MP3 works, how to download this music, what kind of MP3 hardware is available, and what type of player and encoder she could use. She has requested that you and a group of your fellow employees put together a two-page report with this information and other any relevant information you may find. A good place to start searching is at mp3.lycos.com/.

HOW DO I EVALUATE ELECTRONIC INFORMATION?

OBJECTIVES

When you complete this module, you will be able to:

- Identify reasons for evaluating Internet resources.

- Identify parts of a Web page.

- Identify criteria for evaluating electronic information.

- Identify Internet resources.

- Cite Internet resources appropriately.

⏱ **Estimated Time: 1.5 hours**

VOCABULARY

Body
Copyright
Currency
Efficiency
Fair use
Footer
Header
MLA
Navigation

Ms. Perez has been surfing the Internet to find information concerning other video stores and the different types of services they provide. She has also been researching possible new services and merchandise for Vista Multimedia to offer. To her surprise, she has found an abundance of information; so much so that she is beginning to wonder if the information she is finding is accurate and reliable.

Because she knows you are taking a computer class at school, she has asked if you can tell her how to determine if information found on the Internet is always accurate. She would like to know what criteria should be used to determine if information is "good" information; in other words if the information is accurate and reliable.

Information is only as good as the source. Anyone, anywhere, can put anything on the Internet. It may be true; it may not be true. How can you determine if the information is legitimate? Developing the ability to evaluate information critically on the Internet is a very important skill today in this information age!

Ms. Perez is right to want to know if the information she is locating on the Internet is going to be usable before she spends hours and hours researching for it. Choosing reliable sources is critical to the success of your research.

Evaluating Information Found on the Internet

The Internet provides opportunities for students, teachers, scholars, and anyone needing information to find it from all over the world. It is fairly easy to locate information and to publish it electronically. However, because anyone can put information on the Internet, it is not always accurate or reliable. Anyone using information obtained from the Internet needs to develop skills to evaluate what they find.

Hot Tip

The Internet epitomizes the concept of *caveat lector:* Let the reader beware.

Viewing a Page

The pages on the Web have so many different looks. Some pages are full with pictures, sounds, animations, links, and information. Some are very exciting; others may be just plain. Sometimes the appearance of the page alone may draw you to a site, and after reading it, you realize it is not the site you need. Let's take a look at a page on the Web. See Figure 16.1.

Key the URL for the White House in the address line (www.whitehouse.gov). Now that the page is loaded, let's examine it. Here are some questions you may want to consider (you will need to scroll through the page to in order to answer all of the questions):

FIGURE 16.1
The White House Homepage

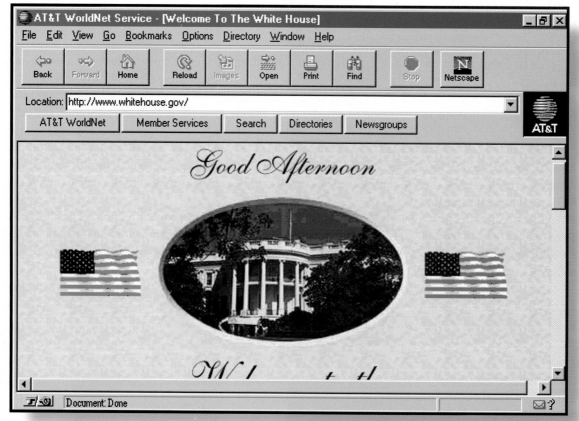

- Did it take a long time to load?

- Are the graphics on the page related to the site?

- Are the sections on the page labeled?

- Who wrote the information on this page?

- How can you communicate with the author?

- When was the page last updated?

- Are there appropriate links?

- Is it easy to follow links?

Based on what you have seen so far, would you think this might be a good site for information? Maybe we need to go just a bit further to really look at the information contained at the site. Here are more questions to consider:

- Can you tell what the page is about from its title?

- Is the information useful for your report?

- How old is the information?

- Are you given other sites/links to visit for additional information?

- Does any of the information contradict information you found someplace else?

- Did the author use words like *always, never, best, worst*?

- Do you think the author knows the information he or she is sharing?

ETHICS IN TECHNOLOGY

SOFTWARE PIRACY

One of the biggest problems facing the computer industry today is software piracy, the illegal copying or using of programs. Copying software is very easy. Some people believe it is alright to copy software and use it for free. They think software is too expensive. And it can be. Some low-level software costs less than $25, but more specialized software can cost up to $500! When users copy the software, they are only giving up access to documentation and tech support; so they decide it is worth it to copy it illegally.

You, too, may ask, "What is the big deal about copying software?" Remember, it is an expensive process that takes highly trained programmers hundreds of hours to develop.

Shareware, free software that can be used for a given period of time, is also being abused. Many people use it with no intention of purchasing it. You will probably be surprised to know that not only individual users copy software illegally—so do businesses. Billions of dollars are lost every year as a result of pirated software.

Software can be pirated in many ways. Of course, the easiest is to copy from the original disks. Software can also be copied from the server of a network and over an e-mail system.

The Copyright Act of 1976 was passed to govern software piracy. In 1983 a Software Piracy and Counterfeiting Amendment was added. It is no longer a misdemeanor to copy software illegally—it is a felony.

267

FIGURE 16.2
Header, body and footer

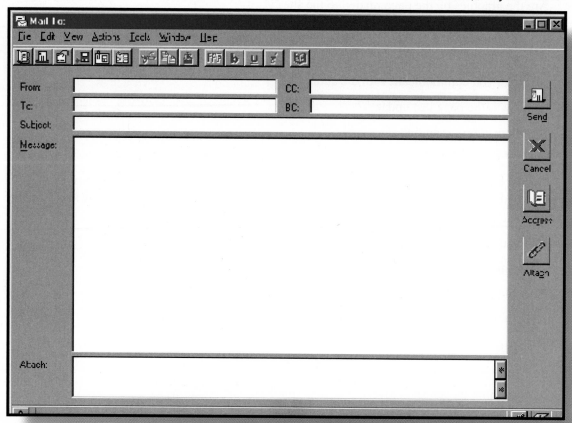

These questions represent just a start at evaluating electronic information.
A Web document has three main elements:

- *Header:* contains a link to the sponsoring institution (may also be in the footer).

- *Footer:* contains the author or contact person, date of revision.

- *Body:* contains information identifying the intended audience, purpose of the information.

 Did You Know?

Links that are no longer active are called *dead links*.

See Figure 16.2.

Sometimes you may see all of these elements on a Web page. If you do not, try entering the URL again and leave off the ending portions. Sometimes the URL may take you further into the page with various links that would cause the page with the information you are looking for to be bypassed. Example: If you could not find the institution or author information at the following site:

www.jack.com/admin/lamb/staff.html

Retype the URL minus the "staff.html," leaving jack.com/admin/lamb.

Criteria for Evaluating Electronic Information

Authorship

A well-developed resource identifies its author and/or producer. You will be given enough information to be able to determine if the originator is a reliable source. What expertise or authority does the author have that qualifies him or her to distribute this information? If you don't see this information, use the BACK key to see if maybe another part of the file contains this information. Look especially for a name and e-mail address of the person who created or maintains the information. You can always contact him or her for information regarding credentials and expertise.

If the information regarding the author is not visible, a search by the author's name using a search engine may provide the information regarding the author. It may also lead to other information by the same author. If an e-mail address is visible, use it to request information regarding the author.

The domain portion of the URL will also give you information concerning the appropriateness of the site for your area of study. Examples:

■ .edu for educational or research information

■ .gov for government resources

■ .com for commercial products or commercially sponsored site

■ .org for nonprofit organizations

■ .mil for military branches

Content

Is the purpose of this Web site stated? Is the information accurate? Is the information in-depth enough? Has the information been reviewed? Don't take any information presented on the Internet at face value. The source of the information should be clearly stated whether it is original or borrowed from somewhere else. As you read through the information, pay close attention to determine if the content covers a specific time period or an aspect of a topic or if it is more broad.

Currency

A very important consideration of an effective site is its *currency*, which refers to the age of the information, how long has it been posted, and how often it is updated. Some sites need to be updated more often than others to reflect changes in the kind of information. Medical or technological information needs to be updated more often than historical information. Out-of-date information may not give you the results you need.

Most sites on the Internet have numerous links that will take you to additional sites of similar information. Sometimes, however, it is not information you can use. Decide if the site you plan to use has useful information or if it is just a site that links you to more and more sites. Does the site contain dead links, links that are no longer active?

The style of writing and the language used can reveal information about the quality of the site. If the style is objective, the chances are the information is worthy of your attention. However, if it is opinionated and subjective, you may want to give second thought to using it. Ideas and opinions supported by references are additional signs of the value of the site.

269

The overall layout of the page is also important. The page should be free of spelling and grammar errors. Even if the page appears to contain valuable information, misspelled words and incorrect grammar usage tend to bias a reader regarding the validity of the information.

Copyright

Most sites have copyright information. *Copyright* is the exclusive right, granted by law for a certain number of years, to make and dispose of literary, musical, or artistic work. Even if the copyright notice isn't displayed prominently on the page, someone wrote or is responsible for the creation of whatever appears on a page. This means that you cannot use the information as your own. You must give credit to the person who created the work that you will use in your research. Some information on the Internet is classified as *public domain*, which means it can be used without citation. *Fair use* refers to short, cited excerpts, usually as an example for research.

Navigation

Navigation is the ability to move through a site. Being able to move quickly through the links on a Web site is a very important element. Having the information laid out in a logical layout so you can locate what you need easily adds to the *efficiency* of the site. The consistency of the layout from page to page adds to the ability to navigate easily. The first page of a Web site indicates how the site is organized and the options available.

Moving through a site is done by clicking on the links on the page. Some pages consist of many links; others may only contain a few. Regardless, the links should:

- be easy to identify.

- be grouped logically.

- be pertinent to the subject of the original page.

There should be a link on each page that will take you back to the home page and one that will allow you to e-mail the author.

Types of Internet Resources

Electronic Journals

The types of electronic resources include the following:

- journals and journal articles

- magazines and magazine articles

- newspapers and newspaper articles

- Web sites

- E-mail

- Mailing lists

- Organizational sites

- Subject-based sites

Some of these are presented in complete form; others are only portions of the document. Regardless of the type, the site should give information concerning:

- the identification of the publisher

- article reviewer information

- special hardware requirements

- availability of older copies of the article, newspaper, or journal

- the currency of the site. See Figure 16.3.

Search Engines

Search engines are programs written to query and retrieve information stored in a database. They differ from database to database and depend on the information stored in the database itself. Examples of search engines are AltaVista, Excite, Mamma, Dogpile, and AskJeeves. If you used one of the many search engines available to locate information on the Internet, you need to know:

- how the search engine decides the order in which it returns information requested. The top spaces (the first sites listed) are sold to advertisers by the search engines. Therefore, the first sites listed are not always the best sites or the most accurate and reliable.

- how the search engine searches for information and how often the information is updated.

Citing Internet Resources

Internet resources used in reports must be cited. You must give proper credit to any information you include in your report that is not your original thought. This will also provide the reader of the document with choices for additional research. It will also allow the information to be retrieved again. You can find general guidelines for citing electronic sources in the *MLA Handbook for Writers of Research Papers. The Chicago Manual of Style* is another source for this information.

FIGURE 16.3
THE Journal Homepage

Here are some samples of citing Internet resources as suggested in the *MLA Handbook for Writers of Research Papers:*

■ ***Online journal article:*** Author's last name, first initial. (date of publication or "NO DATE" if unavailable). Title of article or section used [Number of paragraphs]. Title of complete work. [Form, such as HTTP, CD-ROM, E-MAIL]. Available: complete URL [date of access].

For information concerning using MLA style for citing sources, visit www.mla.com.

■ ***Online magazine article:*** Author's last name, first initial. (date of publication). Title of article. [Number of paragraphs]. Title of work. [Form] Available: complete URL [date of access].

■ ***Web sites:*** Name of Site [date]. Title of document [Form] Available: complete URL [date of access]

■ ***E-mail:*** Author's last name, first name (author's e-mail address) (date). Subject. Receiver of e-mail (receiver's e-mail address).

Remember, anyone can put information on the Internet. Evaluate any resources that you choose to use carefully to ensure you have a high-quality resource that could really be of value to you.

TECHNOLOGY CAREERS

INTERNET WEB DESIGNER/WEB MASTER

Every page on the Internet was designed by someone. Today, that someone is called a web designer. The way a page looks on the Internet is the responsibility of the web designer. The overall goal of the web designer is to design and create a page that is efficient and appealing.

Each page on the Internet has to be maintained and kept up-to-date. The web master is responsible for this task. A typical web master manages a Web site. That usually includes creating content, adapting existing content in a user-friendly format, creating and maintaining a logical structure, running the Web server software.

Not so long ago, both of these functions were the responsibility of the web master. However, today, with growing technology in hardware and software, these tasks are becoming more and more specialized and therefore performed by more than one person. Web masters and web designers can work in any organization that has a Web site. Such organizations include educational institutions, museums, libraries, government agencies, and of course, corporations.

A person working in either of these capacities needs to have skills in graphic design, HTML language, web design software programs, general programming and the ability to adapt to new web technology as it evolves.

An Associate or Bachelor's in Computer Science or Graphic Design is usually required. However, because the field is relatively new, many employers will accept persons with extensive experience in graphic design combined with computer skills.

The salary for a web master or web designer will vary depending on location and experience. The average salary can vary from $20,000 to $36,000.

Internet Detective

There is an on-line tutorial on evaluating the quality of the information you locate on the Internet. It gives specific information regarding evaluating electronic resources. You can access the Internet Detective by visiting www.sosig.ac.uk/desire/internet-detective.html. You can surf though the pages of this site. Your instructor may give you additional directions for using this site.

Evaluation Survey

Let's use the information we discussed in this module to construct a survey to evaluate electronic resources. There are several topics that we discussed and they are all very important. In order to condense our survey, we may need to combine some of the topics.

CRITERIA FOR EVALUATING ELECTRONIC RESOURCES

1. Can you identify the author of the page?   Yes _____   No _____

2. Is an e-mail address listed?   Yes _____   No _____

3. Can you access site in a reasonable time?   Yes _____   No _____

4. Is the text on the screen legible?   Yes _____   No _____

5. Are the commands and directions easy to follow?   Yes _____   No _____

6. Is the information current?   Yes _____   No _____

7. When you perform a search, do you get what you expect? Yes _____   No _____

8. Are instructions clearly visible?   Yes _____   No _____

9. Is the information updated regularly?   Yes _____   No _____

10. Make any comment here you would like concerning the site.

_____

_____

Now that we have constructed our survey, let's identify a site on the Internet and use our survey to evaluate it. You may select a site such as the name of the college you want to attend, a magazine article of interest to you, the White House, or any topic on which you may want to gather information.

Summary

- Web pages have three basic elements: header, body, and footer.

- The criteria for evaluating Internet resources include:
    - authorship
    - content
    - copyright information
    - navigation
    - quality control

- There are various types of Internet resources including electronic journals, magazines, newspapers, Web sites, and e-mail messages.

- It is very important to cite any information that you use from the Internet. The MLA style is widely used for citing electronic resources.

LESSON 16 REVIEW QUESTIONS

MULTIPLE CHOICE

1. The header, footer, and body represent the main _____ of a Web document.
   - **A.** elements
   - **B.** sizes
   - **C.** domains
   - **D.** currency

2. _____ refers to the age of information.
   - **A.** Date
   - **B.** Infancy
   - **C.** Currency
   - **D.** Dead link

3. .Edu, .gov, .org, and .com are examples of the _____ portion of an URL.
   - **A.** name
   - **B.** domain
   - **C.** ending
   - **D.** handle

4. _____ is the exclusive right, granted by law for a certain number of years, to make and dispose of literary, musical, or artist work.
   - **A.** Copyright
   - **B.** Security
   - **C.** Privacy
   - **D.** Resource

5. _____ is the ability to move through a site.
    A. Linking
    B. Grouping
    C. Citing
    D. Navigation

TRUE/FALSE

Circle the T if the statement is true. Circle F if it is false.

T F   **1.** It can be assumed that all information found on the Internet is accurate.

T F   **2.** The age of a article will affect its usefulness to a user.

T F   **3.** Everyone who puts information on the Internet is an authority on the particular subject.

T F   **4.** A Web document has three main elements.

T F   **5.** Spelling and grammar errors on a Web page may affect a user's opinion of a site.

SHORT ANSWERS

1. _____ refers to the age of the article.

2. All sites should have the _____ address of the author so the user can make contact.

3. Some information on the Internet is classified as _____ which means it can be used without citation.

4. _____ refers to the ability to move through a site.

5. A _____ is copy of a paper journal posted to the Internet.

CROSS-CURRICULAR PROJECTS

MATH

Create a list of approximately five to seven questions to ask in evaluating Internet resources. Select a topic in math such as percentages, word problems, and so on, and locate information on your selected topic on the Internet. After reviewing several sites, decide on the one that would be most helpful to you. Use your list of questions to evaluate the site. Your ultimate task is to determine if the site you chose is a valuable site.

SCIENCE

Create a list of approximately five to seven questions to ask in evaluating Internet resources. Select a topic in science such as a health issue, weather conditions, and so on, and locate information on your selected topic on the Internet. After reviewing several sites, decide on the one that would be most helpful to you. Use your list of questions to evaluate the site. Your ultimate task is to determine if the site you chose is a valuable site.

SOCIAL STUDIES

Create a list of approximately five to seven questions to ask in evaluating Internet resources. Select a topic in social studies such as government topics, geography, and so on, and locate information on your selected topic on the Internet. After reviewing several sites, decide on the one that would be most helpful to you. Use your list of questions to evaluate the site. Your ultimate task is to determine if the site you chose is a valuable site.

LANGUAGE ARTS

Using the information contained in this module, create an evaluation checklist that one could use to evaluate Internet resources. You may decide on the format you want to use for this assignment. Locate a topic on the Internet and use your checklist to evaluate it.

WEB PROJECT

Chose a topic to research on the Internet. Print the first two sites that you find. Using the information you studied in this module, critique the two sites and write a report of your findings.

TEAM PROJECT

Ms. Perez, your supervisor, has informed you that she has contacted the services of a Web designer to create a Web page for the store. However, she would like to be able to talk intelligently with the Web designer when telling him or her exactly what she wants on the Web page. She has asked you and the other part-time employee to work together to provide her with samples of Web pages for five video/multimedia stores. She also wants you to provide her with a critique of each page.

How Do I Create a Web Page?

Ms. Perez is very excited about the possibilities of advertising Vista Multimedia on the Web. She would also like to have her own personal Web page. She has one or two ideas about what she would like to do, but she still does not fully understand what is involved. You explain to Ms. Perez that the process of creating a Web page is fairly simple. There are many ways in which to create a Web page and there are special programs one can use. To fully understand Web page creation, however, it is important to first understand HTML. Please keep in mind as you go through this module that only the basic HTML tags are covered. There are many other tags and methods you can use to develop Web pages.

How a Web Page Works

Have you ever wondered how a Web page works? When you consider that there are millions of Web pages on the Internet, you might make the correct assumption that it is really not that difficult to create a Web page. In fact, not only is it incredibly easy to create a Web page, it is also a lot of fun.

Before beginning the process of creating a Web page, you will need an understanding of some basic terminology:

- **Web page:** This is a plain text document on the World Wide Web. Every Web page is identified by a unique address, or URL.

- **HTML:** HTML, or Hypertext Markup Language, is the language of the Web. HTML is a series of tags that are integrated into a text document. These tags describe how the text should be formatted when a Web browser displays it on the screen.

Internet

If you're looking for a Web site with free graphics and information on creating graphics, try Laurie McCanna, author of "Creating Great Web Graphics", Web site. You can find this site located at www.mccannas.com/

- **Web browser:** A Web browser interprets the HTML tags within the page so the text can be displayed on the screen. Two of the most popular Web browsers are Microsoft's Internet Explorer and Netscape's Communicator.

- **Web server:** A Web server displays Web pages and renders them into final form so they can be viewed by anyone with an Internet connection and a Web browser. Every Web server has an unique Web address.

You may infer from these basic terminology definitions that you need a Web server before you can create your Web page. This is not true. The only tools you will need are your Web browser and a text editing program. Your Web browser can easily display your Web page from your personal computer. Once you create your Web page and have it in final format, you will most likely want to publish it to a Web server. We cover publishing your Web page later in the module.

ETHICS IN TECHNOLOGY

UNDERSTANDING E-MAIL ENCRYPTION

When you send an e-mail message, you may not realize that it can literally bounce all over the world before it reaches its final destination. As your e-mail message travels from computer to computer, it may encounter "sniffers," or software programs that are waiting to alter or tamper with your e-mail. Most of the time, the e-mail that you send may not be that important. It could be a note to a friend or a request for information. On the other hand, it could contain your computer network login and password and or maybe even a credit card number.

Several companies have made available programs to encrypt your e-mail. In fact, there are literally hundreds of e-mail encryption programs. If you are using recent versions of Netscape Communicator or Internet Explorer, you have encryption options. Internet Explorer, for example, has two different types of certificates to protect your privacy: a personal certificate and a Web site certificate.

Encryption programs work with cryptographic keys. The user provides a password and the program turns the password into a key. There is both a public key and a private key. The user retains the private key for decryption purposes.

Plan a Document

Many times when we start a project, we have a tendency to jump right in and go full speed ahead. Sometimes this works, but more often than not, we find ourselves having to back up and redo some of our work. Planning may take a small amount of our time in the beginning, but it will pay off in the long run. So before you get started actually creating your personal Web page, let's consider some of the elements you may want to include. See Figure 17.1.

- *Title:* This can be anything you choose; an example is "The personal Web page of Joe Smith" where you would substitute your name for Joe Smith.

- *Page content:* What do you want to include in your Web page? Do you want to share information about your family, your hobbies, your school, or sports? Make a list of what features you would like to include.

- *Hyperlinks:* To what other Web sites would you like to link? Make a note of these. You will need the URL, or Web site address, for each link.

- *Closing comments:* Do you want to include any closing comments? Perhaps you want to add your e-mail address.

FIGURE 17.1
Sample Web page outline

Sample Web page outline
Title: A title for your Web page

Page Content:
  Hobbies
  School Favorites
  Family
  Favorite Vacation destination
  What I did last summer

Hyperlinks:
  Sony Playstation
  My School
  Skateboarding.com
  My favorite sports team

Closing:
  My e-mail address
  My favorite quote

A Basic Page

An HTML page has two components—page content and *HTML tags*. The page content is that part of the document you want to display, such as a list of your hobbies or other information about yourself or your school, and so on. HTML tags are easily identifiable because they are enclosed in brackets: <HTML>.

- Many tags come in pairs with a start tag and an end tag. For instance, <TITLE> is a start tag and </TITLE> is an end tag. You identify an end tag by including the slash (</>) character before the name of the tag. The start and end tag identify the content between them as HTML formatted. These are sometimes called container tags.

- Some tags are a single entity—that is, they don't have an end tag. An example is the <BR> tag, which indicates a line break.

- Tags are not case sensitive, but it is best to select a format and stay with it. In this module, uppercase letters are used for all HTML tags.

- Some tags can contain attributes. For example, the <BODY> tag is required for all HTML documents. But if you wanted the background color of your Web page to be blue, you can add an attribute so your <BODY> tag would look like this: <BODY bgcolor = "Blue">.

Every new page that you create requires a particular set of tags structured in a particular format. See Figure 17.2. The structure of these tags always remain the same. In Figure 17.2, each tag is on a separate line. In HTML, you could type everything in one long single line. However, for readability and editing, typing each command on a separate line is a much better procedure.

- *HTML:* Notice in Figure 17-2 that the first line in the document is <HTML>, a start tag, and that the last line is </HTML>, an end tag. All other tags and page content is contained within these two tags.

- *HEAD:* Contained within the start and end <HEAD> tags is the <TITLE> tag.

- *TITLE:* The title tag gives the page its official title. The content entered between the start and end title tags is displayed on the browser title bar.

- *BODY:* All Web page content is contained between the start and end <BODY> tags.

FIGURE 17.2
Required HTML Tags

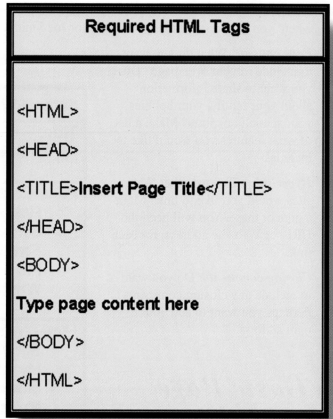

In the examples in this book, we use Windows Notepad to create the HTML documents. However, as mentioned previously, you can use any text editing program to create a Web page. You can even use a word processing program and save your document in ASCII or text format.

Because the tags contained in Figure 17.2 are required for all HTML documents, the first goal is to create a template containing these tags. By doing this, you will only have to type in these tags one time. In the future, just open the template, save it with a new name, and add your page content.

STEP-BY-STEP  17.1

1. Launch your text editing program.

2. Create the template. See Figure 17.3.

3. Save your text file as **HTML template.htm.**

4. Close your editing program.

When you create any future HTML document, you can open this file, save it with a different name, and add your page content.

Your next task is to add a title, add a line of page content, and to view your web page in your browser.

 Hot Tip

You can view the HTML code for documents on the Web. Surf the Internet and find a Web page that you like. On your Browser's menu, click View and then click Source to display the HTML code.

FIGURE 17.3
HTML Template

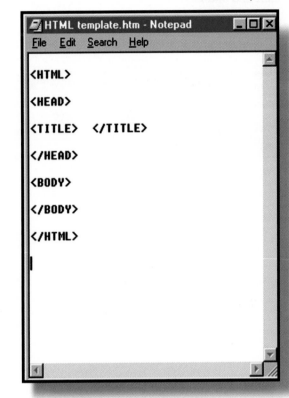

STEP-BY-STEP  17.2

1. Launch your text editing program.

2. Open the HTML template document. Note that most programs save with a particular file type. To display this document name and to open the document, you may have to change Types of files to "All files(*.*)."

3. On the File menu, click Save As. Save the HTML template document as **[Your name]'s Web page.htm**. In our example, we create a Web page for Joe Smith, a student who works part time for Vista Multimedia.

4. Between the start and end TITLE tags, type **[Your name]'s Web page**.

5. Between the two BODY tags, type **Welcome to my Web page**.

6. On the File menu, click Save.

7. Launch your browser.

8. On the File menu, click **Open**.

9. Click Browse, locate your file, and click **OK**.

Congratulations! You have just created and displayed your first Web page. See Figure 17.4.

Look at your Web page and compare it to your HTML document. Notice that none of the HTML tags display. Also notice that displayed in the browser's title bar is the text you typed between the start and end TITLE tags, and that this text does not display as part of the document itself. Notice also that the only text which displays as part of the document is that text you typed in between the start and end BODY tags.

FIGURE 17.4
Web page displayed in browser

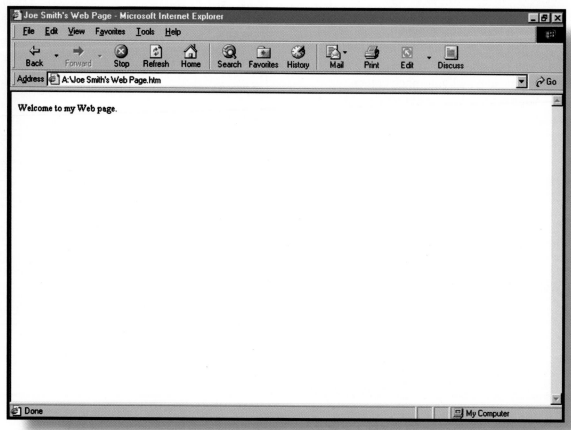

Page Formatting

One of the first things you will discover when creating a Web page is that pressing your keyboard's Enter key has no effect on a Web page. You can press the Enter key a dozen times or more, but it will not make a difference when the page is displayed in the browser. This is because the browser ignores any blank lines you attempt to enter from the keyboard. There are ways, however, that you can create a new line and/or leave spaces between lines.

 **Internet**

There are many places on the Web where you can find free images or graphics. Go to the Ask Jeeves natural language search engine and ask Jeeves "Where can I find free graphics?"

Line Breaks

If you want to start a new line, you can use the break tag: <BR>. The break tag is a single entity. That is, you do not need a start and end tag. You can use the break tag to start a new line or you can even use the break tag to skip a line. See Figure 17.5.

FIGURE 17.5
Using the <BR> tag

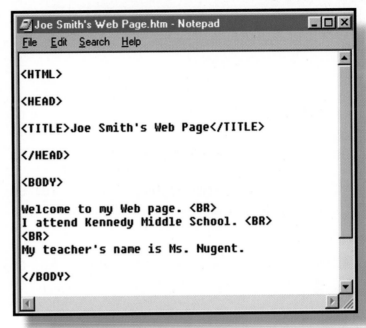

```
Joe Smith's Web Page.htm - Notepad
File   Edit   Search   Help

<HTML>

<HEAD>

<TITLE>Joe Smith's Web Page</TITLE>

</HEAD>

<BODY>

Welcome to my Web page. <BR>
I attend Kennedy Middle School. <BR>
<BR>
My teacher's name is Ms. Nugent.

</BODY>
```

Paragraph Breaks

A second way to create a blank line is with the paragraph tag: <P>. An end tag </P> is not required, but many Web programmers include it as a matter of style. As it appears, a paragraph tag does the same thing as two break tags <BR>. See Figure 17.6.

FIGURE 17.6
Adding the <P> tag

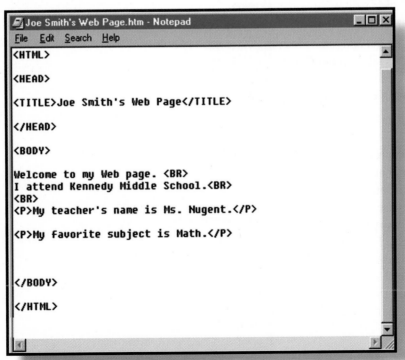

```
Joe Smith's Web Page.htm - Notepad
File   Edit   Search   Help
<HTML>

<HEAD>

<TITLE>Joe Smith's Web Page</TITLE>

</HEAD>

<BODY>

Welcome to my Web page. <BR>
I attend Kennedy Middle School.<BR>
<BR>
<P>My teacher's name is Ms. Nugent.</P>

<P>My favorite subject is Math.</P>



</BODY>

</HTML>
```

283

1. Launch your text editing program and open your Web page document.

2. At the end of the Welcome to My Web page line, add *
*.

3. Press the [ENTER] key. (Remember that pressing Enter does not affect the way in which the Web page displays. Adding extra spaces makes it easier to read and edit your HTML document.

4. Add another *
* and press the [ENTER] key.

5. Type *<P>My teacher's name is Ms. Nugent.</P>*. Press [ENTER].

6. Type *<P>My favorite subject is math.</P>*. Press [ENTER].

7. On the File menu, click *Save*.

8. Launch your browser.

9. On the File menu, click *Open*.

10. Click Browser, locate your file, and click *OK*.

Lists

Another way to arrange and organize text on a Web page is through the use of **lists**. Within HTML, there are three types of lists:

- ***Ordered list:*** This is generally a numbered list and requires start <OL> and end </OL> tags. Each item in the list begins with <LI>.

- ***Unordered list:*** This is generally a bulleted list and requires start <UL> and end </UL> tags. Each item in the list begins with <LI>.

- ***Definition list:*** This is a list of terms with indented definitions. This list requires a start tag <DL> and an end tag </DL>. Additionally, the tag <DT> is required for the term and <DD> is required for the definition. See Figures 17.7 and 17.8. Please note that the entire template is not displayed—only the text that is between the start and end <BODY> tags.

FIGURE 17.7
HTML List examples

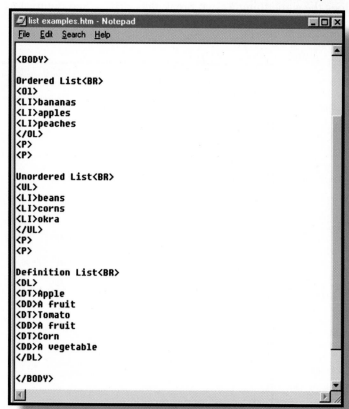

```
list examples.htm - Notepad

File   Edit   Search   Help

<BODY>

Ordered List<BR>
<OL>
<LI>bananas
<LI>apples
<LI>peaches
</OL>
<P>
<P>

Unordered List<BR>
<UL>
<LI>beans
<LI>corns
<LI>okra
</UL>
<P>
<P>

Definition List<BR>
<DL>
<DT>Apple
<DD>A fruit
<DT>Tomato
<DD>A fruit
<DT>Corn
<DD>A vegetable
</DL>

</BODY>
```

FIGURE 17.8
Browser displaying list examples

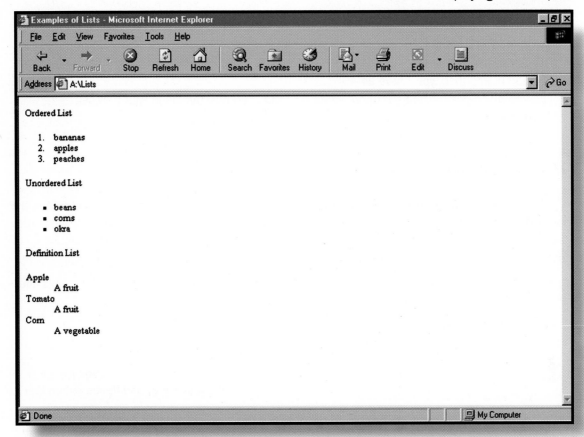

Center

One more way to organize text on the page is through the use of the <CENTER> tag. This tag requires both a start and end tag. Simply enclose whatever text between the two tags and that text is centered. You can center a single word, a sentence, a paragraph, a series of paragraphs, or even an image.

STEP-BY-STEP ▷ 17.4

1. Launch your text editing program and open your Web page.

2. Click under the last sentence you entered in the previous Step-by-Step (My Favorite subject is Math) and type <CENTER> *I like school because:* </CENTER>.

3. Type a BREAK <BR> tag and press [ENTER].

4. Type <OL> to begin your ordered list. Press [ENTER].

5. Type <LI> to begin the first item in the list.

6. Type *It is fun.* Press [ENTER].

(continued on next page)

7. Type <LI> and then type *My teachers are good teachers.* Press [ENTER].

8. Type <LI> and then type *I have an opportunity to learn about the world.* Press [ENTER].

9. Type </OL to end the list.

10. Save your file.

11. Display the file in your browser.

Text Formatting

Now that you've learned some ways in which you can control the placement of text within the browser, it's time to learn how to dress up the text. Just like formatting text within your word processing program, you can also apply formatting to text that is displayed in a Web browser. Some of the text formatting you can apply is as follows:

■ *Bold:* To bold text requires start <B> and </B> end tags. Surround the text with these tags and your text displays as bold in your browser.

■ *Italics:* To display italicized text, use the start <I> and end </I> tags.

■ *Underline:* To underline text, use the start <U> and end </U> tags. See Figure 17.9.

FIGURE 17.9
Bold, underline, and italics examples

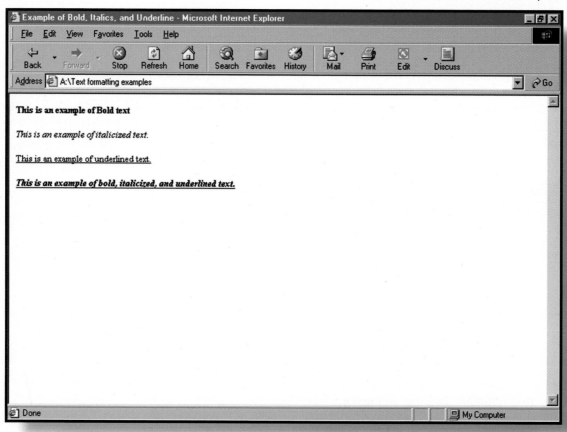

Changing Font Size and Color

When you browse the Internet, your browser displays the text based on a default font size, type, and default color. However, the font size, type, and color can all be changed. This is done through the start <FONT> and end </FONT> tags.

If you've used a word processing program, you know that it is very easy to change text size. You can make the text very small or very large. Your options within HTML are not quite as flexible as they are within word processing. For most browsers, seven different sizes are commonly available. The sizes range from 1, which is the smallest, to 7, which is the largest. To change the font size, you add the SIZE attribute to the FONT tag. Example: <FONT SIZE = 3>. See Figure 17.10.

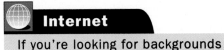

Internet

If you're looking for backgrounds for your Web site, then one of the first places you should go is to Yahoo's Background for Web Pages. Here you will find an extensive list of links to many Web sites. Just go to www.yahoo.com and search for Web Page backgrounds.

FIGURE 17.10
Font tag examples

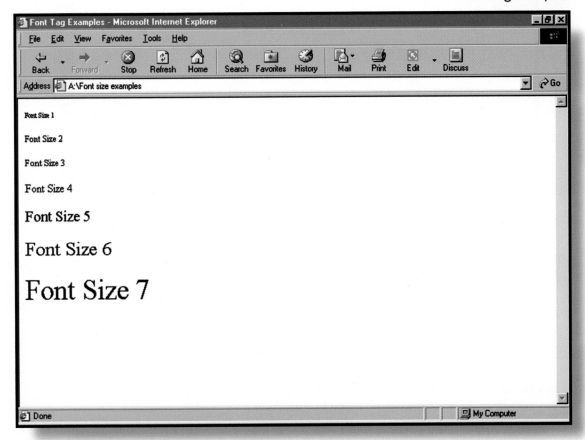

You've seen how easy it is to change the font size. It's just as easy to change the color by using the COLOR attribute. Example: <FONT COLOR = RED>. Or you can combine the font size and font color within one tag. Example: <FONT SIZE = 1 COLOR = RED>. See Figure 17.11.

A third font attribute that you can manipulate is the font type. Example: <FONT FACE = ARIAL>. If you wish, you can even specify color, size, and type all within one start and end tag. See Figures 17.12 and 17.13.

FIGURE 17.11
Font tag colors

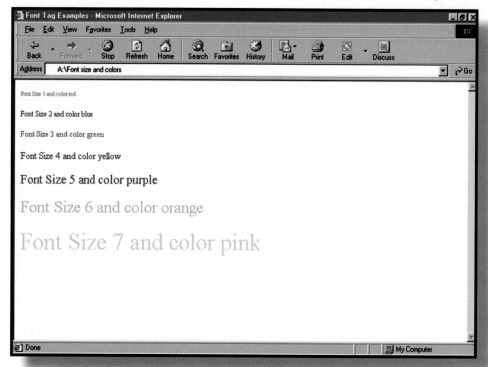

TECHNOLOGY CAREERS

CONSULTANT

A consultant provides professional advice or services. They have specialized knowledge that they can sell to their clients. Many consultants work on short-term projects for companies who may not have employees with the required skills for a particular job. Many consultants telecommute or work from home.

Successful consultants can be found in just about every field imaginable. There are garage-sale consultants and consultants who will help you arrange your closets. However, the Information Technology field has created an entire new line of consultants. There are programming consultants, database consultants, and even Web designer and Web development consultants. So if you enjoy working with computers; and, in particular, developing Web pages, then consulting may be a job field that you would want to investigate.

FIGURE 17.12

Font tag color, size, and type

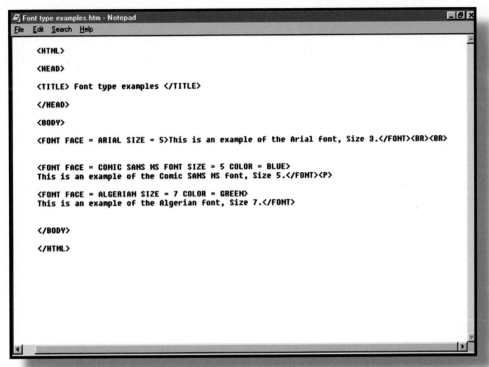

FIGURE 17.13

Font tag examples

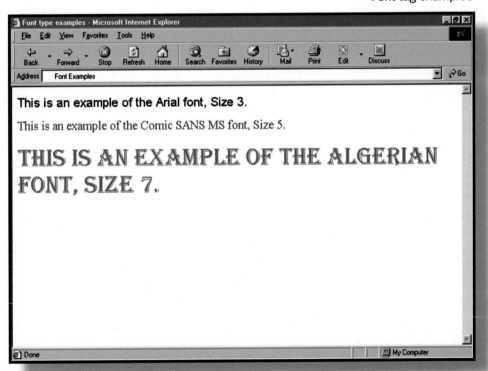

FIGURE 17.14
Heading tags

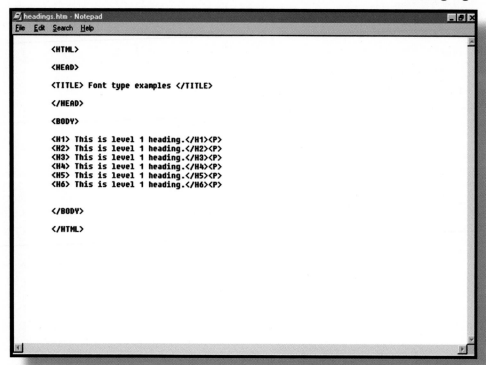

FIGURE 17.15
Heading tag examples

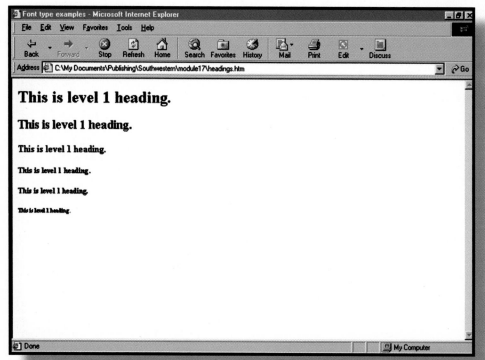

Headings

If you are familiar with word processing, you may have used styles. A style is a set of formatting characteristics that you can apply to text in your document to quickly change its appearance. HTML does not support styles, but the Heading command does some automatic formatting for you. The characteristics of *headings* include the type face, size, and the extra space above or below the heading. However, the browser you use will determine the final appearance.

There are six levels of HTML headings. The start tag for the first level is <H1> and the end tag is </H1>. For the other five levels, just substitute the desired number within the start and end tags. Level 1 is the largest and level 6 is the smallest. See Figures 17.14 and 17.15.

Hyperlinks

A defining feature of any Web document is *hyperlinks*, active references to other parts of the same documents or to other documents. These other documents can be on the same computer, on a network server (intranet), or stored on a computer in another country. As long as you know the location of the document and the address of the computer on which it resides, you can create a hyperlink to it.

Providing hyperlinks between documents gives the user easy access to related information. Hyperlinks are relative or absolute.

Relative Links

When all the files, including the graphics and images, are saved in one folder or will be published on the same Web server, you should probably use relative links. A *relative link* gives the file location in relation to the current document. When you use relative links, you can move the folder and files that contain the hyperlink and maintain the destination of the hyperlink without breaking the path of the relative link.

The tags for a relative hyperlink are <A HREF = "FILENAME"> </A>. The <A> within this tag represents Anchor. Let's assume that Joe Smith's Web page is located in a folder titled Web Documents. Joe Smith creates a second Web page titled Hobbies. He would like to link to this second Web page from his Joe Smith's Web page. To do this, he creates a relative hyperlink. The link would look like the following: <A HREF = "HOBBIES.HTM"> </A>.

STEP-BY-STEP ▷ 17.5

1. Launch your text editing program and open your Web page.

2. Click under the last line you typed (My favorite subject is Math) and type: *Click here for my favorite <A HREF = "HOBBIES.HTM> hobbies.</A>*

3. Save your document and then close it.

4. Open the HTML template.htm file.

5. Save the file as HOBBIES.HTM.

6. In between the start and end <BODY> tags, type *My favorite hobbies are (and list two or three of your favorite hobbies).*

7. Save and close your HOBBIES document.

8. Launch your browser and open your Web page document.

9. Click the hobbies link to display the HOBBIES document.

Absolute Link

Absolute links are hyperlinks to other Web sites. If you wanted to link to a list of your favorite places on the Web, you would use an absolute link. These links use a fixed file location or Web address. The fixed location identifies the destination by its full address. An example of an absolute link is <A HREF = WWW.ROCK-CLIMBING.COM> rock climbing </A>. See Figure 17.16.

FIGURE 17.16
Absolute links example

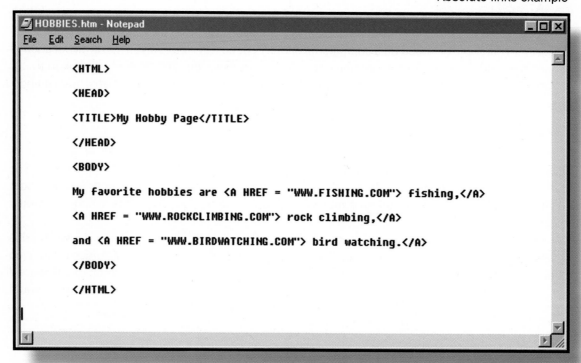

E-Mail

There are several other types of links in addition to those that lead to other Web pages. One of the most common types of non-Web links is e-mail. It is a good idea to include your e-mail address on every page on your site. When the user clicks the e-mail address, the browser starts a mail program. The e-mail address is automatically inserted into the address line. You use the <A> tag to create the link. Example: <A HREF="mailto:joe-smith@hotmail.com">Joe Smith</A>. See Figure 17.17.

FIGURE 17.17
E-mail link

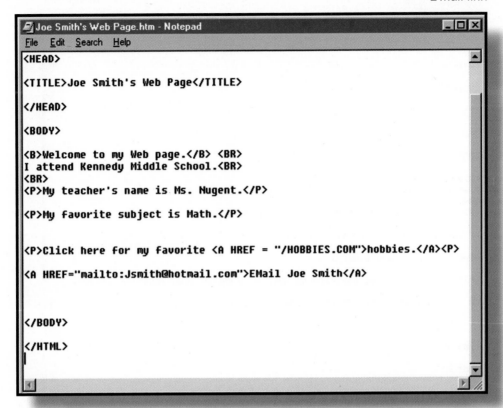

```
Joe Smith's Web Page.htm - Notepad
File   Edit   Search   Help

<HEAD>

<TITLE>Joe Smith's Web Page</TITLE>

</HEAD>

<BODY>

<B>Welcome to my Web page.</B> <BR>
I attend Kennedy Middle School.<BR>
<BR>
<P>My teacher's name is Ms. Nugent.</P>

<P>My favorite subject is Math.</P>


<P>Click here for my favorite <A HREF = "/HOBBIES.COM">hobbies.</A><P>

<A HREF="mailto:Jsmith@hotmail.com">EMail Joe Smith</A>



</BODY>

</HTML>
```

Images

Images or graphics are what add life to your Web site and make it exciting and fun. However, as much as they can add to a page, they can also slow down the downloading of your file, especially for someone with a slow modem. Many times when it takes too long to download a page, the person browsing the Web clicks the browser's Stop button and moves on to another site. Keep this in mind when you are creating your pages.

File Formats

Three different image types are supported by browsers and displayed on the Web:

- *GIF:* This is the most commonly used file type. It stands for Graphic Interchange Format and is pronounced "jif."

- *JPG or JPEG:* Another commonly used file format that results in smaller file sizes than GIF. This format is best used for photographs and other photo-quality images. JPEG stands for Joint Photographic Expert Group.

- *PNG:* This is a fairly new format. It has the advantages of both JPEG and GIF. However, it is not widely used. It is pronounced "ping" and stands for Portable Network Graphics.

To add an image to your Web page, use the <IMG> tag. This is a single tag; that is, there is no end tag. However, many attributes can be used with this tag. Three of the most popular are as follows.

293

FIGURE 17.18
Image tag

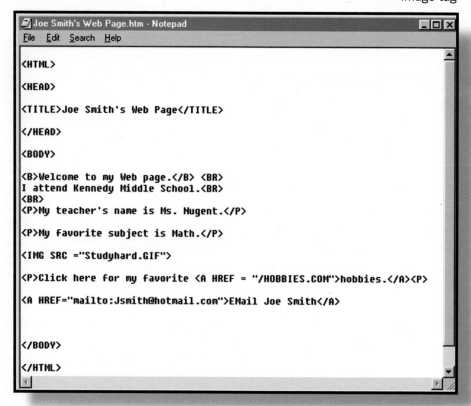

FIGURE 17.19
Browser display of image

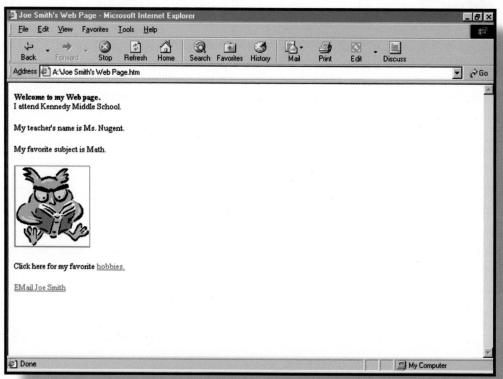

■ The first is SRC and is mandatory. Example: <IMG SRC = "Joe.gif">. SRC stands for source.

■ The second attribute that can be used with this tag is ALT. Use this attribute to provide alternative text. Some people with slow modems turn off images. Using the ALT (alternate) attribute provides them with an indication of the nature of the picture. This is an optional attribute. Example: <IMG SRC = "Joe.gif" ALT = "Joe Smith's picture"> See Figures 17.18 and 17.19.

■ The third attribute is ALIGN. Using this attribute, you can align the image in relation to the location of the image and the text. This is an optional attribute. Example: <IMG SRC = "Joe.gif" ALT = "Joe Smith's picture" ALIGN = LEFT>.

When you look at a Web page with images, the images appear to be part of the page. In reality, however, if your Web page displays three images, you have four separate files—the HTML document and the three image files. When the browser encounters the <IMG> tag, it knows to look for the SRC or source. The image could be located in the same folder as your HTML document or it could be located on a totally different computer on the other side of the world. If this was true, you would specify the address of the computer, just like you specified the absolute link. Example: <IMG SRC = "www.rockclimbing.com/Joe.gif" ALT = "Joe Smith's picture" ALIGN = LEFT>.

Your next question might be "How does the browser know where to display the image on the page?" You can place images almost anywhere within the body of your Web page. They can be on a line by themselves, at the end of a paragraph, at the beginning of a line, in the middle of a line, and so forth. Using the Align tag, you can control to a great extent exactly where they are placed. See Figures 17.20 and 17.21.

FIGURE 17.20
Image example placement

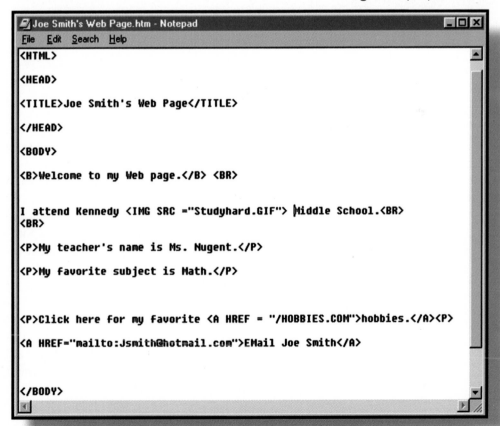

FIGURE 17.21
Image as displayed in browser

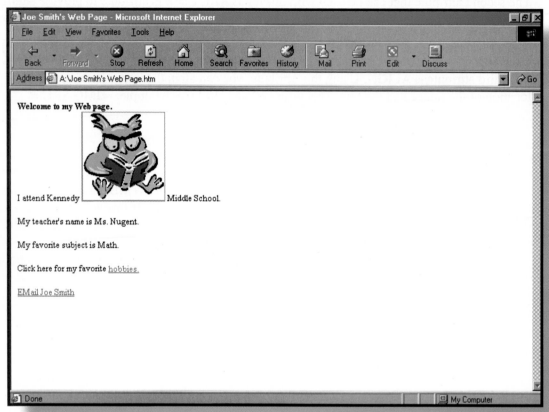

Horizontal Rule and Bulleted Lists

Many Web designers use horizontal lines to separate blocks of texts. The horizontal rule <HR> is a single entry tag that renders a thin line which extends across the width of the browser window. Simply enter the code and the line displays.

Another option for separating blocks of text is to use some type of graphical divider. Many of them are available for download on the Web or you can create your own with a paint or draw program such as PaintShop Pro. To add a graphical horizontal line to your Web page, simply go to the location within the document where you would like it to display. Then use the <IMG SRC> tag to insert it into your page. Example: <IMG SRC = "redline">. See Figures 17.22 and 17.23.

Earlier in this chapter you learned how to create and display bulleted lists. Suppose you prefer graphical bullets instead of the standard bullets. This is also easily accomplished with the <IMG SRC> tag. Simply place the tag before the line of text.

 Did You Know?

There are many free hosting sites on the Web. Some of them even offer free several MBs of free disk space. One of the most popular of these is www.idrive.com. This site advertises that it allows infinite storage space for your files.

FIGURE 17.22
Image tag for line divider

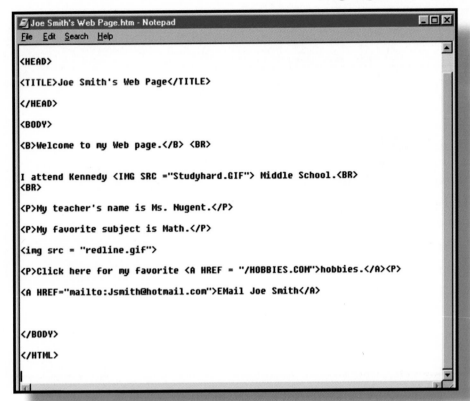

```
Joe Smith's Web Page.htm - Notepad
File  Edit  Search  Help

<HEAD>

<TITLE>Joe Smith's Web Page</TITLE>

</HEAD>

<BODY>

<B>Welcome to my Web page.</B> <BR>

I attend Kennedy <IMG SRC ="Studyhard.GIF"> Middle School.<BR>
<BR>
<P>My teacher's name is Ms. Nugent.</P>

<P>My favorite subject is Math.</P>

<img src = "redline.gif">

<P>Click here for my favorite <A HREF = "/HOBBIES.COM">hobbies.</A><P>

<A HREF="mailto:Jsmith@hotmail.com">EMail Joe Smith</A>



</BODY>

</HTML>
```

FIGURE 17.23
Line divider example

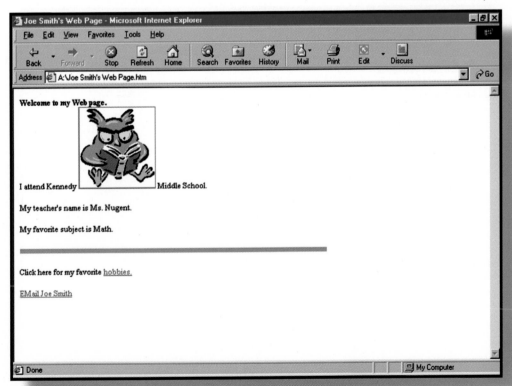

FIGURE 17.24
Web page with background color

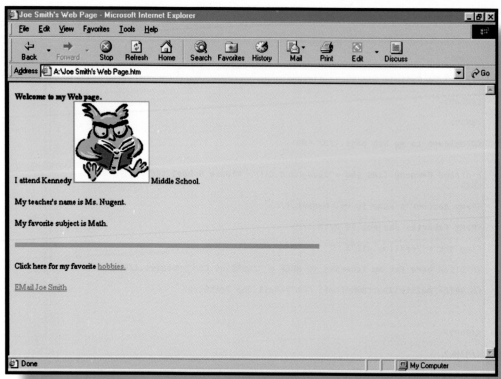

FIGURE 17.25
Web page with background image

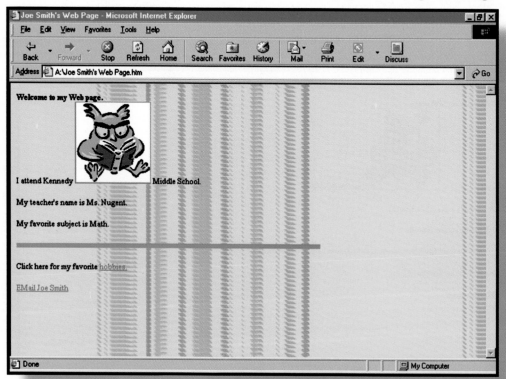

Backgrounds

As you surf the Web, you may notice that the background color of many Web pages is either white or gray. Generally the background color is determined by the browser you are using. You may also have noticed that many Web pages have some type of color or image for the background. You, too, can add color or images to the background of your Web pages. This is easily done by adding the BGCOLOR attribute to the <BODY> tag. Example: <BODY BGCOLOR = "PINK">. See Figure 17.24.

To add a background image to you Web page, you would specify the image. Example: <BODY BGGROUND = "IMAGE.GIF">. See Figure 17.25.

Publishing Your Web page

Your school may have its own Web server that you can use to publish your Web page creations. If not, do not be dismayed. A dozen or more Web sites on the Internet offer free space. Two of the most popular of these are Angelfire, located at www.angelfire.com, and Yahoo's GeoCities, located at geocities.yahoo.com/home/. See Figures 17.26 and 17.27.

Most of the sites that provide free space also provide step-by-step instructions on how to upload your page. Just locate and click on the link that indicates free home page or free space on their server. If you wonder how someone can offer free space for you to save your Web pages, you might want to check out all of the advertising on the page. These companies generate their income by selling banners and other advertising space.

FIGURE 17.26
Free Web page at GeoCities

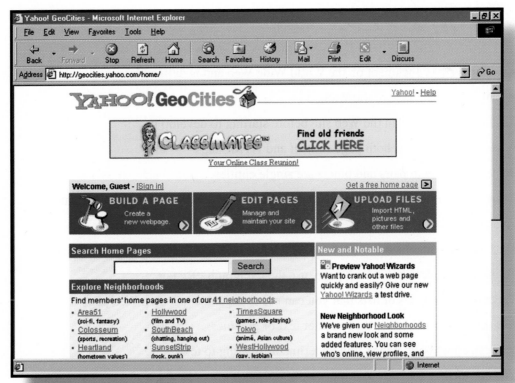

FIGURE 17.27
Free Web page at Angelfire

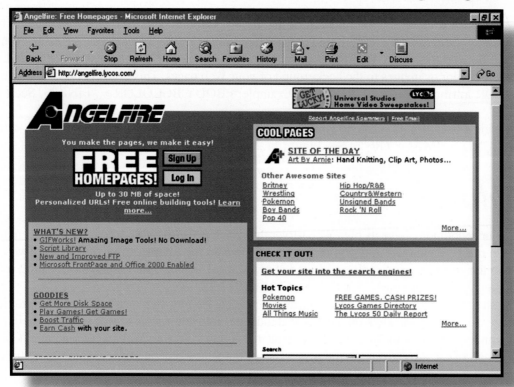

Summary

■ A Web page is a document on the World Wide Web and is defined by a unique URL.

■ HTML is the language of the Web.

■ It is always best to plan the Web site before starting to develop it.

■ A basic Web page has both page content and HTML tags

■ Some tags come in pairs and others are single entities.

■ Every Web page requires a particular set of tags structured in a particular format.

■ Pressing the keyboard Enter key has no affect on how a Web page displays.

■ To start a new line in a Web page, use the break <BR> tag.

■ To insert a blank line in a Web page, use the paragraph <P> tag.

■ There are three types of lists that you can use to organize text on a Web page.

■ Use the Center <Center> tag to center text or graphics.

■ You can apply bold, italics, and underline formatting to text.

■ You can change font size and font color.

- There are seven different font sizes supported by most browsers.

- There are six levels of HTML headings.

- A hyperlink is an active reference to other parts of the same document or to other documents.

- A relative link gives the file location in relation to the current document.

- Absolute links are hyperlinks to other Web sites.

- One of the most common types of non-Web links is e-mail.

- Three different image types are support by browsers – GIF, JPEG, and PNG.

- Use horizontal lines to separate blocks of text.

- You can add a background color to your Web page by using the <BODY BGCOLOR = "color name"> tag.

- You can add a background image to your Web page by using the <BODY BGGROUND = "image.gif"> tag.

- Many Web sites provide free space online for publishing your Web page.

LESSON 17 REVIEW QUESTIONS

MULTIPLE CHOICE

1. _____ is the language of the Web.
   A. Image
   B. BGCOLOR
   C. HTML
   D. HTTP

2. The _____ of your Web page is what appears on the browser title bar.
   A. body
   B. heading
   C. title
   D. closing

3. All Web page content is contained between the start and end _____ tags.
   A. title
   B. head
   C. IMG
   D. body

4. To leave a blank line on a Web page document, use the _____ tag.
   A.
   B. <P>
   C. <END>
   D. <START>

5. There are _____ different font sizes.
   A. one
   B. three
   C. seven
   D. twelve

TRUE/FALSE

Circle the T if the statement is true. Circle F if it is false.

T   F   1. The only way you can view your Web page is to log on to a Web server.

T   F   2. Within a Web page, you can change the color of text.

T   F   3. All Web page backgrounds are either white or gray.

T   F   4. A relative link would link to another Web site.

T   F   5. Use the ALT attribute to display a text description of an image.

SHORT ANSWER

1. A _____ is a thin line that extends across the width of the browser.

2. Use the _____ attribute to display a background color.

3. Use the _____ tag to create bold text.

4. An _____ list is generally a numbered list.

5. To center text or an image on a Web page, use the _____ tag.

CROSS-CURRICULAR PROJECTS

MATH

Create a Web page document for your math class. Include within this document a heading, a numbered list, a background color, and absolute links to two other mathematics Web sites.

SCIENCE

Select a special science project you may be working on. Create two Web pages for this project. Include somewhere within these two pages a H1 heading, a definition list, a background color, relative links from one of the Web pages to the other, and absolute links to at least one other Web site on your selected topic. Include at least two images in your Web page.

SOCIAL STUDIES

Ask your social studies teacher for a list of topics that you will study in the next month. Create a Web page, using a heading and a background color. Use "Links to (topics as provided by your teacher)" for the heading. Search the Web for Web sites related to the topics. Create a list of absolute links to the Web sites. Include at least 10 Web sites and include a short description of what can be found at the Web site.

LANGUAGE ARTS

Your teacher has asked you to write an article about your last vacation. After you write the article, convert it to a Web page document. Illustrate the page with images and graphical dividers.

TEAM PROJECT

Create a page about something relating to your school. It can be about sports, clubs, fund-raising, a special class project, or other topic as approved by your teachers. Use images, graphical bullets, at least two heading levels, two different font faces, and different font colors. Publish your Web page on your school's file server or on one of the free hosting servers.

WEB PROJECT

Now that you have the basic skills necessary to create a Web page, Ms. Perez would like to have at least a three-page Web site for Vista Multimedia. Create the Web site for Ms. Perez. Use as many tags as possible that were introduced in this module. To extend your HTML knowledge, use www.AskJeeves.com for HTML tutorial links. Include some additional HTML tags that you may find in one of these tutorials.

HOW CAN I USE TECHNOLOGY TO SOLVE A PROBLEM?

OBJECTIVES

When you complete this module, you will be able to:

■ Define problem solving.

■ Identify technology tools for solving problems.

■ Identify problem solving steps.

■ Explain how other forms of technology are used to solve problems.

⏱ Estimated Time: 1.5 hours

VOCABULARY

Database
Database software
Distance learning
Problem solving
Search engines
Spreadsheet software
Technology
Telecommunications
Word processing
     software

The staff meeting that Ms. Perez scheduled last week was a disaster! No one showed up at the assigned time. However, everyone came to the conference room an hour later for the meeting. What happened? Ms. Perez had scheduled the meeting at a time she thought would fit the schedule of everyone who needed to attend the meeting. An hour later did not fit her schedule!

This is not the first time that a scheduling mistake has occurred. However, Ms. Perez has had enough of missed meetings and the embarrassment caused by them! She needs to be able to know when everyone is free for meetings, when employees are scheduled to work, when she has meetings and other obligations of her own, and whatever else to keep herself and her staff organized.

She is sure that there must be some type of technology that can help her. She hasn't asked you yet, but you know she probably will ask for help to solve her problem. The technology is out there. However, before you just go out and purchase a piece of software because you think it might be appropriate, you need to analyze exactly what Ms. Perez's problem is and make your selection based on your findings.

How Does Technology Solve Problems for You?

Did your Spanish instructor give you an assignment to write a report in Spanish? Did your math instructor assign you to find the average temperatures for a month in your town? Did your adviser for Future Business Leaders of America ask for a printout of all members who have still not paid their dues or to determine how much candy you would need to sale to make a $250 profit? Do you have a classmate who has a disability that prevents him or her from being able to key information into the computer? If you can answer "yes" to even one of these scenarios, technology is your solution!

Technology is the application of scientific discoveries to the production of goods and services that improve the human environment. The computer is a major element of technology and has aided in improvements in medical research, space travel, and exploration just to name a few.

Technology provides tools for dealing with the many situations that could affect business operations as well as our individual lives. Technology is responsible for transporting us to a make-believe universe when we play arcade games at the mall, making getting cash from our banks any time of the day or night as easy as locating an ATM machine, and making it possible for employees to send messages over networks. The Internet's capabilities are endless.

The computer plays a major role in the technology boom. It addresses and solves many of the technical types of issues and concerns in our society. A basic function of a computer is to solve problems; to answer questions, to provide an easier and better way to perform certain tasks. Computer software controls the versatility of the computer. In other words, with the appropriate software, you can solve just about any problem or simplify any task.

The amount and kinds of technology available are astounding. You can find technology for almost every situation from finding and purchasing stock over the Internet to finding personnel for a space shuttle! See Figure 18.1.

FIGURE 18.1

Clockwise from top left: A technician uses a computer to evaluate data; Students use a variety of of computers for researching and writing papers; This business person is using a general-purpose computer to keep track of inventory; This scientist is using a computer containing a special math processor to conduct an experiment.

Selecting the correct technology to address a specific task or problem requires careful investigation. A logical guideline needs to be followed in order to identify the situation that could use technology to alleviate problems or to enhance a specific task and to identify the exact technology that would address the situation. This is called problem solving and there are steps that should be followed in order to solve problems effectively

What Is Problem Solving?

Problem solving is a systematic approach of going from an initial situation to a desired situation; subject to some resource constraints.

Problem-Solving Steps

To solve a problem successfully, a logical plan should be used. This plan will give you a guide or road map to use. It will assist from defining the problem to gathering information concerning the problem, to identifying possible solutions, to selecting and implementing the best solution. A guide is listed here.

- Define the problem.

- Investigate and analyze the problem.

- Identify possible solutions.

- Select and implement a solution.

- Evaluate solutions.

Each of the listed steps is very important in the problem-solving process. Each step should be fully completed before going to the next step. Let's explore each step closely.

Identify the Problem

In this stage, you ensure there really is a problem and identify what it is. Sometimes the problem may not be as transparent as you might think. You need to really investigate the situation to determine what is the real issue. Ask questions, use what-if statements, eliminate some facts, include others, clarify the current situation, and identify what the situation should be or maybe what you would like it to be. If necessary, make notes or sketches; identify the known and unknown facts. Once you have identified the problem, you can now begin to determine why the problem exists, possible causes, and so on.

Investigate and Analyze the Problem

Before you can begin to solve the problem, you need all the facts. Collect all available data and facts regarding the situation. This step will provide information needed to make an accurate decision. Sometimes during this step, it may be decided that a problem really does not exist at all or that what you thought was the problem really is not, but something else is. However if there is a legitimate problem or need, your detective work at this stage should provide you with this information.

Identify Possible Solutions

Once the problem has been identified, possible solutions need to be identified. What can to be done to alleviate the problem? What needs to be done differently? What needs to be deleted or added? These are the types of questions that would need to be answered in looking for a solution. In exploring possible solutions, several solutions may be identified.

Choose and Implement Chosen Solution

If more than one possible solution is identified, critique and test each solution to determine what the outcome of the situation would be with each solution. Based on this information, you would choose the solution that provides the best outcome. Once the solution is selected, implement it.

Evaluate Solutions

After putting the chosen solution into place, you will need to evaluate its performance on the situation. Did it eliminate the problem? Did it do what you needed to have done? If your answer is "yes," you now have a solution to a situation that caused you concern.

Problem Solving with Computers in Action

Now that we have discussed the guideline for solving problems using technology, let's use it to solve Ms. Perez's scheduling problem.

Identifying the Problem

What needs to be accomplished? What information is needed and how is it to be presented?

- Selecting appropriate software to be used

- Eliminating scheduling conflicts

- Knowing employees' schedules

Investigating and Analyzing Problem

- How can she know all employees' schedules?

- How can she notify all employees of meeting in a timely fashion?

- What type of software is available for her needs?

ETHICS IN TECHNOLOGY

DIGITAL WATERMARKS

A watermark is a faded-looking image in the background of a document. A digital watermark is an image embedded within graphics and audio files and used to identify the owner's rights to these files. In other words, a digital image can be added to music files, pictures, and so on, which identifies the creator's work in a way that is invisible to the human eye.

These watermarks also serve the purposes of identifying quality and assuring that the work is the original. Watermarking technology makes it possible for copyright owners to find illegal copies of the work and take appropriate legal action.

Digital watermarks are also an excellent tool for Web masters. It ensures that only lawful image and audio files are used, so they are not guilty of copyright infringement.

Identify Possible Solutions

■ Use word processing software to type a memo to send to all employees announcing meeting.

■ Manually check everyone's schedule to see when they are scheduled to be at work and available for a meeting.

■ Identify a software program that can be used to enter and maintain employees' schedules and also has the capability to notify employees of meetings and also let her know they have received the message.

Choose Solution and Implement Chosen Solution

■ Identify a software program that can be used to enter and maintain employees' schedules that also has the capability to notify employees of meetings and also let her know they have received the message.

■ There are several scheduling programs on the market. After examining the capabilities of several, it was decided that Microsoft Scheduler+ would be best for the video store.

Evaluate Chosen Solution

After obtaining the software, Microsoft Scheduler+, and learning to use it, Ms. Perez entered everyone's work schedule and other information she needed to have available for herself and each employee. She could hardly wait to "announce" the next staff meeting. When it was time, she created a message and sent it to everyone. She was immediately notified when each employee opened their message whether they responded right away or not. Each employee did eventually respond to the staff meeting message by the deadline and indicated if they would be attending the staff meeting. Problem solved!

Internet

Go to the Microsoft Office web site and find information concerning Microsoft Scheduler+ features.

Using Technology Tools to Solve Problems

Computers and the Internet have made it much easier to find solutions to many of the tasks that individuals and businesses need to address on a daily basis. Typical software programs used are word processing, database, spreadsheet, utility programs, scheduling, collaboration, telecommunications, and multimedia (graphics, animation, digital video, sound, authoring, presentation).

Once you have learned to use the mechanics of computer software, you can determine how you can use this software to perform various types of tasks. Here are some examples:

■ *Word processing software* is used to type data, but it has many applications that it can perform other than just typing. What are these applications and how can you use them to, say, prepare envelopes for a group of customers?

■ Web pages can be designed using HTML codes or using word processing software. You have just started a new small business and want to advertise on the Internet. How can you go about having a Web page prepared?

■ You know that grades can be averaged in a spreadsheet; but how can you determine what grade you would need to make on the final exam to receive an "A" in your math class?

All of these situations pose "problems" that need to be solved or at least situations that could use some type of technology. Each software application mentioned can solve one of the problems. However, you will need to determine which software program to use and how to use its capabilities to solve the problem at hand.

The Internet offers electronic communication, distance learning and teleconferencing, networking, and electronic research tools. These tools are used to collect and analyze data for use in problem-solving activities. As a user, this means you must be adequately familiar with the mechanics or the "know-how" of the software and how to use search engines and other features available for Internet research.

You can see technology in use almost everywhere! It assists in the development of new treatments in the medical field; it guides you through tourist attractions such as museums, it simulates space travels, it assist law enforcement activities, and it makes those special effects in movies seem so real! What ways can you see technology in your life?

Using Software to Solve Problems

There are many different types of software programs available to address various types of applications. There are basic software programs available as well as software programs for specialized areas such as banking, medical, real estate, insurance, law, and so forth.

 Did You Know?

Many word processing programs have advanced features that allow you to perform spreadsheet-like functions and database-like functions. You can create files and use the mathematical functions available like you find in spreadsheet programs. Data files can be created that can sorted, selected and even merged into other documents.

WORD PROCESSING SOFTWARE

Word processing software allows you to create and modify documents. It greatly reduces the need for retyping documents. Most word processing programs have features that make creating various types of documents such as newsletters, reports, and tables an easy task. The merge feature save hours in preparing multiple documents. Do you need an alphabetical listing of members of an organization? This is a simple task for word processing software. Footnotes and endnotes can be entered effortlessly. This software addresses many of the document needs of an organization or individual. See Figure 18.2.

Refer to "Computer Concepts: Systems, Applications, Design" CD-Rom. Select the Databanks section to learn more about word processing.

FIGURE 18.2
Word processing documents

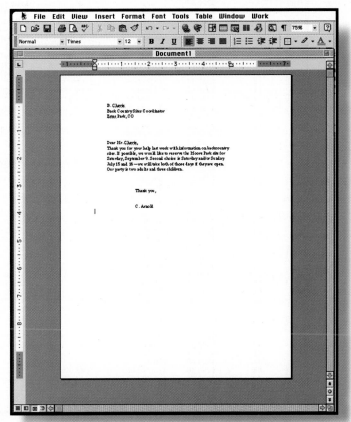

309

SPREADSHEET SOFTWARE

Spreadsheet programs are designed to store and manipulate numeric data. They are used extensively in business to produce financial analyses such as budgets, financial statements, and forecasts. Formulas are entered into a spreadsheet to calculate various conditions. The beauty of the spreadsheet is its ability to recalculate itself when different information is entered.

Spreadsheet software has become a vital tool to businesses because it helps in predicting the outcome of various situations and factors. There are times when businesses need to know what the outcome will be under certain circumstances. Spreadsheet software allows this type for forecasting with "what-if" statements. It is quite evident how this type of software solves problems for businesses. See Figure 18.3.

Refer to "Computer Concepts: Systems, Applications, Design" CD-ROM. Select the Databanks section to learn more about spreadsheet programs.

FIGURE 18.3

Spreadsheets are used for documents such as budgets, inventories, etc.

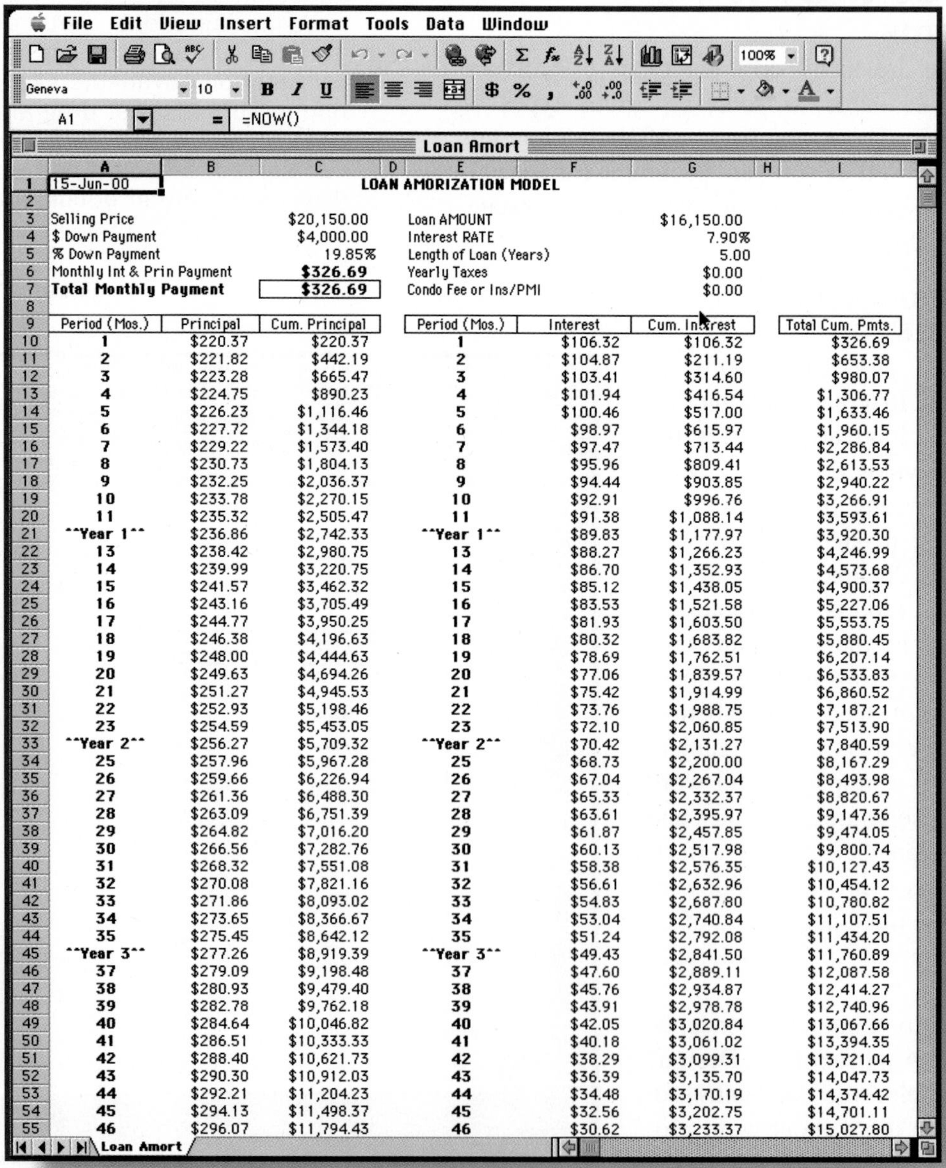

	A	B	C	D	E	F	G	H	I
1	15-Jun-00				**LOAN AMORIZATION MODEL**				
2									
3	Selling Price		$20,150.00		Loan AMOUNT		$16,150.00		
4	$ Down Payment		$4,000.00		Interest RATE		7.90%		
5	% Down Payment		19.85%		Length of Loan (Years)		5.00		
6	Monthly Int & Prin Payment		**$326.69**		Yearly Taxes		$0.00		
7	**Total Monthly Payment**		**$326.69**		Condo Fee or Ins/PMI		$0.00		
8									
9	Period (Mos.)	Principal	Cum. Principal		Period (Mos.)	Interest	Cum. Interest		Total Cum. Pmts.
10	**1**	$220.37	$220.37		**1**	$106.32	$106.32		$326.69
11	**2**	$221.82	$442.19		**2**	$104.87	$211.19		$653.38
12	**3**	$223.28	$665.47		**3**	$103.41	$314.60		$980.07
13	**4**	$224.75	$890.23		**4**	$101.94	$416.54		$1,306.77
14	**5**	$226.23	$1,116.46		**5**	$100.46	$517.00		$1,633.46
15	**6**	$227.72	$1,344.18		**6**	$98.97	$615.97		$1,960.15
16	**7**	$229.22	$1,573.40		**7**	$97.47	$713.44		$2,286.84
17	**8**	$230.73	$1,804.13		**8**	$95.96	$809.41		$2,613.53
18	**9**	$232.25	$2,036.37		**9**	$94.44	$903.85		$2,940.22
19	**10**	$233.78	$2,270.15		**10**	$92.91	$996.76		$3,266.91
20	**11**	$235.32	$2,505.47		**11**	$91.38	$1,088.14		$3,593.61
21	**^^Year 1^^**	$236.86	$2,742.33		**^^Year 1^^**	$89.83	$1,177.97		$3,920.30
22	**13**	$238.42	$2,980.75		**13**	$88.27	$1,266.23		$4,246.99
23	**14**	$239.99	$3,220.75		**14**	$86.70	$1,352.93		$4,573.68
24	**15**	$241.57	$3,462.32		**15**	$85.12	$1,438.05		$4,900.37
25	**16**	$243.16	$3,705.49		**16**	$83.53	$1,521.58		$5,227.06
26	**17**	$244.77	$3,950.25		**17**	$81.93	$1,603.50		$5,553.75
27	**18**	$246.38	$4,196.63		**18**	$80.32	$1,683.82		$5,880.45
28	**19**	$248.00	$4,444.63		**19**	$78.69	$1,762.51		$6,207.14
29	**20**	$249.63	$4,694.26		**20**	$77.06	$1,839.57		$6,533.83
30	**21**	$251.27	$4,945.53		**21**	$75.42	$1,914.99		$6,860.52
31	**22**	$252.93	$5,198.46		**22**	$73.76	$1,988.75		$7,187.21
32	**23**	$254.59	$5,453.05		**23**	$72.10	$2,060.85		$7,513.90
33	**^^Year 2^^**	$256.27	$5,709.32		**^^Year 2^^**	$70.42	$2,131.27		$7,840.59
34	**25**	$257.96	$5,967.28		**25**	$68.73	$2,200.00		$8,167.29
35	**26**	$259.66	$6,226.94		**26**	$67.04	$2,267.04		$8,493.98
36	**27**	$261.36	$6,488.30		**27**	$65.33	$2,332.37		$8,820.67
37	**28**	$263.09	$6,751.39		**28**	$63.61	$2,395.97		$9,147.36
38	**29**	$264.82	$7,016.20		**29**	$61.87	$2,457.85		$9,474.05
39	**30**	$266.56	$7,282.76		**30**	$60.13	$2,517.98		$9,800.74
40	**31**	$268.32	$7,551.08		**31**	$58.38	$2,576.35		$10,127.43
41	**32**	$270.08	$7,821.16		**32**	$56.61	$2,632.96		$10,454.12
42	**33**	$271.86	$8,093.02		**33**	$54.83	$2,687.80		$10,780.82
43	**34**	$273.65	$8,366.67		**34**	$53.04	$2,740.84		$11,107.51
44	**35**	$275.45	$8,642.12		**35**	$51.24	$2,792.08		$11,434.20
45	**^^Year 3^^**	$277.26	$8,919.39		**^^Year 3^^**	$49.43	$2,841.50		$11,760.89
46	**37**	$279.09	$9,198.48		**37**	$47.60	$2,889.11		$12,087.58
47	**38**	$280.93	$9,479.40		**38**	$45.76	$2,934.87		$12,414.27
48	**39**	$282.78	$9,762.18		**39**	$43.91	$2,978.78		$12,740.96
49	**40**	$284.64	$10,046.82		**40**	$42.05	$3,020.84		$13,067.66
50	**41**	$286.51	$10,333.33		**41**	$40.18	$3,061.02		$13,394.35
51	**42**	$288.40	$10,621.73		**42**	$38.29	$3,099.31		$13,721.04
52	**43**	$290.30	$10,912.03		**43**	$36.39	$3,135.70		$14,047.73
53	**44**	$292.21	$11,204.23		**44**	$34.48	$3,170.19		$14,374.42
54	**45**	$294.13	$11,498.37		**45**	$32.56	$3,202.75		$14,701.11
55	**46**	$296.07	$11,794.43		**46**	$30.62	$3,233.37		$15,027.80

DATABASE SOFTWARE

Database software makes it possible to create and maintain large collections of data. This is type of software is critical to the success to just about every business. A *database* is a collection of files. Customer lists and inventory lists are just two examples of how database software is used in business. The data stored in a database can easily be accessed in a variety of ways. Do you need to know how many of your customers have live in a certain Zip code? Your database software can render this information. See Figure 18.4.

Refer to "Computer Concepts: Systems, Applications, Design" CD-ROM. Select the Databanks section to learn more about databases.

FIGURE 18.4
Database documents

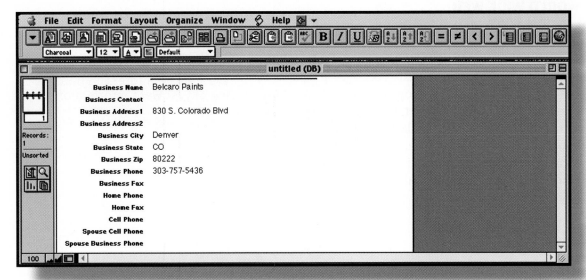

TELECOMMUNICATIONS

Telecommunications is electronically transferring data. Two of the most popular features of telecommunication are *distance learning* and *teleconferencing*. Distance learning addresses the problem of not being able to actually attend classes, and teleconferencing reduces the cost of travel, schedule conflicts, and accommodations for busy executives by providing conferencing capabilities without having to leave their offices. More problems solved.

Hot Tip

The Information Superhighway is the result of cable-television companies and telephone companies, which used to be separate types of companies, beginning to provide the same services.

PERSONAL INFORMATION MANAGEMENT SOFTWARE

Personal information management software (PIMS) is used to organize appointments, telephone messages, projects, and tasks to be completed. Some examples of PIMs are Microsoft Scheduler+, Microsoft Outlook, and Lotus Organizer.

OTHER SOFTWARE PROGRAMS

Many, many more types of software programs on the market provide specific capabilities for specific applications. For example, there is software for real estate agents, builders, doctors, musicians, cooks, and the list goes on and on.

311

Using the Internet to Solve Problems

The capabilities of the Internet are numerous! Users can exchange messages, participate in discussion groups, and transfer files from one location to another. Researchers can access information from remote sources, information can be shared around the world, businesses can sell services and products, and the list goes on and on. A brief discussion of some Internet services follows.

E-MAIL

Electronic mail is the most popular service of the Internet. It allows users to communicate with each other at any time day or night. Businesses find that e-mail makes communication more efficient and eliminates interruptions from telephone calls and also eliminates playing phone tag. E-mail definitely addresses a need.

WORLD WIDE WEB

The WWW, as it is sometimes referred to, is a collection of interlinked multimedia documents stored on tens of thousands of independent servers around the world. In simpler terms, it consists of pages and pages of businesses, individuals, and organizations. Many businesses advertise on the Internet. Do you need to purchase a new car? Linking to the car dealer's Web page will give you all the information you need including cost, options, local dealerships, and so on. If you want to know what kinds of business are in your area, you could go to www.bigbook.com.

 Internet

Link to the maker of a car that you may be interest in purchasing or just want information on. Determine the cost and the availability of pre-owned cars in your locality.

TECHNOLOGY CAREERS

ADMINISTRATIVE ASSISTANT

The administrative assistant oversees the overall functioning of an office. The position requires the person to work with considerable initiative in the absence of the supervisor and to exercise independent judgment within the framework of established policies and objectives.

The computer is the main tool that the administrative assistant uses to complete many of the required tasks. Word processing, database management, spreadsheet, and desktop publishing software programs are used daily. The administrative assistant also uses other types of computer capabilities depending on the type of office in which he or she works. Most companies have networked computers, which are part of the administrative assistant's responsibilities as well.

The qualifications required include excellent communication skills; both verbal and written, knowledge of modern office practices, systems, and equipment, ability to handle multiple projects simultaneously, strong math, interpersonal, and organizational skills, and a professional, friendly, and outgoing personality. A sense of humor is also an asset.

A college degree is usually preferred. Evidence of some training and impressive experience, however, is sometimes acceptable. The average salary for an administrative assistant ranges between $25,000 and $35,000 a year depending on experience and location of company.

FIGURE 18.5
Search engines are helpful in locating needed information on the Web.

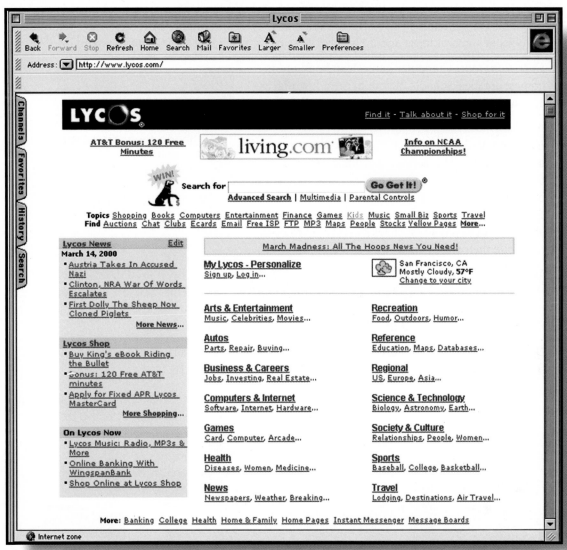

SEARCH ENGINES

Not sure of the name of an organization or business but know the subject or topic on which you need information? Use a search engine. Search engines allow you to enter a keyword to find sites that contain information that you need. Some popular search engines include Excite, Hotboot, Mamma, AskJeeves, and Dogpile. See Figure 18.5.

Hot Tip

You can ask a complete question to locate information on the Internet. Just AskJeeves.com.

Other Technologies

The use of technology has affected our daily lives in so many different ways. This section briefly looks at some of these and their benefits to us as individuals and as businesses.

- **Entertainment:** Computer games can be found in homes, arcades, schools, just to name a few places. These games range from action games to simulations.

- **Electronic banking:** Nearly every bank offers electronic banking. This service permits customers to bank whenever they want. They can take money out of their accounts any place there is an ATM machine. They can also do on-line banking, which allows them to pay bills, check balances, and even reconcile their statements.

 **Hot Tip**

Voice mail is the most popular example of the combination of telephone technology and computer technology. It has proven to be a very important asset to businesses because it help to alleviate the many problems caused in trying to make contact with customers, suppliers, etc.

- **Medical and health care:** For quite some time computers have been used in hospitals for record keeping. Now they have a greater role in the care of patients. Sensors can be attached to patients to indicate when changes occur within their bodies. Tests that used to take a long time to complete now can be done quickly with computers. See Figure 18.6.

- **Dangerous tasks:** Some jobs are too dangerous for humans to perform. Computers can perform these jobs as well or even better than humans. See Figure 18.7.

FIGURE 18.6
Computers help medical personnel provide more effective treatment.

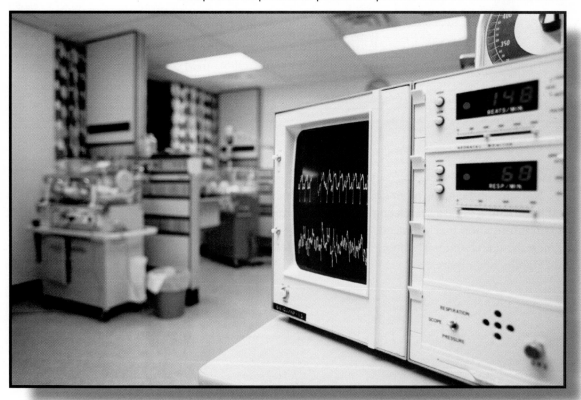

Repetitious tasks are performed by computers. An example is the manufacture of the microprocessor chip. Each one must be made exactly alike. This is done by using computers to control the processing equipment down to the exact timing and chemical mixtures.

Summary

- Technology has made a great impact on our lives.

- The computer plays a major role in the technology boom.

- Computer software controls the versatility of the computer.

- Problem solving involves defining a problem and finding a solution.

- Typical software programs such as word processing, spreadsheet, database management, and telecommunications are used to solve problems.

- The Internet offers electronic communication, distance learning, teleconferencing, networking, and electronic research tools to address solving problems.

- Other technologies that have affected our lives in solving problems for us include the areas of entertainment, medicine, transportation, banking, and the performance of dangerous tasks.

- The sequence of problem solving include defining the problem, investigating and analyzing the problem, identifying possible solutions, selecting and implementing the best solution, and evaluating the chosen solution.

FIGURE 18.7
Computers can perform tasks in environments too dangerous for humans.

LESSON 18 REVIEW QUESTIONS

MULTIPLE CHOICE

1. Word processing, database, spreadsheets, and telecommunications are types of
_____ used to solve problems.
   A. search engines
   B. software
   C. URLs
   D. technology

2. Being able to withdraw cash from your checking account any time you want is made possible through the use of _____.
   A. ATMs
   B. online banking
   C. debit cards
   D. postdated checks

3. Electronic communication, distance learning, and teleconferencing are examples of _____ tools for solving problems.
   A. software
   B. Internet
   C. e-mail
   D. hardware

4. _____ software provides the ability to make what-if statements in order to perform forecasts.
   A. Database
   B. Spreadsheet
   C. Word processing
   D. Web page design

5. A _____ is a collection of files.
   A. database
   B. spreadsheet
   C. search engine
   D. list

TRUE/FALSE

Circle the T if the statement is true. Circle F if it is false.

T F   1. Technology can solve every imaginable problem a person could have.

T F   2. The first step in the problem-solving process is to select a solution.

T F   3. Telecommunications is electronically transferring data.

T F   4. Electronic mail is the most popular service on the Internet.

T F   5. Many businesses advertise on the World Wide Web.

SHORT ANSWER

1. Use _____ when using search engines to locate information.

2. The first step in the problem-solving process is to _____ the problem.

3. The _____ plays a major role in the technology boom.

4. Give the name of one search engine. _____

5. The last step in the problem-solving process is to _____ the chosen solution.

CROSS-CURRICULAR PROJECTS

MATH

Computer games have become a booming business. There are usually two or three that are very popular every year. Locate sales data for the top five computer games for the past two years. Prepare a report indicating the total sales for the two-year period as well as indicating the share of the market each one held. You may find useful information at www.pcdata.com. You may also find information at individual computer games companies.

SCIENCE

You heard one of your instructors say that he needed to take a course next semester but the course was being offered at an inconvenient time for him. He had been told the course was also being offered as a distance learning class, which is sometimes called online learning. Write a report that explains just what this means. How are the computer and other technology involved in making this type of class possible? You may find useful information at www.hoyle.com/distance.htm. Also try using the keyword *distance learning* with several search engines.

SOCIAL STUDIES

Did you ever wonder how the design of stamps are selected? What criteria does the post office use in selecting images for stamps? Select two stamps and write a report on how these stamps were chosen. You can find information at www.usps.com and www.AskJeeves.com

LANGUAGE ARTS

In this module, several tools for solving problems were discussed. Identify a problem related to being secretary of your Future Business Leaders of America chapter. Select one of the tools discussed to address this problem. Prepare a report to share with the class. Be sure to indicate why you chose the tool you did.

WEB PROJECT

Using search engines to locate information on the Internet was discussed in this module. As with anything, there are rules or guidelines to follow in order to use search engines effectively. If you can narrow your search by using precise keywords, you have a better chance of finding just the information you want. Use the Internet to locate information on using search engine effectively. Prepare a handout you can share with your classmates. You may find useful information at www.webreference.com, www.monash.com, and http://daphne.palomar.edu/TGSEARCH.

317

Ms. Perez is pleased that you suggested Microsoft Scheduler+ to help her get organized, and she is very happy with it. However, she knows you were considering another software program called Microsoft Outlook. She would like to compare the features of it with Scheduler+. She has asked you to work with the other part-time employee to prepare a table showing this information. You will find the information you need at the following URL: www.microsoft.com.

WHAT ARE SOME TECHNOLOGICAL ISSUES?

LESSON 19

OBJECTIVES

When you complete this module, you will be able to:

- Identify types of computer crimes.
- Identify the "work" of hackers.
- Identify computer viruses.
- Describe how privacy is invaded because of computer use.
- Identify various security measures.
- Describe software piracy.
- Identify computer-related laws.

⏱ **Estimated Time: 1.5 hours**

VOCABULARY

Biometric security measures
Computer crimes
Computer fraud
Hacking
Logic bomb
Shareware
Software piracy
Time bomb
Trojan horse
Worm

Ms. Perez has just received an e-mail message from a friend warning her about a computer virus. Needless to say, she is very concerned and has decided to discuss this issue and other issues that relate to the security and safety of the computers in the video store. She has asked you to help her gather information.

She wants to focus on how computers have made a very positive impact in our lives, how they have made our daily lives much easier, our jobs more productive, learning more interesting, and so forth. But she also wants to make employees aware that even though the computer provides many positive benefits for us, problems exist such as viruses, security, and various computer crimes.

She has asked you to also locate suggestions for protecting the system that is used in the store and for educating the employees.

Types of Computer Crimes

What is a *computer crime*? It is a criminal act committed through the use of a computer, for example, getting into someone else's system and changing information or creating a computer virus and causing it to damage information on others' computers. It can also involve the theft of a computer and any equipment associated with the computer.

Computer crime is a bigger problem than most people realize. Billions of dollars every year are lost to corporations because of this often undetected, and therefore unpunished, crime. Computer crimes have increased since data communications and computer networks have become popular. Many computer crimes consist of stealing and damaging information and stealing actual computer equipment. Other types of computer crimes can include the following:

- unauthorized use of a computer

- infection of a computer by a malicious program (a virus)

- harassment and stalking on the computer

- theft of computer equipment

- copyright violations of software

- copyright violations of information found on the Internet

> **Hot Tip**
>
> The FBI's National Crime Information Center has a division for computer crimes.

Computer Fraud

Computer fraud is conduct that involves the manipulation of a computer or computer data in order to obtain money, property, or value dishonestly or to cause loss. Examples of computer fraud include stealing money from bank accounts and stealing information from other people's computers for gain.

Managers and supervisors in companies should be aware of certain signs that may be indicators of computer fraud:

 Did You Know?

The first computer crime, electronic embezzlement, was committed in 1958.

- Low staff morale: Unhappy staff members may decide the company owes them.

- Unusual work patterns.

- Staff members who appear to be living beyond their income.

Computer Hacking

Computer hacking involves invading someone else's computer, usually for personal gain or just the satisfaction of invading someone else's computer. Hackers are usually computer experts who enjoy having the power to invade someone else's privacy. They can steal money or change or damage data stored on a computer.

It is estimated that hacking causes millions of dollars of damage each year. There have been several high-profile cases of hacking in the United States.

Computer Viruses

A *virus* is a program that has been written, usually by a hacker, to cause corruption of data on a computer. The virus is attached to an executable file (like a program file) and spreads from one file to another once the program is executed. A virus can cause major damage to a computer's data or it can do something as minor as display messages on your screen. There are different variations of viruses.

- A *worm* makes many copies of itself, resulting in the consumption of system resources that slows down or actually halts tasks. Worms don't have to attach themselves to other files.

- A *time bomb* is a virus that does not cause its damage until a certain date or until the system has been booted a certain number of times.

■ A *logic bomb* is a virus triggered by the appearance or disappearance of specified data.

■ A *trojan horse* is a virus that does something different from what it is expected to do. It may look like it is doing one thing while in actuality it is doing something quite opposite (usually something disastrous).

In order to protect your computer against virus damage:

■ Use antivirus software. This software should always run on your computer and should be updated regularly.

■ Be careful in opening e-mail attachments. It is a good idea to save them to disk before reading them so you can scan them.

■ Don't access files copied from floppy disks or downloaded from the Internet without scanning them first. See Figure 19.1.

FIGURE 19.1
Scanning a file for potential virus

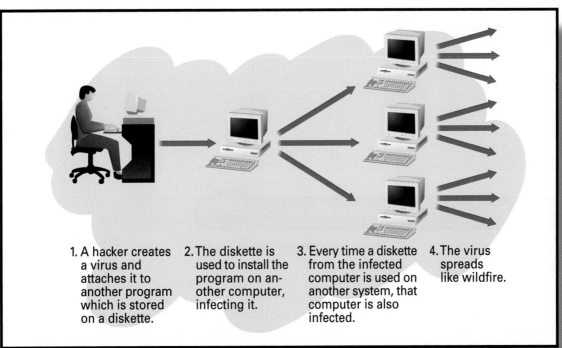

1. A hacker creates a virus and attaches it to another program which is stored on a diskette.

2. The diskette is used to install the program on another computer, infecting it.

3. Every time a diskette from the infected computer is used on another system, that computer is also infected.

4. The virus spreads like wildfire.

Other Computer Crimes

Theft of computer time is also a crime committed regularly on the job. This crime is committed when an employee uses a company's computer for personal use such as running a small side business, keeping records of an outside organization, or keeping personal records. While you are working these types of tasks, you are not being as productive as you could be for your employer.

Using the information you see on someone else's screen or printout to profit unfairly is theft of output.

Changing data before it is entered into the computer or after it has been entered into the computer is called *data diddling*. Anyone who is involved with creating, recording, encoding, and checking data can change data.

Privacy

The amount of personal information available on each of us is astonishing. You would probably be very upset to know the extent to which this information is available and to whom it is available. There are many companies who gather information to create databases and sell or trade this information to others.

Any time you submit information on the Internet, it is possible for this information to be gathered by many persons and used for various situations. Information can also be gathered from online data regarding school, banking, hospitals, insurance, and any other information supplied for such everyday activities.

Much of the information gathered and sold results in your name being added to mailing lists. These lists are used by companies for marketing purposes. Junk e-mails are used for the same purpose. Information regarding one's credit history is also available to be sold.

If you work for a company that provides you with e-mail, you should know that the information you send is available to the company; it is the company's property. It can be accessed from backup copies made by the system.

Hot Tip

The movie "The Net" is an example of how computer viruses can affect computers and our lives.

TECHNOLOGY CAREERS

SYSTEM ANALYST

A system analyst works with the user to develop information systems. They plan and design new systems, recommend changes to existing systems, and participate in implementing changes. They are also responsible for writing manuals for the programs as well as external documentation. They system analyst is responsible for making sure that all users understand and can use the system effectively as well as keeping management informed.

This position requires a good technical knowledge of the computer. The system analyst should be up-to-date in the advances in the computer science field, good with details, and comfortable dealing with difficult people. Effective teaching skills are imperative because the analyst will have to teach the system to the users. A system analyst should be a people-person because they work with a lot of users. They have to be self-motivated, a team worker and a good listener. Many system analysts begin as programmers and work their way up to systems analysts. However, having a four-year degree in computer science will enhance chances of obtaining a higher-paying beginning position. Having a certification, which requires five years of experience as an analyst and passing an exam, will also enhance chances of a higher-paying job.

A system analyst in a big firm can make anywhere from $47,000 to $60,000. In a small firm they can make anywhere from $38,000 to $50,000. These ranges vary based on location and size of the number of users on the system.

Security

Computer security is necessary in order to keep hardware, software, and data safe from harm or destruction. Some risks to computers are natural causes, some are accidents, and some are intentional. It is not always evident that some type of computer crime or intrusion has occurred. Therefore, it is necessary that safeguards for each type of risk be put into place. It is the responsibility of a company or an individual to protect their data.

The best way to protect data is to control access to the data. The most common form of restricting access to data is the use of passwords. Users must have a password in order to log into a system. Companies sometimes restrict access to certain computers. Passwords are usually changed periodically. See Figure 19.2.

Other security measures include the following:

- Making security a priority; maintain and enforce security measures.

- Electronic identification cards to gain access to certain areas within a building or department.

- Firewalls, which consist of special hardware and software, protect individual companies' networks from external networks. A firewall would allow users inside the organization the ability to access computers outside of their organization but keep outside users from accessing their computers.

- Use antivirus software to protect data on your computer.

- Institute a very selective hiring process that includes careful screening of potential employees. Do not keep employees on staff who refuse to follow security rules. This measure will prevent internal theft or sabotage.

FIGURE 19.2
Passwords are used to protect against unauthorized use.

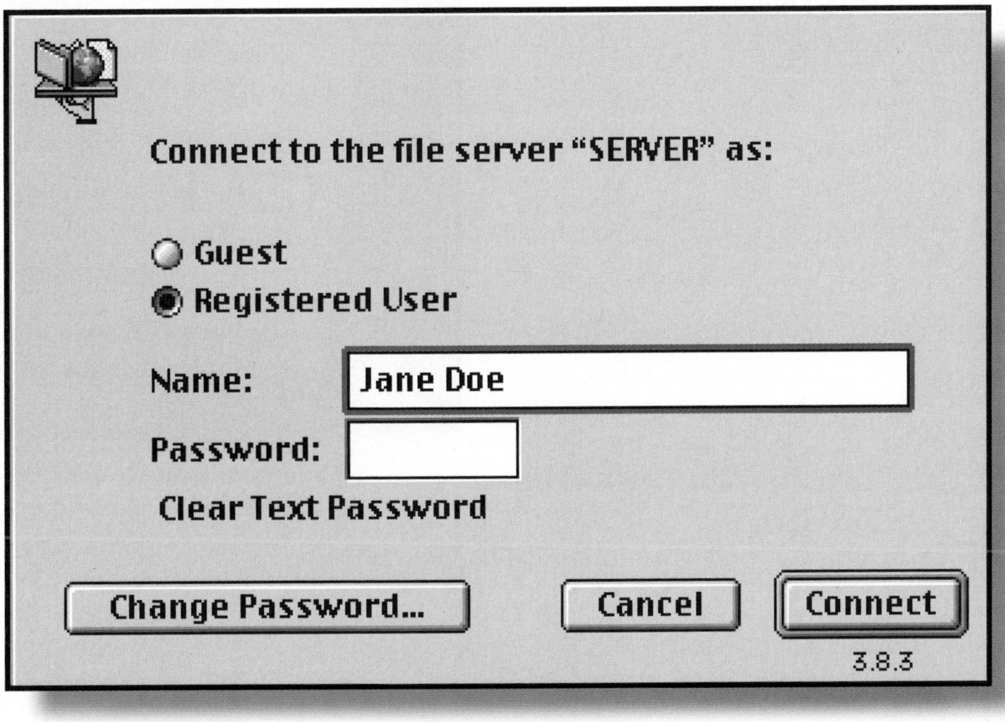

Connect to the file server "SERVER" as:

○ Guest
● Registered User

Name: Jane Doe

Password:

Clear Text Password

[Change Password...] [Cancel] [Connect]

3.8.3

- Regularly backing up data and storing it offsite.

- Employing **biometric security measures**, which examine a fingerprint, a voice pattern, or the iris or retina of the eye. These must match the entry that was originally stored in the system for an employee. This method of security is usually used when high-level security is required. See Figure 19.3.

Software Piracy

Illegal copying and using software is called **software piracy**. It has become a big problem because it is so easy to copy software. It has cost software companies millions of dollars in sales each year. Many persons are misusing shareware as well. **Shareware** is software you can use for free for a specified period to try it out. If you decide you like it and it meets your needs, you are supposed to pay for it.

 Did You Know?

The penalty for copying software can be up to $250,000, five years in prison, or both?

FIGURE 19.3
Biometric security measures

Protection for Technology Injuries

In the rise of computer crimes and other technology issues, many laws have been passed in an effort to assist those injured by these offenses. However, many of the offenses are difficult to prove. Here is a list of some of the laws that protect users.

- The Copyright Act of 1976: Protects the developers of software.

- Computer Matching & Privacy Protection Act, 1988: Regulates how federal data can be used to determine whether am individual is entitled to federal benefits.

- Electronic Communication Privacy Act; 1986: Prohibits the interception of data communications.

- Computer Fraud and Abuse Act, 1986: Prohibits individuals without authorization from knowingly accessing a company computer to obtain records from financial communications.

- Software Piracy and Counterfeiting Amendment of 1983.

- Many states have individual laws governing computer crimes in their states.

Internet

Go to the www.bsa.org site to discover what one organization is doing to prevent software privacy.

ETHICS IN TECHNOLOGY

THE TEN COMMANDMENTS FOR COMPUTER ETHICS

1. Thou shalt not use a computer to harm other people.

2. Thou shalt not interfere with other people's computer work.

3. Thou shalt not snoop around in other people's files.

4. Thou shalt not use a computer to steal.

5. Thou shalt not use a computer to bear false witness.

6. Thou shalt not use or copy software for which you have not paid.

7. Thou shalt not use other people's computer resources without authorization.

8. Thou shalt not appropriate other peoples intellectual output.

9. Thou shalt think about the social consequences of the program you write.

10. Thou shalt use a computer in ways that show consideration and respect.

Summary

■ Computer crime has become a major problem, costing companies billions of dollars annually.

■ Computer fraud is conduct that involves the manipulation of a computer or computer data for dishonest profit.

■ Computer hacking involves invading someone else's computer for personal gain. Sometimes it is done for financial gain and sometimes just as a prank.

■ A computer virus is a program that has been written to cause corruption of data on a computer.

■ There are different variations of viruses. These include worms, time bombs, logic bombs, and trojan horses.

■ To protect yourself against viruses, install and keep an antivirus program running on your computer. Be sure to update it regularly.

■ E-mail attachments can contain viruses. It is a good idea to save any message to disk if you are not familiar with the sender. After saving it to a diskette, you can scan it for viruses.

■ Personal privacy has been invaded by the computer. Information about our personal lives is freely available.

■ Other computer crimes include theft of computer time, data diddling, and using information from another person's screen or printouts.

■ Companies purchase personal information obtained on the Internet to sell to various companies for marketing purposes.

■ Computer security is necessary in order to keep hardware, software, and data safe from harm or destruction.

■ Some risks to computers are from natural causes, some are the result of accidents, and others are intentional.

■ The best way to protect data is to control access to the data.

■ The most common way to control access to data is to use passwords.

■ Illegal copying and using software is called software piracy. It has cost companies millions of dollars in lost sales.

■ Shareware is software you can use for free for a specified period.

■ Laws have been passed in an effort to assist those who have been injured by computer crimes and offenses.

■ Many of these crimes are difficult to prove and prosecute.

LESSON 19 REVIEW QUESTIONS

MULTIPLE CHOICE

1. _____ is a criminal act that is committed through the use of a computer.
   A. Hacking
   B. Piracy
   C. Copyright
   D. Computer crime

2. _____ invade other people's computers.
   A. Hackers
   B. Programmers
   C. Trojan horses
   D. System analysts

3. A _____ is a program that has been written to cause corruption of data on a computer.
   A. Microsoft Word
   B. virus
   C. antivirus software
   D. biometric

4. _____ control access to computer data.
   A. Passwords
   B. Firewalls
   C. Trojan horses
   D. Worms

5. Software that users may use on a trial basis is called _____.
   A. freeware
   B. shareware
   C. antivirus software
   D. Microsoft Office

TRUE/FALSE

Circle the T if the statement is true. Circle F if it is false.

T F 1. A computer crime involves crimes committed through the use of a computer.

T F 2. A computer crime involves the theft of a computer and any equipment associated with the computer.

T F 3. Hackers only invade other people's computers for fun.

T F 4. Laws to police computer use are difficult to enforce.

T F 5. Worms, time bombs, logic bombs, and trojan horses are variations of viruses.

SHORT ANSWERS

1. Mailing lists are sold to various companies for _____ purposes.

2. _____ _____ is necessary in order to keep hardware, software, and data safe from harm or destruction.

3. _____ security measures involve examining a fingerprint, a voice pattern, or the iris or retina of the eye.

4. _____ _____ has become a big problem because it is very easy to copy software.

5. The _____ protects the developers of software.

CROSS-CURRICULAR PROJECTS

LANGUAGE ARTS

Many colleges and universities have formal statements regarding the ethical use of their computer systems. Use the Internet or contact a local college or university to obtain a copy of such a statement. After reading it carefully, rewrite it to include any additional rules you believe should be included.

MATH

Computer crimes have been responsible for the loss of millions of dollars. Some crimes result in more loss than others. Use the Internet and other resources to locate information on lost revenue due to the top five computer crimes. If you have access to spreadsheet software, prepare this information in a spreadsheet and perform formulas that will not only add the totals, but also display the percentage of each crime's portion. Some keywords that may be helpful are *computer crimes, computer crime costs, hackers, viruses,* and *software piracy*. Use various search engines to research each term.

SCIENCE

Use the Internet and other resources to identify early security measures that were used to protect computers and computer data. Describe how these measures counteracted the intrusions made. Write a report of your findings.

Visit some companies that make computer security devices such as www.pcguardian.com. The URL www.looksmart.com may also be helpful in your search.

SOCIAL STUDIES

Viruses have been around for quite a while. Use the Internet and other resources to research the history of early viruses. Prepare a report to share with your classmates on the types of viruses and the damage they caused. Also include any information you may find on the person who programmed the virus if possible. Use a search engine and the keywords *computer viruses* or *early computer viruses*.

WEB PROJECT

The Global Information Infrastructure Awards are designed to recognize innovation and excellence in the use of the Internet. This organization is also responsible for promoting responsible use of the information highway. Go to the organization's site (www.gii-awards.com), choose one organization that has been honored, and write a report on this organization's contribution.

TEAM PROJECT

The video store has been having problems lately with viruses. Ms. Perez has asked you and the other part-time employee to do some research to find out what steps to take to reduce the chances of this continuing. Include in your report the names of software programs that could be used and information on how to train employees to avoid this problem.

HOW IS TECHNOLOGY CHANGING THE WORK-PLACE AND SOCIETY?

OBJECTIVES

When you complete this module, you will be able to:

- Describe the impact of technology on education.

- Describe the impact of technology on science and medicine.

- Describe the impact of technology on work and play.

⏱ **Estimated Time: 1.5 hours**

VOCABULARY

Artificial intelligence
Bot
Computer-based learning
Digital cash
Distance learning
Electronic commerce
Simulation
Virtual reality
WebQuest

As the age of innovation blazes its way into the world of technology, dramatic changes are taking places in every aspect of life—from home to school to the workplace. And the changes are swift and dramatic. Just as soon as we settle in and become comfortable with a new technological change, along comes something more innovative and different. As things look now, the world is in for a lot more of this type of change. Ms. Perez is very interested is how all of these changes could affect Vista Multimedia, her personal life, and the lives of her employees. She has asked you to provide some insight into some of the changes taking place.

Education

There are many similarities between today's schools and those of 40 or 50 years ago. In many classrooms, the students still sit in rows and the teacher stands at the front of the class, lecturing and using a chalkboard. However, in other classrooms, a technological revolution is taking place.

Many people predict that technology will change the entire structure of education. Others believe the way in which most students receive education today—students and teacher in a traditional classroom—will remain for many years. Regardless of who is right, one thing is certain: Technology is having a tremendous impact on education in general and in more and more classrooms around the world.

Internet

The Internet and the World Wide Web are the biggest factors affecting education today. For instance, not so long ago, if a science teacher gave the class a project to find out how a television works, the students would go to the library and do the research. In many of today's classrooms, the students most likely go to the Internet, and maybe to the How Stuff Works Web site to find this information. See Figure 20.1. Using the Internet, it is fast and easy to find the information you need.

FIGURE 20.1
How Stuff Works Web site

Perhaps you're having a geography test next week, and you would like to pretest your geography knowledge. You can again use the Internet as your resource. One site you might visit is the CIA Geography Quiz Page. See Figure 20.2.

FIGURE 20.2
CIA Geography Quiz Page

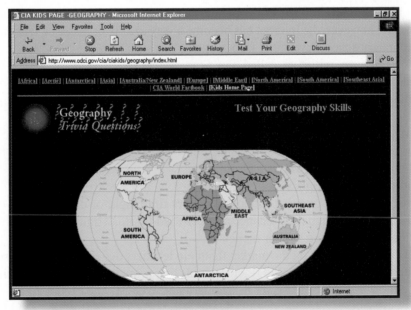

You may have had an opportunity to participate in or work with a ***WebQuest***. Bernie Dodge and Tom developed the WebQuest Model March at San Diego State University. This type of activity uses the Internet for investigation and problem solving. Dozens of WebQuests have been developed by schools all over the country. Example WebQuests include countries around the world, politics, learning about money, and so forth. You can find a list and a link to some of these at www.macomb.k12.mi.us/wq/webqindx.htm. One of the more popular of these is Ancient Egypt. See Figure 20.3.

FIGURE 20.3
Ancient Egypt WebQuest

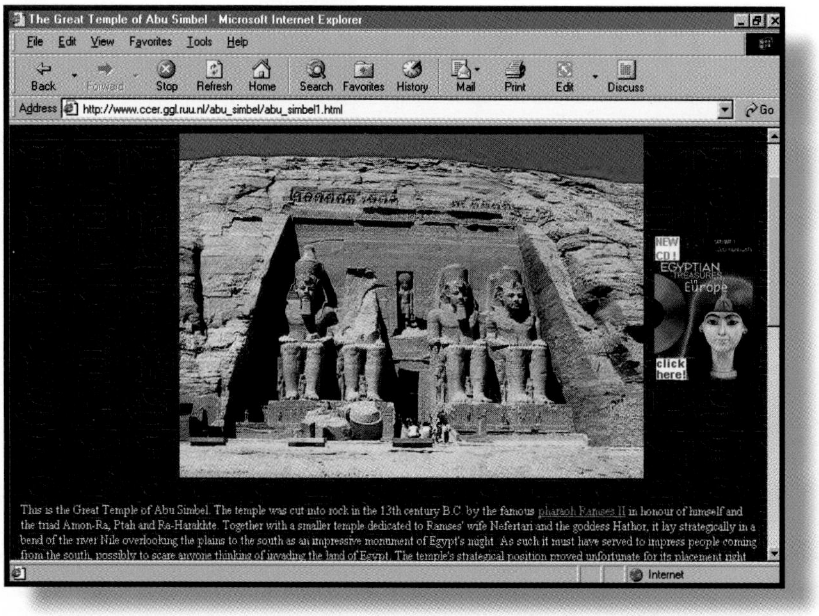

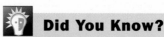

Distance Learning

For years many people have been receiving their education via distance learning methods. These methods include television and correspondence courses that are completed through the mail. In the last few years, however, the Internet has become a way to deliver ***distance learning***. At the elementary and secondary school levels, the Department of Education supports an initiative called the Star Schools Program. This program provides distance education learning to more than millions of learners annually.

Did You Know?

According to the National Center for Education Statistics, 93% of public schools are connected to the Internet.

Imagine, if you will, being able to complete high school from home. This is possible in some states. For instance, any high school student who is a Florida resident can attend the Florida High School Online for free. This a certified diploma-granting school, open any time night or day. Students enroll, log on, and complete their work through the guidance of a certified Florida High School teacher. See Figure 20-4. Other states are developing similar models.

New types of programs are on the market that help teachers develop online courses. These programs are an integrated set of Web-based teaching tools that provide guidance and testing for the student. Two of the most popular of these are Blackboard and WebCT. See Figure 20.5.

FIGURE 20.4
Florida Online High School

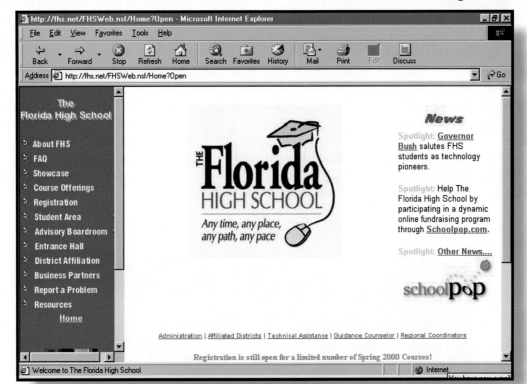

FIGURE 20.5
WebCT example

Computer-Based Learning

There are probably 20 or 30 other students in your class. And each of these students, including you, learns in different ways and at different rates. Likewise, information can be presented in many formats and at different levels. This could be through lecture, homework, group projects, movies, and so forth. The more ways in which information can be presented, the more opportunities everyone has to use their own learning style so they can master the particular topic.

You may have heard the terms *computer-based learning* or computer-assisted instruction (CAI). These are examples of ways your teacher can use the computer for instruction. It is basically using a computer as a tutor. And for many students this is one of the most effective ways for them to learn. For example, you may have difficulty understanding a specific mathematics concept, such as how to calculate percentages. Your teacher may suggest a special computer program to help reinforce that difficult concept. Using such a program provides you with the opportunity to master the idea by reviewing the concept as many times as necessary. See Figure 20.6.

FIGURE 20.6
Students at work in computer lab

Simulations

Learning doesn't have to be all dull, boring work. Learning can actually be fun for everyone, especially if it is done through computer simulation. Simulations are models of real-world activities. They are designed to allow you to experiment and explore environments that may be dangerous or unavailable. Using simulations, you can explore other worlds and settings without leaving your classroom. With this type of model, you learn by doing.

You can find simulations on the Internet or the simulations may come on a CD-ROM disk that you would run from a local computer.

Some example simulations are as follows:

 Internet

For more about medicine and virtual reality, visit the University of Illinois VR Web site located at www.bvis.uic.edu/VRML/VRTechnologies/VRTechnologies.htm.

■ Many of you have probably heard about fortunes being made and lost in the stock market. If you would like to see how good your investing skills are, you might want to try The Stock

Market game located at www.smgww.org/. This simulation is for students of all ages—from middle school to adults. By playing this game, you learn about finance and the American economic system. To participate in this game, you invest a hypothetical $100,000 in the stock market and follow your investments over a 10-week time period. See Figure 20.7.

FIGURE 20.7
Stock Market simulation game

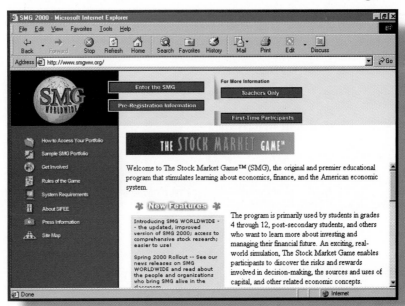

■ Maybe you are interested in outer space and would like to explore Mars. You can do this through simulation. Try the Mars 2200 simulation located at www.inworldvr.com/Mars2200/. Several options and versions are available. You can even select screen size and processor speed. See Figure 20.8.

FIGURE 20.8
Mars 2200 simulation

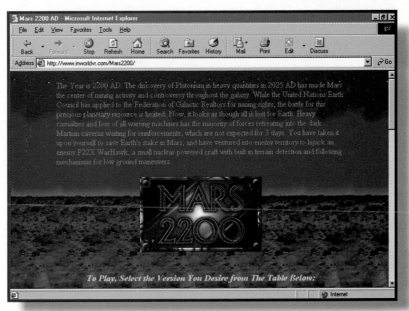

■ One of the earliest and still most popular simulations is SimCity. Several versions of this program have been released. It is used extensively in schools throughout the world. This problem-solving software program allows the user to create a city, including highways, buildings, homes, and so forth. See Figure 20.9.

FIGURE 20.9
SimCity simulation

ETHICS IN TECHNOLOGY

WHO IS RESPONSIBLE?

Increasingly, computers participate in decisions that affect human lives. Consider medical safety, for instance, and consider that just about everything in a hospital is tied to a computer. So what happens if these machines don't produce the expected results? What happens if they have been incorrectly programmed?

When programmers write a program, they check for as many conditions as possible. But there is always the chance they might miss one. So what happens if a computer malfunctions and applies a high dosage of radiation? Or what happens if two medications are prescribed to an individual and the computer doesn't indicate the medications are incompatible? Or what happens when someone calls for an ambulance and the system doesn't work and there is no backup?

Then the question becomes who is responsible for these mishaps. Is it the programmer? Is it the company? Is it the person who administered the radiation treatment?

The incidents described here actually happened. These are ethical issues that are being decided in court.

FIGURE 20.10
The future

Scientific Discovery and Technological Innovations

Our world is changing at an ever-increasing pace. Currently, people around the world are able to communicate with each other almost instantaneously. The amount of available Information is increasing each and every day. In fact it is continuing to increase faster than we can process it. On the positive side, the information and discoveries are contributing to a better lifestyle for many people. Predictions are that we will learn to cure illnesses and to continue to increase our life span.

But there's another aspect to all of this. Within all of this change, other predictions are that an anti-technology backlash is possible. Many people feel technology is creating a world out of control. Moral and cultural dilemmas are becoming more and more common, and many people want to return to a simpler, slower way of life.

If society could and would return to something simpler is highly debatable. Even today, there are very few places in the world one can live that are not being affected by technology. And many scientists say we're "only at the Model-T stage" of what's to come. Let's take a brief look at some of the predicted and possible scientific changes on the horizon. See Figure 20.10.

Artificial Intelligence

Some of you who enjoy science fiction may have read the book or seen the movie 2001: A Space Odyssey. In this movie, originally released in the late 1960s and re-released in 2000, controlling the spaceship on its way to Mars is a computer referred to as HAL. This computer has a type of artificial intelligence so it never makes a mistake. No computer such as HAL yet exists, but the concept of artificial intelligence is still a branch of computer science. Computer scientists have made many advancements in this area.

The concept of *artificial intelligence* (AI) has been around for many years. In fact it was coined in1956 by John McCarthy at the Massachusetts Institute of Technology. The goal for this software is to process information on its own without human intervention. There are many ways in which artificial intelligent applications are being developed and being used today. Some examples are as follows:

- *Games playing:* an area where the most advances have been made.

- *Natural language:* offers the greatest potential rewards by allowing people to interact easily with computers by talking to them.

- *Expert systems:* computer programs that help us make decisions. For instance, an expert system may help your parents determine the best type of insurance for their particular needs.

337

- ***Robotics:*** when we think of robotics, we may think of humanoid robots like those in Star Wars. In real life, however, we do not see this type of robot in our society. Robots, mostly used in assembly plants, are only capable of limited tasks. One of the newest types of robots is called a bot, commonly used by search engines.

Genetic Engineering

The human life span has almost tripled in the last 200 years. We can now expect to live almost 80 years. Implications are that the average life span in the 21st century will continue to increase, possibly dramatically. One of the major factors contributing to this increase is ***genetic engineering***, which refers to changing the DNA in a living organism. There are groups of people who argue against this technology. The supporters, however, point out the many benefits. Here are some examples:

- Increasing resistance to disease

- Enabling a plant or animal to do something it would not typically do

- Enabling a fruit to ripen without getting squashy

One of the most widely known projects within this area is the Human Genome Project. Its goal is to identify all of the approximately 100,000 genes in human DNA, store and analyze this data, and address the ethical, legal, and social issues surrounding the project. The project is coordinated by the Department of Energy and the National Institute of Health. Because of the data and resources resulting from this project, some observers such as Bill Gates and President Clinton predict the 21st century will be the "biology century." See Figure 20.11.

FIGURE 20.11
Human Genome Project web site

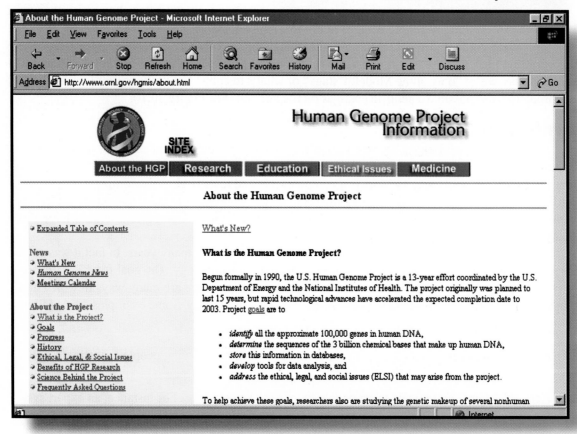

Virtual Reality

The term *virtual reality* (VR) means different things to different people. A general definition is an artificial environment that feels like a real environment. This environment is created with computer hardware and software. Virtual reality and simulation share some common characteristics. Simulation is sometimes referred to as desktop VR. However, with virtual reality, there is more of a feeling of being in the actual environment—of using all or almost all of the five senses. The user is completely immersed inside the virtual world, generally through some head-mounted display. This helmet contains the virtual and auditory displays.

Virtual reality is used in many different ways and areas. Some examples are as follows:

- *Education:* The creation of virtual environments so students may have a better understanding of history, for instance. Imagine experiencing World War II as though you were really there. Or maybe you would like to experience what it would be like to live during the age of dinosaurs. With a virtual world, you feel as though you are really there.

- *Training:* You may have had an opportunity to play Doom or Torok: Dinosaur Hunter or some of the other virtual games. If so, you may have felt you were part of the action. You could control much of the environment and make choices as to what your next move would be. A variation of this type of virtual reality is being used to train pilots, navigators, and even astronauts. These individuals are put into virtual life and death situations, where they must make decisions. This helps prepare them in the event a similar situation occurs in real life.

Did You Know?

A man in Texas wants to prove how wired the world has become. He is spending an entire year in his house. He will use his computer to order groceries and other items. You can find more information at www.dotcomguy.com.

TECHNOLOGY CAREERS

SIMULATION ANALYSTS

Simulation analysts work with large and small companies. Their primary job is to investigate different options to determine which would be the best for a particular situation. For instance, health care company administrators might want to implement a new system for filing and processing insurance claims. Before spending a huge amount of money, they may hire a simulation analyst to determine which system would best meet their needs. Or a bank is going to bring in a new system to process checks. It hires an analyst to do simulation modeling of what the system might and might not do.

Simulation analysts work with all types of companies and industries. Some necessary skills include the ability to see detail in a system and to be a good technical writer. The person should be a logical thinker and have good analytical skills. A good memory is an additional asset.

Opportunities and the need for simulation analysts are increasing. One of the reasons for the increase is that simulation is being applied to a larger variety of problems by more and more companies.

As a consultant, you would probably do some traveling. Consulting fees are generally quite generous, with some simulation analysts making as much as $75,000 or more. You may find some analysts with only a two-year degree, but generally you need at least a bachelor's degree in computer information systems or computer engineering

- *Medicine:* One example of a medical VR application is the "Anatomic VisualizeR," being developed at the University of California, San Diego. This project is a virtual reality–based learning environment that will enable medical students to actively learn human anatomy. Or, at a university in Germany, a VR system allows student surgeons to practice operations.

- *Miniaturized chips:* Researchers at Texas Instruments have developed an advanced semiconductor manufacturing technology. The transistors are so small that more than 400 million of them will fit onto a single chip the size of a fingernail. And we can expect this type of technological advance will continue.

These are just a few examples of activities taking place today. As in the past, it is fairly certain that scientific discovery and technological innovation will greatly affect our economic and military developments in the future. Predictions are that science and technology will continue to advance and become more widely available and utilized around the world. Some people forecast, however, that the benefits derived from these advancements would not be evenly distributed.

Work and Play

How will technology affect us as individuals in our work and social life? Although no one knows what the future will bring, predictions are many. Many people predict that with high-skilled work more in demand, semi-skilled work will start to disappear. We've already discussed some of the changes taking place in education and how genetic engineering is helping increase life expectancy. As a result of these advances, what types of changes can we expect in the economy and in our personal lives?

 Hot Tip

The economy created by the Internet is generating enormous environmental benefits by reducing the amount of energy and materials consumed by businesses. It is predicted that the Internet will revolutionize the relationship between economic growth and the environment.

Global Economy

One thing for certain about the new economy: Knowledge is the greatest asset. However, knowledge will be limited by time—it can be incredibly valuable one moment and worthless the next. The spread and sharing of knowledge, the development of new technologies, and an increased recognition of common world problems present unlimited opportunities for economic growth.

Consider banking, finance, and commerce. Electronic technology is having a dramatic effect on these industries. Think about money. Will it become obsolete? Most likely so. Already, huge amounts of money zip around the globe at the speed of light. Technology is affecting the way information and money is transmitted. See Figure 20.12.

Electronic Commerce

You have probably read about the Industrial Revolution and how it affected our world. The Internet economy is being compared to the Industrial Revolution. *Electronic commerce*, or E-commerce, which means having an online business, is changing the way our world does business.

Within this electronic business, one can buy and sell products through the Internet. We find e-commerce in every corner of the modern business. Predictions are that over a billion people will be connected to the Internet by the year 2005. Internet speed will increase as more people add cable modems or digital subscriber lines (dsl). All of this activity and high-speed connections indicate more online businesses. Some analysts predict that within the next 10 years the value of Internet-based business will account for up to 10% of the world's consumer sales. And the Center for

FIGURE 20.12
Transmitting data

Research in Electronic Commerce at the University of Texas indicates that out of the thousands of online companies, over two thirds of them are not the big Fortune 500 companies—they are smaller companies.

When it comes to buying online, many people hesitate because they fear someone will steal their credit card number. However, *digital cash* is a new technology that may ease some of those fears. The digital cash system allows someone to pay by transmitting a number from one computer to another. The digital cash numbers are issued by a bank and represent a specified sum of real money; each number is unique. When one uses digital cash, there is no way to obtain information about the user.

As you read about electronic commerce, you may wonder about what effects it will have on you personally. You or someone in your family may have already made a purchase online. Buying online will become much more common in the future, and you may find it becomes a way of life.

Rarely a day goes by that you or someone in your family doesn't receive junk mail. In the future, much of the postal junk mail will be replaced by SPAM, junk mail sent to your e-mail address. Several states are already looking at ways to legislate this new junk mail.

Another aspect you might consider is the number of and new categories of jobs being generated due to electronic commerce. This might be something you want to consider as you look toward a future career. Some examples include Webmasters, programmers, network managers, graphic designers, Web developers, and so forth. You may also think about going into an online business for yourself. Individuals with imagination and ambition will discover that the greatest source of wealth is their ideas.

Personal Lives

Will our personal life become almost like Star Trek? Many people predict it will. Just as technology is affecting our work environment, it is also affecting our personal lives.

Hot Tip

Want to find out more about the Internet and electronic commerce? The Internet Economy Indicators Web site located at www.internetindicators.com/ provides lots of statistics and links to other sites on how to start your own online business.

In the 20th century, society witnessed all types of changes in the places people lived. They moved from the farms to the cities and then to the suburbs. The 21st century will also witness changes as the home becomes the center for work, entertainment, learning, and possibly even health care. More and more people will telecommute or run a business from their home. As a result, they will have to manage their lives in a world of uncertainty. This will be a great change for many people. They will have to make decisions about how to separate their business and personal lives.

Some examples of potential technological advances that can affect our personal lives are as follows:

■ ***Clothes that fight odor and bacteria:*** Some clothing companies are manufacturing clothes that keep you comfortable and smelling good. For example, when the temperature drops, jackets grow warmer and sweat socks resist bacteria and odors. Or how about clothing that kills mosquitoes on contact?

■ ***The flying car:*** This has long been a fantasy of the American public, but the question is how long will it be before we all have flying cars? It will probably be a few more years before we're flying around like the Jetsons, but there are possibilities on the horizon. Moller International has developed a personal vertical takeoff and landing vehicle (VTOL). The Skycar is able to operate in a much less restrictive area than a helicopter or airplane and is less expensive and safer. These factors allow this type of future transportation to be addressed and investigated for the first time. See Figure 20.13.

FIGURE 20.13
Moller Web site – Skycar

■ ***Voice recognition:*** Some people forecast that within the next few years written language will be dead and writing may become an ancient art form. Instead we will talk to computers or computerlike devices, and they will reply. We will curl up in the bed with our electronic book, and it will read us to sleep.

■ ***Nonlethal weapons:*** A company in San Diego is working on a nonlethal weapon that uses two ultraviolet laser beams. These two beams of UV radiation ionize paths in the air to create "wires" in the atmosphere. This device is harmless, but it can immobilize people and animals at a distance.

- ***Space travel:*** Would you like to take a trip around the world—that is, by low-earth orbit? You may be able to do so in the near future. The Roton Rocket Company is developing a fleet of commercial vehicles to provide the public the opportunity to access space. See Figure 20.14.

FIGURE 20.14
Roton Rocket Space Flight

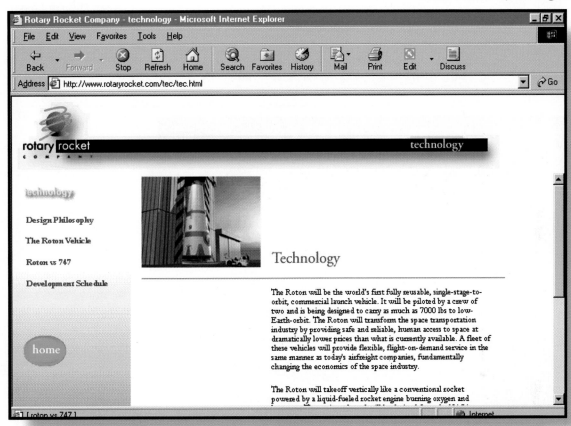

- ***Smart shoes and smart seats:*** When we think of technology, not too many of us consider our shoes. No matter how expensive our shoes are, they can still become uncomfortable after wearing them for long hours. A technology called expansive polymer gel uses a micro voltage to expand or contract the gel. Weight can be evenly distributed and heat dissipated. This technology is also being applied to car seats.

- ***Smart houses:*** The smart house uses computers to help the family live a healthy, happy, and safe life. A smart house, among other things, keeps the temperature at a comfortable level while monitoring the amount of electricity being used, helps the family plan and prepare healthy meals, monitors devices within the home and schedules maintenance, and provides accommodations for individuals with disabilities.

Internet

Electronic ink will have a far-reaching impact on our society. The ink itself is a liquid that can be printed onto nearly any surface. You can learn about electronic ink at www.eink.com/technology/flash.htm.

343

- ***Electronic shopping:*** No longer do we have to fight the crowds and search for parking spaces. We can do all of our shopping online. Regardless of what you are shopping for—electronics, jewelry, flowers, clothes, food, or even a snack from Pizza Hut—you can have it delivered to your door. See Figure 20.15.

So what does the future hold? No one really knows. You can be assured, however, that it will be exciting and ever changing.

FIGURE 20.15
Pizza Hut Web site

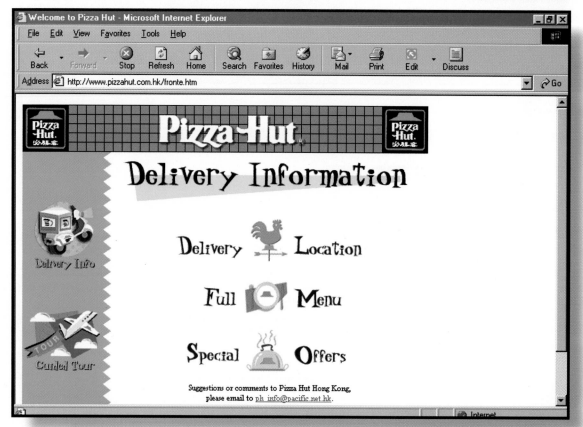

Summary

- Many people predict that technology will change the entire structure of education.
- Technology is having a tremendous impact on education.
- The Internet and the World Wide Web at the biggest factors affecting education today.
- Online courses through the Internet are becoming very popular.
- Many schools use computer-based learning to reinforce concepts.
- Simulations are models of real-world activities.

- Information is continuing to increase faster than we can process it.

- Some people predict an anti-technology backlash.

- Artificial intelligence is software that can process information on its own without human intervention.

- Genetic engineering refers to changing the DNA in a living organism.

- Virtual reality is an artificial environment that feels like a real environment.

- Virtual reality is used in education, training, medicine, research, and other areas.

- In the new global economy, knowledge is the greatest asset.

- Value of knowledge will be determined by time.

- Electronic commerce is the buying and selling of goods and services using the Internet.

- Electronic commerce is predicted to grow at an ever-increasing rate.

- Digital cash allows someone to pay online by transmitting a number from one computer to another.

- New jobs and new job categories are being developed because of the Internet and electronic commerce.

- In the 21st century, many people will work from their homes.

- Some technological advances are clothes that fight odors, flying cars, voice recognition, non-lethal weapons, space travel, smart shoes and smart seats, smart houses, and electronic shopping.

LESSON 20 REVIEW QUESTIONS

MULTIPLE CHOICE

1. New technology is causing _____ changes in our society
   A. some
   B. none
   C. major
   D. a few

2. One of the biggest factors affecting education is the _____.
   A. government
   B. school board
   C. Internet
   D. other students

3. _____ is the delivery of education over the Internet.
   A. Simulation
   B. Distance learning
   C. Virtual reality
   D. None of the above

345

4. If you were participating in a _____ application, you would wear a helmet.
   A. simulated
   B. cloning
   C. virtual reality
   D. computer-based training

5. The buying and selling of goods on the Internet is called _____.
   A. economic commerce
   B. electronic commerce
   C. on-hand business
   D. local commerce

TRUE/FALSE

Circle the T if the statement is true. Circle F if it is false.

T F 1. With digital cash, you can pay someone by transmitting a number from one computer to another.

T F 2. Life in the 21st century will probably be very similar to that of the 20th century.

T F 3. It is a real possibility that within the next 25 years or so individuals will be able to purchase a ticket to orbit the earth.

T F 4. There are only a few applications for virtual reality.

T F 5. Simulations are models of real-world activities.

SHORT ANSWER

1. A _____ uses the Internet for investigation and problem solving.

2. Using _____ you learn by doing.

3. SimCity is a popular _____ activity.

4. _____ is the changing of the DNA in a living organism.

5. _____ is software that works without human intervention.

CROSS-CURRICULAR PROJECTS

MATH/LANGUAGE ARTS

See what information you can find on possible other flying cars. Prepare a report and a chart showing the possibilities for these cars. Include price, speed, size, and any other relevant numbers you can locate.

SCIENCE/LANGUAGE ARTS

Robots, and particularly bots, have become a very important element in searching and finding information online. Do some research, using whatever resources are available, and write a report on what the bots are and how they work. If you have an Internet connection, check out info.webcrawler.com/mak/projects/robots/faq.html.

SOCIAL STUDIES

It is predicted that in the next few years the home and business will merge for many people; more and more people will work from home. Would you consider working from home? Why or why not? What advantages and disadvantages do you see? Give a report or a presentation to your class.

LANGUAGE ARTS

The year is 2070. You were born in 2055. Use your word processing program to write a letter to someone who lived 50 years ago and tell him or her about your life and your community.

WEB PROJECT

Visit the U.S. Geological Survey's Water Science for Schools Web site located at ga.water.usgs.gov/edu/. Review the Web site and then go to the Activity Center. Complete the Surveys and Challenge Questions. Print a copy of these and give them to your teacher.

TEAM PROJECT

Ms. Perez is interested in other information pertaining to the global economy and electronic commerce. She would like you to prepare a report for her on what items she would need to know before setting up an e-commerce Web site.

GLOSSARY

A

Absolute Link hyperlinks to other Web sites

Address bar contains the URL or address of the active Web page; also where you type the location for the Web page you want to visit

Address book where you keep a list of your e-mail contacts

Animation are special visual or sound effects that you can add to text or to an object for a presentation

Applications software widely referred to as productivity software. Applications software is comprised of programs designed for an end user. Some of the more commonly used application programs are word processors, database systems, presentation systems, spreadsheet programs, and desktop publishing programs

Arithmetic/logic unit (ALU) performs arithmetic computations and logical operations. The arithmetic operations include addition, subtraction, multiplication, and division. The logical operations involve comparisons

Audience handouts print options for a presentation that allow the audience to have hard copies

B

Balance An element of desk top publishing. Created by distributing the weight of various elements. This includes graphics, text, or lines.

Biometric Security Measures Using the examination of a fingerprint, a voice pattern, or the iris or retina of the eye. These must match the entry that was originally stored in the system for an employee. This method of security is usually used when high-level security is required.

Bit a zero or one

Body on a web page, contains information identifying the intended audience, purpose of the information.

Boolean Logic is another way that you can search databases. This works on a similar principle as search engine math, but has a little more power. Boolean logic consists of three logical operators:

AND

NOT

OR

Bookmark site or location that you have specially marked so you can locate it again

Browser a software program that you use to retrieve documents from the WWW.

Byte eight bits are called a byte or character. Eight bits or combinations of ones and zeros represent a letter such A

C

Cell the point at which a column and a row intersects or meets

Central processing unit also called the microprocessor, the processor, or central processor, is the "brains" of the computer. The

CPU is housed on a tiny silicon chip. This chip contains millions of switches and pathways that help your computer make important decisions

Cloning the entire genetic complement of either a nucleus or a cell, is copied

Coherence consistent format

Column vertical sections of a spreadsheet. Identified by a letter/s.

Communications Channel type of link through which data can be transmitted from one computer to another

Computer an electronic device that receives data, processes data, stores data, and produces a result (output).

Computer-based Learning using a computer as a tutor

Computer Crimes a criminal act that is committed through the use of a computer, like getting into someone else's system and changing information or creating a computer virus and causing it to damage information on others' computers. It can also involve the theft of a computer and any equipment associated with the computer.

Computer Fraud conduct that involves the manipulation of a computer or computer data in order to dishonestly obtain money, property or value, or to cause loss. Examples of computer fraud include stealing money from bank accounts and stealing information from other persons' computers for gain

Computer System combination of hardware, software, and data working together

Control unit the "boss" so to speak, and coordinates all of the CPU's activities. Using programming instructions, it controls the flow of information through the processor by controlling what happens inside the processor.

Copyright is the exclusive right, granted by law for a certain number of years, to make and dispose of literary, musical or artist work. Even if the copyright notice isn't displayed prominently on the page, someone wrote or is responsible for the creation of whatever

appears on a page. This means that you cannot use the information as you own

Currency on a web page, refers to the age of the information; how long has it been posted, how often it is updated.

Cursor a marker that can be moved about the screen (using the keyboard, a mouse, or a joystick) to indicate where input will appear

Cybernetic Implant this is the implanting of a computer chip into the brain

D

Data is the information that is entered into the computer to be processed. Data consists of

> Text
>
> Numbers
>
> Sounds and images
>
> Database
>
> a collection of related data

Data Communication the technology that enables computers to communicate between each other. Data communications is defined as the transmission of text, numeric, voice or video data from one machine to another. Popular examples are the Internet, electronic messages (e-mail), faxes, and electronic or online banking

Design templates contain color schemes with custom formatting and styled fonts, all designed to create a special look for a presentation

Desktop the first screen you see when the operating system is up and fully running. It is called the desktop because the icons are intended to represent real objects on a real desktop.

Desktop Publishing the process of producing professional-looking documents such as flyers, brochures, reports, newsletters, and pamphlets using a desktop personal computer and a color printer

Digital Cash allows someone to pay by transmitting a number from one computer to another. The digital cash numbers are issued by a bank and represent a specified sum of real money; each number is unique.

Distance Learning using technology as a medium for schooling or learning

Domain name the portion of a website name that identifies the type of site. The .com in www.microsoft.com is the domain name. The .com indicates that this is a commercial site.

DOS (Disk Operating System)a character-based operating system. The user interacts with the system by typing in commands. DOS is a single-user or single-tasking operating system because the user can run only one program at a time.

E

Editing changing an existing document

Efficiency information laid out in a logical layout so that you can locate what you need. Used to grade a web site.

Electronic Commerce having an on-line business

Electronic presentation allows the presenter to bring together and present a variety of special effects and features. Presentation graphics program are excellent for creating on-screen shows

E-Mail the capability to send a message from one person's computer to another person's computer where it is stored until read by the receiving person. E-mail messages can be sent to friends, family members and businesses locally or across the oceans.

F

Fair Use refers to short, cited excerpts, usually as an example for research.

Field an individual piece or item of information

File transfer protocol (FTP) an Internet standard that allows users to download and upload files with other computers on the Internet.

Finder program that displays the Macintosh desktop

Focus the element that pulls the reader's eye to a particular location. This can be a graphic or large headlines or titles.

Folder logical location created by the user to store files

Font a typeface, size, and style, such as Times New Roman 12-point bold

Footer on a web page, contains the author or contact person, date of revision

Form an object you use to maintain, view, and print records in a database. Users can customize the appearance of the form.

Format the process of preparing the disk to receive data. When a disk is formatted, it is organized into tracks and sectors

Formatting the ability to control:

> the appearance of the text
>
> the layout of the text
>
> other objects on the page
>
> spacing
>
> margins
>
> indentations
>
> alignments

You can format characters, paragraphs, or the entire document.

Formula is a statement that performs a calculation

Formula View printing your spreadsheet with the formulas showing instead of the result of the formulas

Function a built-in formula that is a shortcut for common calculations such as addition and average

G

Genetic Engineering refers to changing the DNA in a living organism

Grammar Checker checks each sentence in the document and points out grammatical errors like subject and verb agreement, sentence fragments, sentence structure, sentence length, and punctuation. The checker offers advice on how to re-word the sentence.

Graphical user interface (GUI) a symbolic "desktop" where various objects or icons are displayed. These graphical symbols represent files, disks, programs, and other objects. GUIs permit the user to manipulate these onscreen icons. Most people use a pointing device such as a mouse to click on the icons and execute the commands.

H

Hacking involves invading someone else's computer, usually for personal gain or just the satisfaction of being able to invade someone else's computer. Hackers are usually computer experts who enjoy having the power to invade someone else's privacy.

Hardware is the tangible, physical equipment that can be seen and touched. Examples include the keyboard, processor, monitor, and printer

Head HTML tag. Contained within the start and end <HEAD> tags is the <TITLE> tag.

Header on a web page, contains a link to the sponsoring institution

Headings HTML tag. The characteristics of headings include the type face, size, and the extra space above or below the heading.

History display of a record of all the sites you have visited in the last 20 days

Hits the number of returns on your keywords during a search on the web

Home page the first page that's displayed when you launch your browser

Home row keys keys include a, s, d, f, j, k, l, and ;. These are called the home row because these are the keys from which all keystrokes are made

HTML tags codes used within the hypertext markup language to create a web page

Hyperlinks an area on a web page that, when highlighted and clicked on, will take you to another location on the web

Hypertext markup language (HTML) This text-based program (language) is used to create documents for the WWW . HTML is a series of tags that are integrated into a text document. These tags describe how the text should be formatted when a Web browser displays it on the screen.

I

Input data that is entered into the computer system via an input or storage device

Input Devices enable you to input data and commands into the computer

Internet was originally developed for the government to enable researchers around the world to be able to share information. Today, it is the largest network (computers connected together) in the world.

K

Keyboard the most common input device for entering numeric and alphabetic data into a computer

Keyboarding the ability to enter text by using the correct fingers without looking at the keys. This is also sometimes called touch typing.

Keywords describe the information you are trying to locate while searching for data on the web

L

Label alphabetical text in a spreadsheet

Layout and Design the way graphics and text are used to produce a quality document.

Lists a way to arrange and organize text on a Web page. Within HTML, there are three types of lists:

> **Ordered list** – This is generally a numbered list

351

Unordered list – This is generally a bulleted list

Definition list – This is a list of terms with indented definitions

Local Area Network a series of connected personal computers, workstations, and other devices such as printers, scanners, or other devices within a confined space such as an office or building.

Logic Bomb computer virus which is triggered by the appearance or disappearance of specified data

M

Main memory called random access memory or RAM. Is like short term memory. Data, information, and program instructions are stored on a RAM chip or a set of RAM chips. When the computer is turned off or if there is a loss of power, whatever is stored in the RAM memory chips disappears. Therefore, it is considered volatile. The computer can read from and write to this type of memory. RAM is also referred to as main memory and primary memory.

Math symbols one key symbol used to abbreviate works such as and/or. You can use math symbols in a search on the web to help focus the search

Menu bar location on the screen where the commands that you will use are displayed

MLA MLA Handbook for writers of research papers

Modem communications hardware device that facilitates the transmitting and receiving of data.

Monitors video display screens. They can be either monochromatic or color. A monochromatic (monochrome) monitor screen is a one-color display. It could be white, green or amber. Color monitors display thousands of colors

Mouse a pointing device that rolls around on a flat surface and controls the pointer on the screen

Microcomputer also called a personal computer or desktop computer, is the type of computer that is used at home or at the office, by one person. It's size and shape allow it to fit on top or under a desk. The PC is typically used for writing papers or letters, tracking personal finances, playing games and surfing the Internet.

Motherboard a circuit board that contains many integral components. A circuit board is simply a thin plate or board that contains electronic components. Some of the most important of these components are:

The central processing unit

Memory

Basic Controllers

Expansion ports and expansion slots

N

Navigation is the ability to move through a web site.

Networks connects one computer to other computers and peripheral devices. This connection enables the computers to share data and resources. If the computers are located in a relatively close location of each other; in the same building or department, they are part of a local area network

Network operating system allows a group of two or more microcomputers to be connected.

Newsgroup a discussion forum or a type of bulletin board. Each "board" is dedicated to discussion on a particular topic.

O

Operating systems provide an interface between the user or application program and the computer hardware

Optical Storage Devices use laser technology to read and write data on silver platters.

Output Devices enable the computer to give you the results of the processed data

P

Parallel Port transmit data eight bits at a time. Usually used by the printer.

Presentation graphics program software to create a sequence of ideas and pictures to be shown as a presentation.

Primary Key uniquely identifies a field for each record

Printers an output device that transfers data to a paper format

Problem Solving a logical guideline needs to be followed in order to identify the situation that could use technology to alleviate problems or to enhance a specific task and to identify the exact technology that would address the situation.

Protocols a standard format for transferring data between two devices. TCP/IP is the agreed upon international standard for transmitting data.

Q

Query a question you ask about the data stored in a database. Querying a database means to search a database for specific records that meet a given criteria

R

Random access memory See Main Memory

Read only memory ROM chips are found throughout a computer system. The computer manufacturer uses this type of chip to store specific instructions that are needed for the computer operations. This type of memory is non-volatile. These instructions remain on the chip regardless if the power is turned on or off

Record a collection of fields in a database

Related search pre-programmed queries or questions suggested by the search engine. A related search can dramatically improve your odds of finding the information you are seeking

Relative Link gives the file location in relation to the current document. When you use relative links, you can move the folder and files that contain the hyperlink and maintain the destination of the hyperlink without breaking the path of the relative link.

Report contain the contents of the database. These reports can be used to summarize data, pulling out only what is needed. The formatting, such as headings, spacing, graphics, etc., can be decided by the user

Ribbon area on the screen. The icons in this area allow you to change the appearance of your document. It is sometimes called the Formatting toolbar

Row identified by numbers. Horizontal area on a spreadsheet.

Ruler used to change paragraph indentations and margin settings.

S

Search engine is another Internet tool to help you locate information on the Internet.

Serial Port A connection on the computer through which bits travel in single file. Usually used by the modem and mouse

Shareware software you can use for free for a specified period to try it out. If you decide that you like it and it meets your needs, you are suppose to pay for it.

Simulation models of real-world activities

Site License ability to purchase and install a software program on just the server and pay the vendor based on the number of users of that program.

Software is the intangible set of instructions that tells the computer what to do. These sets of instructions are called programs or software programs. There are two types of software programs. These are system software programs and application software programs

Software Piracy Illegal copying and using software

353

Spell Checker checks each word of the document against a dictionary of known words. If it finds a word that it does not recognize because it is not in its dictionary, it will display this word. The word may be displayed as a different color or a wavy red line under it.

Spider a search engine robot that searches the Internet for the keywords. It feeds the pages it finds to the search engine. It is called a spider because it crawls the Web continually, examining Web sites and finding and looking for links

Spreadsheet a row and column arrangement of data used to enter, calculate, manipulate, and analyze numbers. They are used to prepare budgets, financial statements, and inventory management. They are also used to make forecasts and also to assist in making decisions

Status bar displays information about document including current page number, total pages in document, location of cursor, and the status of some of the specialized key.

Storage a hardware device that permits storage of data.

Subject Directories a method for searching for information on the WWW

Systems software a group of programs that coordinate and control the resources and operations of a computer system. Systems software enables the many components of the computer system to communicate. There are three categories of systems software: Operating systems, utilities, and language translators.

T

Table a group of records in a database

Technology is the application of scientific discoveries to the production of goods and services that improve the human environment. The computer is a major element of technology and has aided in improvements in medical research, and space travel and exploration just to name a few.

Telecommunications is electronically transferring data. Two of the most popular features of telecommunication are distance learning and teleconferencing.

Templates pre-designed documents that are already formatted. Most word processing programs have templates for letters, reports, newsletters, memos, and faxes.

Text area area on the computer screen that will contain the information that you type

Thesaurus assists with using different words in a document by suggesting synonyms.

Thumbnail Sketch a rough draft drawing used to explore layout options of a document you are creating.

Title name of a web page. This can be anything you choose; an example is: "The personal Web page of Joe Smith" where you would substitute your name for Joe Smith.

Time Bomb computer virus that does not cause its damage until a certain date or until the system has been booted a certain number of times.

Title bar area on the screen where document names appear.

Toolbar area on the screen where Icons (little pictures) of commonly used commands are displayed

Topology the way or geometric arrangement of how the network is set up and connected. Example of topology are ring, star or bus.

Transitions special effects that display when you move from slide to slide during a presentation

Transmission Media the physical or wireless system used move data from one location to another. Examples of transmission media are twisted pair wire, coaxial cable or fiber optic cable.

Trojan Horse computer virus that does something different from what it is expected to do. It may look like it is doing one thing while in actuality it is doing something quite opposite (usually something disastrous).

Typeface a set of characters with a common design and shape. Typefaces can add mood or "feeling" to a document.

Updating is the process of adding, changing, and deleting records in a table to keep them current and accurate.

U

URL web site address is referred to as URL or Universal Resource Locator.

Usenet a worldwide network of computers that facilitates the transmission of messages among the news servers.

V

Value is a number entered on a spreadsheet

Virtual Reality an artificial environment that appears to feel like a real environment.

Voice Recognition devices that are used to "speak" commands into the compute and to enter text. These devices are usually microphones and require supporting software.

W

WebQuest a type of activity that uses the Internet for investigation and problem solving

Web Page plain text document on the World Wide Web. Every Web page is identified by a unique address or URL.

Web server displays Web pages and renders them into final form so that they can be viewed by anyone with an Internet connection and a Web browser. Every Web server has an unique Web address.

What-if-analysis spreadsheet tool used to play out different situations to determine outcome

Wide Area Network a computer network that covers a large geographical area. Most WANs are made up of several connected LANs

Wildcard character the * symbol or aster-isk is considered a wildcard character. If you don't know the spelling of a word or you want to search plurals or variations of a word, use the wildcard character

Window rectangular area of the screen; used to display a program, data, or other information. Windows can be resized and moved around the screen.

Windows the title given to the graphical user interface operating system for the PC

Wizards walk you through a series of steps in completing a task or document

Word Processing one of the most common software applications for computers today. It provides the capability to handle text which makes it easy to create (and modify) all kinds of documents from simple one-page documents, to multi-page reports, to flyers, to brochures, to books.

Word wrap text will wrap around the right margin and continue on the next line.

World Wide Web a subset or an application that makes use of the Internet. The Internet can exist without the Web, but the Web cannot exist without the Internet

Worm a type of computer virus that makes many copies of itself resulting in the consumption of system resources which slows down or actually halt tasks.   Worms don't have to attach themselves to other files.

WYSIWYG "What You See Is What You Get."

INDEX

Absolute links, in Web pages, 291

Access indicator, with browsers, 218

Active cells, in spreadsheets, 120–121

Add-ins, 24–25

Addition, 20

Add-ons, 24–25

Address bar, with browsers, 218, 219–220

Address book, for e-mail, 236, 237

Address boxes, in spreadsheets, 121

Addresses
   for e-mail, 203–204
   in Internet, 198–199

Address List feature, with browsers, 220

Administrative Assistant, 313

Advanced Research Projects Agency (ARPA), Internet and, 195

Advertising
   impact of technology on, 341
   in Web pages, 299–300

AIX, 56

ALIGN attribute, in <IMG> tag, 295–297

Alignment of text, with word processors, 109

All-In-One-Search-Page, 251

Alphanumeric keys, 64
   learning, 68–69

Alt (alternate) key, 31, 64

AltaVista search engine, 247, 249, 251

America Online (AOL), 197
   chat rooms with, 205

AND logical operator, in Web searches, 258–259

And operator, 140

Andreessen, Marc, 201

Angelfire Web site, 299–300

Animation, for presentations, 158–159

Announcements, mailing lists for, 207

Antivirus software, 321, 323

AOL Messenger, 205. *See also* Messenger

Apple Guide Help Balloons, 97

Apple Macintosh computers. *See* Macintosh computers

Apple Museum, Web site for, 90

Applications software, 49
   keyboarding and, 63
   for word processing, 101–103

Arguments, of spreadsheet functions, 124

Arithmetic/logic units (ALUs), 18, 20, 22, 23

Arithmetic operations, 3
   in spreadsheets, 124

ARPANET, Internet and, 195–196

Arrow keys, 32

Artificial intelligence (AI), 337–338

Ascenders, of characters, 170

Ascending sort, of databases, 138

ASCII (American Standard Code for Information Interchange), 25

Askanexpert, Web site for, 205

AskJeeves search engine, 245–247, 313

Asterisk (*), as wildcard character, 259

Astrolab, Web site for, 183

<A> tag, 291–293

@ symbol, in e-mail addresses, 203

Attributes, in HTML tags, 280

Audience handouts, 150

AudioFind Web site, 251

Authorship, of Web pages, 269

AutoComplete feature, with browsers, 219

AutoCorrect feature
   with browsers, 219
   with word processors, 106

AutoLayout dialog box, 150, 151

AutoSearch feature, with browsers, 219, 222

Avatars, 206

Average function, in spreadsheets, 125

Babbage, Charles, 3

Backgrounds, in Web pages, 298–299

Back key, in navigating Web pages, 220, 269

Backspace key, error correction with, 70, 106, 123

Backups
   in computer security, 323–324
   utility programs for, 50–51

Bad sectors, 83

Balance, in desktop publishing, 169

Banking, impact of technology on, 340, 341

Bar code scanners, 35, 36

Beaucoup Web site, 250–251

Beginners Central, Web site for, 200

Berners-Lee, Tim, 200

Between operator, 140

BGCOLOR attribute, in <BODY> tag, 299

Binary representation, 20

Biometric security measures, 324

BIOS (Basic Input Output System), 57

BIOS ROM, 19, 23, 57

Bits, 20, 25
   and serial and parallel ports, 24

Blackboard Web site, 332

Body
   of HTML documents, 279, 282
   of Web pages, 268

<BODY> tag, 280

Bold attribute, for characters, 108, 170, 286

Bookmarks
   with browsers, 220, 224–225
   organizing, 225

Boolean logic, 258

Boolean searching, 258–259

Booting computers, 57

Boot records, 57

Borders, in desktop publishing, 174

Bottom Dollar Web site, 250

Brackets, in HTML tags, 279

Break key, 65

Break tag. *See*
 tag

Bridges, in networks, 186

Britannica Web site, 253–256

Browser software, 197, 200–203, 215–233. *See also* Web browser software
  basic operations of, 218–229
  cleaning caches of, 226–229
  displaying HTML documents with, 281–282
  function of, 215–217
  saving text, Web pages, and images with, 229–233
  terminology for, 217–218

BrowserWatch, Web site for, 217

 tag, 279, 283, 284

<B> tag, 286

Buddy lists, 205

Bulleted lists, in Web pages, 284–285, 296

Bulletin boards, in Internet, 208–209

Bus topology, 189

Bytes, 25

Cable, for networks, 182–183

Cable modems
  for Internet connection, 198
  in networks, 185

Cache memory, 23

Caches, with browsers, 226–229

Camcorders, 36

Cap height, of characters, 170

Caps Lock key, 32

Career finding, search engines for, 252

CareerPath Web site, 251

Cars, impact of technology on, 342

Catalog City Web site, 250

Category-oriented search engines, 250

CD-R (compact disk recordable) drives, 44

CD-ROM (compact disk, read only memory), 43

CDS (compact disks), 41, 43–44

Cells
  formatting, 127
  in spreadsheets, 120–121, 122, 123–126

Centered text, with word processors, 109

Centering, in Web pages, 285–286

<CENTER> tag, 285–286

Central processing unit (CPU), 18, 20
  execution and instruction cycles of, 22
  in motherboard, 19

Certified systems engineers, 183

Channels, in data communications, 9, 181, 182

Character formatting, with word processors, 107–108

Charts, in presentations, 154–155

Chart Type dialog box, 155

Chat rooms, in Internet, 204–206

Chicago Manual of Style, The, 271

CIA Geography Quiz Web site, 331

Circuit boards, 19

Clicking, with mouse, 33

Clients, in networks, 181, 185, 187–188

Client/server network, 187–188

Clip art, in desktop publishing, 172, 173

Clip Art Gallery, 152

Clipboard, selecting text and, 106–107

Close button, 81

Closed lists, 207

Close option, with word processors, 113

Close Window, 81

Closing comments, in Web pages, 279

Clothing, impact of technology on, 342, 343

Coaxial cable, 182–183
  Internet connection via, 198

Coherence, in desktop publishing, 169

Color
  in desktop publishing, 174
  of Web page backgrounds, 298–299
  of Web page text, 287–289

COLOR attribute, of <FONT> tag, 288–289

Color ink jet printers, 39

Color laser printers, 38

Columns
  deleting from spreadsheets, 127
  inserting into spreadsheets, 127
  in spreadsheets, 119, 120–121, 124–125, 126

with word processors, 110

Column widths, changing in spreadsheets, 127

Command-line interfaces, to operating systems, 52

Commands, with word processors, 102, 112, 113

Communication, among computers, 9–12

Communications channels, 182

Communications hardware, 185

Communications media, in networks, 182–184

Communicator. *See* Netscape Communicator

Company finding, search engines for, 252

Comparison operators, with databases, 140

Compressed files, 209–210

CompuServe, 197

Computer-based learning, 334

Computer crimes, 319–321, 324
  legal protection from, 325

Computer fraud, 320

Computer Fraud and Abuse Act of 1986, 325

Computer games, training via, 339

Computer Matching and Privacy Protection Act of 1988, 325

Computer Museum Network, Web site of, 4

Computer programs, 8
  control unit and, 20
  downloading from Internet, 232–233
  ethics of incorrect, 336
  software as, 48–49
  starting, 86–90

Computers, 1–13
  applications of, 1, 3, 4–5, 13, 17–18, 308–313, 314–315
  in ARPANET, 195–196
  booting, 57
  communication between, 9
  components of, 19–24
  connecting to Internet, 196–198, 199
  and data input, output, and storage, 30
  displaying Web pages with, 278
  early generation, 3–4, 63

ethics and, 58
functions of, 2
future of, 13
graphical user interfaces for, 78
hardware and software for, 48
history of, 3–4
in Internet, 11–12
keyboarding and, 63
in networks, 10–12, 180–181, 185–187, 187–188, 189–190
operating systems for, 49, 50
popularity of, 3
problem solving with, 305, 307–308
security of, 122, 323–324
as systems, 8
types of, 6–7
unauthorized use of, 319–320
Web site for early, 63
Computer systems, 8
components of, 17–24
Computer time, theft of, 321
Computer viruses, 43, 319, 320–321
Concept-based searching, 244
Connectivity, among computers, 13
Consultant, 288
Container tags, 279
Content
in desktop publishing, 169
of Web pages, 269, 279
Content Advisor, with Internet Explorer, 226
Controllers, in motherboard, 24
Control units, 18, 20, 22, 23
in motherboard, 19
Copy command, selecting text and, 106
Copying files, 92
Copying formulas, into spreadsheets, 125–126
Copying software, ethics of, 267
Copying text
with Internet Explorer, 231–232
with Netscape Communicator, 229–230
Copyright Act of 1976, 267, 325
Copyrights, 320
ethics and, 163
of Web pages, 270
Corbis search engine, 251
Corel Presentations, 150

Count function, in spreadsheets, 125
Crawlers, in search engines, 247
"Creating Great Web Graphics" (McCanna), 278
Credit, for Web-page information, 270
Credit card numbers, security for, 227
Cropping, of graphics, 172
Cryptographic keys, passwords as, 278
Ctrl (control) key, 31, 64
with spreadsheets, 121
Currency, of Web pages, 269–270
Cursor, with word processors, 105. See also Insertion point
Cursor movement keys, 65
Cut command, selecting text and, 107

Dangerous tasks, technology for, 314–315
Data, 8
computers and, 2, 3, 8, 30
in databases, 135–136
entering into spreadsheets, 123–126
entering into tables, 138–139, 142, 143
erasing, 83
hidden in spreadsheets, 128
in Internet, 199
in problem solving, 306
theft of, 321
Database management system (DBMS), 135–136. See also Databases; Database systems
Databases, 135–136
creating, 136–138
creating forms for, 142
creating reports from, 142–143
entering records into, 138–139, 142, 143
modifying table structure of, 140
printing, 142
in problem solving, 311
querying, 140, 141
for search engines, 247
for spreadsheets, 120
updating, 142
Web Developers and, 203
Database software, 311
Database structure, 136–138

Database systems, 49, 135–143. See also Spreadsheets
Data communications, 9
in Internet, 11–12
in networks, 10, 181
Data diddling, as computer crime, 321
Data processing, 2, 3, 17–25, 30
examples of, 17–18
Datasheets, in presentations, 154–155
Data storage, 2, 18, 41–44
Dead links, 268
Decorative fonts, in desktop publishing, 171
Dedicated desktop publishing software, 168
Definition lists, in Web pages, 284–285
Delete key, error correction with, 70, 106
Deleting columns and rows from spreadsheets, 127
Deleting files, 93
Descenders, of characters, 170
Descending sort, of databases, 138
Design
in desktop publishing, 169, 170–171, 174–175
of presentations, 158–160
Design templates, for presentations, 158
Desktop Publisher, 173
Desktop publishing, 167–168
design and layout in, 169, 170–171, 174–175
graphics in, 172–173
guidelines for, 176
stages in, 168–169
Desktop publishing programs, 49, 167–176
Desktops
closing windows in, 81–82
in graphical user interfaces, 52, 79–80
opening windows in, 80–81
Details, of files, 93, 94
Digest, from mailing lists, 207
Digital cameras, 36
Digital cash, 341
Digital signatures, ethics of, 115
Digital watermarks, 307
Directional keys, 31, 64, 65

Director of Information Technology, 127

Directory searches, 243

Discussion lists, 207

Diskettes, 8, 42, 43
care of, 68
saving documents on, 111–112

Distance learning, 311, 332–333

Ditto search engine, 251

Division, 20

<DL> tag, 284–285

Document areas ,with word processors, 103. *See also* Text areas

Documents
closing, 113
desktop publication of, 167–168
formatting of, 71, 109–110
in HTML, 279–299
integrating spreadsheets into, 128
printing of, 112
in problem solving, 309
proofreading of, 110–111
saving, 111–112
spell checking of, 70
storing, 79
for Web pages, 113, 279–299

Document title, in screens, 66

Dogpile search engine, 252

Domain names
abbreviations in (table), 202
in e-mail addresses, 203
in Internet, 199, 201

DOS (Disk Operating System), 52, 53, 54

Dot matrix printers, 37–38, 40

Dot pitch, 37

Double clicking, with mouse, 33

Double-spaced text, with word processors, 109

Downloading files and programs, 232–233

DPI (dots per inch) pin resolution, of dot matrix printers, 40

Dragging, with mouse, 33

Drawing toolbar, 157

Drivers, 57

Drop-down menus, with word processors, 104

DSL (Digital Subscriber Line), Internet connection via, 198

<DT> tag, 284–285

DVD (Digital Versatile Disk), 44, 148

Early generation computers, 3–4

EBCDIC (Extended Binary Coded Decimal Interchange Code), 25

E-cycle, 22

Editing text, with word processors, 106–111

Edit WordArt Text dialog box, 156

Education
impact of technology on, 330–336
virtual environments in, 339

Educational software, 49

Efficiency, of Web pages, 270

Electromagnetic waves, data communications via, 184

Electronic banking, 314

Electronic commerce, 340–341, 344

Electronic Communication Privacy Act of 1986, 325

Electronic identification
biometric, 324
in computer security, 323

Electronic ink, 343

Electronic journals, on Internet, 270–271

Electronic mail. *See* E-mail

Electronic presentations, 149–150

Electronic shopping, 344

E-mail, 12, 234–237
addresses for, 203–204
addresses in Web pages, 269
in ARPANET, 196
attaching documents to, 112
citing of, 272
computer viruses in, 321
digital signatures in, 115
encryption of, 278
etiquette for, 198
with Internet, 203–204
junk, 139, 244
mailing lists with, 206
organizing, 236–237
problem solving with, 312

E-mail links, in Web pages, 292–293

E-mail software, 203

Employee screening, in computer security, 323

Encryption software, 139

for e-mail, 278
for Internet security, 227

Encyclopedia Britannica. *See* Britannica Web site

End tags, 279

Entering text, with word processors, 105–106

Enter key, 68
with spreadsheets, 123

Entertainment, technology in, 314

Equal to operator, 140

Erasing data, 83

Ergonomic keyboards, 32, 64

Error messages, from Internet searches, 223

Esc (escape) key, 32, 65
with spreadsheets, 123

Ethernet protocol, 191

Ethics, 58, 73, 97, 115, 122, 139, 163, 175, 187, 198, 227, 267, 278, 307, 336
ten commandments for, 325

Etiquette, for e-mail, 198

Excite search engine, 205, 244

Execution cycle, 22, 23

Exit option, with word processors, 104, 113

Expansion boards, 24–25

Expansion cards, 24–25, 41

Expansion ports, in motherboard, 19, 24

Expansion slots, in motherboard, 19, 24

Expedia Maps, 223

Expert systems, 337

External modems, 197

Extranets, 12

Fair use, of Web-page information, 270

Fast Search search engine, 249

Favorites, 220
with Internet Explorer, 224–225

Fax machines, 39

Fiber optic cable, 183, 184

Field names, in databases, 137

Fields, in databases, 136, 137–138

Field size, in databases, 137

File allocation table (FAT), of disk drive, 42

File Download dialog box, 232

File menu, with word processors, 104
Files, 85–86
  attaching to e-mail, 235
  copying, 92
  in databases, 136, 137
  deleting, 93
  downloading from Internet, 232–233
  for graphics, 293
  lists of, 93, 94
  managing, 91–96
  moving, 91
  printing, 69
  recovering deleted and erased, 83
  retrieving, 69
  saving, 69
  selecting, 94–96
  sorting names of, 94, 95, 96
  storing documents as, 79
  transferring across Internet, 209–210
  utility programs for managing, 50–51
  viewing, 93–94
  with word processors, 104
File servers, 10, 10
Finder, for Macintosh user interface, 79
Firewalls, in computer security, 323
Flat-panel displays, 37
Floppy disk drives, 18, 19, 41, 42
  creating folders on, 85–86
  formatting, 50, 82–85
  saving documents on, 111–112
Florida High School, Web site for, 206, 332–333
Focus, in desktop publishing, 169, 172
Folders, 85
  bookmarks and favorites in, 224–225
  creating, 85–86
  for e-mail, 236–237
  managing, 91–96
  selecting files for, 96
  sorting names of, 94, 96
  storing documents in, 79
Font attributes, 108, 171
Fonts
  in desktop publishing, 170–171
  in Web pages, 287–289

with word processors, 107–108
Font sizes, 108, 171
  in Web pages, 287–291
Font style
  with Web pages, 291
  with word processors, 107–108
<FONT> tag, 287–289
Footers
  in Web pages, 268
  with word processors, 110
Footnotes, with word processors, 110
Format dialog box, 84
Format Menu, 108
Formatting cells in spreadsheets, 127
Formatting characters, in word processing, 107–108
Formatting disks, 50, 82–85, 83–85
Formatting documents, 71
  for Web pages, 282–291
Formatting lines, in word processing, 109
Formatting paragraphs
  in Web pages, 283–284
  in word processing, 109
Formatting Results dialog box, 84
Formatting spreadsheets, 128–129
Formatting text, in word processing, 107
Formatting toolbox, in screens, 66
Forms, with databases, 142
Formula bars, in spreadsheets, 121
Formulas, as spreadsheet data, 123–124, 125
Formula View, of spreadsheets, 127
Forward function, with browsers, 220
FTP (File Transfer Protocol), with Internet, 209–210
Full justified text, with word processors, 109
Function keys, 31, 64
  selecting spreadsheet cells with, 122
Functions, in spreadsheets, 123–126

Galaxy Web site, 257
GameCenter, Web site for, 207
Game playing, computer technology for, 337
Gates, Bill, 3
Gateways, in networks, 186
General search engines, 244–249

table of popular, 249
Genetic engineering, technology of, 338
GeoCities Web site, 299
GIF (Graphic Interchange Format) files, 293
Global economy, impact of technology on, 340
Go button, with browsers, 218
Google search engine, 249
Grammar checking, 70
  with word processors, 111
Graphical user interfaces (GUIs), 78–82
  in booting computers, 57
  exploring windows of, 89
  for Mac OS, 53, 54
  to operating systems, 52
  shutting down, 79, 80
  starting programs from, 86–90
  starting up, 79
  switching between windows in, 90
  Windows as, 54–55
Graphic Designer, 173
Graphics
  in database reports, 142–143
  in desktop publishing, 172–173
  with presentation systems, 148–162
  in Web pages, 278, 293–299
  with word processors, 113
Graphics tablets, 34
Graphs
  in presentations, 154–155
  from spreadsheets, 128–129
Greater than operator, 140
Greater than or equal to operator, 140
Grids, in spreadsheets, 120–121
Groups, of e-mail addresses, 237

Hackers, 175, 187, 320
HAL computer, 337
Hamsterdance Web site, 201
Hard disk drives, 18, 19, 41, 42
  formatting, 50
  saving documents on, 111–112
Hard return, 68
Hardware, 8
  for Internet connection, 198
  for networks, 185–187
  software versus, 48–49

Hardware sharing, with networks, 182

Head, of HTML documents, 279

Headers
in Web pages, 268
with word processors, 110

Headings, in Web pages, 290–291

<HEAD> tag, 280

Health care, technology in, 314

Help, 97

Hiding data in spreadsheets, 128

Hierarchies, USENET, 209

High-speed digital lines, Internet connection via, 198

History feature, with browsers, 220, 221, 223–224

Hits, in Internet searches, 244, 248

Homebusinessmag, Web site for, 209

Home computers, 6
origin of, 3–4

Home function, with browsers, 220

Home key, selecting spreadsheet cells with, 122

Home pages. *See also* Web pages
of browsers, 218–219
of White House, 266

Home row keys, 66

Home software, 49

Horizontal lines, in desktop publishing, 174

Horizontal rule, in Web pages, 296–297

Horizontal scroll bar, in screens, 66, 79

Host node computers, in ARPANET, 195–196

HotBot search engine, 258–259

How Stuff Works, Web site for, 202, 331

HREF attribute, in <A> tag, 291–293

<HR> tag, 296–297

<H> tags, 290–291

HTML (Hypertext Markup Language)
browsers and, 215
in creating Web pages, 277, 278, 279–299
title searching and, 259–260
with word processors, 113
as World Wide Web protocol, 200–203

HTML markup tags, 202, 279–299

required, 280–282

<HTML> tag, 280

HTML template, 281

HTTP (Hypertext Transfer Protocol), 201

Hubs, in networks, 186, 190

Human Genome Project, 338

"Hunt and peck" typing, 64

Hybrid topologies, 190

Hyperlink lists, from Internet searches, 245

Hyperlinks. *See* Hypertext links

Hypertext, 202

Hypertext links, 279
dead, 268
in Web pages, 269, 270, 291–292

IBM PC (personal computer), operating systems for, 53, 54–55

ICE (intelligent concept extraction), search engines with, 244

Icons, in graphical user interfaces, 52, 53, 54, 66, 79–80, 93–94

ICQ, 205

I-cycle, 22

IEEE (Institute of Electrical and Electronics Engineers), code of ethics by, 58

If function, in spreadsheets, 125, 129–130

Image scanners, 35

<IMG> tag, 293–297

Impact printers, 37–38, 40

Indexes, for search engines, 247

Information, 265–273
evaluating Internet, 265, 266–268, 269–270, 273
searching Internet for, 242–243

"Information highway," 195

Information sharing, with networks, 182

InfoSeek search engine, 248–249

Injuries, protection against, 325

Ink jet printers, 37, 38, 39

Input, into computers, 2, 8, 18

Input devices, 18, 30, 31–36
connecting computers to, 41

Inserting columns and rows into spreadsheets, 127

Insertion point. *See also* Cursor
in correcting text, 106
in entering text, 105

Insert key, error correction with, 106

Instruction cycle, 22, 23

Interfaces, to operating systems, 52

Internet, 11–12, 195–210, 215–237.
See also Browser software
accessing, 196–198
citing resources on, 271–272
computer viruses from, 321
connecting to, 196–198
downloading programs from, 232–233
educational impact of, 330–333
electronic commerce and, 340–341
evaluating information from, 265, 266–268, 269–270, 273
evaluation survey for, 273
features of, 200–210
history of, 195–196
privacy and, 322
problem solving with, 305, 308–309, 312–313
protocols for, 191, 199
searching, 242–260
structure of, 198–199
types of resources on, 270–271
uses of, 195, 196

Internet Detective, 273

Internet Explorer, 197, 201, 215–217, 278
address bar for, 219–220
address list for, 220
bookmarking with, 224–225
changing default home page of, 218–219
cleaning caches of, 226–227
controlling Web access with, 226
copying and saving text with, 231–232
e-mail with, 234
History feature with, 223–224
search function with, 222–223
toolbars for, 220–221

Internet Keywords feature, with browsers, 222

Inter-Net-Network, 196

Internet Options dialog box, 227

Internet Relay Chat (IRC), 205

Internet Service Providers (ISPs), 197

Internet Web Designer, 272

Intranets, 12

Inventories, computer maintenance of, 5

IP addresses, 201

IPOS (input, process, output, storage) functions, 18

IP protocol. *See* TCP/IP (Transmission Control Protocol/Internet Protocol)

ISDN (Integrated Services Digital Network) lines, Internet connection via, 198

<I> tag, 286

Italic attribute, for characters, 108, 286

Jaz drives, 41, 43

Job interviews, 231

Jobs, Steve, 3

Jones Telecommunications and Multimedia Encyclopedia, Web site for, 20

Joysticks, 34

JPEG (Joint Photographic Expert Group) files, 293

JPG files, 293

Junk e-mail, 139, 244

Justification, with word processors, 109

Keyboarding, 31, 63–73
  developing basic skill at, 67–69

Keyboards, 8, 18, 30, 31–32, 63–64
  correct positioning of, 66–67
  layout of, 64–65
  selecting spreadsheet cells with, 122

Key fields, in databases, 137

Keystrokes
  in macros, 125
  for selecting spreadsheet cells, 122

Keystroking, 66

Keywords, 245

Keyword searches, 242–243, 244–249

Labels, as spreadsheet data, 123

Landscape orientation, with word processors, 109

Language translators, 51

Large icons, in graphical user interfaces, 93

Laser printers, 37, 38

in desktop publishing, 168

LaserWriter printer, 168

Layout
  in desktop publishing, 169, 170–171, 174–175
  of Web pages, 269–270

Learn the Net Web site, 259

Left justified text, with word processors, 109

Less than operator, 140

Less than or equal to operator, 140

Librarian's Index Web site, 257

Linear bus topology, 189

Line break
  HTML tag for, 279
  in Web pages, 283

Line formatting, in word processing, 109

Lines, in desktop publishing, 174

Line spacing, with word processors, 109

Links. *See* Hypertext links

Linux, 56

List owners, 206

Lists, in Web pages, 284–285

Lists of files, 93, 94

<LI> tag, 284–286

Local area networks (LANs), 10, 180–181, 187–188
  for Internet connection, 196
  protocols in, 191
  transmission hardware for, 186–187

Location bar, with browsers, 219–220

Logical operations, 3
  with databases, 140
  with search engines, 257–259

Logic bombs, as computer viruses, 321

Logos, in database forms, 142

Lotus Freelance presentation system, 150

Lycos search engine, 251, 313

Machine language, 20
  translation of programs into, 51

Macintosh computers
  copying files with, 92
  creating folders for, 86
  deleting files on, 93
  desktop publishing and, 168

formatting floppy disks for, 85
  getting help on, 97
  graphical user interface for, 79
  moving files with, 91
  operating system for, 50, 53
  selecting file on, 96
  shutting down, 80
  sorting file names on, 94
  starting programs on, 88, 89, 89

Macintosh Desktop, 81

Mac OS, 50, 53
  networks and, 191

Macros, in spreadsheets, 125

Magnetic scanners, 35, 36

Magnetic storage devices, 41–43, 82

Magnetic tape cartridges, 41

Magnetic tape drives, 43

Mailing lists, 139
  with Internet, 206–208

Mail merge command, with word processors, 113

Mainframe computers, 7

Main memory, 21. *See also* Random access memory (RAM)

Manager of information systems, 71

Maps, search engines for, 252

Margins, with word processors, 109

Mars 2220 simulation, 335

Math symbols, in Web searches, 257–258

Max function, in spreadsheets, 125

Maximizing windows, 89

McCanna, Laurie, 278

McCarthy, John, 337

Medical care, technology in, 314

Medicine
  impact of technology on, 337–340
  virtual reality in, 340

Memory, 2, 18, 21–23
  cache, 23
  in motherboard, 19, 21
  random access, 21–22
  read-only, 23

Menu bars
  with browsers, 218, 220–221
  in screens, 66
  with word processors, 103

Menus
  in graphical user interfaces, 52, 79
  with word processors, 104, 108

Messenger, 234–235. *See also* AOL Messenger

MetaCrawler search engine, 252

Meta-search engines, 246, 252

Meta tags, in Web pages, 244–245

Microcomputers, 6
  operating systems for, 53–56
  user interfaces for, 52

Microprocessors, 19, 20

Microseconds, 22

Microsoft Certified Systems Engineer (MCSE), 183

Microsoft Chat, 205, 206

Microsoft Internet Explorer. *See* Internet Explorer

Microsoft Windows. *See* Windows operating systems

Microwaves, data communications via, 184

MIDI ports, 41

Min function, in spreadsheets, 125

Miniaturization, in technology, 340

Minicomputers, 7

Minimizing windows, 89

Minus sign, in Web searches, 257–258

MLA Handbook for Writers of Research Papers, on citing Internet resources, 271–272

Modems
  as input and output devices, 30
  Internet connection via, 196–197
  in networks, 181, 185
  serial ports and, 24

Modifier keys, 31, 64

Modifying databases, 140–142

Moller International, 342

Money, impact of technology on, 340, 341

Monitors, 18, 37

Mosaic browser, 201
  Web site for, 200

Motherboards, 19–24

Mouse (mice), 33
  keyboard in place of, 71
  selecting spreadsheet cells with, 122
  with spreadsheets, 121

Moving, of graphics, 172

Moving files, 91

Moving windows, 89

MP3 search engines, 251

MS-DOS operating system, 52

MSN, as Internet Service Provider, 197

Multimedia search engines, 251, 251

Multimedia software, 49

Multiplication, 20

Multitasking operating systems, 55

Music search engines, 251

Nanoseconds, 22

NASA (National Aeronautics and Space Administration), Web site for, 11

Natural language, computer technology for understanding, 337

Navigation, within Web pages, 270

Navigator. *See* Netscape Navigator

NetMeeting program, 149

Netscape Communicator, 215–217, 278
  bookmarking with, 224–225
  changing default home page of, 218–219
  cleaning caches of, 228–229
  controlling Web access with, 226
  copying and saving text with, 229–230
  e-mail with, 234–235
  History feature with, 224
  search function with, 222–223
  toolbars for, 220–221

Netscape Navigator, 197, 201

Net Search Web site, 222

Netware operating system, 57

NetWatch, with Netscape Communicator, 226

Network Administrator, 183

Network interface cards (NICs), 186
  for Internet connection, 196

Network News Transfer Protocol (NNTP), newsgroups and, 208–209

Network operating systems (NOS), 57, 191

Networks, 10–12, 180–191. *See also* ARPANET; Internet; Local area networks (LANs); Wide area networks (WANs); World Wide Web (WWW)
  benefits of, 182
  communications media in, 182–184
  described, 180–182
  hardware for, 185–187
  operating system software for, 191
  protocols in, 190–191
  security in, 187
  topologies of, 189–190
  types of, 187–188
  Windows 95 and, 55

Network transmission hardware, 186–187

New dialog box, for presentation systems, 150

Newsgroups, in Internet, 208–209

Newsreader software, 208–209

News servers, 208

Nonimpact printers, 38–40

Nonlethal weapons, 342–343

Nonvolatile memory, 23

Normal view, of presentation, 153

Northern Light search engine, 249

Notebook computers, 6

Notepad, creating HTML documents with, 280

Not equal to operator, 140

NOT logical operator, in Web searches, 258–259

Novell, Web site for, 187

Novell Certified Systems Engineer (CSE), 183

Numbered lists, in Web pages, 284–285

Numeric keypad, in keyboards, 31, 64

Num Lock key, 32

Oikarinen, Jarkko, 205

<OL> tag, 284–286

Online journal articles, citing of, 272

Online magazine articles, citing of, 272

Online meetings, 149

Operating systems, 49, 50, 52. *See also* DOS (Disk Operating System); Mac OS; MS-DOS operating system; Network operating systems (NOS); Unix operating system; Windows operating systems
  for microcomputers, 53–56
  for networks, 191
  software for, 49, 50–56, 57

Optical storage devices, 43–44
Ordered lists, in Web pages, 284–285
OR logical operator, in Web searches, 258–259
Ornamental typefaces, in desktop publishing, 170–171
Outline attribute, for characters, 108
Outline view, of presentation, 153
Outlook Express, 234
  e-mailing with, 235, 236
Output, from computers, 2, 8, 18
Output devices, 18, 30, 37–40
  connecting computers to, 41
Overhead transparencies, 150
Overtype key, error correction with, 106

Packets, for e-mail, 234
Page borders, in desktop publishing, 174
PageMaker software, 168
Page numbers, with word processors, 110
Page Setup option, with word processors, 104
Page size, with word processors, 109
Palace, The, as virtual world, 206, 207
Palm-top computers, 6–7
Paragraph formatting, in word processing, 109
Paragraph tags, in Web pages, 283–284
Parallel ports, 41
  in motherboard, 24
Passwords
  in computer security, 323
  controlling Internet access with, 226
  as cryptographic keys, 278
Paste command, selecting text and, 107
Paths, in data communications, 181
Pause key, 65
Payroll, spreadsheets for, 119
PC cards, 41
PC Support Specialist, 33
Peer-to-peer network, 188
People finding, search engines for, 252
Peripheral devices
  in networks, 10

Universal Serial Bus for, 24
Personal computers. See Home computers
Personal digital assistants (PDAs), 6–7
Personal information, privacy of, 322
Personal information management software (PIMS), 311
Personal lives, impact of technology on, 341–344
Personal software, 49
PgDn key, selecting spreadsheet cells with, 122
PgUp key, selecting spreadsheet cells with, 122
PhotoCD, 44
Photocopiers
  ink jet printers as, 39
  laser printers as, 38
Phrase searching, 257
Physical media, in networks, 182–183
Picoseconds, 22
PICS (Platform for Internet Content Selection) standard, 226
Pins, in dot matrix printers, 40
Pirates, 175
  of software, 267, 324
Pizza Hut Web site, 344
Plagiarism, ethics and, 73
Planning
  in desktop publishing, 169
  of Web pages, 279
Play, impact of technology on, 340–344
Plug and Play technology, 55
Plus sign, in Web searches, 257–258
PNG (Portable Network Graphics) files, 293
Pointers
  in graphical user interfaces, 79
  with mouse, 33
  in spreadsheets, 121
Pointing, with mouse, 33
Pointing device, in graphical user interfaces, 79
Points, measuring font sizes with, 108, 171
Portable operating systems, 56
Portrait orientation, with word processors, 109
Posture, at keyboard, 66–67

PowerPoint presentation system, 150–152
  charts and, 154–155
  design templates in, 158–160
  printing presentations with, 160
  views with, 153
  WordArt and, 156–157
Preferences dialog box, 228
Presentation broadcasting, 149
Presentation Expert, 161
Presentations
  adding charts to, 154–155
  adding WordArt to, 156–157
  creating, 150–152
  delivering, 162
  design of, 158–160
  preparing effective, 161–162
  printing of, 160
  rule of thirds for, 162
  viewing, 153
Presentations graphics programs, 149
Presentation skills, 162
Presentation systems, 49, 148–162
Pretty Good Privacy software, 139
Prices, of printers, 37, 38
Primary key, in databases, 137
Primary memory, 21. See also Random access memory (RAM)
Printers, 18, 30, 37–40
  parallel ports and, 24
Printheads, of dot matrix printers, 40
Printing
  of databases, 142
  of documents, 112
  of files, 69
  of presentations, 160
  of spreadsheets, 126, 127
  of Web pages, 220
Print option, with word processors, 104
Print Preview, with word processors, 104
Print quality, 37
Print Screen key, 32, 65
Privacy, 322
  ethics and, 139
Private lists, 207
Problem solving, 304–315, 306
  computers in, 307–308
  methods of, 306–308

technology in, 304–306, 308–315
Processing cycle, 22
Prodigy, 197
    chat rooms with, 205
Productivity software, 49
Programming, as career, 252
Programming languages, 20, 252
    for Web Developers, 203
Programs. *See* Computer programs
Project Management, 96
Projectors, in presentations, 149
Proofreading text, with word
    processors, 110–111
Proprietary chat rooms, 205, 206
Protocols, 199
    in data communications, 9,
    190–191
    for Internet, 199, 201, 208–209,
    209–210
    for World Wide Web, 200–203
<P> tag, 283–284
Public domain, Web pages in, 270
Public lists, 207
Publishing Web pages, 299–300

Qualifiers, in Web searches, 257–258
Querying, of databases, 140, 141
Quit option, with word processors,
    104
QWERTY layout, 64

Radio, data communications via, 184
Random access memory (RAM), 19,
    21–22
Ranges, of spreadsheet cells, 124
Read-only memory (ROM), 23
Receivers, in data communications,
    9, 181
Records, in databases, 136, 138–139
Recreation, impact of technology on,
    340–344
Recycle Bin, 80, 82
    deleted files in, 93
Reformatting, of floppy disk drives,
    83
Refresh function, with browsers, 220,
    226
Related searches, 260
Relative links, in Web pages, 291
Reliability, of Internet information,
    265, 266–268

Reload function, with browsers, 226
Removable storage media, caring for,
    44
Reports
    from databases, 142–143
    with presentation systems,
    148–162
Resizing windows, 89
Resolution
    of dot matrix printers, 40
    of monitors, 37
Responsibility, ethics of, 336
Restoring windows, 89
Retrieval, 3, 18
    of documents, 79
    of files, 69
Ribbons, in dot matrix printers, 40
Right clicking, with mouse, 33
Right justified text, with word
    processors, 109
Ring topology, 189–190
Robotics, 338
ROM chips, 23
Rotating, of graphics, 172
Round function, in spreadsheets, 125
Routers, in networks, 187
Rows
    deleting from spreadsheets, 127
    inserting into spreadsheets, 127
    in spreadsheets, 119, 120–121
RSACi standard, 226
Rule of thirds, for presentations, 162
Rulers
    with word processors, 103
    in screens, 66

SafeSurf standard, 226
Sans serif fonts
    in desktop publishing, 170–171
    with word processors, 107–108
Satellites, data communications via,
    184
Save As command
    with spreadsheets, 126
    with word processors, 111–112
Save As dialog box, 233
Save command, with word
    processors, 111–112
Saving documents
    as spreadsheets, 126
    with word processors, 111–112

Saving files, 69
    with word processors, 104
Saving text
    with Internet Explorer, 231–232
    with Netscape Communicator,
    229–230
Scanners, 24, 35–36
    in desktop publishing, 172
Science, impact of technology on,
    337–340
Screening, in computer security, 323
Screens, 65–66
    with AskJeeves search engine,
    245–247
    for Beaucoup Web site, 250
    for Britannica Web site, 253, 254,
    255, 256
    for browsers, 217, 220, 221, 222,
    223, 224, 225, 227, 228, 229, 230,
    232, 233
    for chat rooms, 205, 206, 207
    for CIA Geography Quiz Web site,
    331
    for databases, 136, 138, 139, 141,
    143, 311
    in desktop publishing, 168, 171,
    172
    for educational Web sites, 332, 333
    for e-mail, 204, 234, 235, 236, 237
    in graphical user interfaces, 52
    for HotBot search engine, 258
    for How Stuff Works Web site, 331
    for Human Genome Project Web
    site, 338
    for InfoSeek search engine,
    248–249
    for Internet Explorer, 216, 217,
    220, 221, 222, 223, 224, 225, 227,
    234
    for THE Journal Homepage, 271
    for Learn the Net, 259
    for Lycos search engine, 313
    for mailing lists, 208
    for multimedia search engines, 251
    for Netscape Communicator, 216,
    221, 225, 228, 229, 230, 235
    for Pizza Hut Web site, 344
    with presentation systems, 150,
    151, 152, 153, 154, 155, 156–157,
    158–159, 160
    for simulations Web sites, 335, 336
    for Skycar Web site, 342

for spreadsheets, 120, 121, 124, 126, 128, 129, 130, 310

for WebCrawler search engine, 260

for Web pages, 268, 280, 281, 282, 283, 284, 285, 286, 287, 288, 289–290, 292, 293, 294, 295, 296, 297–298, 299, 300

for WebQuest Web site, 332

for Web sites, 200, 201

for White House home page, 266

for word processors, 103–104, 105, 107, 108, 110, 111, 112, 309

with WS_FTP program, 210

Screen size, of monitors, 37

Scroll bars

with browsers, 218

in graphical user interfaces, 66, 79

with word processors, 103

Scroll Lock key, 32, 65

SCSI (small computer system interface) ports, 41

Search Assistant, with Internet Explorer, 222–223

Search engines, 244–249

on Internet, 271

problem solving with, 313

table of popular, 249

Web chats hosted by, 205

World Wide Web and, 243

Search Engine Watch Web site, 247

Search function, with browsers, 220, 222–223

Searching the Internet, 242–260

general search engines for, 244–249

keywords in, 242–243, 244–249

reasons for, 243

specialty search engines for, 250–252

by subject directory, 253–257

techniques for, 257–260

Sectors, 82–83

bad, 83

Security, 323–324

of computers and data, 122, 187

Internet, 227

Selecting cells, in spreadsheets, 122, 125

Selecting files, 94–96

Selecting text, in word processing, 106–107

Self-running presentations, 149

Senders, in data communications, 9, 181

Serial ports, 41

in motherboard, 24

Serif fonts

in desktop publishing, 170–171

with word processors, 107–108

Servers, in networks, 181, 185, 187–188

Settings dialog box, 229

Shareware, 267, 324

Shareware Web site, 250

Shift key, 31, 64

Sholes, Christopher, 63

Shortcuts, with browsers, 219

Shut Down Windows dialog box, 80

Sierramm.com, Web site for, 203

SimCity Web site, 336

Simplicity, in desktop publishing, 169

Simulation analysts, 339

Simulations, in education, 334–336

Single-spaced text, with word processors, 109

SIZE attribute, with <FONT> tag, 287–289

Size Box, 89

Sizing, of graphics, 172

Skycar Web site, 342

Slash character </>

in HTML tags, 279

Slide show, of presentation, 153

Slide sorter view, of presentation, 153, 159

Slide view, of presentation, 153

Small icons, in graphical user interfaces, 93, 94

Smart houses, 343

Smart seats, 343

Smart shoes, 343

Snap search engine, 205

Social changes, technology and, 330–344

Software, 8, 48–57. *See also* Search engines

for accessing Internet, 197

antivirus, 321, 323

for creating presentations, 148–162

for database systems, 135–143

development of, 54

encryption, 139, 227

ethics and, 58

hardware versus, 48–49

keyboarding and, 63

for network operating systems, 57, 191

for operating systems, 52–57

problem solving with, 305–306, 307–308, 309–313

spreadsheet, 119–130

types of, 49–51

word processing, 101–114

Software developers, 54

Software drivers, 57

Software piracy, 267, 324

Software Piracy and Counterfeiting Amendment of 1983, 325

Software sharing, with networks, 182

Sorting

of databases, 138

of file and folder names, 94, 95, 96

Space bar, 68

Space travel, 343

Spamming, 139

ethics of, 97, 244

Special-purpose keys, 32, 65

selecting spreadsheet cells with, 122

Specialty search engines, 250–252

table of popular, 252

Speed, of printers, 37

Spell checking, 70, 110–111

in spreadsheets, 128

Speller dialog box, 70

Spiders, in search engines, 247

Spoofing, 139

Sports Search Web site, 250

Spreadsheets, 49, 119–130

components of, 120–121

editing, 127–129

entering data into, 123–126

formatting, 128–129

integrating into documents, 128

navigating in, 122

in problem solving, 308–309, 310

purposes of, 119–120

using, 129–130

Spreadsheet software, 310

SRC attribute, in <IMG> tag, 295–297

Standard toolbar, in screens, 66

Star Schools Program, 332

Star topology, 190
Start tags, 279
Status bar
  with browsers, 218
  in screens, 66
  with word processors, 103
Stemming, in Internet searches, 244
Stock Market Game, 334–335
Storage, 2, 3
  of documents, 79
Storage devices, 41–44
  caring for, 44
Style. *See* Font style
Subject directories, 253
  table of popular, 257
Subject directory searching, 253–257
Subscribers, to mailing lists, 207–208
Subtraction, 20
Sum function, in spreadsheets, 125
Supercomputers, 7
Super floppy disk drives, 41
"Surfing" the Internet, 195, 226
Switchboard Web site, 250
Switching between windows, 90
System Analyst, 322
Systems software, 49, 50–56

Tables, in databases, 136, 137,
  138–139, 140–142
Taskbars, 89, 90
TCP/IP (Transmission Control
  Protocol/Internet Protocol), 191,
  199
Technology
  described, 305
  ethics in, 307, 336
  issues raised by, 319–325
  problem solving with, 304–306,
  308–315
  social changes via, 330–344
Telecommunications, 311
Teleconferencing, 311
Telephone lines, Internet connection
  via, 196–197
Templates
  in desktop publishing, 174
  with word processors, 113
Ten commandments for computer
  ethics, 325
Text

artistic, 156–157, 173
blocks of, 106–107
copying and saving with Internet
  Explorer, 231–232
copying and saving with Netscape
  Communicator, 229–230
in desktop publishing, 170–171
formatting of, 107, 286–291
with word processors, 105–113
Text areas, in screens, 66. *See also*
  Document areas
TextArt, 156–157, 173
Text boxes, in desktop publishing,
  174
Thesaurus, with word processors, 111
35mm slides, 150
"Three-in-one" office machines, 39
Thumbnail sketches, in desktop
  publishing, 169, 175
Time bombs, as computer viruses,
  320
Time magazine, Web page for, 271
Title
  of HTML documents, 279
  HTML tag for, 279
  of Web page, 279
Title bar
  with browsers, 218
  in screens, 66
  with word processors, 103
Title searching, 259–260
<TITLE> tag, 279, 280
Token ring protocol, 191
Toner, in laser printers, 38
Toolbars
  with browsers, 218, 220–221
  in screens, 66
  with spreadsheets, 121
  for WordArt, 157
  with word processors, 103
Topology, 189
  of networks, 189–190
Touch display screens, 35
Touch typing, 63
Trackballs, 34
Tracks, of disk drives, 42, 82–83
Training, technology in, 339
Transitions, for presentations,
  158–159
Transmission hardware, for networks,

186–187
Transmission media, 182
Trash Bin, 80, 82
  deleted files in, 93
Travel information, search engines
  for, 252
Trojan horses, as computer viruses,
  321
Twisted-pair cable, 182
Typefaces, in desktop publishing,
  170–171
Typesetting, desktop publishing and,
  168
Typewriter keyboard, 31, 64
Typing techniques, 66–67

<UL> tag, 284–285
Underline attribute
  for characters, 108, 286
United States, Internet in, 11, 195
Universal Serial Bus (USB), in
  motherboard, 24
University of Albany, Web site for,
  226
Unix operating system, 56
  networks and, 191
Unordered lists, in Web pages,
  284–285
Updating databases, 142
URLs (Universal Resource Locators),
  201, 268, 269
  in browser address bar, 219–220
  from Internet searches, 248
USENET, newsgroups and, 208–209
USENET hierarchies, 209
User interfaces, to operating systems,
  52
User names, in e-mail addresses, 203
<U> tag, 286
Utility programs, 50–51
  table of, 50

Values, as spreadsheet data, 123
Vertical lines, in desktop publishing,
  174
Vertical scroll bar, in screens, 66, 79
Vertical takeoff and landing (VTOL)
  craft, personal, 342
Video input devices, 36
Viewing files, 93–94
Views, of presentations, 153

Virtual characters, 206
Virtual chat rooms, 204
Virtual Library (VL) Web site, 251
Virtual reality (VR), technology of, 339–340
Virtual worlds, 206
Viruses. *See* Computer viruses
Visual chatting, 206, 207
Visuals. *See* Graphics
Voice activation, 8
Voice recognition devices, 35, 342
Volatile memory, 21

Wallpaper, Web pages as, 234
Warp Server operating system, 57
Watermarks
    in desktop publishing, 174
    digital, 307
Web browser software, 197, 200–203, 278. *See also* Browser software
    displaying HTML documents with, 281–282
    HTML and, 202
Web chat, 205
WebCrawler search engine, 260
Web CT Web site, 332–333
Web Developer, 204
Web Master, 272
Web pages, 201, 202, 277–300
    backgrounds in, 298–299
    citing of, 272
    copying and saving with Internet Explorer, 231–232
    copying and saving with Netscape Communicator, 229–230
    creation of, 277, 279–282
    defined, 278
    efficiency of, 270
    evaluating content of, 269–270
    evaluation survey for, 273
    formatting of, 282–291
    free hosting for, 296
    lists in, 284–285
    navigation within, 270
    offensive content on, 226
    operation of, 277–278
    organization of, 268
    planning of, 279
    in problem solving, 308–309

publishing, 299–300
    viewing of, 266–268
    as wallpaper, 234
    with word processors, 113
Web presentations, 149
Web protocols, 201–202
WebQuest Web site, 332
Web servers, 201, 278
    browsers and, 215
Web sites. *See* Web pages
WebTV, Internet connection via, 198
What-if analysis, with spreadsheets, 129–130
White House, home page of, 266
White space, in desktop publishing, 169
Wide area networks (WANs), 10, 180–181, 187, 188
    ARPANET and Internet as, 195–196
    protocols in, 191
    transmission hardware for, 186–187
Wildcard characters, 259
Wildcard searching, 259
Windows
    changing, 89
    closing, 81–82
    in graphical user interfaces, 79, 87, 88, 89, 90
    opening, 80–81
    with spreadsheets, 121
    switching between, 90
    for WordPad, 87, 88
Windows 95 operating system, 55
Windows 98 operating system, 55
Windows 2000 operating system, 55
Windows CE operating system, 55
Windows Desktop, 80
Windows Explorer, viewing files with, 93–94, 95
Windows NT operating system, 55, 57
Windows operating systems, 50, 53, 54–55, 79
    creating folders for, 85–86
    formatting floppy disks with, 83–84
    getting help with, 97
    managing files with, 91–96
    networks and, 191

starting programs with, 86–88
Wireless media, in networks, 182, 184
Wizards, in desktop publishing, 174
WordArt, 156–157, 173
WordArt Gallery, 156
WordArt toolbar, 157
Word counts, with word processors, 111
WordPad, 86–88, 89, 90
WordPad Save As dialog box, 87
Word processing operator, 114
Word processing software, 309
Word processors, 49, 101–114
    advantages of, 101
    described, 101–102
    desktop publishing with, 168
    editing text with, 106–111
    entering text with, 105–106
    exiting from, 113
    formatting text with, 107–110
    printing text with, 112
    in problem solving, 308–309
    proofreading text with, 110–111
    screens for, 103–104
    selecting text with, 106–107
Word wrapping, in screens, 66, 105
Work, impact of technology on, 340–344
Workgroup computing software, 49
Worksheets. *See* Spreadsheets
Workstations, organization of, 67
World data, search engines for obtaining, 252
World Wide Web (WWW). *See also* Internet
    browsers for, 215–217
    educational impact of, 330–333
    Internet and, 196, 200–203
    keyword searches of, 244–249
    problem solving with, 312
    searching, 243
WORM (write once, ready many) disks, 41, 44
Worms, as computer viruses, 320
WS_FTP program, for file compression, 210
WYSIWYG (What You See Is What You Get) formatting, 106
    in desktop publishing, 167

X-height, of characters, 170

Yahoo! search engine, 205, 250, 257,
  287
Yahoo! Web site, publishing Web
  pages at, 299

Zip drives, 41, 43
Zipped files, 209–210
Zoom Box, 89